ANNUAL EDITIONS

Global Issues

Twenty-Fourth Edition

08/09

D1278124

EDITOR

Robert M. Jackson

California State University, Chico

Robert M. Jackson is a professor emeritus of political science and past dean of the School of Graduate, International and Sponsored Programs at California State University, Chico. In addition to teaching courses on third world politics and globalization, he has published articles on the international political economy, international relations simulations, and political behavior. Dr. Jackson has been responsible for numerous international training programs for professionals throughout the world. International educational exchanges and study abroad programs also have been an area of special interest. His research and professional travels include China, Japan, Hong Kong, Taiwan, Singapore, Malaysia, Spain, Portugal, Morocco, Belgium, Germany, the Czech Republic, the Netherlands, Russia, Mexico, Guatemala, Honduras, Costa Rica, El Salvador, Brazil, Chile, and Argentina.

 **Higher Education**

Boston   Burr Ridge, IL   Dubuque, IA   New York   San Francisco   St. Louis
Bangkok   Bogotá   Caracas   Kuala Lumpur   Lisbon   London   Madrid   Mexico City
Milan   Montreal   New Delhi   Santiago   Seoul   Singapore   Sydney   Taipei   Toronto

Higher Education

ANNUAL EDITIONS: GLOBAL ISSUES, TWENTY-FOURTH EDITION

1 2 3 4 5 6 7 8 9 0 QPD/QPD 0 9 8

ISBN 978–0–07–339763–4
MHID 0–07–339763–6
ISSN 1093–278X

Managing Editor: *Larry Loeppke*
Senior Managing Editor: *Faye Schilling*
Developmental Editor: *Jade Benedict/Debra A. Henricks*
Editorial Assistant: *Nancy Meissner*
Production Service Assistant: *Rita Hingtgen*
Permissions Coordinator: *Shirley Lanners*
Senior Marketing Manager: *Julie Keck*
Marketing Communications Specialist: *Mary Klein*
Marketing Coordinator: *Alice Link*
Project Manager: *Sandy Wille*
Design Specialist: *Tara McDermott*
Senior Administrative Assistant: *DeAnna Dausener*
Senior Production Supervisor: *Laura Fuller*
Cover Graphics: *Kristine Jubeck*

Compositor: Laserwords Private Limited
Cover Images: both: Corbis/Royalty Free

Library in Congress Cataloging-in-Publication Data
Main entry under title: Annual Editions: Global Issues 2008/2009.
 1. Global Issues—Periodicals by Jackson, Robert, *comp.* II. Title: Global Issues
658'.05

www.mhhe.com

Editors/Advisory Board

Members of the Advisory Board are instrumental in the final selection of articles for each edition of ANNUAL EDITIONS. Their review of articles for content, level, currentness, and appropriateness provides critical direction to the editor and staff. We think that you will find their careful consideration well reflected in this volume.

Preface

In publishing ANNUAL EDITIONS we recognize the enormous role played by the magazines, newspapers, and journals of the public press in providing current, first-rate educational information in a broad spectrum of interest areas. Many of these articles are appropriate for students, researchers, and professionals seeking accurate, current material to help bridge the gap between principles and theories and the real world. These articles, however, become more useful for study when those of lasting value are carefully collected, organized, indexed, and reproduced in a low-cost format, which provides easy and permanent access when the material is needed. That is the role played by ANNUAL EDITIONS.

The beginning of the new millennium was celebrated with considerable fanfare. The prevailing mood in much of the world was that there was a great deal for which we could congratulate ourselves. The very act of sequentially watching on television live celebrations from one time zone to the next was proclaimed as a testimonial to globalization and the benefits of modern technology. The tragic events of September 11, 2001, however, were a stark reminder of the intense emotions and methods of destruction available to those determined to challenge the status quo. The subsequent wars in Afghanistan and Iraq along with continuing acts of terror have dampened the optimism that was expressed at the outset of the twenty-first century.

While the mass media may focus on the latest crisis for a few weeks or months, the broad forces that are shaping the world are seldom given the in-depth analysis that they warrant. Scholarly research about these historic forces of change can be found in a wide variety of publications, but these are not readily accessible. In addition, students just beginning to study global issues can be discouraged by the terminology and abstract concepts that characterize much of the scholarly literature. In selecting and organizing the materials for this book, we have been mindful of the needs of beginning students and have, thus, selected articles that invite the student into the subject matter.

Each unit begins with an introductory article(s) providing a broad overview of the subject area to be studied. The following articles examine in more detail specific case studies that often identify the positive steps being taken to remedy problems. Recent events are a continual reminder that the world faces many serious challenges, the magnitude of which would discourage even the most stouthearted individual. While identifying problems is easier than solving them, it is encouraging to know that many are being addressed.

Perhaps the most striking feature of the study of contemporary global issues is the absence of any single, widely held theory that explains what is taking place. As a result, we have made a conscious effort to present a wide variety of points of view. The most important consideration has been to present global issues from an international perspective, rather than from a purely American or Western point of view. By encompassing materials originally published in different countries and written by authors of various nationalities, the anthology represents the great diversity of opinions that people hold. Two writers examining the same phenomenon may reach very different conclusions. It is not just a question of who is right or wrong, but rather understanding that people from different vantage points can have differing perspectives on an issue.

Another major consideration when organizing these materials was to explore the complex interrelationship of factors that produce social problems such as poverty. Too often, discussions of this problem (and others like it) are reduced to arguments about the fallacies of not following the correct economic policy or not having the correct form of government. As a result, many people overlook the interplay of historic, cultural, environmental, economic, and political factors that form complex webs that bring about many different problems. Every effort has been made to select materials that illustrate this complex interaction of factors, stimulating the beginning student to consider realistic rather than overly simplistic approaches to the pressing problems that threaten the existence of civilization.

In addition to an annotated *table of contents* and a *topic guide,* included in this edition of *Annual Editions: Global Issues* are *World Wide Web* sites that can be used to further explore topics addressed in the articles.

This is the twenty-fourth edition of *Annual Editions: Global Issues.* When looking back over more than two decades of work, a great deal has taken place in world affairs, and the contents and organization of the book reflect these changes. Nonetheless there is one underlying constant. It is my continuing goal to work with the editors and staff at McGraw-Hill Contemporary Learning Series to provide materials that encourage the readers of this book to develop a life-long appreciation of the complex and rapidly changing world in which we live. I want to thank Rebecca Wenter for her timely research assistance. This collection of articles is an invitation to further explore the global issues of the twenty-first century and become personally involved in the great issues of our time.

Finally, materials in this book were selected for both their intellectual insights and readability. Timely and well-written materials should stimulate good classroom lectures and discussions. I hope that students and teachers will enjoy using this book. Readers can have input into the next edition by completing and returning the postage-paid *article rating form* in the back of the book.

Robert M. Jackson
Editor

Contents

UNIT 1
Global Issues in the Twenty-First Century: An Overview

The concepts in bold italics are developed in the article. For further expansion, please refer to the Topic Guide.

UNIT 2
Population and Food Production

UNIT 3
The Global Environment and Natural Resources

The concepts in bold italics are developed in the article. For further expansion, please refer to the Topic Guide.

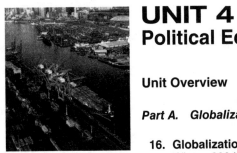

UNIT 4
Political Economy

The concepts in bold italics are developed in the article. For further expansion, please refer to the Topic Guide.

UNIT 5
Conflict

The concepts in bold italics are developed in the article. For further expansion, please refer to the Topic Guide.

UNIT 6
Cooperation

UNIT 7
Values and Visions

The concepts in bold italics are developed in the article. For further expansion, please refer to the Topic Guide.

The concepts in bold italics are developed in the article. For further expansion, please refer to the Topic Guide.

Correlation Guide

The *Annual Editions* series provides students with convenient, inexpensive access to current, carefully selected articles from the public press. **Annual Editions: Global Issues 08/09** is an easy-to-use reader that presents articles on important topics such as *population, environment, political economy,* and many more. For more information on *Annual Editions* and other *McGraw-Hill Contemporary Learning Series* titles, visit www.mhcls.com.

This convenient guide matches the units in **Annual Editions: Global Issues 08/09** with the corresponding chapters in one of our best-selling McGraw-Hill Political Science textbooks by Rourke.

Annual Editions: Global Issues 08/09	International Politics on the World Stage, 12/e by Rourke
Unit 1: Global Issues in the Twenty-First Century	**Chapter 1:** Thinking and Caring about World Politics **Chapter 5:** Globalism: The Alternative Orientation
Unit 2: Population and Food Production	**Chapter 14:** Preserving and Enhancing Human Rights and Dignity
Unit 3: The Global Environment and Natural Resources	**Chapter 15:** Preserving and Enhancing the Biosphere
Unit 4: Political Economy	**Chapter 7:** Intergovernmental Organizations: Alternative Governance **Chapter 8:** National Power and Statecraft: The Traditional Approach **Chapter 12:** National Economic Competition: The Traditional Road
Unit 5: Conflict	**Chapter 8:** National Power and Statecraft: The Traditional Approach **Chapter 10:** National Security: The Traditional Road **Chapter 11:** International Security: The Alternative Road
Unit 6: Cooperation	**Chapter 9:** International Law and Justice: An Alternative Approach **Chapter 13:** International Economic Cooperation: The Alternative Road
Unit 7: Values and Visions	**Chapter 3:** Levels of Analysis and Foreign Policy

Topic Guide

This topic guide suggests how the selections in this book relate to the subjects covered in your course. You may want to use the topics listed on these pages to search the Web more easily.

On the following pages a number of Web sites have been gathered specifically for this book. They are arranged to reflect the units of this *Annual Edition*. You can link to these sites by going to the student online support site at *http://www.mhcls.com/online/*.

ALL THE ARTICLES THAT RELATE TO EACH TOPIC ARE LISTED BELOW THE BOLD-FACED TERM.

Agriculture
1. A Special Moment in History
3. Can Extreme Poverty Be Eliminated?
4. The Ideology of Development
9. Continuing the Green Revolution
11. Deflating the World's Bubble Economy

Communication
1. A Special Moment in History
2. It's a Flat World, After All
40. The Politics of God
41. What Lurks in its Soul?

Conservation
1. A Special Moment in History
11. Deflating the World's Bubble Economy
12. The Great Leap Backward?
14. Plastic Bags Are Killing Us
15. Cry of the Wild
22. Ensuring Energy Security
23. Nuclear Now!
24. Looking into the Sun

Cultural Customs and Values
2. It's a Flat World, After All
3. Can Extreme Poverty Be Eliminated?
4. The Ideology of Development
5. Feminists and Fundamentalists
7. The Century Ahead
16. Globalization and Its Contents
18. The Lost Continent
19. Political Graft: The Russian Way
29. Lifting the Veil
33. Men of Principle
36. The Grameen Bank
39. Humanity's Common Values
40. The Politics of God
42. A Deeper Shade of Green

Demographics
1. A Special Moment in History
7. The Century Ahead
8. Africa's Restless Youth
38. Teamwork Urged on Bird Flu

Dependencies, International
2. It's a Flat World, After All
16. Globalization and Its Contents
17. Why the World Isn't Flat
20. Promises and Poverty
22. Ensuring Energy Security
38. Teamwork Urged on Bird Flu

Development, economic
2. It's a Flat World, After All
3. Can Extreme Poverty Be Eliminated?
4. The Ideology of Development
5. Feminists and Fundamentalists
9. Continuing the Green Revolution
12. The Great Leap Backward?
16. Globalization and Its Contents
17. Why the World Isn't Flat
18. The Lost Continent
19. Political Graft: The Russian Way
20. Promises and Poverty
36. The Grameen Bank

Development, social
3. Can Extreme Poverty Be Eliminated?
4. The Ideology of Development
5. Feminists and Fundamentalists
8. Africa's Restless Youth
18. The Lost Continent
19. Political Graft: The Russian Way
20. Promises and Poverty
36. The Grameen Bank
39. Humanity's Common Values
41. What Lurks in its Soul?

Ecology
1. A Special Moment in History
2. It's a Flat World, After All
3. Can Extreme Poverty Be Eliminated?
9. Continuing the Green Revolution
11. Deflating the World's Bubble Economy
12. The Great Leap Backward?
14. Plastic Bags Are Killing Us
15. Cry of the Wild
22. Ensuring Energy Security
23. Nuclear Now!
24. Looking into the Sun
42. A Deeper Shade of Green

Economics
1. A Special Moment in History
2. It's a Flat World, After All
3. Can Extreme Poverty Be Eliminated?
4. The Ideology of Development
11. Deflating the World's Bubble Economy
12. The Great Leap Backward?
16. Globalization and Its Contents
17. Why the World Isn't Flat
18. The Lost Continent
19. Political Graft: The Russian Way
20. Promises and Poverty
22. Ensuring Energy Security
23. Nuclear Now!
24. Looking into the Sun
36. The Grameen Bank
41. What Lurks in its Soul?

Energy: Exploration, Production, Research, and Politics
11. Deflating the World's Bubble Economy
12. The Great Leap Backward?
22. Ensuring Energy Security
23. Nuclear Now!
24. Looking into the Sun

Environment
1. A Special Moment in History
9. Continuing the Green Revolution
11. Deflating the World's Bubble Economy
12. The Great Leap Backward?
14. Plastic Bags Are Killing Us
15. Cry of the Wild
20. Promises and Poverty
22. Ensuring Energy Security
23. Nuclear Now!
24. Looking into the Sun
42. A Deeper Shade of Green

Internet References

The following Internet sites have been carefully researched and selected to support the articles found in this reader. The easiest way to access these selected sites is to go to our student online support site at *http://www.mhcls.com/online/*.

AE: Global Issues 08/09

The following sites were available at the time of publication. Visit our Web site—we update our student online support site regularly to reflect any changes.

General Sources

U.S. Information Agency (USIA)
http://www.america.gov/

USIA's home page provides definitions, related documentation, and discussions of topics of concern to students of global issues. The site addresses today's Hot Topics as well as ongoing issues that form the foundation of the field.

World Wide Web Virtual Library: International Affairs Resources
http://www.etown.edu/vl/

Surf this site and its extensive links to learn about specific countries and regions, to research various think tanks and international organizations, and to study such vital topics as international law, development, the international economy, human rights, and peacekeeping.

UNIT 1: Global Issues in the Twenty-First Century: An Overview

The Henry L. Stimson Center
http://www.stimson.org

The Stimson Center, a nonpartisan organization, focuses on issues where policy, technology, and politics intersect. Use this site to find varying assessments of U.S. foreign policy in the post–cold war world and to research other topics.

The Heritage Foundation
http://www.heritage.org

This page offers discussion about and links to many sites having to do with foreign policy and foreign affairs, including news and commentary, policy review, events, and a resource bank.

IISDnet
http://www.nsi-ins.ca/

The International Institute for Sustainable Development presents information through links to business, sustainable development, and developing ideas. "Linkages" is its multimedia resource for policymakers.

The North-South Institute
http://www.nsi-ins.ca/

Searching this site of the North-South Institute, which works to strengthen international development cooperation and enhance gender and social equity, will help you find information and debates on a variety of global issues.

UNIT 2: Population and Food Production

The Hunger Project
http://www.thp.org

Browse through this nonprofit organization's site, whose goal is the sustainable end to global hunger through leadership at all levels of society. The Hunger Project contends that the persistence of hunger is at the heart of the major security issues threatening our planet.

Penn Library: Resources by Subject
http://www.library.upenn.edu/cgi-bin/res/sr.cgi

This vast site is rich in links to information about subjects of interest to students of global issues. Its extensive population and demography resources address such concerns as migration, family planning, and health and nutrition in various world regions.

World Health Organization
http://www.who.int

This home page of the World Health Organization will provide you with links to a wealth of statistical and analytical information about health and the environment in the developing world.

WWW Virtual Library: Demography & Population Studies
http://demography.anu.edu.au/VirtualLibrary/

A definitive guide to demography and population studies can be found at this site. It contains a multitude of important links to information about global poverty and hunger.

UNIT 3: The Global Environment and Natural Resources Utilization

National Geographic Society
http://www.nationalgeographic.com

This site provides links to material related to the atmosphere, the oceans, and other environmental topics.

National Oceanic and Atmospheric Administration (NOAA)
http://www.noaa.gov

Through this home page of NOAA, part of the U.S. Department of Commerce, you can find information about coastal issues, fisheries, climate, and more. The site provides many links to research materials and to other Web resources.

SocioSite: Sociological Subject Areas
http://www.pscw.uva.nl/sociosite/TOPICS/

This huge site provides many references of interest to those interested in global issues, such as links to information on ecology and the impact of consumerism.

Internet References

United Nations Environment Programme (UNEP)
http://www.unep.ch

Consult this home page of UNEP for links to critical topics of concern to students of global issues, including desertification, migratory species, and the impact of trade on the environment.

UNIT 4: Political Economy

Belfer Center for Science and International Affairs (BCSIA)
http://ksgwww.harvard.edu/csia/

BCSIA is the hub of Harvard University's John F. Kennedy School of Government's research, teaching, and training in international affairs related to security, environment, and technology.

U.S. Agency for International Development
http://www.usaid.gov

Broad and overlapping issues such as democracy, population and health, economic growth, and development are covered on this Web site. It provides specific information about different regions and countries.

The World Bank Group
http://www.worldbank.org

News, press releases, summaries of new projects, speeches, publications, and coverage of numerous topics regarding development, countries, and regions are provided at this World Bank site. It also contains links to other important global financial organizations.

UNIT 5: Conflict

DefenseLINK
http://www.defenselink.mil

Learn about security news and research-related publications at this U.S. Department of Defense site. Links to related sites of interest are provided. The information systems BosniaLINK and GulfLINK can also be found here. Use the search function to investigate such issues as land mines.

Federation of American Scientists (FAS)
http://www.fas.org

FAS, a nonprofit policy organization, maintains this site to provide coverage of and links to such topics as global security, peace, and governance in the post–cold war world. It notes a variety of resources of value to students of global issues.

ISN International Relations and Security Network
http://www.isn.ethz.ch

This site, maintained by the Center for Security Studies and Conflict Research, is a clearinghouse for information on international relations and security policy. Topics are listed by category (Traditional Dimensions of Security, New Dimensions of Security, and Related Fields) and by major world region.

The NATO Integrated Data Service (NIDS)
http://www.nato.int/structur/nids/nids.htm

NIDS was created to bring information on security-related matters to within easy reach of the widest possible audience. Check out this Web site to review North Atlantic Treaty Organization documentation of all kinds, to read *NATO Review,* and to explore key issues in the field of European security and transatlantic cooperation.

UNIT 6: Cooperation

Carnegie Endowment for International Peace
http://www.ceip.org

An important goal of this organization is to stimulate discussion and learning among both experts and the public at large on a wide range of international issues. The site provides links to *Foreign Policy,* to the Moscow Center, to descriptions of various programs, and much more.

OECD/FDI Statistics
http://www.oecd.org/statistics/

Explore world trade and investment trends and statistics on this site from the Organization for Economic Cooperation and Development. It provides links to many related topics and addresses the issues on a country-by-country basis.

U.S. Institute of Peace
http://www.usip.org

USIP, which was created by the U.S. Congress to promote peaceful resolution of international conflicts, seeks to educate people and to disseminate information on how to achieve peace. Click on Highlights, Publications, Events, Research Areas, and Library and Links.

UNIT 7: Values and Visions

Human Rights Web
http://www.hrweb.org

The history of the human rights movement, text on seminal figures, landmark legal and political documents, and ideas on how individuals can get involved in helping to protect human rights around the world can be found in this valuable site.

InterAction
http://www.interaction.org

InterAction encourages grassroots action and engages government policymakers on advocacy issues. The organization's Advocacy Committee provides this site to inform people on its initiatives to expand international humanitarian relief, refugee, and development-assistance programs.

We highly recommend that you review our Web site for expanded information and our other product lines. We are continually updating and adding links to our Web site in order to offer you the most usable and useful information that will support and expand the value of your Annual Editions. You can reach us at: *http://www.mhcls.com/ annualeditions/.*

World Map

N
W E
S

160° 140° 120° 100° 80° 60°
80°

U.S.

CANADA

60°

NORTH
PACIFIC
OCEAN

40°

UNITED STATES

NORTH
ATLANTIC
OCEAN

Tropic of Cancer
20°

MEXICO

U.S.

GUYANA
SURINAME
FRENCH
GUIANA
(FR)

0°

Equator

COLOMBIA

ECUADOR

VENEZUELA

WESTERN
SAMOA

PERU

BRAZIL

TONGA
20°

BOLIVIA

PARAGUAY

Tropic of Capricorn

CHILE

URUGUAY

ARGENTINA

SOUTH
ATLANTIC
OCEAN

SOUTH
PACIFIC
OCEAN

Antarctic Circle

90° U.S. 0° 70°
THE
BAHAMAS

CUBA

MEXICO
20°

DOMINICAN
REPUBLIC

JAMAICA

HAITI

PUERTO RICO

BELIZE

ST. KITTS AND NEVIS
ANTIGUA AND BARBUDA
DOMINICA

GUATEMALA

HONDURAS

CARIBBEAN
SEA

MARTINIQUE

ST. LUCIA

EL
SALVADOR

NICARAGUA

ST. VINCENT AND THE GRENADINES

BARBADOS
GRENADA

10°

COSTA RICA

PANAMA

TRINIDAD AND TOBAGO

COLOMBIA

VENEZUELA

0 1000 2000 Miles
0 1000 2000 3000 Kilometers

Scale: 1 to 125,000,000

xvi

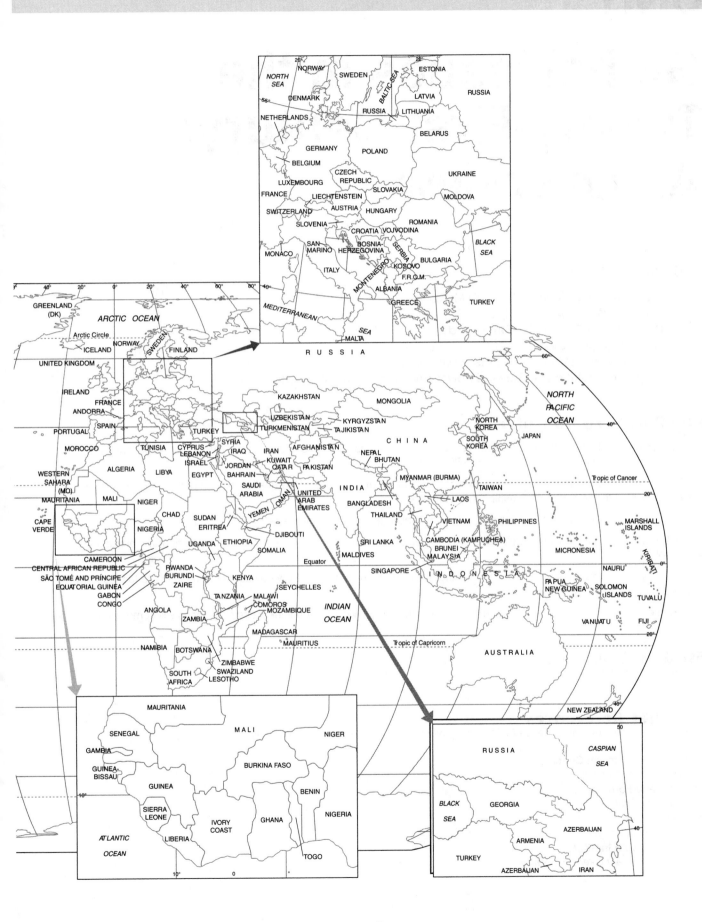

UNIT 1

Global Issues in the Twenty-First Century: An Overview

Unit Selections

Key Points to Consider

- Do the analyses of any of the authors in this section employ the assumptions implicit in the allegory of the balloon? If so, how? If not, how are the assumptions of the authors different?

- All the authors point to interactions among different factors. What are some of the relationships that they cite? How do the authors differ in terms of the relationships they emphasize?

- What assets that did not exist 100 years ago do people now have to solve problems?

- What events during the past 60 years have had the greatest impact on shaping the realities of contemporary international affairs?

- What do you consider to be the five most pressing global problems of today? How do your answers compare to those of your family, friends, and classmates?

- Describe how international affairs might different in the year 2050. Why do you think these differences will come about?

Student Web Site
www.mhcls.com/online

Internet References
Further information regarding these Web sites may be found in this book's preface or online.

The Henry L. Stimson Center
http://www.stimson.org
The Heritage Foundation
http://www.heritage.org
IISDnet
http://www.nsi-ins.ca/
The North-South Institute
http://www.nsi-ins.ca/ensi/index.html

Imagine yellow paint being brushed onto an inflated, clear balloon. The yellow color, for purposes of this allegory, represents *people*. In many ways the study of global issues is first and foremost the study of people. Today, there are more human beings occupying Earth than ever before. In addition, we are in the midst of a period of unprecedented population growth. Not only are there many countries where the majority of people are under age 16, but also due to improved health care, there are more older people alive than ever before. The effect of a growing global population, however, goes beyond sheer numbers, for this trend has unprecedented impacts on natural resources and social services. An examination of population trends and the related topic of food production is a good place to begin an in-depth study of global issues.

Imagine that our fictional artist next dips the brush into a container of blue paint to represent *nature.* The natural world plays an important role in setting the international agenda. Shortages of raw materials, climate change, regional droughts, and pollution of waterways are just a few examples of how natural resources can have global implications.

Adding blue paint to the balloon reveals one of the most important underlying concepts found in this book. Although the balloon originally was covered by both yellow and blue paint (people and nature as separate conceptual entities), the two combined produce an entirely different color: green. Talking about nature as a separate entity or people as though they were somehow removed from the forces of the natural world is a serious intellectual error. The people-nature relationship is one of the keys to understanding many of today's most important global issues.

The third color to be added to the balloon is red. This color represents *social structures.* Factors falling into this category include whether a society is urban or rural, industrial or agrarian, and consumer-oriented or dedicated to the needs of the state. The relationship between this component and the others is extremely important. The impact of political decisions on the environment, for example, is one of the most significant features of the contemporary world. Will the whales or bald eagles survive? Historically, the forces of nature determined which species survived or perished. Today, survival depends on political decisions—or indecision. Understanding the complex relationship between social structure and nature (known as "ecopolitics") is central to the study of global issues.

Added to the three primary colors is the fourth and final color of white. It represents the *meta* component (i.e., those qualities that make human beings different from other life forms). These include new ideas and inventions, culture and values, religion and spirituality, and art and literature. The addition of the white paint immediately changes the intensity and shade of the mixture of colors, again emphasizing the relationship among all four factors.

If the painter continues to ply the paintbrush over the miniature globe, a marbling effect becomes evident. From one area to the next, the shading varies because one element is more dominant than another. Further, the miniature system appears dynamic. Nothing is static; relationships are continually changing. This leads to a number of important insights: (1) there are no such things as separate elements, only connections or relationships; (2) changes in one area (such as the climate) will result in changes in all other areas; and (3) complex and dynamic relationships make it difficult to predict events accurately, so observers and policy makers are often surprised by unexpected events.

This book is organized along the basic lines of the balloon allegory. The first unit provides a broad overview of a variety of perspectives on the major forces that are shaping the world of the twenty-first century. From this "big picture" perspective more in-depth analyses follow. Unit 2, for example, focuses on population and food production. Unit 3 examines the environment and related natural resource issues. The next three units look at different aspects of the world's social structures. They explore issues of economics, national security, conflict, and international cooperation. In the final unit, a number of "meta" factors are presented.

The reader should keep in mind that, just as it was impossible to keep the individual colors from blending into new colors on the balloon, it is also impossible to separate global issues into discrete chapters in a book. Any discussion of agriculture, for example, must take into account the impact of a growing population on soil and water resources, as well as new scientific breakthroughs in food production. Therefore, the organization of this book focuses attention on issue areas; it does not mean to imply that these factors are somehow separate.

With the collapse of the Soviet empire and the end of the cold war, the outlines of a new global agenda have emerged. Rather than being based on the ideology and interests of the two superpowers, new political, economic, environmental, cultural and security issues are interacting in an unprecedented fashion. Rapid population growth, environmental decline, uneven economic progress, and global terrorist networks are all parts of a complex state of affairs for which there is no historic parallel. As we proceed through the first decade of the twenty-first century, signs abound that we are entering a new era. In the words of Abraham Lincoln, "As our case is new, so we must think anew." Compounding this situation, however, is a whole series of old problems such as ethnic and religious rivalries.

The authors in this first unit provide a variety of perspectives on the trends that they believe are the most important to understanding the historic changes at work at the global level. This discussion is then pursued in greater detail in the following units.

Although the authors look at the same world, they often come to different conclusions. This raises an important issue of values and beliefs, for it can be argued that there really is no objective reality, only differing perspectives. In short, the study of global issues will challenge each thoughtful reader to examine her or his own values and beliefs.

A Special Moment in History

BILL MCKIBBEN

We may live in the strangest, most thoroughly different moment since human beings took up farming, 10,000 years ago, and time more or less commenced. Since then time has flowed in one direction—toward *more*, which we have taken to be progress. At first the momentum was gradual, almost imperceptible, checked by wars and the Dark Ages and plagues and taboos; but in recent centuries it has accelerated, the curve of every graph steepening like the Himalayas rising from the Asian steppe. . . .

But now—now may be the special time. So special that in the Western world we might each of us consider, among many other things, having only one child—that is, reproducing at a rate as low as that at which human beings have ever voluntarily reproduced. Is this really necessary? Are we finally running up against some limits?

To try to answer this question, we need to ask another: *How many of us will there be in the near future?* Here is a piece of news that may alter the way we see the planet—an indication that we live at a special moment. At least at first blush the news is hopeful. *New demographic evidence shows that it is at least possible that a child born today will live long enough to see the peak of human population.*

Around the world people are choosing to have fewer and fewer children—not just in China, where the government forces it on them, but in almost every nation outside the poorest parts of Africa. . . . If this keeps up, the population of the world will not quite double again; United Nations analysts offer as their mid-range projection that it will top out at 10 to 11 billion, up from just under six billion at the moment. . . .

The good news is that we won't grow forever. The bad news is that there are six billion of us already, a number the world strains to support. One more near-doubling—four or five billion more people—will nearly double that strain. Will these be the five billion straws that break the camel's back? . . .

Looking at Limits

The case that the next doubling, the one we're now experiencing, might be the difficult one can begin as readily with the Stanford biologist Peter Vitousek as with anyone else. In 1986 Vitousek decided to calculate how much of the earth's "primary productivity" went to support human beings. He added together the grain we ate, the corn we fed our cows, and the forests we cut for timber and paper; he added the losses in food as we overgrazed grassland and turned it into desert. And when he was finished adding, the number he came up with was 38.8 percent. We use 38.8 percent of everything the world's plants don't need to keep themselves alive; directly or indirectly, we consume 38.8 percent of what it is possible to eat. "That's a relatively large number," Vitousek says. "It should give pause to people who think we are far from any limits." Though he never drops the measured tone of an academic, Vitousek speaks with considerable emphasis: "There's a sense among some economists that we're *so* far from any biophysical limits. I think that's not supported by the evidence."

For another antidote to the good cheer of someone like Julian Simon, sit down with the Cornell biologist David Pimentel. He believes that we're in big trouble. Odd facts stud his conversation—for example, a nice head of iceberg lettuce is 95 percent water and contains just fifty calories of energy, but it takes 400 calories of energy to grow that head of lettuce in California's Central Valley, and another 1,800 to ship it east. ("There's practically no nutrition in the damn stuff anyway," Pimentel says. "Cabbage is a lot better, and we can grow it in upstate New York.") Pimentel has devoted the past three decades to tracking the planet's capacity, and he believes that we're already too crowded—that the earth can support only two billion people over the long run at a middle-class standard of living, and that trying to support more is doing damage. He has spent considerable time studying soil erosion, for instance. Every raindrop that hits exposed ground is like a small explosion, launching soil particles into the air. On a slope, more than half of the soil contained in those splashes is carried downhill. If crop residue—cornstalks, say—is left in the field after harvest, it helps to shield the soil: the raindrop doesn't hit hard. But in the developing world, where firewood is scarce, peasants burn those cornstalks for cooking fuel. About 60 percent of crop residues in China and 90 percent in Bangladesh are removed and burned, Pimentel says. When planting season comes, dry soils simply blow away. "Our measuring stations pick up African soils in the wind when they start to plough."

The very things that made the Green Revolution so stunning—that made the last doubling possible—now cause trouble. Irrigation ditches, for instance, water 27 percent of all arable land and help to produce a third of all crops. But when flooded soils are baked by the sun, the water evaporates and the minerals in the irrigation water are deposited on the land. A hectare (2.47 acres) can accumulate two to five tons of salt annually, and eventually plants won't grow there. Maybe 10 percent of all irrigated land is affected.

. . . [F]ood production grew even faster than population after the Second World War. Year after year the yield of wheat and corn and rice rocketed up about three percent annually. It's a favorite statistic of the eternal optimists. In Julian Simon's book *The Ultimate Resource* (1981), charts show just how fast the growth was, and how it continually cut the cost of food. Simon wrote, "The obvious implication of this historical trend toward cheaper food—a trend that probably extends back to the beginning of agriculture—is that real prices for food will continue to drop. . . . It is a fact that portends more drops in price and even less scarcity in the future."

A few years after Simon's book was published, however, the data curve began to change. That rocketing growth in grain production ceased; now the gains were coming in tiny increments, too small to keep pace with population growth. The world reaped its largest harvest of grain per capita in 1984; since then the amount of corn and wheat and rice per person has fallen by six percent. Grain stockpiles have shrunk to less than two months' supply.

No one knows quite why. The collapse of the Soviet Union contributed to the trend—cooperative farms suddenly found the fertilizer supply shut off and spare parts for the tractor hard to come by. But there were other causes, too, all around the world—the salinization of irrigated fields, the erosion of topsoil, and all the other things that environmentalists had been warning about for years. It's possible that we'll still turn production around and start it rocketing again. Charles C. Mann, writing in *Science*, quotes experts who believe that in the future a "gigantic, multi-year, multi-billion-dollar scientific effort, a kind of agricultural 'person-on the-moon project,' " might do the trick. The next great hope of the optimists is genetic engineering, and scientists have indeed managed to induce resistance to pests and disease in some plants. To get more yield, though, a cornstalk must be made to put out another ear, and conventional breeding may have exhausted the possibilities. There's a sense that we're running into walls.

. . . What we are running out of is what the scientists call "sinks"—places to put the by-products of our large appetites. Not garbage dumps (we could go on using Pampers till the end of time and still have empty space left to toss them away) but the atmospheric equivalent of garbage dumps.

It wasn't hard to figure out that there were limits on how much coal smoke we could pour into the air of a single city. It took a while longer to figure out that building ever higher smokestacks merely lofted the haze farther afield, raining down acid on whatever mountain range lay to the east. Even that, however, we are slowly fixing, with scrubbers and different mixtures of fuel. We can't so easily repair the new kinds of pollution. These do not come from something going wrong—some engine without a catalytic converter, some waste-water pipe without a filter, some smokestack without a scrubber. New kinds of pollution come instead from things going as they're supposed to go—but at such a high volume that they overwhelm the planet. They come from normal human life—but there are so many of us living those normal lives that something abnormal is

happening. And that something is different from the old forms of pollution that it confuses the issue even to use the word.

Consider nitrogen, for instance. But before plants can absorb it, it must become "fixed"—bonded with carbon, hydrogen, or oxygen. Nature does this trick with certain kinds of algae and soil bacteria, and with lightning. Before human beings began to alter the nitrogen cycle, these mechanisms provided 90–150 million metric tons of nitrogen a year. Now human activity adds 130–150 million more tons. Nitrogen isn't pollution—it's essential. And we are using more of it all the time. Half the industrial nitrogen fertilizer used in human history has been applied since 1984. As a result, coastal waters and estuaries bloom with toxic algae while oxygen concentrations dwindle, killing fish; as a result, nitrous oxide traps solar heat. And once the gas is in the air, it stays there for a century or more.

Or consider methane, which comes out of the back of a cow or the top of a termite mound or the bottom of a rice paddy. As a result of our determination to raise more cattle, cut down more tropical forest (thereby causing termite populations to explode), and grow more rice, methane concentrations in the atmosphere are more than twice as high as they have been for most of the past 160,000 years. And methane traps heat—very efficiently.

Or consider carbon dioxide. In fact, concentrate on carbon dioxide. If we had to pick one problem to obsess about over the next fifty years, we'd do well to make it CO_2—which is not pollution either. Carbon *mon*oxide is pollution: it kills you if you breathe enough of it. But carbon *di*oxide, carbon with two oxygen atoms, can't do a blessed thing to you. If you're reading this indoors, you're breathing more CO_2 than you'll ever get outside. For generations, in fact, engineers said that an engine burned clean if it produced only water vapor and carbon dioxide.

Here's the catch: that engine produces a *lot* of CO_2. A gallon of gas weighs about eight pounds. When it's burned in a car, about five and a half pounds of carbon, in the form of carbon dioxide, come spewing out the back. It doesn't matter if the car is a 1958 Chevy or a 1998 Saab. And no filter can reduce that flow—it's an inevitable by-product of fossil-fuel combustion, which is why CO_2 has been piling up in the atmosphere ever since the Industrial Revolution. Before we started burning oil and coal and gas, the atmosphere contained about 280 parts CO_2 per million. Now the figure is about 360. Unless we do everything we can think of to eliminate fossil fuels from our diet, the air will test out at more than 500 parts per million fifty or sixty years from now, whether it's sampled in the South Bronx or at the South Pole.

This matters because, as we all know by now, the molecular structure of this clean, natural, common element that we are adding to every cubic foot of the atmosphere surrounding us traps heat that would otherwise radiate back out to space. Far more than even methane and nitrous oxide, CO_2 causes global warming—the greenhouse effect—and climate change. Far more than any other single factor, it is turning the earth we were born on into a new planet.

. . . For ten years, with heavy funding from governments around the world, scientists launched satellites, monitored weather balloons, studied clouds. Their work culminated in a long-awaited report from the UN's Intergovernmental Panel on

Climate Change, released in the fall of 1995. The panel's 2,000 scientists, from every corner of the globe, summed up their findings in this dry but historic bit of understatement: "The balance of evidence suggests that there is a discernible human influence on global climate." That is to say, we are heating up the planet—substantially. If we don't reduce emissions of carbon dioxide and other gases, the panel warned, temperatures will probably rise 3.6° Fahrenheit by 2100, and perhaps as much as 6.3°.

You may think you've already heard a lot about global warming. But most of our sense of the problem is behind the curve. Here's the current news: the changes are already well under way. When politicians and businessmen talk about "future risks," their rhetoric is outdated. This is not a problem for the distant future, or even for the near future. The planet has already heated up by a degree or more. We are perhaps a quarter of the way into the greenhouse era, and the effects are already being felt. From a new heaven, filled with nitrogen, methane, and carbon, a new earth is being born. If some alien astronomer is watching us, she's doubtless puzzled. This is the most obvious effect of our numbers and our appetites, and the key to understanding why the size of our population suddenly poses such a risk.

Stormy and Warm

What does this new world feel like? For one thing, it's stormier than the old one. Data analyzed last year by Thomas Karl, of the National Oceanic and Atmospheric Administration, showed that total winter precipitation in the United States has increased by 10 percent since 1900 and that "extreme precipitation events"—rainstorms that dumped more than two inches of water in twenty-four hours and blizzards—had increased by 20 percent. That's because warmer air holds more water vapor than the colder atmosphere of the old earth; more water evaporates from the ocean, meaning more clouds, more rain, more snow. Engineers designing storm sewers, bridges, and culverts used to plan for what they called the "hundred-year storm." That is, they built to withstand the worst flooding or wind that history led them to expect in the course of a century. Since that history no longer applies, Karl says, "there isn't really a hundred-year event anymore . . . we seem to be getting these storms of the century every couple of years." When Grand Forks, North Dakota, disappeared beneath the Red River in Spring, 1997, some meteorologists referred to it as "a 500-year flood"—meaning, essentially, that all bets are off. Meaning that these aren't acts of God. "If you look out your window, part of what you see in terms of weather is produced by ourselves," Karl says. "If you look out the window fifty years from now, we're going to be responsible for more of it."

Twenty percent more bad storms, 10 percent more winter precipitation—these are enormous numbers. It's like opening the newspaper to read that the average American is smarter by 30 IQ points. And the same data showed increases in drought, too. With more water in the atmosphere, there's less in the soil, according to Kevin Trenberth, of the National Center for Atmospheric Research. Those parts of the continent that are normally dry—the eastern sides of mountains, the plains and deserts—are even drier, as the higher average temperatures evaporate more of what rain does fall. "You get wilting plants and eventually drought faster than you would otherwise," Trenberth says. And when the rain does come, it's often so intense that much of it runs off before it can soak into the soil.

So—wetter and drier. *Different.* . . .

The effects of . . . warming can be found in the largest phenomena. The oceans that cover most of the planet's surface are clearly rising, both because of melting glaciers and because water expands as it warms. As a result, low-lying Pacific islands already report surges of water washing across the atolls. "It's nice weather and all of a sudden water is pouring into your living room," one Marshall Islands resident told a newspaper reporter. "It's very clear that something is happening in the Pacific, and these islands are feeling it." Global warming will be like a much more powerful version of El Niño that covers the entire globe and lasts forever, or at least until the next big asteroid strikes.

If you want to scare yourself with guesses about what might happen in the near future, there's no shortage of possibilities. Scientists have already observed large-scale shifts in the duration of the El Niño ocean warming, for instance. The Arctic tundra has warmed so much that in some places it now gives off more carbon dioxide than it absorbs—a switch that could trigger a potent feedback loop, making warming ever worse. And researchers studying glacial cores from the Greenland Ice Sheet recently concluded that local climate shifts have occurred with incredible rapidity in the past—18° in one three-year stretch. Other scientists worry that such a shift might be enough to flood the oceans with fresh water and reroute or shut off currents like the Gulf Stream and the North Atlantic, which keep Europe far warmer than it would otherwise be. (See "The Great Climate Flip-flop," by William H. Calvin, January (*Atlantic*.) In the words of Wallace Broecker, of Columbia University, a pioneer in the field, "Climate is an angry beast, and we are poking it with sticks."

But we don't need worst-case scenarios: best-case scenarios make the point. The population of the earth is going to nearly double one more time. That will bring it to a level that even the reliable old earth we were born on would be hard-pressed to support. Just at the moment when we need everything to be working as smoothly as possible, we find ourselves inhabiting a new planet, whose carrying capacity we cannot conceivably estimate. We have no idea how much wheat this planet can grow. We don't know what its politics will be like: not if there are going to be heat waves like the one that killed more than 700 Chicagoans in 1995; not if rising sea levels and other effects of climate change create tens of millions of environmental refugees; not if a 1.5° jump in India's temperature could reduce the country's wheat crop by 10 percent or divert its monsoons. . . .

We have gotten very large and very powerful, and for the foreseeable future we're stuck with the results. The glaciers won't grow back again anytime soon; the oceans won't drop. We've already done deep and systemic damage. To use a human analogy, we've already said the angry and unforgivable words that will haunt our marriage till its end. And yet we can't simply walk out the door. There's no place to go. We have to salvage what we can of our relationship with the earth, to keep things from getting any worse than they have to be.

If we can bring our various emissions quickly and sharply under control, we *can* limit the damage, reduce dramatically the chance of horrible surprises, preserve more of the biology we were born into. But do not underestimate the task. The UN's Intergovernmental Panel on Climate Change projects that an immediate 60 percent reduction in fossil-fuel use is necessary just to stabilize climate at the current level of disruption. Nature may still meet us halfway, but halfway is a long way from where we are now. What's more, we can't delay. If we wait a few decades to get started, we may as well not even begin. It's not like poverty, a concern that's always there for civilizations to address. This is a timed test, like the SAT: two or three decades, and we lay our pencils down. It's *the* test for our generations, and population is a part of the answer. . . .

The numbers are so daunting that they're almost unimaginable. Say, just for argument's sake, that we decided to cut world fossil-fuel use by 60 percent—the amount that the UN panel says would stabilize world climate. And then say that we shared the remaining fossil fuel equally. Each human being would get to produce 1.69 metric tons of carbon dioxide annually—which would allow you to drive an average American car nine miles a day. By the time the population increased to 8.5 billion, in about 2025, you'd be down to six miles a day. If you carpooled, you'd have about three pounds of CO_2 left in your daily ration—enough to run a highly efficient refrigerator. Forget your computer, your TV, your stereo, your stove, your dishwasher, your water heater, your microwave, your water pump, your clock. Forget your light bulbs, compact fluorescent or not.

I'm not trying to say that conservation, efficiency, and new technology won't help. They will—but the help will be slow and expensive. The tremendous momentum of growth will work against it. Say that someone invented a new furnace tomorrow that used half as much oil as old furnaces. How many years would it be before a substantial number of American homes had the new device? And what if it cost more? And if oil stays cheaper per gallon than bottled water? Changing basic fuels—to hydrogen, say—would be even more expensive. It's not like running out of white wine and switching to red. Yes, we'll get new technologies. One day last fall *The New York Times* ran a special section on energy, featuring many up-and-coming improvements: solar shingles, basement fuel cells. But the same day, on the front page, William K. Stevens reported that international negotiators had all but given up on preventing a doubling of the atmospheric concentration of CO_2. The momentum of growth was so great, the negotiators said, that making the changes required to slow global warming significantly would be like "trying to turn a supertanker in a sea of syrup."

There are no silver bullets to take care of a problem like this. Electric cars won't by themselves save us, though they would help. We simply won't live efficiently enough soon enough to solve the problem. Vegetarianism won't cure our ills, though it would help. We simply won't live simply enough soon enough to solve the problem.

Reducing the birth rate won't end all our troubles either. That, too, is no silver bullet. But it would help. There's no more practical decision than how many children to have. (And no more mystical decision, either.)

The bottom-line argument goes like this: The next fifty years are a special time. They will decide how strong and healthy the planet will be for centuries to come. Between now and 2050 we'll see the zenith, or very nearly, of human population. With luck we'll never see any greater production of carbon dioxide or toxic chemicals. We'll never see more species extinction or soil erosion. Greenpeace recently announced a campaign to phase out fossil fuels entirely by mid-century, which sounds utterly quixotic but could—if everything went just right—happen.

So it's the task of those of us alive right now to deal with this special phase, to squeeze us through these next fifty years. That's not fair—any more than it was fair that earlier generations had to deal with the Second World War or the Civil War or the Revolution or the Depression or slavery. It's just reality. We need in these fifty years to be working simultaneously on all parts of the equation—on our ways of life, on our technologies, and on our population.

As Gregg Easterbrook pointed out in his book *A Moment on the Earth* (1995), if the planet does manage to reduce its fertility, "the period in which human numbers threaten the biosphere on a general scale will turn out to have been much, much more brief" than periods of natural threats like the Ice Ages. True enough. But the period in question happens to be our time. That's what makes this moment special, and what makes this moment hard.

BILL McKibben is the author of several books about the environment, including *The End of Nature* (1989) and *Hope, Human and Wild* (1995). His article in this issue appears in somewhat different form in his book *Maybe One: A Personal and Environmental Argument for Single-Child Families*, published in 1998 by Simon & Schuster.

It's a Flat World, After All

Thomas L. Friedman

In 1492 Christopher Columbus set sail for India, going west. He had the Nina, the Pinta and the Santa Maria. He never did find India, but he called the people he met "Indians" and came home and reported to his king and queen: "The world is round." I set off for India 512 years later. I knew just which direction I was going. I went east. I had Lufthansa business class, and I came home and reported only to my wife and only in a whisper: "The world is flat."

And therein lies a tale of technology and geoeconomics that is fundamentally reshaping our lives—much, much more quickly than many people realize. It all happened while we were sleeping, or rather while we were focused on 9/11, the dot-com bust and Enron—which even prompted some to wonder whether globalization was over. Actually, just the opposite was true, which is why it's time to wake up and prepare ourselves for this flat world, because others already are, and there is no time to waste.

I wish I could say I saw it all coming. Alas, I encountered the flattening of the world quite by accident. It was in late February [2004], and I was visiting the Indian high-tech capital, Bangalore, working on a documentary for the Discovery Times channel about outsourcing. In short order, I interviewed Indian entrepreneurs who wanted to prepare my taxes from Bangalore, read my X-rays from Bangalore, trace my lost luggage from Bangalore and write my new software from Bangalore. The longer I was there, the more upset I became—upset at the realization that while I had been off covering the 9/11 wars, globalization had entered a whole new phase, and I had missed it. I guess the eureka moment came on a visit to the campus of Infosys Technologies, one of the crown jewels of the Indian outsourcing and software industry. Nandan Nilekani, the Infosys C.E.O., was showing me his global video-conference room, pointing with pride to a wall-size flat-screen TV, which he said was the biggest in Asia. Infosys, he explained, could hold a virtual meeting of the key players from its entire global supply chain for any project at any time on that supersize screen. So its American designers could be on the screen speaking with their Indian software writers and their Asian manufacturers all at once. That's what globalization is all about today, Nilekani said. Above the screen there were eight clocks that pretty well summed up the Infosys workday: 24/7/365. The clocks were labeled U.S. West, U.S. East, G.M.T., India, Singapore, Hong Kong, Japan, Australia.

"Outsourcing is just one dimension of a much more fundamental thing happening today in the world," Nilekani explained. "What happened over the last years is that there was a massive investment in technology, especially in the bubble era, when hundreds of millions of dollars were invested in putting broadband connectivity around the world, undersea cables, all those things." At the same time, he added, computers became cheaper and dispersed all over the world, and there was an explosion of e-mail software, search engines like Google and proprietary software that can chop up any piece of work and send one part to Boston, one part to Bangalore and one part to Beijing, making it easy for anyone to do remote development. When all of these things suddenly came together around 2000, Nilekani said, they "created a platform where intellectual work, intellectual capital, could be delivered from anywhere. It could be disaggregated, delivered, distributed, produced and put back together again—and this gave a whole new degree of freedom to the way we do work, especially work of an intellectual nature. And what you are seeing in Bangalore today is really the culmination of all these things coming together."

At one point, summing up the implications of all this, Nilekani uttered a phrase that rang in my ear. He said to me, "Tom, the playing field is being leveled." He meant that countries like India were now able to compete equally for global knowledge work as never before—and that America had better get ready for this. As I left the Infosys campus that evening and bounced along the potholed road back to Bangalore, I kept chewing on that phrase: "The playing field is being leveled."

"What Nandan is saying," I thought, "is that the playing field is being flattened. Flattened? Flattened? My God, he's telling me the world is flat!"

Here I was in Bangalore—more than 500 years after Columbus sailed over the horizon, looking for a shorter route to India using the rudimentary navigational technologies of his day, and returned safely to prove definitively that the world was round—and one of India's smartest engineers, trained at his country's top technical institute and backed by the most modern technologies of his day, was telling me that the world was flat, as flat as that screen on which he can host a meeting of his whole global supply chain. Even more interesting, he was citing this development as a new milestone in human progress and a great opportunity for India and the world—the fact that we had made our world flat!

This has been building for a long time. Globalization 1.0 (1492 to 1800) shrank the world from a size large to a size medium, and the dynamic force in that era was countries globalizing for resources and imperial conquest. Globalization 2.0 (1800 to 2000) shrank the world from a size medium to a size small, and it was spearheaded by companies globalizing for markets and labor. Globalization 3.0 (which started around 2000) is shrinking the world from a size small to a size tiny and flattening the playing field at the same time. And while the dynamic force in Globalization 1.0 was countries globalizing and the dynamic force in Globalization 2.0 was companies globalizing, the dynamic force in Globalization 3.0—the thing that gives it its unique character—is individuals and small groups globalizing. Individuals must, and can, now ask: where do I fit into the global competition and opportunities of the day, and how can I, on my own, collaborate with others globally? But Globalization 3.0 not only differs from the previous eras in how it is shrinking and flattening the world and in how it is empowering individuals. It is also different in that Globalization 1.0 and 2.0 were driven primarily by European and American companies and countries. But going forward, this will be less and less true. Globalization 3.0 is not only going to be driven more by individuals but also by a much more diverse—non-Western, nonwhite—group of individuals. In Globalization 3.0, you are going to see every color of the human rainbow take part.

"Today, the most profound thing to me is the fact that a 14-year-old in Romania or Bangalore or the Soviet Union or Vietnam has all the information, all the tools, all the software easily available to apply knowledge however they want," said Marc Andreessen, a co-founder of Netscape and creator of the first commercial Internet browser. "That is why I am sure the next Napster is going to come out of left field. As bioscience becomes more computational and less about wet labs and as all the genomic data becomes easily available on the Internet, at some point you will be able to design vaccines on your laptop."

Andreessen is touching on the most exciting part of Globalization 3.0 and the flattening of the world: the fact that we are now in the process of connecting all the knowledge pools in the world together. We've tasted some of the downsides of that in the way that Osama bin Laden has connected terrorist knowledge pools together through his Qaeda network, not to mention the work of teenage hackers spinning off more and more lethal computer viruses that affect us all. But the upside is that by connecting all these knowledge pools we are on the cusp of an incredible new era of innovation, an era that will be driven from left field and right field, from West and East and from North and South. Only 30 years ago, if you had a choice of being born a B student in Boston or a genius in Bangalore or Beijing, you probably would have chosen Boston, because a genius in Beijing or Bangalore could not really take advantage of his or her talent. They could not plug and play globally. Not anymore. Not when the world is flat, and anyone with smarts, access to Google and a cheap wireless laptop can join the innovation fray.

When the world is flat, you can innovate without having to emigrate. This is going to get interesting. We are about to see creative destruction on steroids.

How did the world get flattened, and how did it happen so fast?

It was a result of 10 events and forces that all came together during the 1990's and converged right around the year 2000. Let me go through them briefly. The first event was 11/9. That's right—not 9/11, but 11/9. Nov. 9, 1989, is the day the Berlin Wall came down, which was critically important because it allowed us to think of the world as a single space. "The Berlin Wall was not only a symbol of keeping people inside Germany; it was a way of preventing a kind of global view of our future," the Nobel Prize-winning economist Amartya Sen said. And the wall went down just as the windows went up—the breakthrough Microsoft Windows 3.0 operating system, which helped to flatten the playing field even more by creating a global computer interface, shipped six months after the wall fell.

The second key date was 8/9. Aug. 9, 1995, is the day Netscape went public, which did two important things. First, it brought the Internet alive by giving us the browser to display images and data stored on Web sites. Second, the Netscape stock offering triggered the dot-com boom, which triggered the dot-com bubble, which triggered the massive overinvestment of billions of dollars in fiber-optic telecommunications cable. That overinvestment, by companies like Global Crossing, resulted in the willy-nilly creation of a global undersea-underground fiber network, which in turn drove down the cost of transmitting voices, data and images to practically zero, which in turn accidentally made Boston, Bangalore and Beijing next-door neighbors overnight. In sum, what the Netscape revolution did was bring people-to-people connectivity to a whole new level. Suddenly more people could connect with more other people from more different places in more different ways than ever before.

No country accidentally benefited more from the Netscape moment than India. "India had no resources and no infrastructure," said Dinakar Singh, one of the most respected hedge-fund managers on Wall Street, whose parents earned doctoral degrees in biochemistry from the University of Delhi before emigrating to America. "It produced people with quality and by quantity. But many of them rotted on the docks of India like vegetables. Only a relative few could get on ships and get out. Not anymore, because we built this ocean crosser, called fiber-optic cable. For decades you had to leave India to be a professional. Now you can plug into the world from India. You don't have to go to Yale and go to work for Goldman Sachs." India could never have afforded to pay for the bandwidth to connect brainy India with high-tech America, so American shareholders paid for it. Yes, crazy overinvestment can be good. The overinvestment in railroads turned out to be a great boon for the American economy. "But the railroad overinvestment was confined to your own country and so, too, were the benefits," Singh said. In the case of the digital railroads, "it was the foreigners who benefited." India got a free ride.

The first time this became apparent was when thousands of Indian engineers were enlisted to fix the Y2K—the year 2000—computer bugs for companies from all over the world. (Y2K should be a national holiday in India. Call it "Indian Interdependence Day," says Michael Mandelbaum, a foreign-policy analyst at Johns Hopkins.) The fact that the Y2K work could be outsourced to Indians was made possible by the first two flatteners, along with a third, which I call "workflow." Workflow is shorthand for all the software applications, standards and electronic transmission pipes, like middleware, that connected all those computers and fiber-optic cable. To put it another way, if the Netscape moment connected people to people like never before, what the workflow revolution did was connect applications to applications so that people all over the world could work together in manipulating and shaping words, data and images on computers like never before.

Indeed, this breakthrough in people-to-people and application-to-application connectivity produced, in short order, six more flatteners—six new ways in which individuals and companies could collaborate on work and share knowledge. One was "outsourcing." When my software applications could connect seamlessly with all of your applications, it meant that all kinds of work—from accounting to software-writing—could be digitized, disaggregated and shifted to any place in the world where it could be done better and cheaper. The second was "offshoring." I send my whole factory from Canton, Ohio, to Canton, China. The third was "open-sourcing." I write the next operating system, Linux, using engineers collaborating together online and working for free. The fourth was "insourcing." I let a company like UPS come inside my company and take over my whole logistics operation—everything from filling my orders online to delivering my goods to repairing them for customers when they break. (People have no idea what UPS really does today. You'd be amazed!). The fifth was "supply-chaining." This is Wal-Mart's specialty. I create a global supply chain down to the last atom of efficiency so that if I sell an item in Arkansas, another is immediately made in China. (If Wal-Mart were a country, it would be China's eighth-largest trading partner.) The last new form of collaboration I call "informing"—this is Google, Yahoo and MSN Search, which now allow anyone to collaborate with, and mine, unlimited data all by themselves.

So the first three flatteners created the new platform for collaboration, and the next six are the new forms of collaboration that flattened the world even more. The 10th flattener I call "the steroids," and these are wireless access and voice over Internet protocol (VoIP). What the steroids do is turbocharge all these new forms of collaboration, so you can now do any one of them, from anywhere, with any device.

The world got flat when all 10 of these flatteners converged around the year 2000. This created a global, Web-enabled playing field that allows for multiple forms of collaboration on research and work in real time, without regard to geography, distance or, in the near future, even language. "It is the creation of this platform, with these unique attributes, that is the truly important sustainable breakthrough that made what you call the flattening of the world possible," said Craig Mundie, the chief technical officer of Microsoft.

No, not everyone has access yet to this platform, but it is open now to more people in more places on more days in more ways than anything like it in history. Wherever you look today—whether it is the world of journalism, with bloggers bringing down Dan Rather; the world of software, with the Linux code writers working in online forums for free to

challenge Microsoft; or the world of business, where Indian and Chinese innovators are competing against and working with some of the most advanced Western multinationals—hierarchies are being flattened and value is being created less and less within vertical silos and more and more through horizontal collaboration within companies, between companies and among individuals.

Do you recall "the IT revolution" that the business press has been pushing for the last 20 years? Sorry to tell you this, but that was just the prologue. The last 20 years were about forging, sharpening and distributing all the new tools to collaborate and connect. Now the real information revolution is about to begin as all the complementarities among these collaborative tools start to converge. One of those who first called this moment by its real name was Carly Fiorina, the former Hewlett-Packard C.E.O., who in 2004 began to declare in her public speeches that the dot-com boom and bust were just "the end of the beginning." The last 25 years in technology, Fiorina said, have just been "the warm-up act." Now we are going into the main event, she said, "and by the main event, I mean an era in which technology will truly transform every aspect of business, of government, of society, of life."

As if this flattening wasn't enough, another convergence coincidentally occurred during the 1990's that was equally important. Some three billion people who were out of the game walked, and often ran, onto the playing field. I am talking about the people of China, India, Russia, Eastern Europe, Latin America and Central Asia. Their economies and political systems all opened up during the course of the 1990s so that their people were increasingly free to join the free market. And when did these three billion people converge with the new playing field and the new business processes? Right when it was being flattened, right when millions of them could compete and collaborate more equally, more horizontally and with cheaper and more readily available tools. Indeed, thanks to the flattening of the world, many of these new entrants didn't even have to leave home to participate. Thanks to the 10 flatteners, the playing field came to them!

It is this convergence—of new players, on a new playing field, developing new processes for horizontal collaboration—that I believe is the most important force shaping global economics and politics in the early 21st century. Sure, not all three billion can collaborate and compete. In fact, for most people the world is not yet flat at all. But even if we're talking about only 10 percent, that's 300 million people—about twice the size of the American work force. And be advised: the Indians and Chinese are not racing us to the bottom. They are racing us to the top. What China's leaders really want is that the next generation of underwear and airplane wings not just be "made in China" but also be "designed in China." And that is where things are heading. So in 30 years we will have gone from "sold in China" to "made in China" to "designed in China" to "dreamed up in China"—or from China as collaborator with the worldwide manufacturers on nothing to China as a low-cost, high-quality, hyperefficient collaborator with worldwide manufacturers on everything. Ditto India. Said

Craig Barrett, the C.E.O. of Intel, "You don't bring three billion people into the world economy overnight without huge consequences, especially from three societies"—like India, China and Russia—"with rich educational heritages."

That is why there is nothing that guarantees that Americans or Western Europeans will continue leading the way. These new players are stepping onto the playing field legacy free, meaning that many of them were so far behind that they can leap right into the new technologies without having to worry about all the sunken costs of old systems. It means that they can move very fast to adopt new, state-of-the-art technologies, which is why there are already more cellphones in use in China today than there are people in America.

If you want to appreciate the sort of challenge we are facing, let me share with you two conversations. One was with some of the Microsoft officials who were involved in setting up Microsoft's research center in Beijing, Microsoft Research Asia, which opened in 1998—after Microsoft sent teams to Chinese universities to administer I.Q. tests in order to recruit the best brains from China's 1.3 billion people. Out of the 2,000 top Chinese engineering and science students tested, Microsoft hired 20. They have a saying at Microsoft about their Asia center, which captures the intensity of competition it takes to win a job there and explains why it is already the most productive research team at Microsoft: "Remember, in China, when you are one in a million, there are 1,300 other people just like you."

The other is a conversation I had with Rajesh Rao, a young Indian entrepreneur who started an electronic-game company from Bangalore, which today owns the rights to Charlie Chaplin's image for mobile computer games. "We can't relax," Rao said. "I think in the case of the United States that is what happened a bit. Please look at me: I am from India. We have been at a very different level before in terms of technology and business. But once we saw we had an infrastructure that made the world a small place, we promptly tried to make the best use of it. We saw there were so many things we could do. We went ahead, and today what we are seeing is a result of that. There is no time to rest. That is gone. There are dozens of people who are doing the same thing you are doing, and they are trying to do it better. It is like water in a tray: you shake it, and it will find the path of least resistance. That is what is going to happen to so many jobs—they will go to that corner of the world where there is the least resistance and the most opportunity. If there is a skilled person in Timbuktu, he will get work if he knows how to access the rest of the world, which is quite easy today. You can make a Web site and have an e-mail address and you are up and running. And if you are able to demonstrate your work, using the same infrastructure, and if people are comfortable giving work to you and if you are diligent and clean in your transactions, then you are in business."

Instead of complaining about outsourcing, Rao said, Americans and Western Europeans would "be better off thinking about how you can raise your bar and raise yourselves into doing something better. Americans have consistently led in innovation over the last century. Americans whining—we have never seen that before."

Rao is right. And it is time we got focused. As a person who grew up during the cold war, I'll always remember driving down the highway and listening to the radio, when suddenly the music would stop and a grim-voiced announcer would come on the air and say: "This is a test. This station is conducting a test of the Emergency Broadcast System." And then there would be a 20-second high-pitched siren sound. Fortunately, we never had to live through a moment in the cold war when the announcer came on and said, "This is a not a test."

That, however, is exactly what I want to say here: "This is not a test."

The long-term opportunities and challenges that the flattening of the world puts before the United States are profound. Therefore, our ability to get by doing things the way we've been doing them—which is to say not always enriching our secret sauce—will not suffice any more. "For a country as wealthy as we are, it is amazing how little we are doing to enhance our natural competitiveness," says Dinakar Singh, the Indian-American hedge-fund manager. "We are in a world that has a system that now allows convergence among many billions of people, and we had better step back and figure out what it means. It would be a nice coincidence if all the things that were true before were still true now, but there are quite a few things you actually need to do differently. You need to have a much more thoughtful national discussion."

If this moment has any parallel in recent American history, it is the height of the cold war, around 1957, when the Soviet Union leapt ahead of America in the space race by putting up the Sputnik satellite. The main challenge then came from those who wanted to put up walls; the main challenge to America today comes from the fact that all the walls are being taken down and many other people can now compete and collaborate with us much more directly. The main challenge in that world was from those practicing extreme Communism, namely Russia, China and North Korea. The main challenge to America today is from those practicing extreme capitalism, namely China, India and South Korea. The main objective in that era was building a strong state, and the main objective in this era is building strong individuals.

Meeting the challenges of flatism requires as comprehensive, energetic and focused a response as did meeting the challenge of Communism. It requires a president who can summon the nation to work harder, get smarter, attract more young women and men to science and engineering and build the broadband infrastructure, portable pensions and health care that will help every American become more employable in an age in which no one can guarantee you lifetime employment.

We have been slow to rise to the challenge of flatism, in contrast to Communism, maybe because flatism doesn't involve ICBM missiles aimed at our cities. Indeed, the hot line, which used to connect the Kremlin with the White House, has been replaced by the help line, which connects everyone in America to call centers in Bangalore. While the other end of the hot line might have had Leonid Brezhnev threatening nuclear war, the other end of the help line just has a soft voice eager to help you sort out your AOL bill or collaborate with you on a new piece of software. No, that voice has none of the menace of Nikita Khrushchev pounding a shoe on the table at the United Nations, and it has none of the sinister snarl of the bad guys in "From Russia with Love." No, that voice on the help line just has a friendly Indian lilt that masks any sense of threat or challenge. It simply says: "Hello, my name is Rajiv. Can I help you?"

No, Rajiv, actually you can't. When it comes to responding to the challenges of the flat world, there is no help line we can call. We have to dig into ourselves. We in America have all the basic economic and educational tools to do that. But we have not been improving those tools as much as we should. That is why we are in what Shirley Ann Jackson, the 2004 president of the American Association for the Advancement of Science and president of Rensselaer Polytechnic Institute, calls a "quiet crisis"—one that is slowly eating away at America's scientific and engineering base.

"If left unchecked," said Jackson, the first African-American woman to earn a Ph.D. in physics from M.I.T., "this could challenge our pre-eminence and capacity to innovate." And it is our ability to constantly innovate new products, services and companies that has been the source of America's horn of plenty and steadily widening middle class for the last two centuries. This quiet crisis is a product of three gaps now plaguing American society. The first is an "ambition gap." Compared with the young, energetic Indians and Chinese, too many Americans have gotten too lazy. As David Rothkopf, a former official in the Clinton Commerce Department, puts it, "The real entitlement we need to get rid of is our sense of entitlement." Second, we have a serious numbers gap building. We are not producing enough engineers and scientists. We used to make up for that by importing them from India and China, but in a flat world, where people can now stay home and compete with us, and in a post-9/11 world, where we are insanely keeping out many of the first-round intellectual draft choices in the world for exaggerated security reasons, we can no longer cover the gap. That's a key reason companies are looking abroad. The numbers are not here. And finally we are developing an education gap. Here is the dirty little secret that no C.E.O. wants to tell you: they are not just outsourcing to save on salary. They are doing it because they can often get better-skilled and more productive people than their American workers.

These are some of the reasons that Bill Gates, the Microsoft chairman, warned the governors' conference in a Feb. 26 speech that American high-school education is "obsolete." As Gates put it: "When I compare our high schools to what I see when I'm traveling abroad, I am terrified for our work force of tomorrow. In math and science, our fourth graders are among the top students in the world. By eighth grade, they're in the middle of the pack. By 12th grade, U.S. students are scoring near the bottom of all industrialized nations. . . . The percentage of a population with a college degree is important, but so are sheer numbers. In 2001, India graduated almost a million more students from college than the United States did. China graduates twice as many students with bachelor's degrees as the U.S., and they have six times as many graduates majoring in engineering. In the international competition to have the biggest and best supply of knowledge workers, America is falling behind."

We need to get going immediately. It takes 15 years to train a good engineer, because, ladies and gentlemen, this really is rocket science. So parents, throw away the Game Boy, turn off the television and get your kids to work. There is no sugar-coating this: in a flat world, every individual is going to have to run a little faster if he or she wants to advance his or her standard of living. When I was growing up, my parents used to say to me, "Tom, finish your dinner—people in China are starving." But after sailing to the edges of the flat world for a year, I am now telling my own daughters, "Girls, finish your homework—people in China and India are starving for your jobs."

I repeat, this is not a test. This is the beginning of a crisis that won't remain quiet for long. And as the Stanford economist Paul Romer so rightly says, "A crisis is a terrible thing to waste."

THOMAS L. FRIEDMAN is the author of *"The World Is Flat: A Brief History of the Twenty-First Century,"* to be published this week by Farrar, Straus & Giroux and from which this article is adapted. His column appears on the Op-Ed page of *The Times,* and his television documentary "Does Europe Hate Us?" was shown on the Discovery Channel on April 7, 2005.

Can Extreme Poverty Be Eliminated?

Market economics and globalization are lifting the bulk of humanity out of extreme poverty, but special measures are needed to help the poorest of the poor.

JEFFREY D. SACHS

Almost everyone who ever lived was wretchedly poor. Famine, death from childbirth, infectious disease and countless other hazards were the norm for most of history. Humanity's sad plight started to change with the Industrial Revolution, beginning around 1750. New scientific insights and technological innovations enabled a growing proportion of the global population to break free of extreme poverty.

Two and a half centuries later more than five billion of the world's 6.5 billion people can reliably meet their basic living needs and thus can be said to have escaped from the precarious conditions that once governed everyday life. One out of six inhabitants of this planet, however, still struggles daily to meet some or all of such critical requirements as adequate nutrition, uncontaminated drinking water, safe shelter and sanitation as well as access to basic health care. These people get by on $1 a day or less and are overlooked by public services for health, education and infrastructure. Every day more than 20,000 die of dire poverty, for want of food, safe drinking water, medicine or other essential needs.

For the first time in history, global economic prosperity, brought on by continuing scientific and technological progress and the self-reinforcing accumulation of wealth, has placed the world within reach of eliminating extreme poverty altogether. This prospect will seem fanciful to some, but the dramatic economic progress made by China, India and other low-income parts of Asia over the past 25 years demonstrates that it is realistic. Moreover, the predicted stabilization of the world's population toward the middle of this century will help by easing pressures on Earth's climate, ecosystems and natural resources—pressures that might otherwise undo economic gains.

EXTREME POVERTY could become a thing of the past in a few decades if the affluent countries of the world pony up a small percentage of their wealth to help the planet's 1.1 billion indigent populations out of conditions of dire poverty.

Although economic growth has shown a remarkable capacity to lift vast numbers of people out of extreme poverty, progress is neither automatic nor inevitable. Market forces and free trade are not enough. Many of the poorest regions are ensnared in a poverty trap: they lack the financial means to make the necessary investments in infrastructure, education, health care systems and other vital needs. Yet the end of such poverty is feasible if a concerted global effort is undertaken, as the nations of the world promised when they adopted the Millennium Development Goals at the United Nations Millennium Summit in 2000. A dedicated cadre of development agencies, international financial institutions, nongovernmental organizations and communities throughout the developing world already constitute a global network of expertise and goodwill to help achieve this objective.

This past January my colleagues and I on the U.N. Millennium Project published a plan to halve the rate of extreme poverty by 2015 (compared with 1990) and to achieve other quantitative targets for reducing hunger, disease and environmental degradation. In my recent book, *The End of Poverty,* I argue that a large-scale and targeted public investment effort could in fact eliminate this problem by 2025, much as smallpox was eradicated globally. This hypothesis is controversial, so I am pleased to have the opportunity to clarify its main arguments and to respond to various concerns that have been raised about it.

Beyond Business as Usual

Economists have learned a great deal during the past few years about how countries develop and what roadblocks can stand in their way. A new kind of development economics needs to emerge, one that is better grounded in science—a "clinical economics" akin to modern medicine. Today's medical professionals understand that disease results from a vast array of interacting factors and conditions: pathogens, nutrition, environment, aging, individual and population genetics, lifestyle. They also know that one key to proper treatment is the ability

Crossroads for Poverty

The Problem:

- Much of humankind has succeeded in dragging itself out of severe poverty since the onset of the Industrial Revolution in the mid-18th century, but about 1.1 billion out of today's 6.5 billion global inhabitants are utterly destitute in a world of plenty.
- These unfortunates, who get by on less than $1 a day, have little access to adequate nutrition, safe drinking water and shelter, as well as basic sanitation and health care services. What can the developed world do to lift this huge segment of the human population out of extreme poverty?

The Plan:

- Doubling affluent nations' international poverty assistance to about $160 billion a year would go a long way toward ameliorating the terrible predicament faced by one in six humans. This figure would constitute about 0.5 percent of the gross national product (GNP) of the planet's rich countries. Because these investments do not include other categories of aid, such as spending on major infrastructure projects, climate change mitigation or post conflict reconstruction, donors should commit to reaching the long stand target of 0.7 percent of GNP by 2015.
- These donations, often provided to local groups, would need to be closely monitored and audited to ensure that they are correctly targeted toward those truly in need.

to make an individualized diagnosis of the source of illness. Likewise, development economists need better diagnostic skills to recognize that economic pathologies have a wide variety of causes, including many outside the traditional ken of economic practice.

Public opinion in affluent countries often attributes extreme poverty to faults with the poor themselves—or at least with their governments. Race was once thought the deciding factor. Then it was culture: religious divisions and taboos, caste systems, a lack of entrepreneurship, gender inequities. Such theories have waned as societies of an ever widening range of religions and cultures have achieved relative prosperity. Moreover, certain supposedly immutable aspects of culture (such as fertility choices and gender and caste roles) in fact change, often dramatically, as societies become urban and develop economically.

Most recently, commentators have zeroed in on "poor governance," often code words for corruption. They argue that extreme poverty persists because governments fail to open up their markets, provide public services and clamp down on bribe taking. It is said that if these regimes cleaned up their acts, they, too, would flourish. Development assistance efforts have become largely a series of good governance lectures.

The availability of cross-country and time-series data now allows experts to make much more systematic analyses. Although debate continues, the weight of the evidence indicates that governance makes a difference but is not the sole determinant of economic growth. According to surveys conducted by Transparency International, business leaders actually perceive many fast-growing Asian countries to be more corrupt than some slow-growing African ones.

Geography—including natural resources, climate, topography, and proximity to trade routes and major markets—is at least as important as good governance. As early as 1776, Adam Smith argued that high transport costs inhibited development in the inland areas of Africa and Asia. Other geographic features, such as the heavy disease burden of the tropics, also interfere. One recent study by my Columbia University colleague Xavier Sala-i-Martin demonstrated once again that tropical countries saddled with malaria have experienced slower growth than those free from the disease. The good news is that geographic factors shape, but do not decide, a country's economic fate. Technology can offset them: drought can be fought with irrigation systems, isolation with roads and mobile telephones, diseases with preventive and therapeutic measures.

The other major insight is that although the most powerful mechanism for reducing extreme poverty is to encourage overall economic growth, a rising tide does not necessarily lift all boats. Average income can rise, but if the income is distributed unevenly the poor may benefit little, and pockets of extreme poverty may persist (especially in geographically disadvantaged regions). Moreover, growth is not simply a free-market phenomenon. It requires basic government services: infrastructure, health, education, and scientific and technological innovation. Thus, many of the recommendations of the past two decades emanating from Washington—that governments in low-income countries should cut back on their spending to make room for the private sector—miss the point. Government spending, directed at investment in critical areas, is itself a vital spur to growth, especially if its effects are to reach the poorest of the poor.

The Poverty Trap

So what do these insights tell us about the region most afflicted by poverty today, Africa? Fifty years ago tropical Africa was roughly as rich as subtropical and tropical Asia. As Asia boomed, Africa stagnated. Special geographic factors have played a crucial role.

Foremost among these is the existence of the Himalaya Mountains, which produce southern Asia's monsoon climate and vast river systems. Well-watered farmlands served as the starting points for Asia's rapid escape from extreme poverty during the past five decades. The Green Revolution of the 1960s and 1970s introduced high-yield grains, irrigation and fertilizers, which ended the cycle of famine, disease and despair.

It also freed a significant proportion of the labor force to seek manufacturing jobs in the cities. Urbanization, in turn, spurred growth, not only by providing a home for industry and innovation but also by prompting greater investment in a healthy and skilled labor force. Urban residents cut their fertility rates and

Globalization, Poverty and Foreign Aid

Average citizens in affluent nations often have many questions about the effects of economic globalization on rich and poor nations and about how developing countries spend the aid they receive. Here are a few brief answers:

Is Globalization Making the Rich Richer and the Poor Poorer?

Generally, the answer is no. Economic globalization is supporting very rapid advances of many impoverished economies, notably in Asia. International trade and foreign investment inflows have been major factors in China's remarkable economic growth during the past quarter century and in India's fast economic growth since the early 1990s. The poorest of the poor, notably in sub-Saharan Africa, are not held back by globalization; they are largely bypassed by it.

Is Poverty the Result of Exploitation of the Poor by the Rich?

Affluent nations have repeatedly plundered and exploited poor countries through slavery, colonial rule and unfair trade practices. Yet it is perhaps more accurate to say that exploitation is the result of poverty (which leaves impoverished countries vulnerable to abuse) rather than the cause of it. Poverty is generally the result of low productivity per worker, which reflects poor health, lack of job-market skills, patchiness of infrastructure (roads, power plants, utility lines, shipping ports), chronic malnutrition and the like. Exploitation has played a role in producing some of these conditions, but deeper factors [geographic isolation, endemic disease, ecological destruction, challenging conditions for food production] have tended to be more important and difficult to overcome without external help.

Will Higher Incomes in Poor Countries Mean Lower Incomes in Rich Countries?

By and large, economic development is a positive-sum process, meaning that all can partake in it without causing some to suffer. In the past 200 years, the world as a whole has achieved a massive increase in economic output rather than a shift in economic output to one region at the expense of another. To be sure, global environmental constraints are already starting to impose themselves. As today's poor countries develop, the climate, fisheries and forests are coming under increased strain. Overall global economic growth is compatible with sustainable management of the ecosystems on which all humans depend—indeed, wealth can be good for the environment—but only if public policy and technologies encourage sound practices and the necessary investments are made in environmental sustainability.

Do U.S. Private Contributions Make Up for the Low Levels of U.S. Official Aid?

Some have claimed that while the U.S. government budget provides relatively little assistance to the poorest countries, the private sector makes up the gap. In fact, the Organization for Economic Cooperation and Development has estimated that private foundations and nongovernmental organizations give roughly $6 billion a year in international assistance, or 0.05 percent of U.S. gross national product (GNP). In that case, total U.S. international aid is around 0.21 percent of GNP—still among the lowest ratios of all donor nations.

—J.D.S.

thus were able to spend more for the health, nutrition and education of each child. City kids went to school at a higher rate than their rural cousins. And with the emergence of urban infrastructure and public health systems, city populations became less disease-prone than their counterparts in the countryside, where people typically lack safe drinking water, modern sanitation, professional health care and protection from vector-borne ailments such as malaria.

Africa did not experience a green revolution. Tropical Africa lacks the massive floodplains that facilitate the large-scale and low-cost irrigation found in Asia. Also, its rainfall is highly variable, and impoverished farmers have been unable to purchase fertilizer. The initial Green Revolution research featured crops, especially paddy rice and wheat, not widely grown in Africa (high-yield varieties suitable for it have been developed in recent years, but they have not yet been disseminated sufficiently). The continent's food production per person has actually been falling, and Africans' caloric intake is the lowest in the world; food insecurity is rampant. Its labor force has remained tethered to subsistence agriculture.

Compounding its agricultural woes, Africa bears an overwhelming burden of tropical diseases. Because of climate and the endemic mosquito species, malaria is more intensively transmitted in Africa than anywhere else. And high transport costs isolate Africa economically. In East Africa, for example, the rainfall is greatest in the interior of the continent, so most people live there, far from ports and international trade routes.

Much the same situation applies to other impoverished parts of the world, notably the Andean and Central American highlands and the landlocked countries of Central Asia. Being economically isolated, they are unable to attract much foreign investment (other than for the extraction of oil, gas and precious minerals). Investors tend to be dissuaded by the high transport costs associated with the interior regions. Rural areas therefore remain stuck in a vicious cycle of poverty, hunger, illness and illiteracy. Impoverished areas lack adequate internal savings to make the needed investments because most households live hand to mouth. The few high-income families, who do accumulate savings, park them overseas rather than at home. This capital flight includes not only financial capital but also the human variety, in the form of skilled workers—doctors, nurses, scientists and engineers, who frequently leave in search of improved economic opportunities abroad. The poorest countries are often, perversely, net exporters of capital.

Put Money Where Mouths Are

The technology to overcome these handicaps and jump-start economic development exists. Malaria can be controlled using bed nets, indoor pesticide spraying and improved medicines. Drought-prone countries in Africa with nutrient depleted soils can benefit enormously from drip irrigation and greater use of fertilizers. Landlocked countries can be connected by paved highway networks, airports and fiber-optic cables. All these projects cost money, of course.

Many larger countries, such as China, have prosperous regions that can help support their own lagging areas. Coastal eastern China, for instance, is now financing massive public investments in western China. Most of today's successfully developing countries, especially smaller ones, received at least some backing from external donors at crucial times. The critical scientific innovations that formed the underpinnings of the Green Revolution were bankrolled by the Rockefeller Foundation, and the spread of these technologies in India and elsewhere in Asia was funded by the U.S. and other donor governments and international development institutions.

We in the U.N. Millennium Project have listed the investments required to help today's impoverished regions cover basic needs in health, education, water, sanitation, food production, roads and other key areas. We have put an approximate price tag on that assistance and estimated how much could be financed by poor households themselves and by domestic institutions. The remaining cost is the "financing gap" that international donors need to make up.

For tropical Africa, the total investment comes to $110 per person a year. To place this into context, the average income in this part of the world is $350 per annum, most or all of which is required just to stay alive. The full cost of the total investment is clearly beyond the funding reach of these countries. Of the $110, perhaps $40 could be financed domestically, so that $70 per capita would be required in the form of international aid.

Adding it all up, the total requirement for assistance across the globe is around $160 billion a year, double the current rich-country aid budget of $80 billion. This figure amounts to approximately 0.5 percent of the combined gross national product (GNP) of the affluent donor nations. It does not include other humanitarian projects such as postwar Iraqi reconstruction or Indian Ocean tsunami relief. To meet these needs as well, a reasonable figure would be 0.7 percent of GNP, which is what all donor countries have long promised but few have fulfilled. Other organizations, including the International Monetary Fund, the World Bank and the British government, have reached much the same conclusion.

When polled, Americans greatly overestimate how much foreign aid the U.S. gives—by as much as 30 times.

Foreign Aid: How Should the Money Be Spent?

Here is a breakdown of the needed investment for three typical low-income African countries to help them achieve the Millennium Development Goals. For all nations given aid, the average total annual assistance per person would come to around $110 a year. These investments would be financed by both foreign aid and the countries themselves.

Investment Area	Average per Year between 2005–2015 ($ per capita)		
	Ghana	Tanzania	Uganda
Hunger	7	8	6
Education	19	14	5
Gender equality	3	3	3
Health	25	35	34
Water supply and sanitation	8	7	5
Improving slum conditions	2	3	2
Energy	15	16	12
Roads	10	22	20
Other	10	10	10
Total	100	117	106

Calculated from data from Investing in Development [U.N. Millennium Project, Earth Scan Publications, 2005]. Numbers do not sum to totals because of rounding.

We believe these investments would enable the poorest countries to cut poverty by half by 2015 and, if continued, to eliminate it altogether by 2025. They would not be "welfare payments" from rich to poor but instead something far more important and durable. People living above mere subsistence levels would be able to save for their futures; they could join the virtuous cycle of rising incomes, savings and technological inflows. We would be giving a billion people a hand up instead of a handout.

If rich nations fail to make these investments, they will be called on to provide emergency assistance more or less indefinitely. They will face famine, epidemics, regional conflicts and the spread of terrorist havens. And they will condemn not only the impoverished countries but themselves as well to chronic political instability, humanitarian emergencies and security risks.

The debate is now shifting from the basic diagnosis of extreme poverty and the calculations of financing needs to the practical matter of how assistance can best be delivered. Many people believe that aid efforts failed in the past and that care is needed to avoid the repetition of failure. Some of these concerns are well grounded, but others are fueled by misunderstandings.

When pollsters ask Americans how much foreign aid they think the U.S. gives, they greatly overestimate the amount by as much as 30 times. Believing that so much money has been donated and so little has been done with it, the public concludes that these programs have "failed." The reality is rather different.

U.S. official assistance to sub-Saharan Africa has been running at $2 billion to $4 billion a year, or roughly $3 to $6 for every African. Most of this aid has come in the form of "technical cooperation" (which goes into the pockets of consultants), food contributions for famine victims and the cancellation of unpaid debts. Little of this support has come in a form that can be invested in systems that improve health, nutrition, food production and transport. We should give foreign aid a fair chance before deciding whether it works or not.

A second common misunderstanding concerns the extent to which corruption is likely to eat up the donated money. Some foreign aid in the past has indeed ended up in the equivalent of Swiss bank accounts. That happened when the funds were provided for geopolitical reasons rather than development; a good example was U.S. support for the corrupt regime of Mobutu Sese Seko of Zaire (now the Democratic Republic of the Congo) during part of the cold war. When assistance has been targeted at development rather than political goals, the outcomes have been favorable, ranging from the Green Revolution to the eradication of smallpox and the recent near-eradication of polio.

The aid package we advocate would be directed toward those countries with a reasonable degree of good governance and operational transparency. In Africa, these countries include Ethiopia, Ghana, Mali, Mozambique, Senegal and Tanzania. The money would not be merely thrown at them. It would be provided according to a detailed and monitored plan, and new rounds of financing would be delivered only as the work actually got done. Much of the funds would be given directly to villages and towns to minimize the chances of their getting diverted by central governments. All these programs should be closely audited.

Western society tends to think of foreign aid as money lost. But if supplied properly, it is an investment that will one day yield huge returns, much as U.S. assistance to Western Europe and East Asia after World War II did. By prospering, today's impoverished countries will wean themselves from endless charity. They will contribute to the international advance of science, technology and trade. They will escape political instability, which leaves many of them vulnerable to violence, narcotics trafficking, civil war and even terrorist takeover. Our own security will be bolstered as well. As U.N. Secretary-General Kofi Annan wrote earlier this year: "There will be no development without security, and no security without development."

The author, **JEFFREY D. SACHS,** directs the Earth Institute at Columbia University and the United Nations Millennium Project. An economist, Sachs is well known for advising governments in Latin America, Eastern Europe, the former Soviet Union, Asia and Africa on economic reforms and for his work with international agencies to promote poverty reduction, disease control and debt reduction in poor countries. A native of Detroit, he received his BA, MA and PhD degrees from Harvard University.

The Ideology of Development

WILLIAM EASTERLY

A dark ideological specter is haunting the world. It is almost as deadly as the tired ideologies of the last century—communism, fascism, and socialism—that failed so miserably. It feeds some of the most dangerous trends of our time, including religious fundamentalism. It is the half-century-old ideology of Developmentalism. And it is thriving.

Like all ideologies, Development promises a comprehensive final answer to all of society's problems, from poverty and illiteracy to violence and despotic rulers. It shares the common ideological characteristic of suggesting there is only one correct answer, and it tolerates little dissent. It deduces this unique answer for everyone from a general theory that purports to apply to everyone, everywhere. There's no need to involve local actors who reap its costs and benefits. Development even has its own intelligentsia, made up of experts at the International Monetary Fund (IMF), World Bank, and United Nations.

The power of Developmentalism is disheartening, because the failure of all the previous ideologies might have laid the groundwork for the opposite of ideology—the freedom of individuals and societies to choose their destinies. Yet, since the fall of communism, the West has managed to snatch defeat from the jaws of victory, and with disastrous results. Development ideology is sparking a dangerous counterreaction. The "one correct answer" came to mean "free markets," and, for the poor world, it was defined as doing whatever the IMF and the World Bank tell you to do. But the reaction in Africa, Central Asia, Latin America, the Middle East, and Russia has been to fight against free markets. So, one of the best economic ideas of our time, the genius of free markets, was presented in one of the worst possible ways, with unelected outsiders imposing rigid doctrines on the xenophobic unwilling.

The backlash has been so severe that other failed ideologies are gaining new adherents throughout these regions. In Nicaragua, for instance, IMF and World Bank structural adjustments failed so conspicuously that the pitiful Sandinista regime of the 1980s now looks good by comparison. Its leader, Daniel Ortega, is back in power. The IMF's actions during the Argentine financial crisis of 2001 now reverberate a half decade later with Hugo Chavez, Venezuela's illiberal leader, being welcomed with open arms in Buenos Aires. The heavy-handed directives of the World Bank and IMF in Bolivia provided the soil from which that country's neosocialist president, Evo Morales, sprung. The disappointing payoff following eight structural adjustment loans to Zimbabwe and $8 billion in foreign aid during the 1980s and 1990s helped Robert Mugabe launch a vicious counterattack on democracy. The IMF-World Bank-Jeffrey Sachs application of "shock therapy" to the former Soviet Union has created a lasting nostalgia for communism. In the Middle East, $154 billion in foreign aid between 1980 and 2001, 45 structural adjustment loans, and "expert" advice produced zero per capita GDP growth that helped create a breeding ground for Islamic fundamentalism.

This blowback against "globalization from above" has spread to every corner of the Earth. It now threatens to kill sensible, moderate steps toward the freer movement of goods, ideas, capital, and people.

Development's Politburo

The ideology of Development is not only about having experts design your free market for you; it is about having the experts design a comprehensive, technical plan to solve all the problems of the poor. These experts see poverty as a purely technological problem, to be solved by engineering and the natural sciences, ignoring messy social sciences such as economics, politics, and sociology.

Sachs, Columbia University's celebrity economist, is one of its main proprietors. He is now recycling his theories of overnight shock therapy, which failed so miserably in Russia, into promises of overnight global poverty reduction. "Africa's problems," he has said, "are . . . solvable with practical and proven technologies." His own plan features hundreds of expert interventions to solve every last problem of the poor—from green manure, breast-feeding education, and bicycles to solar-energy systems, school uniforms for AIDS orphans, and windmills. Not to mention such critical interventions as "counseling and information services for men to address their reproductive health needs." All this will be done, Sachs says, by "a united and effective United Nations country team, which coordinates in one place the work of the U.N. specialized agencies, the IMF, and the World Bank."

So the admirable concern of rich countries for the tragedies of world poverty is thus channeled into fattening the international aid bureaucracy, the self-appointed priesthood of Development. Like other ideologies, this thinking favors collective goals such as national poverty reduction, national economic growth, and the global Millennium Development Goals, over the aspirations of individuals. Bureaucrats who write poverty-reduction frameworks outrank individuals who actually reduce poverty by, say, starting a business. Just as Marxists favored world revolution and socialist internationalism, Development stresses world goals over the autonomy of societies to choose their own path. It favors doctrinaire abstractions such as "market-friendly policies," "good investment climate," and "pro-poor globalization" over the freedom of individuals.

Development also shares another Marxist trait: It aspires to be scientific. Finding the one correct solution to poverty is seen as a scientific problem to be solved by the experts. They are always sure they know the answer, vehemently reject disagreement, and then later change their answers. In psychiatry, this is known as Borderline Personality Disorder. For the Development Experts, it's a way of life. The answer at first was aid-financed investment and industrialization in poor countries, then it was market-oriented government policy reform, then it was fixing institutional problems such as corruption, then it was globalization, then it was the Poverty Reduction Strategy to achieve the Millennium Development Goals.

One reason the answers keep changing is because, in reality, high-growth countries follow a bewildering variety of paths to development, and the countries with high growth rates are constantly changing from decade to decade. Who could be more different than successful developers such as China and Chile, Botswana and Singapore, Taiwan and Turkey, or Hong Kong and Vietnam? What about the many countries who tried to emulate these rising stars and failed? What about the former stars who have fallen on hard times, like the Ivory Coast, which was one of the fastest developers of the 1960s and 1970s, only to become mired in a civil war? What about Mexico, which saw rapid growth until 1980 and has had slow growth ever since, despite embracing the experts' reforms?

The experts in Developmentalism's Politburo don't bother themselves with such questions. All the previous answers were right; they were just missing one more "necessary condition" that the experts have only just now added to the list. Like all ideologies, Development is at the same time too rigid to predict what will work in the messy real world and yet flexible enough to forever escape falsification by real-world events. The high church of Development, the World Bank, has guaranteed it can never be wrong by making statements such as, "different policies can yield the same result, and the same policy can yield different results, depending on country institutional contexts and underlying growth strategies." Of course, you still need experts to figure out the contexts and strategies.

Resistance is Futile

Perhaps more hypocritical yet is Development's simple theory of historical inevitability. Poor societies are not just poor, the experts tell us, they are "developing" until they reach the final stage of history, or "development," in which poverty will soon end. Under this historiography, an end to starvation, tyranny, and war are thrown in like a free toaster on an infomercial. The experts judge all societies on a straight line, per capita income,

with the superior countries showing the inferior countries the image of their own future. And the experts heap scorn on those who resist the inevitabilities on the path to development.

One of today's leading Developmentalists, *New York Times* columnist Thomas Friedman, can hardly conceal his mockery of those who resist the march of history, or "the flattening of the world." "When you are Mexico," Friedman has written, "and your claim to fame is that you are a low-wage manufacturing country, and some of your people are importing statuettes of your own patron saint from China, because China can make them and ship them all the way across the Pacific more cheaply than you can produce them . . . you have got a problem. [T]he only way for Mexico to thrive is with a strategy of reform . . . the more Mexico just sits there, the more it is going to get run over." Friedman seems blissfully unaware that poor Mexico, so far from God yet so close to American pundits, has already tried much harder than China to implement the experts' "strategy of reform."

The self-confidence of Developmentalists like Friedman is so strong that they impose themselves even on those who accept their strategies. This year, for instance, Ghana celebrated its 50th anniversary as the first black African nation to gain independence. Official international aid donors to Ghana told its allegedly independent government, in the words of the World Bank: "We Partners are here giving you our pledge to give our best to make lives easier for you in running your country." Among the things they will do to make your life easier is to run your country for you.

Unfortunately, Development ideology has a dismal record of helping any country actually develop. The regions where the ideology has been most influential, Latin America and Africa, have done the worst. Luckless Latins and Africans are left chasing yesterday's formulas for success while those who ignored the Developmentalists found homegrown paths to success. The nations that have been the most successful in the past 40 years did so in such a variety of different ways that it would be hard to argue that they discovered the "correct answer" from development ideology. In fact, they often conspicuously violated whatever it was the experts said at the time. The East Asian tigers, for instance, chose outward orientation on their own in the 1960s, when the experts' conventional wisdom was industrialization for the home market. The rapid growth of China over the past quarter century came when it was hardly a poster child for either the 1980s Washington Consensus or the 1990s institutionalism of democracy and cracking down on corruption.

What explains the appeal of development ideology despite its dismal track record? Ideologies usually arise in response to tragic situations in which people are hungry for clear and comprehensive solutions. The inequality of the Industrial Revolution bred Marxism, and the backwardness of Russia its Leninist offshoot. Germany's defeat and demoralization in World War I birthed Nazism. Economic hardship accompanied by threats to identity led to both Christian and Islamic fundamentalism. Similarly, development ideology appeals to those who want a definitive, complete answer to the tragedy of world poverty and inequality. It answers the question, "What is to be done?" to borrow the title of Lenin's 1902 tract. It stresses collective social outcomes that must be remedied by collective, top-down action by the intelligentsia, the revolutionary vanguard, the development expert. As Sachs explains, "I have . . . gradually come to understand through my scientific research and on the ground advisory work the awesome power in our generation's hands to end the massive suffering of the extreme poor . . . although introductory economics textbooks preach individualism and decentralized markets, our safety and prosperity depend at least as much on collective decisions."

Freeing the Poor

Few realize that Americans in 1776 had the same income level as the average African today. Yet, like all the present-day developed nations, the United States was lucky enough to escape poverty before there were Developmentalists. In the words of former IMF First Deputy Managing Director Anne Krueger, development in the rich nations "just happened." George Washington did not have to deal with aid partners, getting structurally adjusted by them, or preparing poverty-reduction strategy papers for them. Abraham Lincoln did not celebrate a government of the donors, by the donors, and for the donors. Today's developed nations were free to experiment with their own pragmatic paths toward more government accountability and freer markets. Individualism and decentralized markets were good enough to give rise to penicillin, air conditioning, high-yield corn, and the automobile—not to mention better living standards, lower mortality, and the iPod.

The opposite of ideology is freedom, the ability of societies to be unchained from foreign control. The only "answer" to poverty reduction is freedom from being told the answer. Free societies and individuals are not guaranteed to succeed. They will make bad choices. But at least they bear the cost of those mistakes, and learn from them. That stands in stark contrast to accountability-free Developmentalism. This process of learning from mistakes is what produced the repositories of common sense that make up mainstream economics. The opposite of Development ideology is not anything goes, but the pragmatic use of time-tested economic ideas—the benefits of specialization, comparative advantage, gains from trade, market-clearing prices, trade-offs, budget constraints—by individuals, firms, governments, and societies as they find their own success.

History proves just how much good can come from individuals who both bear the costs and reap the benefits of their own choices when they are free to make them. That includes local politicians, activists, and businesspeople who are groping their way toward greater freedom, contrary to the Developmentalists who oxymoronically impose freedom of choice on other people. Those who best understood the lessons of the 20th century were not the ideologues asking, "What is to be done?" They were those asking, "How can people be more free to find their own solutions?"

The ideology of Development should be packed up in crates and sent off to the Museum of Dead Ideologies, just down the hall from Communism, Socialism, and Fascism. It's time to recognize that the attempt to impose a rigid development ideology on the world's poor has failed miserably. Fortunately, many poor societies are forging their own path toward greater freedom and prosperity anyway. That is how true revolutions happen.

WILLIAM EASTERLY is professor of economics at New York University.

Feminists and Fundamentalists

"Reassertions of an idealized past and a restored 'women's place' are occurring, from Kabul to Cambridge, at a time when the international community has concurred that women's rights are a global good."

KAVITA RAMDAS

The women's movement, as we refer to it now, was one of the most successful movements of the past century. It has been successful in many ways. Perhaps the most tangible evidence is that women's rights have become a desirable commodity, something that in the company of civilized nations people are proud to hold up as a model of what they have achieved, much in the way that democracy has become a global good.

In 1995, 189 countries signed a pact accepting the Beijing Declaration and Platform for Action as an expression of their goals. The platform called itself "an agenda for women's empowerment. It aims at removing obstacles to women's active participation in all spheres of public and private life, through a full and equal share in economic, social, cultural, and political decision making. This means the principle of shared power and responsibility should be established at home, in the workplace, and in wider national and international communities. Equality between women and men is a matter of human rights and a condition for social justice. It is also a necessary and fundamental prerequisite for equality, development, and peace."

These are, indeed, the ideals to which we as an international community should aspire. And in achieving this recognition of women's rights as a global good, we have arguably accomplished one of the most essential outcomes for any social movement: a broad and diverse constituency now concurs that it shares certain values and that we should all collectively promote them.

The women's movement has also been successful, maybe a little less so, with respect to a narrower definition of accomplishment: legal progress in a variety of areas. Today we see—and we sometimes take it for granted—that women are admitted to educational institutions where years ago they were not accepted; that women enjoy opportunities to pursue careers in fields formerly closed to them; that they have inheritance rights, the right to open their own bank accounts, and so forth.

Of course, women still have a long way to go in achieving the narrower legal definition of equality, even in America. Something that seems fairly basic—equal pay for equal work—has not been and probably will not be approved. The Equal Rights Amendment languishes still in the halls of the US Congress. And the United States remains one of the few countries that has not signed the Convention on the Elimination of All Forms of Discrimination against Women.

It does seem, however, that most of the world's nations have accepted women's rights as a global good. And yet the question arises: Is this achievement permanent? Is there some development that might threaten this and future advances of the women's movement?

Social Insecurity

While many of us have arrived at an apparent consensus about the good sense of making women's rights central to our enterprise as forward-looking communities, we are also seeing that the world is coping with unprecedented and unbelievably rapid change—change in science and technology, in social structures, in the movement of people and ideas across borders. As a consequence, all kinds of relationships that once were given are today up for grabs: relationships between individuals and communities, between citizens and states, between parents and children, between husbands and wives. Because of this, millions of people at some fundamental level feel less secure.

Now, the world as we know it has been run to this point by men. Therefore, today's pervasive insecurity is also challenging the prevailing structures in which men set the rules, including the rules of public discourse and political engagement. So what we are seeing is a reaction. The world has mostly agreed that women's rights are a good thing. But, at the same time, this frightening sense of change is condensing into one particular evidence of that change. And that evidence is the transformed position of women in our societies.

The result is a variety of efforts to reassert idealized notions of the past. Islamic fundamentalism is one example that attracts considerable attention. But the assertion of an idealized past is happening across the world, across cultures, within different religious traditions, in different countries and languages, and at all levels of society.

Sistani and Summers

Consider the cases of Iraq's Ali al-Sistani and America's Lawrence Summers. Obviously, these are very different men. They do not share a similar worldview, and they come from very different contexts. Grand Ayatollah Sistani, who wants to impose fundamentalist Islamic constraints on Iraqi women, lives in a rapidly transforming postcolonial society. His is a Muslim country, where the past is alive. Summers—the president of Harvard University who infamously wondered aloud whether women have the same innate abilities in math and science as men—lives in a highly developed capitalist society.

Yet America is also a society in which women increasingly challenge academia and male privilege within academia. Both Iraq and the United States are attempting to respond to where women are located within their social structures. I would argue that both Sistani and Summers are trying, at some level, to place boundaries around what women's roles ought to be.

They are doing so because these roles are up for grabs, and because the aspirations of women pose a widespread dilemma. Having more or less signed on in general to the global good of women's rights, many people around the world feel insecure about what women's advances might mean for their own lives, for their own relationships, for decision making in their own institutions.

This is the global threat: the feeling that somehow, if we let women just take off with this idea about women's rights, who knows where it could go? The last US presidential election highlighted a classic example of this fear, with a number of state ballot referendums drawing voters determined to defend the institution of marriage against perceived erosion.

Indeed, for some the very relevance of men to the reproductive process seems under assault. State governments in America continue to impose restrictions on abortion. But what significance do male partners retain if, outside of marriage between "man and wife," a woman can go to a sperm bank and make an independent choice to have a child? And what does this mean for society? And how do you begin to control this?

The Way We Were

It is not an accident that mass rapes became a symbol of the Bosnian war during the 1990s. An estimated 20,000 to 50,000 Bosnian women were raped during that genocidal conflict. Indeed, mass rape has become a feature of modern warfare—a strange phenomenon, when you consider that warfare has also become so highly technologically developed. We have all these amazing smart bombs, yet we also witness one of the most medieval forms of exerting power. What does this represent, in a society, more broadly?

And how do we think about this reassertion of an idealized past, these "fundamentalisms?" They are certainly not unique to one religion; I have watched Hindu fundamentalists in India spend the past eight years eulogizing one male god in a society that has long prided itself on worshipping numerous goddesses as well as gods.

Predictably, the idealized tradition, the fundamentalist challenge, is borne everywhere on the backs of women, and there is widespread reluctance to oppose it. This is what we found in Afghanistan under the Taliban, a brutal form of gender apartheid that was allowed to exist until the United States invaded in the aftermath of 9-11. Even today, we hear many arguments for why we should not impose human rights on societies that have other cultural traditions—why, if women are treated badly, we ought to be careful about making demands because that may be how things are done in those societies.

The kind of violence that women and girls experience on a day-to-day basis around the world, the kind of entrenched discrimination they face—if this behavior were applied against almost any ethnic or national minority, there would be loud and persistent calls for intervention. After the US invasion of Afghanistan, some rhetoric was heard about the liberation of that country's women. But, as Afghan women would point out, that liberation did not happen until two edifices, two towers, were attacked in the United States.

The variety of fundamentalisms notwithstanding, the one thread they share is the attempt to control women's bodies, the ability of women to move freely, and their ability to speak with any kind of free voice within their societies. It is ironic but telling that these reassertions of an idealized past and a restored "women's place" are occurring, from Kabul to Cambridge, at a time when the international community has concurred that women's rights are a global good. They are occurring at a time when every major international foundation and financial institution has agreed that no development goals—whether in economics, political development, or social development—can be achieved without investing in girls' education and the full and equal participation of women.

The Feminist Vanguard

Fortunately, while there is a threat, there is also hope. The hope is that the women's movement and the advancement of women's rights will be the vanguard in the international community's struggle to overcome fundamentalisms.

You can see this hope in the dilemma the US government is struggling with right now. The Bush administration is caught in a tricky contradiction. Because we have all agreed that women's rights are a global good, the administration cannot say that women's rights do not matter. Yet it is deeply beholden to a Christian fundamentalist movement within the United States that truly believes we must return to an idealized notion of the past.

The Southern Baptist Church, for example, has decided to put the word "obey" back in marriage vows; a woman should obey her husband (it is not in the man's vows). Promise Keepers is another movement that harkens back to eighteenth- and nineteenth-century definitions of husbands as hunter-gatherers and women as loyal wives who stay at home and raise the family. President Bush himself has made a number of speeches that evoke idealized images of a time when, as my husband would say, "men were men, and women were women."

The harkening back to a more constrictive order for women continues while the United States claims to be liberating women overseas from uncivilized nations that do not support women's equality. Human rights are held up as a global good even as they are undermined in the everyday lives of women. At the level of implementation, what you actually see are increasing restrictions on the freedom and control that women have—over their reproductive choices and access to contraception, for example—along with cutbacks in spending on health and education that harm women the most.

This is the global threat: the feeling that somehow, if we let women just take off with this idea about women's rights, who knows where it could go?

Some think Title IX has gone too far and want to turn it back. When many hear the term "Title IX," they think it has to do with women in sports. In fact, it has everything to do with President Summers' comments about women in the sciences. Title IX of the 1972 Education Amendments to the 1964 Civil Rights Act required fair access to a wide variety of educational resources—from soccer playing fields to science laboratories.

There are many levels at which, in the face of rhetorical acceptance of women's rights, policies and proposals are being pursued that would undermine achievements that took decades to accomplish. The women's movement has a vital role in resisting rollbacks.

Changing Culture

I work in the international arena, and people often ask me, "Why do other cultures not value women's rights?" And I like to remind them that there is nothing unique about cultures, and that there is no culture I can think of that intrinsically values women's rights.

Reformers in the United States fought for a very long time for women to be recognized as more than just the property of men, just as they struggled for the rights of black people to be recognized as human beings. Cultures are not static. There is nothing that says Western culture is inherently thoughtful and considerate and inclusive of women, minorities, or anyone else.

Why have some cultures evolved to a place where equal rights are regarded as desirable? Because those who have been most oppressed within these cultures have chosen to fight for the right to be treated with equality and dignity. And this is the same thing that is happening today in most of the world. In India, in Afghanistan, in Iraq, in Peru, in the indigenous communities of Mexico, people are struggling to have their culture evolve as a living, breathing thing, and to have women and girls who have not traditionally had voice in those cultures to now have voice.

There is hope in this—in women's rights as a fulcrum on which societies can tip toward modernity, not in the narrowly defined sense of Westernization, but true modernity, in terms of imagining a different conception of how the world can be organized. Women's movements struggle precisely at this fulcrum between modernity and the fundamentalist pressures to regress, and here there is promise.

In my work I have seen women in the most oppressive and closed societies take extraordinary risks and truly challenge the status quo. I have seen them find ways to make their culture more inclusive, more accepting, and more fundamentally equal for all people within their societies.

My organization, the Global Fund for Women, worked with Afghan women's groups during the Taliban's rule, both in refugee camps in Pakistan and in secret schools for girls—and for boys, I might add, inside Afghanistan. (One of the things people often do not think about is that the success of the women's movement accrues to both women and men. When the Taliban pulled women out of schools in Afghanistan, 65 percent of primary school teachers in the country were women. The government's action jeopardized the education of a whole generation of Afghan boys, who then had no alternative but to go to Islamic religious schools.)

What we found in our work over those years with a number of Afghan women's groups is that they are incredibly strategic about building alliances with male allies within their communities. They do not see their fight as a struggle against men. They see it as a struggle against the patriarchal system. They have been extraordinarily creative about choosing their priorities.

I was in Afghanistan in 2003 after the Taliban had been toppled. Like everyone else, I had seen the pictures of women throwing off their burqas, which everyone in the United States was very excited about (but which most women in Afghanistan, in fact, have not done; while in Iraq many more women have put them back on). To me, far more a sign of liberation in Afghanistan was a scene I witnessed in a small classroom in Kabul, where three women taught a class of 45 male teachers—village school teachers from different provinces around Afghanistan.

These three women, their heads covered in scarves, were discussing the pedagogy of successful education. Amid building blocks made out of recycled cigarette cartons, they were talking to the male teachers about how educators need to make learning joyful and pleasurable, something that children can be enthused about.

When it was time for questions and answers, I asked, "What does it feel like to be sitting in a classroom and listening to three women teachers teaching you?" One man raised his hand and said, "I'm a professor of mathematics and science, and for 25 years, Afghan schoolchildren are boys who have learned how to hold an AK-47 before they learned how to do basic math. I haven't been in a school that has had a science laboratory for 25 years." He said, "During these 25 years, it was women who kept education alive in our country, and I think it's time we should be learning from the women." It was an extraordinary statement, and to me, more powerful than any picture of a woman pulling off her burqa.

"Equal to What?"

Across much of the world the leadership of the women's movement has shifted from the kinds of experiences that Western feminists underwent in the 1960s and 1970s, which were very important and in many ways necessary, but which were very much filled with conflict. There is a willingness now in the developing world to be more inclusive, an approach born out of necessity and also from a sense that this is a struggle we have to be in together.

Women's groups in different parts of the world are showing an increasing ability to build on the notion that their states and the international institutions have all signed onto—this idea that women's rights are a global good—while at the same time finding a way to make it real in their own communities, finding a way to say, "Well, so what happens when the old traditions die?"

In Ethiopia, for example, over 90 percent of women go through female genital mutilation (FGM) as a rite of passage, and women's organizations are challenging the practice. But they are not challenging it from the perspective of "this is an evil, ancient, tribal tradition." Rather, they are looking to the root causes of the tradition.

As I heard an Ethiopian mother explain it, "If you know that the only economic security for your daughter is to ensure that she gets married, and if you know that no one will marry her unless she has gone through the process of FGM, because you cannot assure her purity otherwise, then you have no choice as a mother but to make your daughter go through it, even though you don't have to explain to us how painful it is and what the health consequences are, because each of us has lived those experiences."

If, however, we create an environment in which girls can go to school and stay in school longer, and women have opportunities to earn an income and contribute to their families, then girls will not have to depend for their economic prospects on being married off at age 12 or 13. And if we look at the status of widows in Ethiopia and attend to their security, we can also make a difference, because it turns out that it is the widows who get paid for performing the circumcision ceremony. They depend on this ritual as a means of support because people abandon them at the edges of villages.

The environment fostered by educational and microenterprise initiatives is one that emphasizes joint efforts among men and women within a community. It is not one that says men are the problem. Indeed, women often are just as much the perpetrators of traditional values and practices as men are. What has come through clearly for women's organizations in the rest of the world is that we are struggling against a system, and this system oppresses both women and men who are caught within it.

In the 1960s and 1970s, feminists in the United States were saying, "We want to be equal to you, we want to play on your playing fields, we want to play the same game." Today the women's movement internationally is saying something very different. It is asking the question: "Equal to what?" What do we want to be equal to? And what is the game we should be playing together, men and women, to ensure a freer, more just world that offers more opportunities for all of us?

Kavita Ramdas is president and CEO of the Global Fund for Women.

Unipolar Stability
The Rules of Power Analysis

WILLIAM WOHLFORTH

The potential for the rise of a multipolar world order certainly seems far more plausible now than it did several years ago. In 2003, pundits considered the term "unipolar" to be too modest; only "empire" could capture the extraordinary position of power that the United States appeared to occupy. Indeed, in the eyes of the foreign policy commentariat, the United States has fallen from global empire to hapless Gulliver in a mere four years. When Charles Krauthammer—the columnist who originally coined the term "unipolar moment"—has announced the end of unipolarity, it is hardly a leap to suggest that multipolarity is nigh.

Perceptions of rapid polarity shifts of this sort are not unusual. In the early 1960s, only a decade after analysts had developed the notion of bipolarity, scholars were already proclaiming the return of multipolarity as postwar recoveries in Europe and Japan took off. After the fall of Saigon in 1975, they again announced the advent of multipolarity. The most influential scholarly book on international relations of the past generation, Kenneth N. Waltz's *Theory of International Politics,* was written in part to dispel these flighty views and show that bipolarity still endured. If one looks past the headlines to the deep material structure of the world, Waltz argued, one will see that bipolarity is still the order of the day. Yet in the early 1990s, Waltz himself proclaimed that the return of multipolarity was around the corner. Such perceived polarity shifts are usually accompanied by decline scares—concern that as other powers rise, the United States will lose its competitive edge in foreign relations. The current decline scare is the fourth since 1945—the first three occurred during the 1950s (Sputnik), the 1970s (Vietnam and stagflation), and the 1980s (the Soviet threat and Japan as a potential challenger).

In all of these cases, real changes were occurring that suggested a redistribution of power. But in each case, analysts' responses to those changes seem to have been overblown. Multipolarity—an international system marked by three or more roughly equally matched major powers—did not return in the 1960s, 1970s, or early 1990s, and each decline scare ended with the United States' position of primacy arguably strengthened.

It is impossible to know for sure whether or not the scare is for real this time—shifts in the distribution of power are notoriously hard to forecast. Barring geopolitical upheavals on the scale of Soviet collapse, the inter-state scales of power tend to change slowly. The trick is to determine when subtle quantitative shifts will lead to a major qualitative transformation of the basic structure of the international system. Fortunately, there are some simple rules of power analysis that can help prevent wild fluctuations in response to current events. Unfortunately, arguments for multipolarity's rapid return usually run afoul of them.

Rule No. 1: Be Clear About Definitions of Power

It is important to ask why opinion has gyrated so wildly from bullishness to bearishness in conversations on US power. It is not—as in some of the earlier cases—that perceptions of actual US capabilities or resources have changed. The United States is still widely recognized to be the most powerful state in a material sense since the modern international system took shape in the sixteenth century. I have conducted many of these measurements myself, and I can report that there has been no change in these "objective" indicators over the past three years sufficient enough to explain a shift in elite perspectives of US power.

What have shifted are peoples' views of the real utility of these resources and capabilities. Current discussions of the limits of US power are really focused on the limited usefulness of large amounts of military and economic capabilities. Political scientists generally use the term "power" to refer to a relationship of influence. As Robert Dahl put it, power is "A's ability to get B to do something it would not otherwise have done" (or, of course, to prevent B from doing something it otherwise would have done). In international relations, the same term of "power" is often equated with resources: measurable elements that states possess and use to influence others. In popular commentary, these two meanings of power are often conflated, with unfortunate results.

To begin with, the challenge of converting power-as-resources into power-as-influence is not a uniquely US problem. All great powers confront these challenges. If the cause of the new gloominess concerning US power had to be reduced to one word, it would be "Iraq." In 2003, fresh from apparent military victories in Afghanistan and Iraq, the United States appeared to be a colossus. Yet in 2007, its inability to suppress the Iraqi counterinsurgency and civil war seems to have revealed feet of clay. All the hard data on US military superiority—it is over one-half of global defense spending, some 70 percent of global military R&D, and dominance in information-intensive warfare—now appear in a new light. The world's most vaunted military machine is not even able to tame disorganized Sunni and Shi'a militias in Mesopotamia.

But the example of Iraq exhibits a balance of power dynamic between states and non-state insurgents, not one between several different states. There is no reason to believe that China, Russia, India, or the European Union would perform any better if faced with the challenges that the US military confronts in Iraq. Some scholars argue that Iraq demonstrates new information about the state versus non-state balance. They contend that counterinsurgency campaigns have become much more difficult to execute than what used to be the case. But if this is so, then it applies to all the great powers, not just the United States. According to numerous recent studies conducted by the US military and independent scholars, this argument is not correct. Insurgency has always been difficult to thwart. Once an insurgency takes root, governments rarely prevail. When they do—as in the case of Britain in South Africa at the turn of the last century and more recently, Russia in Chechnya—it is usually the result of deploying very large military forces willing to use ferocious violence on a mass scale against innocent civilians. With a comparatively small force in a large and populous country, the United States' inability to foster stability in Iraq is tragic, but not surprising.

The bottom line is that the world did not suddenly become multipolar when the United States' counterinsurgency in Vietnam failed. And simply because high-technology weaponry has not altered the centuries-old power balance between governments and armed insurgents, it does not necessarily follow that unipolarity is about to end.

Rule No. 2: Watch the Goalposts

The larger problem with conflating power-as-resources with power-as-influence is that it leads to a constant shifting of the goalposts. The better the United States becomes at acquiring resources, the greater the array of global problems it is expected to be able to resolve, and the greater the apparent gap between its material capabilities and the ends it can achieve. The result is an endless raising of the bar for what it takes to be a unipolar power. Samuel Huntington defined a unipolar state as one able "effectively to resolve all important international issues alone, and no combination of other states would have the power to prevent it from doing so." This is an extraordinary standard that essentially conflates unipolarity with universal empire. Great European powers did not lose great power status when they failed to have their way, in, for example, the Balkans in the nineteenth century. In turn, the United States did not cease to be a superpower when it failed to overthrow Fidel Castro in the 1960s. The fact that Washington cannot prevent Hugo Chavez from thumbing his nose at US power is interesting and perhaps even important, but it does not have bearing on the polarity of the international system.

Defining power as the ability to solve whatever global problem is currently in the headlines virtually guarantees highly volatile prognostications about polarity. This sort of headline chasing led to talk of "empire" in 2002 and 2003, just as it feeds today's multipolar mania. Assessing active attempts by the United States to employ its power capabilities may well be the most misleading way to think about power. This approach inevitably leads to a selection bias against evidence of the indirect, "structural" effects of US power that are not dependent upon active management. Many effects that can be attributed to the unipolar distribution of power are developments that never occur: counter-balancing coalitions, Cold War-scale arms races, hegemonic rivalry for dominance, security dilemmas among Asian powers, and decisions by Japan and others to nuclearize. Clearly, assessing unipolarity's potential effects involves weighing such non-events against the more salient examples in which active attempts to use power resources are stymied.

But the selection bias goes much further. Not only are non-events downplayed in comparison to salient events that appear to demonstrate the powerlessness of the United States, but patterns of events that do go its way are often missed. Consider, for example, how often Washington's failure to have its way in the United Nations is cited as compared to its experience in the IMF. And, even in the United Nations, a focus on highly contested issues, such as the attempt at a second resolution authorizing the invasion of Iraq, fails to note how the institution's entire agenda has shifted to address concerns, such as terrorism, that are particularly important to the United States.

Rule No. 3: Do Not Rely on a Single Indicator

When analysts forecast the coming of multipolarity, they often talk of how the rising BRIC countries (Brazil, Russia, India, and China) will alter the global balance of power. If we carefully examine the numbers, what drives most of these projections is China. And if examined even more closely, we will likely see that one indicator alone is being used to project China's rise: the growth of its gross domestic product (GDP). China's global clout will certainly rise with the relative size of its economy. But economic size is only one indicator of power, and it can be a misleading one.

When a huge number of poor people are gathered together in one country, they can create a large economy that is much less capable of generating power than the raw numbers would suggest. After all, India is estimated to have had a much larger economy than the British Isles when it was colonized in the nineteenth century. Studies of national power in the post-industrial age find that what matters most today is not just economic size, but wealth and technological development. Indeed, even if China's overall GDP did come to equal that of the United States, its per-capita GDP would still be only one-quarter that of the United States.

Current projections of China's economic rise may well be overstated. Iraq aside, what is most responsible for the virtual shift to multipolarity is not a word but an acronym: PPP. PPP stands for the "purchasing power parity" estimate of countries' exchange rates—the size of their economies in dollar terms. Although the prices of many manufactured products tend to be equalized by international trade, the price of labor is not, and therefore labor-intensive products and services tend to be relatively cheap in poor countries. PPP corrects for this discontinuity by using prices for a locally selected basket of goods to adjust the exchange rate for converting local currency into dollars. As University of Pennsylvania professor Avery Goldstein notes, "the World Bank's decision in 1994 to shift to a PPP estimate for China's economy was crucial in propelling perceptions of that country's imminent rise to great power status."

Economists universally agree that, properly applied, this method provides better estimates of comparative living standards. But forecasts about China's rise should not be based on predictions of its living standards. They should discuss China's presence as a great power in international politics—its ability to use money to purchase goods and influence matters abroad. PPP clearly exaggerates this sort of power. No one knows how much to discount the PPP numbers for the purposes of making comparisons of national power. What is certain, economist Albert Keidel notes, is that one should not "use projections of national accounting growth rates from a PPP base. This common practice seriously inflates estimates of China's future economic size—exaggerating the speed with which China's economy will overtake that of the United States in total size." Projections must take into account the fact that growth will cause prices to converge with international norms, and thus the PPP to converge with the market exchange rate. Using such a methodology, Keidel estimates that it will take until 2050 for China's total economic size to equal the United States.

National power is a complex phenomenon. We all know that relying on one simple indicator of power is not a good idea. Yet research by political scientists, psychologists, and historians continues to demonstrate that decisionmakers and analysts tend to break this basic rule. Projections of China's rise are a case in point. Even setting aside the manifold challenges that this country faces on the road to superpowerdom—including a looming demographic crisis, a shaky financial system, and the political challenges inherent in a capitalist country ruled by a communist party—extrapolating its rise based on GDP and PPP estimates of its current size is a dubious analytical exercise.

Rule No. 4: Consider Latent Power

US military forces are stretched thin, its budget and trade deficits are high, and the country continues to finance its profligate ways by borrowing from abroad—notably from the Chinese government. These developments have prompted many analysts to warn that the United States suffers from "imperial overstretch." And if US power is overstretched now, the argument goes, unipolarity can hardly be sustainable for long. The problem with this argument is that it fails to distinguish between actual and latent power. One must be careful to take into account both the level of resources that can be mobilized and the degree to which a government actually tries to mobilize them. And how much a government asks of its public is partly a function of the severity of

the challenges that it faces. Indeed, one can never know for sure what a state is capable of until it has been seriously challenged.

Yale historian Paul Kennedy coined the term "imperial overstretch" to describe the situation in which a state's actual and latent capabilities cannot possibly match its foreign policy commitments. This situation should be contrasted with what might be termed "self-inflicted overstretch"—a situation in which a state lacks the sufficient resources to meet its current foreign policy commitments in the short term, but has untapped latent power and readily available policy choices that it can use to draw on this power. This is arguably the situation that the United States is in today.

But the US government has not attempted to extract more resources from its population to meet its foreign policy commitments. Instead, it has moved strongly in the opposite direction by slashing personal and corporate tax rates. Although it is fighting wars in Afghanistan and Iraq and claims to be fighting a global "war" on terrorism, the United States is not acting like a country under intense international pressure. Aside from the volunteer servicemen and women and their families, US citizens have not been asked to make sacrifices for the sake of national prosperity and security. The country could clearly devote a greater proportion of its economy to military spending: today it spends only about 4 percent of its GDP on the military, as compared to 7 to 14 percent during the peak years of the Cold War. It could also spend its military budget more efficiently, shifting resources from expensive weapons systems to boots on the ground. Even more radically, it could reinstitute military conscription, shifting resources from pay and benefits to training and equipping more soldiers. On the economic front, it could raise taxes in a number of ways, notably on fossil fuels, to put its fiscal house back in order.

No one knows for sure what would happen if a US president undertook such drastic measures, but there is nothing in economics, political science, or history to suggest that such policies would be any less likely to succeed than China is to continue to grow rapidly for decades. Most of those who study US politics would argue that the likelihood and potential success of such power-generating policies depends on public support, which is a function of the public's perception of a threat. And as unnerving as terrorism is, there is nothing like the threat of another hostile power rising up in opposition to the United States for mobilizing public support.

With latent power in the picture, it becomes clear that unipolarity might have more built-in self-reinforcing mechanisms than many analysts realize. It is often noted that the rise of a peer competitor to the United States might be thwarted by the counterbalancing actions of neighboring powers. For example, China's rise might push India and Japan closer to the United States—indeed, this has already happened to some extent. There is also the strong possibility that a peer rival that comes to be seen as a threat would create strong incentives for the United States to end its self-inflicted overstretch and tap potentially large wellsprings of latent power.

Conclusion: Remember Power Analysis

When one notices opinions gyrating wildly from year to year, one should immediately question whether commentators are following the basic rules of power analysis. A failure to factor in the fundamental rules of power analysis can lead to a distinctly skewed conception of the future balance of power scenario.

To be sure, the reverse is also true. A failure to update in the face of new information also suggests biases at work. There is certainly a distinct possibility that the recent wave of multipolarity predictions may turn out to be correct. But to anyone familiar with past virtual polarity shifts, the current mood swing toward multipolarity betrays some very familiar hallmarks: slippery definitions of power, mobile benchmarks, over-reliance on a flawed indicator, and failure to distinguish between actual and latent power. Such deficiencies in analysis may turn out to be the difference between an accurate prediction of future geopolitical dynamics and simply another wave of fears and hopes that never comes to fruition.

WILLIAM WOHLFORTH is an Olin Fellow in International Security Studies at Yale University.

UNIT 2

Population and Food Production

Unit Selections

Key Points to Consider

• What are the basic characteristics and trends of the world's population? How many people are there? How long do people typically live?

• How fast is the world's population growing? What are the reasons for this growth? How do population dynamics vary from one region to the next?

• In many regions of the world, the graying of the population is an important trend. What are some of the political implications of this trend?

• How does rapid population growth affect the quality of the environment, social structures, and the ways in which humanity views itself?

• In an era of global interdependence, how much impact can individual governments have on demographic changes?

• What are some of the threats to the human population that might cause it to decline or collapse?

• There is a growing debate about genetically modified food. What are the differing perspectives on this debate and what issues are likely to be contested in the near future?

• How can economic and social policies be changed in order to reduce the impact of population growth on environmental quality?

Student Web Site
www.mhcls.com/online

Internet References
Further information regarding these Web sites may be found in this book's preface or online.

The Hunger Project
http://www.thp.org
Penn Library: Resources by Subject
http://www.library.upenn.edu/cgi-bin/res/sr.cgi
World Health Organization
http://www.who.int
WWW Virtual Library: Demography & Population Studies
http://demography.anu.edu.au/VirtualLibrary/

After World War II, the world's population reached an estimated 2 billion people. It had taken 250 years to triple to that level. In the six decades following World War II, the population tripled again to 6 billion. When the typical reader of this book reaches the age of 50, demographers estimate that the global population will have reached 8 1/2 billion! By 2050, or about 100 years after World War II, some experts forecast that 10 to 12 billion people may populate the world. A person born in 1946 (a so-called baby boomer) who lives to be 100 could see a six-fold increase in population.

Nothing like this has ever occurred before. To state this in a different way: In the next 50 years there will have to be twice as much food grown, twice as many schools and hospitals available, and twice as much of everything else just to maintain the current and rather uneven standard of living. We live in an unprecedented time in human history.

One of the most interesting aspects of this population growth is that there is little agreement about whether this situation is good or bad. The government of China, for example, has a policy that encourages couples to have only one child. In contrast, there are a few governments that use various financial incentives to promote large families.

In the first decade of the new millennium, there are many population issues that transcend numerical or economic considerations. The disappearance of indigenous cultures is a good example of the pressures of population growth on people who live on the margins of modern society. Finally, while demographers develop various scenarios forecasting population growth, it is important to remember that there are circumstances that could lead not to growth but to a significant decline in global population. The spread of AIDS and other infectious diseases reveals that confidence in modern medicine's ability to control these scourges may be premature. Nature has its own checks and balances to the population dynamic. This factor is often overlooked in an age of technological optimism.

The lead article in this section provides an overview of the general demographic trends in the contemporary world, with a

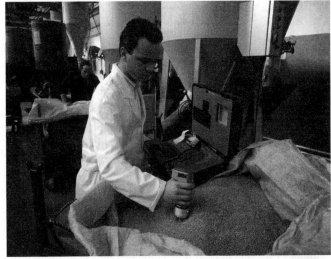

Royalty-Free/CORBIS

special focus on issues related to aging. In the second article, the African demographic youth bulge (which is a trend much different than found in most other regions of the world) is described along with its social and political implications. There is, of course, no greater check on population growth than the ability to produce an adequate food supply. Some experts question whether current technologies are sustainable over the long run. How much food are we going to need in the decades to come, and how are farmers and fishermen going to produce it? The debate about genetically modified crops is the lightning rod for this critical topic.

Making predictions about the future of the world's population is a complicated task, for there are a variety of forces at work and considerable variation from region to region. The danger of oversimplification must be overcome if governments and international organizations are going to respond with meaningful policies. Perhaps one could say that there is not a global population problem but rather many population challenges that vary from country to country and region to region.

The Century Ahead

CHRIS WILSON

The twentieth century was, above all else, a century of population growth; the twenty-first century will be a century of aging. Between 1900 and 2000 the world's population quadrupled, from around 1.5 billion to over 6 billion. Most of this increase occurred after World War II. At present, it seems unlikely that the population will grow by more than about a further 50 percent. The most plausible forecasts see a population numbering between 9 and 10 billion by about 2050, with stability or decline in total population thereafter.

However, the population at older ages will increase far more quickly in the coming century than in the last. Indeed, the end of population growth and its replacement by aging are logically related. All rapidly growing populations are young. If each birth cohort is larger than the one before, there will always be plenty of young people.

Population growth was so characteristic of the recent past that we tend to regard it as the norm. However, for most of human history the long-run rate of population growth has been very close to zero. From the biblical Adam and Eve, it would have taken only thirty-two doublings of the population to reach over 8 billion. At the rate of population growth seen in the 1960s and early 1970s—over 2 percent a year, implying a doubling time of around thirty years—and given that the gap between generations is also usually about thirty years, such an increase could have taken place inside a millennium. Even James Ussher's 1650 estimate of October 23, 4004 B.C. as the date of creation implies we have been around much longer than that. And since *Homo sapiens* actually emerged one hundred and fifty thousand or so years ago, the rate of growth has obviously been close to zero.

Similarly, extrapolating the growth rates of the recent past into the future soon yields logically impossible figures. Ansley Coale once calculated that a growth rate of 2 percent a year sustained for five thousand years would lead to the sheer volume of human beings exceeding that of the solar system.

The absence of growth is a necessary but not sufficient condition for aging; we also need long life expectancy. In populations before the modern medical era, relatively few people survived to reach three score years and ten. Thus, population aging is a novelty requiring both long lives and a low growth rate (i.e., low fertility). Though rare in the past, these conditions are now becoming the norm around the world.

When demographers try to understand the determinants of aging, they use one of social science's great generalizing models: the demographic transition. When a population modernizes, it undergoes, along with many other aspects of development, a set of interconnected changes called the demographic transition. According to this model, every population at some point has high fertility (mostly between four and six children per woman) and low life expectancy (mostly between twenty-five and forty years). With the spread of modern medicine and public health, mortality improves; as family planning and contraceptive use become the norm, fertility falls. Usually life expectancy rises first, with a delay before fertility declines. This difference in timing leads to substantial population growth before the two processes come back into balance.

This process of transition began in the late eighteenth and nineteenth centuries in Europe, the United States, and the other neo-Europes; it became a global phenomenon after World War II. Today, more than half of the world's people live in places where fertility is at or below the level needed for long-run intergenerational replacement (about 2.1 children per woman), and global life expectancy is approaching seventy years.

Trends in mortality can be followed in considerable detail for many European countries from the mid-nineteenth century, and for a few especially well-documented cases, as far back as the late 1700s. For Japan and the United States detailed information dates back to the early twentieth century. What these statistics reveal is both simple and striking. There has been an enormous reduction in mortality, with life expectancy for the two sexes combined now approaching, or even exceeding, eighty in most developed countries. Even more remarkably, this progress has been very regular for many decades. Jim Oeppen and James Vaupel have shown, for example, that the trend in "best-practice" life expectancy (i.e., the country with the longest life expectancy in each year) has been linear for more than 150 years.[1] In each decade the "state of the art" has increased about 2.5 years. Moreover, although there has been some variation at the national level, most developed countries have demonstrated strongly linear trends in life expectancy for the whole of the twentieth century.

Paradoxically, although this trend has been evident in mortality statistics for many decades, it is only in the last few years that it has been recognized. Demographers, actuaries, and others concerned with forecasting mortality had always hitherto assumed that life expectancy was approaching some asymptotic limit and would thus level off in the near future. But if there is some biological limit to extending longevity, there is no sign of it yet. As Oeppen and Vaupel point out, estimates of the maximum possible life expectancy made throughout the twentieth century were, on average, surpassed within five years of being made. This consistent error is of more than purely academic interest—pension- and health-care systems have been funded on the basis of large underestimates of the number of elderly people in the future.

The linearity of the upward climb in life expectancy has occurred in spite of the fact that very different age groups and causes of death have been involved in different eras. Before World War II, almost all progress took place in reducing infectious diseases, with the biggest impact for infants and children. In contrast, today much of the improvement is concentrated at old ages. Perhaps the best analogy for these remarkable changes is to be found in models of economic growth. Just as modern theory hypothesizes the existence of an endogenous rate of growth that is in some sense built into our economic system, so too there may be an endogenous rate of improvement in health, as measured by life expectancy. In any event, we have every reason to expect that continued increases in the average length of life will augment population aging.

There are, of course, exceptions to this optimistic picture. In the Soviet Union and its client states in Eastern and Central Europe, life expectancy stagnated from the 1960s until the end of Communism. It then worsened still further in many cases, in the immediate aftermath of the revolution. In Russia and many of the post-Soviet states it remains low, especially for men. Male life expectancy in Russia today is roughly the same as it was in 1950: about sixty years. To put this stagnation into perspective, the equivalent figure for the United States has increased since 1950 by almost ten years from sixty-six to seventy-six.

In the post-Communist countries further west, however, the last decade has seen rapid improvements; life expectancy there will likely converge to levels seen in Western Europe within a few decades. The origins of the health crisis under Communism and its persistence in Russia, Ukraine, and the other post-Soviet states is a matter of heated debate in both the scientific and general literature. Whatever the cause, the crisis serves as a warning against unqualified Panglossian optimism. Likewise, the emergence of HIV/AIDS and the associated reemergence of tuberculosis make clear that all future estimates of improvement in public health must take into account the potential for severe reversals.

Overall, however, the last half-century has seen unprecedented convergence in mortality patterns around the world. While rich countries still lead in life expectancy, the gap between these leaders and most developing countries has shrunk substantially. In fact, there has been more convergence in demography than in any other aspect of modernization. For example, consider Latin America as a whole, where the United Nations estimates current life expectancy is seventy-two years, and GDP per head (adjusted for inflation and other factors) is below $4,000, according to the Organization for Economic Cooperation and Development. Now consider the United States. Life expectancy in the United States was seventy-two years as recently as the early 1970s. In contrast, the U.S. GDP per head exceeded $4,000 by 1900. Latin America is a century behind the United States in income growth, but only thirty to thirty-five years behind in life expectancy. We can make similar comparisons for most developing countries. And though the gaps in educational attainment or urbanization are somewhat smaller than in GDP per head, none of the other conventional quantitative indices of development has converged as rapidly as demography.

In recent decades there has also been a striking convergence in fertility, which has declined rapidly in most countries. More than half of the world's population now lives in countries or regions in which fertility is below the level needed for intergenerational replacement.[2] In most of Southern Europe (including Italy and Spain) and in most of Central and Eastern Europe, the total fertility rate (the number of children born per woman) is below 1.3. Similar values are now seen in Japan, South Korea, and many of the more developed parts of China. Even some countries that might seem unlikely candidates have experienced rapid fertility decline. In Iran, for example, fertility fell from over six children per woman to just over two between the mid-1980s and mid-1990s. In contrast, fertility in the United States has seemed to defy gravity, staying close to or even above the replacement level for the last two decades. Among the developing countries in which fertility is now lower than in the United States are China, Brazil, Thailand, and Tunisia. If the trends of the last twenty-five years continue for another decade or so, the U.S. fertility level will be well above the median for the human population as a whole.

The very speed of fertility decline in many countries will produce an exaggerated form of aging. While aging is an inevitable and global phenomenon, countries in which fertility has fallen rapidly will experience a form of 'super aging' in the middle decades of this century. The baby boom cohorts of Southern Europe or the pretransition cohorts in China are very large compared to those that followed, and their getting old will greatly exacerbate any problems that aging generates.

There is also a sense in which aging can be 'locked in' as part of a country's demographic regime through a form of negative momentum. For example, in Southern Europe, the large number of baby boomers moving through the childbearing ages has disguised the very low fertility rate of recent decades. The largest age groups at present are those ages 25 to 39. In the coming decades, however, the much smaller cohorts born since the mid-1980s will be in the reproductive ages. Unless these cohorts (currently ages 0 to 19) have much higher fertility than their parents, the number of births in countries such as Italy and Spain will shrink even more rapidly in the future than it has so far. In contrast, the United States and other countries in which fertility has stabilized at close to the replacement level (in Europe, they include France and the Nordic countries) will face much less severe challenges from demographic disruption.

The future is always uncertain to some degree, but when trends have been so clear and so consistent for decades, they form a solid basis for prediction. It is very close to certain that aging will be one of the defining global phenomena in the twenty-first century. The ways in which societies choose to adapt to this new reality will test the old adage that "demography is destiny." Fatalism, however, is uncalled for—to a substantial degree we can still choose our future. However, demography does impose strong constraints on the range of feasible options. Taking these constraints into account is the basis for informed reactions to the challenges posed by aging.

Notes

1. Jim Oeppen and James W. Vaupel, "Broken Limits to Life Expectancy," *Science 296* (2002): 1030–1031.

2. Chris Wilson, "Fertility Below Replacement Level," *Science 304* (2004): 207–209.

CHRIS WILSON is a staff member of the World Population Program at the International Institute for Applied Systems Analysis in Laxenberg, Austria. One of Europe's most widely cited demographers, he is currently researching the causes and consequences of global demographic convergence.

From *Daedalus,* 135:1, Winter 2006, pp. 5–9. Copyright © 2006 by the American Academy of Arts and Sciences. Reprinted by permission of MIT Press Journals.

Africa's Restless Youth

"People interested in Africa's future ought to concern themselves not just with potential conflict, but also potential political change. Youth populations are at the heart of these possibilities."

MICHELLE GAVIN

Scanning the horizon for insight as to what will influence the future of sub-Saharan Africa, one can immediately point to several broad baskets of important indicators. Obviously contributing to the picture are economic growth (or the lack thereof), insecure borders, increasing resource scarcity, the HIV/AIDS pandemic, and the balance of power within nations among ethnic and regional groups. However, a close look at the political engagement and political agendas of youth should also be included in the mix. Young Africans' quest for empowerment will make them significant catalysts for change.

Africa is currently in the midst of what demographers call a youth bulge. A youth bulge typically occurs when less-developed countries, with both high fertility and high mortality rates, begin to bring infant and child mortality rates down. Eventually, development gains tend to bring fertility rates down as well. But in the lag time before this occurs, a population boom of children who survive to adulthood reshapes the demographic landscape.

In Africa today, this dynamic translates into some startling figures. More than 70 percent of all Zimbabweans, for example, are now under 30; the same is true in Kenya, Uganda, Ethiopia, Liberia, and Nigeria, among other countries. Over one-third of the entire population of Zimbabwe, and over 56 percent of the adult (over 15) population, is between 15 and 29 years old. In fact, young adults (aged 15 to 29) make up 40 percent or more of the total adult population in the vast majority of sub-Saharan countries; in roughly 30 African countries, they constitute more than half of the adult population. In contrast, approximately 40 percent of the population in the United States is under 30, and young adults constitute less than 30 percent of the adult population as a whole.

Any discussion of the youth bulge in Africa risks veering into the land of breathless alarmism—*young men and street gangs and guns, oh my!*—or overcorrecting and wandering into the territory of commencement-speech clichés about how the children are indeed the future. But there is room for a closer examination of African youth that emphasizes their political role, and this should be a priority in future research. The young are more inclined to take risks, but vast youthful populations are not going to engage in violence simply for its own sake. On the other hand, violence may be a symptom of clashing political agendas.

In a region where the state has been the source of most power and economic opportunity, but governing institutions are often weak, the desires and grievances of youth are very likely to have political implications. Governments and international actors probably cannot control the degree to which youth bulges shape societies for good or for ill, but they can at least influence outcomes. Focusing too narrowly on violence and conflict rather than on underlying political tensions tends to yield a fairly sickly crop of policy prescriptions, all variations on the theme of "brace yourself." By seeking to understand youth political engagement more clearly, policy makers may be able to create conditions conducive to youth movements that do not leave a legacy of trauma and dysfunction in their wake.

Forever Young?

For the purposes of this article, I am defining youth as anyone from 15 to 29 years old. However, definitions of youth are tricky and often culturally specific. They are also subject to revision and even manipulation. Sierra Leone's National Youth Policy, for instance, targets citizens ages 15 to 35, and Sierra Leoneans sometimes use the term "youth" to describe people in their 40s—this in a country where average life expectancy for males is about 38. Last November, Zimbabwe's *Financial Gazette* questioned the youth credentials of Absolom Sikhosana, the ruling party's Youth League Secretary, suggesting that he was masquerading as a member of the 35-and-under set and that he might in fact be "past his sell-by date." In 2002, South Africa's National Youth Development Policy Framework included a youth definition of 15 to 28, but the National Youth Policy adopted in 1997 had targeted the 14-to-35 range. In any case, according to the International Council on National Youth Policy, various South African government departments use different definitions, which rarely correspond to either of the official policies.

These variable and amorphous definitions point to an interesting phenomenon: in some African countries it is getting increasingly difficult to make the transition from youth to adulthood. Inadequate education systems combine with stratospheric unemployment rates to foreclose the possibility of securing a job that could provide financial security. This in turn makes it unfeasible to marry and start one's own family. Meanwhile, population growth has contributed to a land squeeze, and as desirable land has been divided many times over to accommodate heirs, younger siblings in particular are cut off from the prospect of inheriting workable plots.

Youths are pushed into the continent's urban centers seeking a pathway to a viable future, only to find themselves among the unemployed and alienated masses of young people already looking for the same thing. Here, they are increasingly exposed to many of the same media images of material success that bombard young people in the most developed countries—messages often crafted by marketers to explicitly target the youth demographic. The contrast between these images and their own circumstances and prospects is hard to ignore, amplifying a sense of relative deprivation.

Some young people continue their quest for opportunity by leaving their country and even the continent altogether, risking their lives by placing themselves in the hands of sophisticated and dangerous human smuggling networks that profit from the vast divide between the prospects for African and European youth. But practical and legal constraints ensure that this pathway, like the others, is often blocked. In these situations, many of Africa's youth are caught in a Peter Pan scenario gone terribly wrong. Try as they might, they cannot seem to become adults.

Many African cultures place an extremely high premium on respect for elders. Young people are expected to know their place and to abide by the wisdom of those rich in life experience. Yet, if youth are trapped—indefinitely—in some sort of preparatory state, awaiting the time when they are accorded the respect, responsibility, and opportunity associated with being full-fledged adults in their society, it seems unreasonable to assume that they will wait patiently for a day that is nowhere in sight.

Youths have something to prove, and given opportunity, they will assert themselves. Just how violently or constructively that might happen depends on a range of factors, including the existence and nature of manipulation from older elites, the amount of political space available for civic action, and the capacity of the state and the private sector to hear and understand youth aspirations and to deliver opportunities in a relatively timely fashion.

In one way or another, young Africans are in the market for alternatives to the status quo.

Of course, no country's youth is monolithic. Ethnic, religious, and regional schisms can split demographic cohorts just as they can split a population at large. Also, it is often hard to discern where young women fit into the picture. This is so in part because many become mothers during this period of life, culturally moving into adulthood and a lifetime of domestic responsibility. In addition, young women's leadership and civic engagement opportunities, even within the context of youth movements, often are limited on the basis of gender alone.

Even among young men, agitation for power and respect—be it peaceful or violent—will not be the preoccupation of all youth in any setting. Nevertheless, a vocal, visible, organized segment of the youth population, particularly if it is concentrated in Africa's urban centers, can make for a movement with profound political consequences, and these political actors will be on the stage for many years to come.

Change Agents

In Africa's independence movements and struggles against colonial powers, young people played an important role in case after case. The party that governed Somalia on independence was even called the Somali Youth League. More recently, youth were pivotal in the anti-apartheid struggle in South Africa. Nelson Mandela was 26 when he and other young leaders came together to form the African National Congress Youth League in 1944; their work transformed the ANC. Later, in 1968, 22-year-old Steve Biko led the newly formed and highly influential South African Students Organization. The Soweto uprising of 1976 was grounded in secondary school students' resistance to apartheid policies, and students mobilized en masse to demand change throughout the rest of the struggle.

But today, when their demographic weight is much greater relative to older Africans' than it has been in the past, young people are most often cast in the role of a diffusely destabilizing threat, rather than as potential agents of political and social transformation. The strain of analysis that sees the youth bulge as a fundamentally threatening phenomenon often points to research that suggests a strong relationship between the likelihood of civil conflict and the existence of an urbanized youth bulge. In 2001, the U.S. Central Intelligence Agency released a report on global demographic trends, saying of the projected youth bulges in Africa and parts of the Middle East that:

> "The failure to adequately integrate youth populations is likely to perpetuate the cycle of political instability, ethnic wars, revolutions, and anti-regime activities. . . . Increases in youth populations will aggravate problems with trade, terrorism, anti-regime activities, warfare, and crime and add to the many existing factors that already are making the region's problems increasingly difficult to surmount."

In an influential 2003 report titled *The Security Demographic*, researchers with the nongovernmental organization Population Action International found that countries experiencing a youth bulge were more than twice as likely as other countries to experience civil strife. The numbers are compelling, and so are the recent histories of devastating conflict in states like Liberia and Sierra Leone, where youth were both perpetrators and victims of appalling violence on a massive scale. It is easy to develop a generalized sense that "youth bulge" is code for marauding, angry young men.

Certainly it is not hard to understand why many African youths might have a highly developed sense of grievance. In addition to the frustrating struggle for adult status, shocking numbers of young Africans have at some point in their short lives fallen into one or more of the following unhappy categories: combatants, victims of atrocities, refugees, internally displaced persons, forced laborers, or street children.

AIDS orphans are expected to number 18 million in sub-Saharan Africa in 2010. In the worst-affected areas, their numbers are already overwhelming the capacity of extended family networks to care for them, and alternative support structures are weak or non-existent. According to UNAIDS, 6.2 million Africans 15 to 24 years old are already HIV-positive, and half of all new infections in the region occur in this age group.

> **There is a strong temptation to write off a "lost generation," but there is no avoiding the fact that those currently holding power will not be able to wield it forever.**

The vast majority of Africa's young people have an intimate knowledge of poverty. Even elite youths are faced with a shortage of jobs in which to apply the skills they may have acquired at tremendously overcrowded, underfunded universities. Overall, according to the International Labor Organization (ILO), there are more than 17.4 million unemployed 15- to 24-year-olds in Africa, leading to a regional youth unemployment rate of 18 percent. And even the young people who do have jobs are hardly financially secure: the ILO notes that over 57 percent of African youth are working at the $1-per-day level. One can easily imagine that this cohort as a whole would be quick to blame someone or something—a governing regime or an ethnic group—for a rough past and an uncertain future.

The relationship between youth bulges and violence is important, but it speaks to just one manifestation of youth frustrations and desires. Other avenues for affecting the future include partisan political action, participation in civil society organizations, student activism, and engagement in transnational religious movements. Regardless of whether these manifold forms of expression are accompanied by violent tactics, in light of youths' demographic dominance, all of them will affect the region's future. In one way or another, young Africans are in the market for alternatives to the status quo.

This could mean significant change. In many African countries, the actors dominating the political scene have been on stage (if not in power) for quite some time. President Mwai Kibaki of Kenya is over 75 years old. President Abdoulaye Wade of Senegal is over 80. President Robert Mugabe of Zimbabwe is 83. Most existing state structures, such as party youth wings, do not actually function as entry points to party leadership. The nearly ubiquitous ministries of "youth and sports" are marginal and marginalizing institutions. They are ill-equipped to function as sustainable mechanisms for accommodating and responding to the size and potential strength of youth political activism. When voters under 29 constitute 40 percent of all registered voters, as they did in the last Liberian election, their issues and demands cry out to be mainstream priorities, not sideshows.

Tools of the Elite

Building a capacity to respond to youth demands for empowerment, rather than simply trying to keep a lid on unrest, starts with understanding the dynamics of contemporary youth's political engagement. African youth in the market for alternatives to their current situation will either generate their own vision, or adopt ones supplied by others.

Instances in which youth are manipulated and mobilized to serve an elite agenda are all too easy to come by. Military movements throughout the continent have recruited children and youth on a massive scale. Vast numbers of young Rwandans complied with the most hideous instructions during the 1994 genocide. In Zimbabwe, the ruling party established brutal camps to indoctrinate young people in the party's ideology and to train the party's youth militia.

The camps were organized in 2001 under the auspices of the National Youth Service Training Program, an initiative ostensibly aimed at improving job skills and awareness of civic responsibility. In fact, young Zimbabweans were coerced into attending training camps that taught torture techniques and exposed them to beatings and rapes in the course of molding them into new party loyalists. As the main opposition force in the country, the Movement for Democratic Change, has faltered and split, factions of it, too, have deployed young thugs to intimidate rivals. Meanwhile, the outlook for young Zimbabweans grows increasingly dim, as the national unemployment rate soars to an estimated 80 percent and the economy continues to shrink.

In 2004, disturbing reports emerged from the city of Mbuji-Mayi in the Democratic Republic of Congo. Street children and youths eager for any kind of employment had been mobilized by political elites to demonstrate in rallies and protests and to intimidate opposition figures and supporters in exchange for payment. But these young people went from being political militants for hire to becoming the victims of a massacre. Angry mobs, fed up with the crimes being committed by young people who felt empowered by their political patrons, rampaged through the city, beating and in many instances killing street children and youths.

These horrifying incidents speak to the time-honored tradition of rounding up young people and, by offering short-term opportunity (payment, license to loot, and so forth) and some proximity to power, convincing them to act as violent, visible backers of a given political power. Youth often are enlisted to support political repression and to occupy political space so as to deny it to others. From Kenya to Cameroon, the recruitment of young people to reinforce ethnic divisions, intimidate voices of dissent, and send signals about who possesses strength and power—whatever is most useful for the elites doing the recruiting—has been a regular feature of Africa's political landscape. In some cases, the formation of militant party youth wings is explicit. In other cases, direct ties to the party are less formal, perhaps protecting the party from being held accountable for disruptive youth action.

In the Driver's Seat

But instances in which youth pursue their own agendas can be found as well, and the nature of these efforts ranges from non-threatening to extremely confrontational. The sub-Saharan region is rich in dynamic, creative youth groups with a public service focus, from theater troupes dramatizing HIV/AIDS prevention techniques in Uganda to peace-building programs sustained by Tutsi and Hutu youth in Burundi. Some student groups are clearly co-opted by elites. But others, like the Kenyan University Students Organization that existed in the mid-1990s to demand democratic change, challenge the ruling class and operate as independent civil society actors.

Consider the action of some Sierra Leonean youths, including ex-combatants, in the wake of that country's devastating civil war. These youths wanted power, but rather than focusing exclusively on personal enrichment, the Movement of Concerned Kono Youth, or MOCKY, tried to stand in for what its members perceived to be an absent or ineffective law enforcement presence. As the country's civil war wound down, MOCKY tried to fill roles one would normally associate with government—conducting patrols, monitoring mining activity, and attempting to negotiate with a multinational mining company operating in the region in an effort to secure community development commitments. Dissatisfied by what the state had to offer and longing to assert themselves in positions of leadership and authority, these youths tried to organize an alternative.

Some youth-dominated armed groups in the Niger Delta claim to have a similar agenda. Interestingly, former Nigerian dictator Sani Abacha's "two million man march" in 1998 was a turning point for youth activism. A group calling itself Youths Earnestly Ask for Abacha ostensibly organized this display of support for the regime, although the government clearly directed the entire affair. Young people from around the country were bussed to the gleaming capital city of Abuja to participate, where they saw state-of-the-art infrastructure and facilities presumably financed with Nigeria's oil wealth. The contrast between the wealth on display in Abuja and the desperately poor oil-producing communities in the Niger Delta helped to radicalize a generation.

Being used as Abacha's instruments drove the young people to develop and pursue their own agenda. No longer content to let local chiefs negotiate with the government or oil companies on behalf of communities, youth formed pressure groups and, in many cases, armed militias. Some groups remain available for hire to politicians around election time, but it is clear that these armed youth movements cannot be controlled by the state. Today, media-savvy, youth-dominated militant groups like the Movement for the Emancipation of the Niger Delta (MEND) engage in operations ranging from kidnapping foreign oil workers to hosting CNN correspondents. Their actions have consequences not only for local security, but also for international oil markets.

The Case of Ivory Coast

The distinction between youth acting as instruments and youth acting as agents is not always clear, and power between elites and youth leaders can ebb and flow. Perhaps nowhere are the lines as blurry today as they are in Ivory Coast. Once a proud island of stability and economic growth, over the past decade the country has descended into a toxic mix of civil conflict, violent xenophobia, and political stalemate—with youth as major actors throughout.

When longtime President Felix Houphouet Boigny died in 1993, he was replaced by Henri Konan Bedie, who sought to consolidate his power by marginalizing his primary political rival, Alassane Ouattara. Bedie's method was to promote *"ivoirité"*—an ultranationalist vision of the country's identity that excluded many of the migrant workers from Burkina Faso, Mali, and Guinea who had long labored in Ivory Coast's northern agricultural fields. Not coincidentally, it also excluded Ouattara, whose main base of support was in the north, because of complicated questions about where his parents were born.

Bedie was soon overthrown in a coup, but his formula for neutralizing any political threat from Ouattara was later embraced by the current president, Laurent Gbagbo, who came to power in 2000 in a dubious election in which the two major parties' candidates were prevented from participating. A rebellion broke out in 2002, eventually splitting the country into two parts—the north and west controlled by rebels known as the *Forces Nouvelles,* and the south and east under the control of the Gbagbo government, state security forces, and their militia allies. Notably, both sides' ranks were strengthened by former combatants hardened by youth-dominated conflict in Liberia and Sierra Leone. These roving soldiers-for-hire are a new part of the regional youth landscape.

While these political machinations and the resulting conflict unfolded, global economic conditions that had been squeezing the Ivorian economy throughout the 1980s and 1990s—particularly falling prices for coffee and cocoa—began to bite ferociously. *Ivoirité* fed many elite youths' hunger for someone to blame for the scarcity of jobs, land, and opportunities. Meanwhile, northern youth became increasingly agitated about the prospect of being systematically excluded from the few opportunities available within the country. Both youth groups acted on their anxieties, led by young men who had risen to prominence as students in Ivory Coast's highly political university setting.

In fact, Guillaume Soro, the leader of the *Forces Nouvelles,* and Charles Ble Goude, leader of the pro-Gbagbo Young Patriots militia, were consecutive secretaries general of the Student Federation of Ivory Coast (FESCI) in the period from 1995 to 2001. Other militia leaders also have backgrounds as FESCI officers. FESCI was founded in the early 1990s to advocate for improved conditions at increasingly overcrowded and under-resourced university campuses; it was a movement of youth resisting the shrinking opportunities presented to them and protesting favoritism in the distribution of scholarship funds. In those early days, FESCI's dissatisfaction with government policies aligned it with the movement that advocated for multiparty politics—a movement in which the political party founded by Gbagbo (a former university lecturer himself) played an important part.

Today, the Young Patriots and allied youth militias are among the primary enforcement arms of Gbagbo's state. They can mobilize masses of youth with astonishing speed, and their activities range from the conventionally political (collecting signatures on petitions calling for the *Forces Nouvelles* to be disarmed) to the clearly repressive (prohibiting the distribution of newspapers deemed insufficiently loyal to the ruling party) to the extremely violent (brutally beating opposition supporters or simply those who appear to be of Burkinabe or Malian descent).

The International Crisis Group has documented how rural youth, some of whom had left the city after finding no employment despite having attained university degrees, have been inspired by intense state-controlled media coverage of the Young Patriots' activities to take actions that give them their own social and economic power. They set up barricades to monitor movement in and out of villages, enabling them to collect fees and attempt to reform the land tenure system according to the dictates of *ivoirité*. For their part, the *Forces Nouvelles* act as a de facto government in the territory they control, and profit from trade in cotton and arms, maintaining their own trans-boundary economic networks.

Meanwhile, FESCI lives on, allied to the Young Patriots and the Gbagbo regime. It dominates campus life by controlling access to housing, extorting money and goods, and intimidating students and professors who do not toe the ruling party line. A student organization once devoted to holding government more accountable to youth has become a zealous pro-government force. Those who have tried to form an alternative student organization have been attacked and even killed.

Thus, many youths in Ivory Coast have maneuvered through a complex political environment to establish leadership positions and sources of income for themselves in an arrangement that suits the needs and desires of the ruling political class. Others have abandoned the state structure entirely through rebellion. The country has a long history of student activism, but whereas student leaders used to graduate and move on to senior posts in government or the private sector, students more recently have constructed entirely new spaces to occupy—quite literally, in the case of the *Forces Nouvelles*.

While the ruling party and its youth enforcers are unquestionably linked, it is no longer plain that the power of the youth militias depends on patronage from the state. Political elites may be just as much hostage to the desires of the militia leaders as the other way around. Youth violence features in the case of Ivory Coast primarily as a tool married to youth leaders' own political and economic agendas. The latest peace agreement, under which Soro will serve as prime minister, offers hope of reuniting the country. But until now the country has been in a stalemate in part because the impasse benefits old and young elites in both sectors of the country, despite the fact that Ivory Coast as a whole is growing poorer.

Appeals to a Higher Power

Elsewhere in Africa, increasingly influential transnational religious movements, both Christian and Muslim, are largely fueled by African youth's enthusiastic response to alternative paths to empowerment. Faith can provide surrogate social structures and supports for those who have been through traumatic experiences and have lost other moorings. In some cases, it can also provide a form of education, which may not be available from any other source. Religious movements offer prescriptions for how to improve one's life and transform society, and in Africa today, these prescriptions have explicit political significance.

Many of Africa's youth are caught in a Peter Pan scenario gone terribly wrong. Try as they might, they cannot seem to become adults.

Revivalist Christian movements are thriving in much of Africa. From Malawi to Ghana, Pentecostal churches are encouraging youths to reject the "old ways" that led to poverty and despair and to embrace a faith that promises social networking opportunities, promotes links to fellow worshippers around the world, uses mass media to impressive effect, and embraces the quest for prosperity. The renewal inherent in being "born again" also speaks to the desire for an alternative to the status quo. Prominent figures within these churches can be very young themselves, exemplifying how African youth can attain respect and prominence despite the limited opportunities they may be confronted with. Moreover, unlike university-based movements, religious youth movements are accessible to non-elites.

These religious networks are not divorced from politics. A recent survey by the Pew Forum on Religion and Public Life found that 83 percent of renewalists in Kenya and 75 percent in Nigeria believe that religious groups should express views on social and political questions. And they have put this belief into action—for example, when Christians organized to help defeat a referendum on a new constitution in Kenya in 2005.

At the same time, Muslim youths may find in an Islamic revival movement a vehicle for their rejection of the status quo and desire for an alternative. In a 2005 article in the *Journal of the Royal Anthropological Institute,* Adeline Masquelier described how unemployed young men in Niger embrace a Muslim movement that condemns extravagant customs surrounding marriage (a helpful point that brings the prospect of marriage closer to their modest reach). Foreign Muslim clerics, often from Pakistan or the Middle East, have established a notable presence in the Sahel, drawing in young people to be educated in an ideology that advocates enforcing Islamic law and abandoning the secular state.

Longstanding local movements may move in new directions as young members try to effect radical change, sometimes taking cues from abroad, as with the Al Sunna Wal Jamma group of students in Nigeria that staged attacks in several northern towns in 2004. They claimed to be inspired by Afghanistan's Taliban, and apparently wished to create an Islamic state. In countries where both Christian and Muslim movements are operating, tension is inevitable. It comes as no surprise, for example, that youth have been primary players in the religiously charged communal conflicts that have plagued Nigeria in recent years.

What Next?

People interested in Africa's future ought to concern themselves not just with potential conflict, but also potential political change. Youth populations are at the heart of these possibilities. There is a strong temptation to write off a "lost generation" in the most battle-scarred, traumatized countries, but there is no avoiding the fact that those currently holding power will not be able to wield it forever. Even those who aim to cope with vast, dissatisfied youth populations by pressing young people into the service of the ruling elite may find that, in time, their youthful foot soldiers cease to answer to their elders. Today's young people will, sooner or later, play a dominant role in society.

For policy makers, job creation clearly must be an urgent priority. A focus on educating and socializing children so that they are prepared to play a positive civic role should be another priority, particularly since so many African countries are still at an early phase of their demographic transition. In addition, by understanding youth as political actors rather than simply drivers of conflict, policy makers can aim to manage the challenge to existing orders posed by youth rather than, unrealistically, try to avoid it entirely. A viable way forward involves a thorough understanding of the various youth dynamics on the ground, and also involves a serious effort to give youth the tools, opportunities, and political space in which to pursue their interests and aspirations.

More needs to be done to shed light on how specific variables affect the capacity of youth movements to engage, reshape, and even strengthen the state. What can be done to give Africa's young people reason to believe in governing institutions or to trust that peaceful civic action can effectively address their grievances? How might a closing of the digital divide empower African youth to form new networks for change? The answers will undoubtedly vary from country to country, but the significance of the questions, and the importance of youth political engagement, will remain constant for quite some time to come.

MICHELLE GAVIN is an international affairs fellow at the Council on Foreign Relations.

Continuing the Green Revolution

**Agricultural biotech has greatly improved human life.
But we've still got a long way to go.**

NORMAN E. BORLAUG

Persistent poverty and environmental degradation in developing countries, changing global climatic patterns, and the use of food crops to produce biofuels, all pose new and unprecedented risks and opportunities for global agriculture in the years ahead.

Agricultural science and technology, including the indispensable tools of biotechnology, will be critical to meeting the growing demands for food, feed, fiber and biofuels. Plant breeders will be challenged to produce seeds that are equipped to better handle saline conditions, resist disease and insects, droughts and waterlogging, and that can protect or increase yields, whether in distressed climates or the breadbaskets of the world. This flourishing new branch of science extends to food crops, fuels, fibers, livestock and even forest products.

Over the millennia, farmers have practiced bringing together the best characteristics of individual plants and animals to make more vigorous and productive offspring. The early domesticators of our food and animal species—most likely Neolithic women—were also the first biotechnologists, as they selected more adaptable, durable and resilient plants and animals to provide food, clothing and shelter.

In the late 19th century the foundations for science-based crop improvement were laid by Darwin, Mendel, Pasteur and others. Pioneering plant breeders applied systematic cross-breeding of plants and selection of offspring with desirable traits to develop hybrid corn, the first great practical science-based products of genetic engineering.

Early crossbreeding experiments to select desirable characteristics took years to reach the desired developmental state of a plant or animal. Today, with the tools of biotechnology, such as molecular and marker-assisted selection, the ends are reached in a more organized and accelerated way. The result has been the advent of a "Gene" Revolution that stands to equal, if not exceed, the Green Revolution of the 20th century.

Consider these examples:

- Since 1996, the planting of genetically modified crops developed through biotechnology has spread to about 250 million acres from about five million acres around the world, with half of that area in Latin America and Asia. This has increased global farm income by $27 billion annually.
- Ag biotechnology has reduced pesticide applications by nearly 500 million pounds since 1996. In each of the last six years, biotech cotton saved U.S. farmers from using 93 million gallons of water in water-scarce areas, 2.4 million gallons of fuel and 41,000 person-days to apply the pesticides they formerly used.
- Herbicide-tolerant corn and soybeans have enabled greater adoption of minimum-tillage practices. No-till farming has increased 35% in the U.S. since 1996, saving millions of gallons of fuel, perhaps one billion tons of soil each year from running into waterways and significantly improving moisture conservation as well.
- Improvements in crop yields and processing through biotechnology can accelerate the availability of biofuels. While the current emphasis is on using corn and soybeans to produce ethanol, the long-term solution will be cellulosic ethanol made from forest industry by-products and products.

However, science and technology should not be viewed as a panacea that can solve all of our resource problems. Biofuels can reduce dependence on fossil fuels, but are not a substitute for greater fuel efficiency and energy conservation. Whether we like it or not, gas-guzzling SUVs will have to go the way of the dinosaurs.

So far, most biotechnology research and development has been carried out by the private sector and on crops and traits of greatest interest to relatively wealthy farmers. More biotechnology research is needed on crops and traits most important to the world's poor—crops such as beans, peanuts, tropical roots, bananas, and tubers like cassava and yams. Also, more biotech research is needed to enhance the nutritional content of food crops for essential minerals and vitamins, such as vitamin A, iron and zinc.

The debate about the suitability of biotech agricultural products goes beyond issues of food safety. Access to biotech seeds by poor farmers is a dilemma that will require interventions by governments and the private sector. Seed companies can help improve access by offering preferential pricing for small quantities of biotech seeds to smallholder farmers. Beyond that, public-private partnerships are needed to share research and development costs for "pro-poor" biotechnology.

Finally, I should point out that there is nothing magic in an improved variety alone. Unless that variety is nourished with fertilizers—chemical or organic—and grown with good crop management, it will not achieve much of its genetic yield potential.

NORMAN E. BORLAUG, the 1970 Nobel Peace Prize laureate, was awarded the Congressional Gold Medal, America's highest civilian honor.

Bittersweet Harvest
The Debate over Genetically Modified Crops

HONOR HSIN

In 1982 scientists on the 4th floor of the Monsanto Company U Building successfully introduced a foreign gene into a plant cell for the first time in history. These plants were genetically modified: they continued to express the new gene while exhibiting normal plant physiology and producing normal offspring. This breakthrough spawned the field of genetically modified (GM) crop production. Since the discovery, however, the international response to GM crops has been mixed. Along with the tremendous potential that lies vested in this technology, there are many risks and uncertainties involved as well. Arguments have centered on the health implications and environmental impact of cultivating GM crops and have raised disputes over national interests, global policy, and corporate agendas. Although there are many sides to this debate, discussions on GM crop regulation should be held within the context of scientific evidence, coupled with a careful weighing of present and future agricultural prospects.

Benefits and Costs

The possibility of environmental benefits first spurred the development of GM crops. The environmental issues at stake can be illustrated by one example of a potent genetic modification, the introduction of an endotoxin gene from *Bacillus thuringiensis* (Bt), a soil micro-organism used for decades by organic growers as an insecticide, into soybeans, corn, and cotton. These GM crops promise to reduce the need to spray large amounts of chemicals into a field's ecosystem since the toxins are produced by the plants themselves. The Bt crops pose environmental risks, however, and could possibly harm other organisms. Bt corn was shown to harm monarch butterfly caterpillars in the laboratory, although later studies performed with more realistic farming conditions found this result conclusively only with Syngenta Company's Bt maize, which expressed up to 40 percent more toxin than other brands. Another pertinent environmental issue is the possible evolution of Bt resistance in pests. Since the Bt toxin expressed by the crops is ubiquitous in the field, there is positive selection for resistance against it, which would quickly make Bt's effect obsolete. Experimentation has begun, however, that involves regulating the percentage of Bt crops in a field so that a balance can be achieved between high yields and survival

of Bt-sensitive pests. Although there are still multiple layers of ecosystem complexity that need to be considered, careful scientific research can begin to address these questions.

Another potential area of risk that needs to be analyzed is the effect of GM crops on human health. A possible consequence of Bt expression in crops is the development of allergic reactions in farmers since the toxin is more highly concentrated in the crops than in the field. Furthermore, the method used to insert foreign genes into GM crops always risks manipulation of unknown genes in the plant, resulting in unforeseen consequences. The effects of GM crops on humans therefore must be tested rigorously. Fortunately, no solid evidence yet exists for adverse physiological reactions to GM crops in humans, and some scientists argue that these same genetic-modification techniques are also currently being used in the development of pharmaceutical and industrial products.

A prevailing theme in the GM debate is that when discrepancies between scientific consensus and government policy result in unwanted consequences, the blame is often placed directly on GM crop technology itself. In 2000 about 300,000 acres of StarLink corn, a Bt crop produced by Aventis CropScience, were being cultivated in the United States. Since the US Environmental Protection Agency had declared its uncertainty over the allergenic potential of StarLink, the crops were grown with the understanding that they would be used solely as animal feed. Later that year news broke that StarLink corn had found its way into numerous taco food products around the world. This incident received wide press coverage and brought instant attention to the debate over GM crop safety. More at issue, though, were the United States' lax policies of GM crop approval and regulation. For nearly a decade, the US government made no distinction between GM crops and organically grown crops, and allergenicity safety tests were not mandatory. Only recently has the US Food and Drug Administration begun to reconsider its policies.

Canada is another leading producer of GM crops, with regulatory policies similar to those of the United States. Recent controversy surrounding Canada's cultivation of GM rapeseed, or canola, brought attention to another major environmental risk of GM crops. Unlike wheat and soybeans, which can self-pollinate to reproduce, the pollen of rapeseed plants spreads up to 800 meters beyond the field. There have been concerns in Ottawa over the government's refusal to reveal the location of ongoing GM wheat testing by Monsanto, resulting in fear of unwanted pollen spreading. This issue demonstrates one of the most potent risks of GM crops: uncontrolled breeding and the introduction of foreign genes into the natural ecosystem. An example of such an incident is Mexico's discovery of transgenic genes in non-GM strains of maize, although this result is still under scrutiny. More measures must be tested to restrain these possibilities. Current research on introducing the foreign genes into chloroplasts, which are only carried in the maternal line and not in pollen, offers a promising example.

Unfortunately, activist organizations rarely cite credible scientific evidence in their positions and have won much public sympathy by exploiting popular fears and misconceptions about genetic-engineering technology.

Europe's policy toward GM crops lies on the opposite end of the spectrum. In 1996 Europe approved the import of Monsanto's Roundup Ready soybeans and in 1997 authorized the cultivation of GM corn from Novartis. At around this time, however, there were rising concerns in Britain over BSE (bovine spongiform encephalopathy), or mad cow disease, which was thought to have killed more than two dozen people and cost the country the equivalent of billions of US dollars. The public was enraged over what it believed was a failure of government regulation, and in 1998 the European Commission voted to ban the import and cultivation of new GM crops. Besides the disappointment of private GM corporations like Monsanto, the United States claims to have lost US$600 million in corn exports to the European Union. Recently, several European countries have considered lifting the ban contingent on the establishment of adequate labeling practices. The United States has complained to EU officials that labeling requirements discriminate against its agricultural exports, bringing the GM debate into the midst of a world trade dispute. In late January 2000, a tentative agreement was reached on the Montreal Biosafety Protocol in which the United States, Canada, Australia, Argentina, Uruguay, and Chile agreed to preliminary labeling of international exports and a precautionary principle allowing EU countries to reject imports if a scientific risk assessment of the imported crop is provided. This agreement, however, does not override decisions made by the World Trade Organization.

Corporate Control

The European public's anti-GM crop stance stems primarily from the success of environmental advocacy groups such as Greenpeace and Friends of the Earth. Numerous demonstrations have occurred throughout Britain, France, and other EU countries where GM crops have been uprooted and destroyed.

Unfortunately, activist organizations rarely cite credible scientific evidence in their positions and have won much public sympathy by exploiting popular fears and misconceptions about genetic-engineering technology.

One issue they highlight that might prove significant, however, is the role of corporate interests in the GM-crop debate. A few years ago, Monsanto's attempt to acquire the "terminator" technology sparked tremendous controversy. This patent consisted of an elaborate genetically engineered control system designed to inhibit the generation of fertile seeds from crops. In essence, it was developed so that farmers would need to purchase new GM seeds each year, although arguments were raised that this technology could help prevent uncontrolled GM crop breeding. After much pressure from the nonprofit advocacy group Rural Advancement Foundation International, however, Monsanto announced in late 1999 that it would not market the "terminator" technology.

The "terminator" ordeal attracted so much attention because it placed Monsanto's corporate interest directly against the strongest argument in favor of genetic-engineering technology: potential cost savings and nutritional value of GM crops to developing countries. The UN Development Programme recently affirmed that GM crops could be the key to alleviating global hunger. Although the United Nations has expressed concern over precautionary testing of crops (through agencies like the World Health Organization), some contend that Western opposition to this technology ignores concerns of sub-Saharan and South Asian countries where malnutrition and poverty are widespread.

India is among those nations that could benefit from GM-crop technology. India's population has been growing by 1.8 percent annually; by 2025 India will need to produce 30 percent more grain per year to feed the twenty million new mouths added to its population. The need for higher food productivity is highlighted by incidents of poor farmers in Warangal and Punjab who have committed suicide when faced with devastated crops and huge debts on pesticides. The Indian government has approved several GM crops for commercial production, and testing has also commenced on transgenic cotton, rice, maize, tomato, and cauliflower, crops that would reduce the need for pesticides. A recent furor erupted over the discovery of around 11,000 hectares of illegal Bt cotton in Gujarat. The Gujarat administration responded immediately by ordering the fields stripped, the crops burned, and the seeds destroyed. There is still uncertainty over who will repay the farmers, who claim that Mahyco, a Monsanto subsidiary, is attempting to monopolize the distribution of Bt crops in India, and that the Indian government is also yielding to pressure from pesticide manufacturers. Corporate battles still abound in a nation where many farmers appear to be in need of agricultural change.

Feed the World

Many opponents of GM crops argue that the technology is not needed to help solve the problem of world hunger, with 800 million people who do not have enough to eat. They often argue that the world produces enough food to feed nine billion people while there are only six billion people today, implying that global hunger is simply a matter of distribution and not food productivity. Unfortunately, fixing the distribution problem is a complex issue. Purchasing power would need to increase in developing countries, coupled with increased food production in both developing and developed countries so that crops can be marketed at a price the underprivileged can afford. Since land for farming is limited, the remaining option for increasing crop productivity is to increase yield. While GM-crop technology is not the only method that can be used to achieve this end, it can contribute greatly toward it.

On Dr. Shiva's argument for supporting local knowledge in agricultural practices, Dr. Prakash argues that, from experience, "[local knowledge] is losing one third of your children before they hit the age of three. Is that the local knowledge that you want to keep reinforcing and keep perpetuating?"

Some consider GM crops part of a series of corporate attempts to control markets in developing countries and thus they brand GM technology another globalization "evil." Dr. Vandana Shiva of the Research Foundation for Science, Technology, and Ecology argues that globalization has pressured farmers in developing countries to grow monocultures—single-crop farming—instead of fostering sustainable agricultural diversity. Genetic engineering, in this view, is the next industrialization effort after chemical pesticides, and would also bear no greater benefit than indigenous polycultural farming. The Food and Agricultural Organization of the United Nations also notes the leaning of research investment toward monocultures, spurred on by the profit potential of GM crops.

On the other hand, GM-crop technology serves to increase crop yield on land already in use for agricultural purposes, thereby preserving biodiversity in unused land. In the words of Dr. C. S. Prakash "using genetics helped [to] save so much valuable land from being under the plow." On Shiva's argument for supporting local knowledge in agricultural practices, Dr. Prakash argues that, from experience, "[local knowledge] is losing one third of your children before they hit the age of three. Is that the local knowledge that you want to keep reinforcing and keep perpetuating?"

Continuing along these lines and bringing GM technology in developing countries into the broader context of morality, leaders including Per Pinstrup-Andersen, director of the International Food Policy Research Institute, and Hassan Adamu,

Nigeria's minister of agriculture, emphasize the importance of providing freedom of access, education, and choice in GM technology to the individual farmer himself. In Africa, for example, many local farmers have benefited from hybrid seeds obtained from multinational corporations. On a larger scale, however, Africa's agricultural production per unit area is among the lowest in the world, and great potential lies in utilizing GM crops to help combat pestilence and drought problems. On the issue of local knowledge, Dr. Florence Wambugu of the International Service for the Acquisition of Agribiotech Applications in Kenya (ISAAA) asserts that GM crops consist of "packaged technology in the seed" that can yield benefits without a change in local agricultural customs.

On another front of the world hunger debate, a promising benefit that GM-crop technology brings to developing countries is the introduction or enhancement of nutrients in crops. The first product to address this was "golden rice," an engineered form of rice that expresses high levels of beta-carotene, a precursor of Vitamin A, which could be used to combat Vitamin A deficiency found in over 120 million children worldwide. Although many advocacy groups claim that the increased levels of Vitamin A from a golden rice diet are not high enough to fully meet recommended doses of Vitamin A, studies suggest that a less-than-full dose can still make a difference in an individual whose Vitamin A intake is already deficiently low. Currently the International Rice Research Institute is evaluating environmental and health concerns. After such tests are completed, however, there remains one final hurdle in the marketing process that advocates on both sides of the GM debate do agree on: multilateral access and sharing between public and private sectors. The International Undertaking on Plant Genetic Resources was established to foster such relationships for the world's key crops, but more discussions will have to take place on the intellectual-property rights of GM-crop patents.

Science First

Monsanto recently drafted a pledge of Five Commitments: Respect, Transparency, Dialogue, Sharing, and Benefits. These are qualities that all multinational organizations should bring to the debate over GM crops. In the meantime, the technology of genetic engineering has already emerged and bears promising potential. On the question of world hunger, GM crops are not the full solution, but they can play a part in one. There are possible risks which must be examined and compared to the risks associated with current agricultural conditions, and progress must not be sought too hastily. It is important to base considerations of the benefits and risks of GM crops on careful scientific research, rather than corporate interest or public fears.

HONOR HSIN, Staff Writer, *Harvard International Review.*

From *Harvard International Review,* Spring 2002, pp. 38–41. Copyright © 2002 by Harvard International Review. Reprinted by permission.

UNIT 3

The Global Environment and Natural Resources

Unit Selections

Key Points to Consider

- What are the basic environmental challenges that confront both governments and individual consumers?

- Has the international community adequately responded to problems of pollution and threats to our common natural heritage? Why or why not?

- What is the natural resource picture going to look like thirty years from now?

- How is society, in general, likely to respond to the conflicts between lifestyle and resource conservation?

- The rapid industrialization of China and India has significant impacts beyond their borders. What are some of the environmental impacts?

- Can a sustainable economy be organized and what changes in behavior and values are necessary to accomplish this?

Student Web Site

www.mhcls.com/online

Internet References

Further information regarding these Web sites may be found in this book's preface or online.

National Geographic Society
http://www.nationalgeographic.com

National Oceanic and Atmospheric Administration (NOAA)
http://www.noaa.gov

SocioSite: Sociological Subject Areas
http://www.pscw.uva.nl/sociosite/TOPICS/

United Nations Environment Programme (UNEP)
http://www.unep.ch

Beginning in the eighteenth century, the modern nation-state began to emerge, and over many generations it evolved to the point where it is now difficult to imagine a world without national governments. These legal entities have been viewed as separate, self-contained units that independently pursue their "national interests." Scholars often described the world as a political community of independent units that interact with each other (a concept that has been described as a billiard ball model).

This perspective of the international community as comprised of self-contained and self-directed units has undergone major rethinking in the past 35 years. One of the reasons for this are the international consequences of the growing demands being placed on natural resources The Middle East, for example, contains a large majority of the world's known oil reserves. The United States, Western Europe, China and Japan are very dependent on this vital source of energy. This unbalanced supply and demand equation has created an unprecedented lack of self-sufficiency for the world's major economic powers.

The increased interdependence of countries is further illustrated by the fact that air and water pollution do not respect political boundaries. One country's smoke is often another country's acid rain. The concept that independent political units control their own destiny, in short, makes less sense than it may have 100 years ago. In order to fully understand why this is so, one must first look at how Earth's natural resources are being utilized and how this may be affecting the global environment.

The initial article in the unit examines the broad dimensions of the uses and abuses of natural resources. The central theme in this article is the unsustainable use of natural resources in essential economic activities such as agriculture. In many regions an alarming decline in the quality of the natural resource base is taking place.

An important conclusion resulting from this analysis is that contemporary methods of resource utilization often create problems that transcend national boundaries. Global climate changes, for example, will affect everyone, and if these changes are to be successfully addressed, international collaboration will be required. The consequences of basic human activities such as growing and cooking food are profound when multiplied billions of times every day. A single country or even a few countries working together cannot have a significant impact on redressing these problems. Solutions will have to be conceived that are truly global in scope. Just as there are shortages of natural resources, there are also shortages of new ideas for solving many of these problems.

Unit 3 continues by examining specific case studies that explore in greater detail the issues raised in the first article. Implicit in these discussions is the challenge of moving from

Royalty-Free/CORBIS

the perspective of the environment as primarily an economic resource to be consumed to a perspective that has been defined as "sustainable development." This change is easily called for, but in fact it goes to the core of social values and basic economic activities. Developing sustainable practices, therefore, is a challenge of unprecedented magnitude.

Nature is not some object "out there" to be visited at a national park. It is the food we eat and the energy we consume. Human beings are joined in the most intimate of relationships with the natural world in order to survive from one day to the next. It is ironic how little time is spent thinking about this relationship. This lack of attention, however, is not likely to continue, for rapidly growing numbers of people and the increased use of energy-consuming technologies are placing unprecedented pressures on Earth's carrying capacity.

Deflating the World's Bubble Economy

"Unless the damaging trends that have been set in motion are reversed quickly, we could see vast numbers of environmental refugees abandoning areas scarred by depleted aquifers and exhausted soils. . . ."

LESTER R. BROWN

Throughout history, humans have lived on the Earth's sustainable yield—the interest from its natural endowment. Now, however, we are consuming the endowment itself. In ecology, as in economics, we can consume principal along with interest in the short run, but, for the long term, that practice leads to bankruptcy. By satisfying our excessive demands through overconsumption of the Earth's natural assets, we are in effect creating a global bubble economy. Bubble economies are not new. American investors got an up-close view of this when the bubble in high-tech stocks burst in 2000, and the Nasdaq, an indicator of the value of these stocks, declined by some 75%. Japan had a similar experience in 1989 when its real estate bubble collapsed, depreciating assets by 60%. The Japanese economy has been reeling ever since.

These two events primarily affected those living in the U.S. and Japan, but the global bubble economy that is based on the overconsumption of the Earth's natural capital will affect the entire planet. The trouble is, since Sept. 11, 2001, political leaders, diplomats, and the media have been preoccupied with terrorism and, more recently, the conflict in Iraq. These certainly are matters of concern, but if they divert us from addressing the environmental trends that are undermining our future, Osama bin Laden and his followers will have achieved their goal of disrupting our way of life in a way they could not have imagined.

Of all the sectors affected by the bubble economy, food may be the most vulnerable. Today's farmers are dealing with major new challenges: their crops must endure the highest temperatures in 11,000 years as well as widespread aquifer depletion and the resulting loss of irrigation water unknown to previous generations. The average global temperature has risen in each of the last three decades. The 16 warmest years since record-keeping began in 1880 have occurred since 1980. With the three warmest years on record—1998, 2001, and 2002—coming in the last five years, crops are facing unprecedented heat stress. Higher temperatures reduce yields through their effect on photosynthesis, moisture balance, and fertilization. As the temperature rises above 34° Celsius (94° Fahrenheit), evaporation increases and photosynthesis and fertilization are impeded. Scientists at the International Rice Research Institute in the Philippines and at the U.S. Department of Agriculture together have developed a rule of thumb that each 1° Celsius rise in temperature above the optimum during the growing season reduces grain yields by 10%.

Findings indicate that if the temperature reaches the lower end of the range projected by the Intergovernmental Panel on Climate Change, grain harvests in tropical regions could be reduced by an average of five percent by 2020 and 11% by 2050. At the upper end of the range, yields could drop 11% by 2020 and 46% by 2050. Avoiding these declines will be difficult unless scientists can develop crop strains that are not vulnerable to thermal stress.

The second challenge facing farmers—falling water tables—also is a recent phenomenon. Using traditional animal- or human-powered waterlifting devices, it was virtually impossible to exhaust aquifers. With the spread of powerful diesel and electric pumps during the last half-century, however, overuse has become commonplace. As the world demand for water has climbed, water tables have fallen in scores of countries, including China, India, and the U.S., which together produce nearly half of the world's grain. Many other nations are straining their water reserves, too, setting the stage for dramatic cutbacks in water resources. The more populous among these are Pakistan, Iran, and Mexico. Overpumping creates an illusion of food security, enabling farmers to support a growing population with a practice that virtually ensures an eventual decline in food production and skyrocketing prices.

Food is fast becoming a national security issue as growth in the world harvest slows and falling water tables and rising temperatures hint at upcoming shortages. More than 100 countries import wheat. Some 40 import rice. While a handful of nations are only marginally dependent on imports, many could not survive without them. Iran and Egypt, for example, rely on imports for 40% of their grain supply. Algeria, Japan, South Korea, and Taiwan each import 70% or more. For Israel and Yemen, over 90%. Six countries—the U.S., Canada, France, Australia, Argentina, and Thailand—supply 90% of grain exports. The U.S. alone controls close to half the planet's grain exports, a larger share than Saudi Arabia does of oil.

Thus far, the countries that import heavily are small and mid-sized. China, however, the most populous nation, soon is likely to turn to international markets in a major way. When the former Soviet Union unexpectedly moved in that direction in 1972 for roughly one-tenth of its grain supply following a weather-reduced harvest, wheat prices climbed from $1.90 to $4.89 a bushel. Bread prices soon rose, too. A politics of food scarcity emerged. Pressure from within grain-exporting countries to restrict exports in order to check the rise in domestic food prices was common.

If China depletes its wheat reserves and looks elsewhere to cover the shortfall, now 40,000,000 tons per year, the situation could destabilize overnight, because it would mean petitioning the U.S., thus presenting a potentially delicate geopolitical situation in which 1,300,000,000 Chinese consumers boasting a $100,000,000,000 trade surplus with the U.S. will be competing with U.S. consumers for American grain. If that leads to rising food prices in this country, how will the government respond? In times past, it could have restricted exports, even imposing a trade embargo, as it did with soybeans to Japan in 1974. Today, though, the U.S. has a huge stake in a politically stable China. Growing at seven to eight percent a year, China is the engine that is powering not only the Asian economy but, to some degree, the global economy as well.

For the world's poor—the millions living in cities on one dollar per day or less and already spending 70% of their income on food—escalating grain prices would be life-threatening. A doubling of prices could impoverish vast numbers in a shorter period of time than any event in history. With desperate individuals holding their governments responsible, such a price spike also could destabilize governments of low-income, grain-importing nations.

Historically, there were two food reserves: the global carryover stocks of grain and the cropland idled under the U.S. farm policy to limit production. The latter could be cultivated within a year. Since the U.S. land set-aside initiative ended in 1996, however, there have been only carryover stocks as a reserve.

Food security has changed in other ways. Traditionally, it was largely an agricultural matter. Now, though, it is something that our entire society is responsible for. National population and energy policies may have a greater impact on food security than agricultural policies do. With most of the 3,000,000,000 additional individuals forecasted by 2050 being born in countries already facing water shortages, population control may have a larger influence on food security than crop planting proposals. Achieving an acceptable balance between food and consumers depends on family planners and farmers working together.

Climate change is the wild card in the food security deck. It is perhaps a measure of the complexity of our time that decisions reached in the Ministry of Energy may have more to do with future food security than those in the Ministry of Agriculture. The effects of population and energy policies on food security differ in one important respect: population stability can be achieved by a country acting unilaterally; climate stability cannot.

While the food sector may be the first to reveal the true size of the bubble economy, other wake-up calls, including more destructive storms, deadly heat waves, and collapsing fisheries, also could signal the extent to which we have overshot our ecological limitations. Unless the damaging trends that have been set in motion are reversed quickly, we could see vast numbers of environmental refugees abandoning areas scarred by depleted aquifers and exhausted soils, as well as fleeing advancing deserts and rising seas. In a world where civilization is being squeezed between expanding deserts from the interior continents and rising seas on the periphery, refugees are likely to number not in the millions, but in the tens of millions.

Preventing the bubble from bursting will require an unprecedented degree of international cooperation. Indeed, in both scale and urgency, the effort required is comparable to the U.S. mobilization during World War II. Rapid systemic change—alteration based on market signals that tell the ecological truth—is needed. This means lowering income taxes while raising tariffs on environmentally destructive activities, such as fossil fuel burning, to incorporate the ecological costs. Unless the market can be made to send signals that reflect reality, we will continue making faulty decisions as consumers, corporate planners, and government policymakers.

Stabilizing world population at around 7,500,000,000 is central to avoiding economic breakdowns in countries with large projected population increases that are already overconsuming their natural capital assets. No less than 36 nations, all in Europe (except Japan), essentially have done so. The challenge is to create the economic and social conditions—and to adopt the priorities—that will lead to population stability in the remaining lands. The keys here are offering primary education to every child, providing vaccinations along with basic and reproductive health care, and offering family planning services.

Shifting from a carbon- to a hydrogen-based economy to stabilize climate is quite feasible. Advances in wind turbine design and solar cell manufacturing, the availability of hydrogen generators, and the evolution of fuel cells provide the technologies necessary to build a climate-benign hydrogen economy. Moving quickly to renewable energy sources and improving efficiency depend on incorporating the indirect costs of burning fossil fuels into the market price.

On the energy front, Iceland is the first nation to adopt a national plan to convert its carbon-based energy economy to one of hydrogen. It is starting with the conversion of the Reykjavik bus fleet to fuel cell engines, then will proceed with converting automobiles, and, eventually, the fishing fleet. Iceland's first hydrogen service station opened in April.

Denmark and Germany, meanwhile, are leading proponents of wind power. Denmark, the pioneer, gets 18% of its electricity from turbines and plans to upgrade to 40% by 2030. Germany has developed some 12,000 megawatts of wind-generating capacity. Its northernmost state of Schleswig-Holstein receives 28% of its electricity in that fashion. Spain also is on the fast track in this area.

Japan has emerged as the number-one manufacturer and consumer of solar cells. With its commercialization of a solar roofing material, it now leads the world in electricity generated from solar cells and is well positioned to assist in the electrification of villages in developing areas.

"Preventing the bubble from bursting will require an unprecedented degree of international cooperation. Indeed, in both scale and urgency, the effort required is comparable to the U.S. mobilization during World War II."

The Netherlands leads the industrial world in utilizing the bicycle as an alternative to the automobile. In Amsterdam's pedal-friendly environment, up to 40% of all trips are taken by that mode of transportation. This reflects the priority given to bikes in the design and operation of the country's urban transport systems. At many traffic signals, for example, cyclists are allowed to go first when the light changes.

The Canadian province of Ontario is one of the leaders in phasing out coal. It plans to replace its five coal-fired power plants with gas-fired plants, wind farms, and efficiency gains. This initiative calls for the first plant to close in 2005 and the last one by 2015. The resulting reduction in carbon emissions will be the equivalent of taking 4,000,000 cars off the road. This approach is a model for local and national governments everywhere.

Meanwhile, in pioneering drip irrigation technology, Israel has become the world leader in the efficient use of agricultural water. This unusually labor-intensive irrigation practice is ideally suited where water is scarce and labor is abundant. Water pricing also can be effective in encouraging efficiency. In South Africa, for example, households receive a fixed amount of water for basic needs at a low price, but when water use exceeds this level, the price escalates. This helps ensure that basic needs are met while discouraging waste. Doesn't it make sense to reduce urban and industrial water demand by managing waste without discharging it into the local environment, thereby allowing water to be recycled indefinitely?

In stabilizing soils, South Korea stands out, as its once denuded mountainsides and hills are now covered with trees. The nation's level of flood control, water storage, and hydrological stability is an example for other countries. Although the two Koreas are separated by just a narrow, demilitarized zone, the contrast between them is stark. In North Korea, where little permanent vegetation remains, droughts and floods alternate and hunger is chronic.

The U.S. record in soil conservation is an impressive one. Beginning in the late 1980s, American farmers systematically retired roughly 10% of the most erodible cropland, planting grass on the bulk of it. In addition, they've adopted various soil-conserving initiatives, including minimum- and no-till practices. Consequently, the U.S. has reduced soil erosion by almost 40% in less than two decades.

There is a growing sense among the more thoughtful political and opinion leaders worldwide that business as usual no longer is a viable option. Unless we respond to the social and environmental issues that are undermining our future, we may not be able to avoid economic decline and social disintegration. The prospect of weakened states is growing as the HIV epidemic, water shortages, and land hunger threaten to overwhelm countries on the lower rungs of the global economic ladder. Failed states are a matter of concern not only because of the social costs to their people, but because they serve as ideal bases for international terrorist organizations.

It is easy to spend hundreds of billions in response to terrorist threats, but the reality is that the resources needed to disrupt a modern economy are small, and a Department of Homeland Security, however heavily funded, provides only minimum protection from suicidal extremists. The challenge is not just to provide a high-tech military response to terrorism, but to build a global society that is environmentally sustainable, socially equitable, and democratically based—where there is hope for everyone. Such an effort would more effectively undermine the spread of terrorism than a doubling of military expenditures.

We can construct an economy that does not destroy its natural support systems, a community where the basic needs of all the Earth's people are satisfied, and a world that will allow us to think of ourselves as civilized. The choice is ours—yours and mine. We can stay with the status quo and preside over a global bubble economy that will keep expanding until it finally bursts, or we can be the generation that stabilizes population, eradicates poverty, and alleviates climate change. Historians will record the choice, but it is ours to make.

LESTER R. BROWN is president of the Earth Policy Institute, Washington, D.C., and author of *Plan B: Rescuing a Planet Under Stress and a Civilization in Trouble*.

The Great Leap Backward?

ELIZABETH C. ECONOMY

China's environmental problems are mounting. Water pollution and water scarcity are burdening the economy, rising levels of air pollution are endangering the health of millions of Chinese, and much of the country's land is rapidly turning into desert. China has become a world leader in air and water pollution and land degradation and a top contributor to some of the world's most vexing global environmental problems, such as the illegal timber trade, marine pollution, and climate change. As China's pollution woes increase, so, too, do the risks to its economy, public health, social stability, and international reputation. As Pan Yue, a vice minister of China's State Environmental Protection Administration (SEPA), warned in 2005, "The [economic] miracle will end soon because the environment can no longer keep pace."

With the 2008 Olympics around the corner, China's leaders have ratcheted up their rhetoric, setting ambitious environmental targets, announcing greater levels of environmental investment, and exhorting business leaders and local officials to clean up their backyards. The rest of the world seems to accept that Beijing has charted a new course: as China declares itself open for environmentally friendly business, officials in the United States, the European Union, and Japan are asking not whether to invest but how much.

Unfortunately, much of this enthusiasm stems from the widespread but misguided belief that what Beijing says goes. The central government sets the country's agenda, but it does not control all aspects of its implementation. In fact, local officials rarely heed Beijing's environmental mandates, preferring to concentrate their energies and resources on further advancing economic growth. The truth is that turning the environmental situation in China around will require something far more difficult than setting targets and spending money; it will require revolutionary bottom-up political and economic reforms.

For one thing, China's leaders need to make it easy for local officials and factory owners to do the right thing when it comes to the environment by giving them the right incentives. At the same time, they must loosen the political restrictions they have placed on the courts, nongovernmental organizations (NGOs), and the media in order to enable these groups to become independent enforcers of environmental protection. The international community, for its part, must focus more on assisting reform and less on transferring cutting-edge technologies and developing demonstration projects. Doing so will mean diving into the trenches to work with local Chinese officials, factory owners, and environmental NGOs; enlisting international NGOs to help with education and enforcement policies; and persuading multinational corporations (MNCs) to use their economic leverage to ensure that their Chinese partners adopt the best environmental practices.

Without such a clear-eyed understanding not only of what China wants but also of what it needs, China will continue to have one of the world's worst environmental records, and the Chinese people and the rest of the world will pay the price.

Sins of Emission

China's rapid development, often touted as an economic miracle, has become an environmental disaster. Record growth necessarily requires the gargantuan consumption of resources, but in China energy use has been especially unclean and inefficient, with dire consequences for the country's air, land, and water.

The coal that has powered China's economic growth, for example, is also choking its people. Coal provides about 70 percent of China's energy needs: the country consumed some 2.4 billion tons in 2006—more than the United States, Japan, and the United Kingdom combined. In 2000, China anticipated doubling its coal consumption by 2020; it is now expected to have done so by the end of this year. Consumption in China is huge partly because it is inefficient: as one Chinese official told *Der Spiegel* in early 2006, "To produce goods worth $10,000 we need seven times the resources used by Japan, almost six times the resources used by the U.S. and—a particular source of embarrassment—almost three times the resources used by India."

Meanwhile, this reliance on coal is devastating China's environment. The country is home to 16 of the world's 20 most polluted cities, and four of the worst off among them are in the coal-rich province of Shanxi, in northeastern China. As much as 90 percent of China's sulfur dioxide emissions and 50 percent of its particulate emissions are the result of coal use. Particulates are responsible for respiratory problems among the population, and acid rain, which is caused by sulfur dioxide emissions, falls on one-quarter of China's territory and on one-third of its agricultural land, diminishing agricultural output and eroding buildings.

Yet coal use may soon be the least of China's air-quality problems. The transportation boom poses a growing challenge to China's air quality. Chinese developers are laying more than 52,700 miles of new highways throughout the country. Some 14,000 new cars hit China's roads each day. By 2020, China is expected to have 130 million cars, and by 2050—or perhaps as early as 2040—it is expected to have even more cars than the United States. Beijing already pays a high price for this boom. In a 2006 survey, Chinese respondents rated Beijing the 15th most livable city in China, down from the 4th in 2005, with the drop due largely to increased traffic and pollution. Levels of airborne particulates are now six times higher in Beijing than in New York City.

China's grand-scale urbanization plans will aggravate matters. China's leaders plan to relocate 400 million people—equivalent to well over the entire population of the United States—to newly developed urban centers between 2000 and 2030. In the process, they will erect half of all the buildings expected to be constructed in the world during that period. This is a troubling prospect considering that Chinese buildings are not energy efficient—in fact, they are roughly two and a half times less so than those in Germany. Furthermore, newly urbanized Chinese, who use air conditioners, televisions, and refrigerators, consume about three and a half times more energy than do their rural counterparts. And although China is one of the world's largest producer of solar cells, compact fluorescent lights, and energy-efficient windows, these are produced mostly for export. Unless more of these energy-saving goods stay at home, the building boom will result in skyrocketing energy consumption and pollution.

China's land has also suffered from unfettered development and environmental neglect. Centuries of deforestation, along with the overgrazing of grasslands and overcultivation of cropland, have left much of China's north and northwest seriously degraded. In the past half century, moreover, forests and farmland have had to make way for industry and sprawling cities, resulting in diminishing crop yields, a loss in biodiversity, and local climatic change. The Gobi Desert, which now engulfs much of western and northern China, is spreading by about 1,900 square miles annually; some reports say that despite Beijing's aggressive reforestation efforts, one-quarter of the entire country is now desert. China's State Forestry Administration estimates that desertification has hurt some 400 million Chinese, turning tens of millions of them into environmental refugees, in search of new homes and jobs. Meanwhile, much of China's arable soil is contaminated, raising concerns about food safety. As much as ten percent of China's farmland is believed to be polluted, and every year 12 million tons of grain are contaminated with heavy metals absorbed from the soil.

Water Hazard

And then there is the problem of access to clean water. Although China holds the fourth-largest freshwater resources in the world (after Brazil, Russia, and Canada), skyrocketing demand, overuse, inefficiencies, pollution, and unequal distribution have produced a situation in which two-thirds of China's approximately 660 cities have less water than they need and 110 of them suffer severe shortages. According to Ma Jun, a leading Chinese water expert, several cities near Beijing and Tianjin, in the northeastern region of the country, could run out of water in five to seven years.

Growing demand is part of the problem, of course, but so is enormous waste. The agricultural sector lays claim to 66 percent of the water China consumes, mostly for irrigation, and manages to waste more than half of that. Chinese industries are highly inefficient: they generally use 10–20 percent more water than do their counterparts in developed countries. Urban China is an especially huge squanderer: it loses up to 20 percent of the water it consumes through leaky pipes—a problem that China's Ministry of Construction has pledged to address in the next two to three years. As urbanization proceeds and incomes rise, the Chinese, much like people in Europe and the United States, have become larger consumers of water: they take lengthy showers, use washing machines and dishwashers, and purchase second homes with lawns that need to be watered. Water consumption in Chinese cities jumped by 6.6 percent during 2004–5. China's plundering of its ground-water reserves, which has created massive underground tunnels, is causing a corollary problem: some of China's wealthiest cities are sinking—in the case of Shanghai and Tianjin, by more than six feet during the past decade and a half. In Beijing, subsidence has destroyed factories, buildings, and underground pipelines and is threatening the city's main international airport.

Pollution is also endangering China's water supplies. China's ground water, which provides 70 percent of the country's total drinking water, is under threat from a variety of sources, such as polluted surface water, hazardous waste sites, and pesticides and fertilizers. According to one report by the government-run Xinhua News Agency, the aquifers in 90 percent of Chinese cities are polluted. More than 75 percent of the river water flowing through China's urban areas is considered unsuitable for drinking or fishing, and the Chinese government deems about 30 percent of the river water throughout the country to be unfit for use in agriculture or industry. As a result, nearly 700 million people drink water contaminated with animal and human waste. The World Bank has found that the failure to provide fully two-thirds of the rural population with piped water is a leading cause of death among children under the age of five and is responsible for as much as 11 percent of the cases of gastrointestinal cancer in China.

One of the problems is that although China has plenty of laws and regulations designed to ensure clean water, factory owners and local officials do not enforce them. A 2005 survey of 509 cities revealed that only 23 percent of factories properly treated sewage before disposing of it. According to another report, today one-third of all industrial wastewater in China and two-thirds of household sewage are released untreated. Recent Chinese studies of two of the country's most important sources of water—the Yangtze and Yellow rivers—illustrate the growing challenge. The Yangtze River, which stretches all the way from the Tibetan Plateau to Shanghai, receives 40 percent of the country's sewage, 80 percent of it untreated. In 2007, the Chinese government announced that it was delaying, in part because of pollution, the development of a $60 billion plan to divert the river in order to supply the water-starved cities of Beijing and Tianjin. The Yellow River supplies water to more than 150 million people and 15 percent of China's agricultural land, but two-thirds of its water is considered unsafe to drink and 10 percent of its water is classified as sewage. In early 2007, Chinese officials announced that over one-third of the fish species native to the Yellow River had become extinct due to damming or pollution.

China's leaders are also increasingly concerned about how climate change may exacerbate their domestic environmental situation. In the spring of 2007, Beijing released its first national assessment report on climate change, predicting a 30 percent drop in precipitation in three of China's seven major river regions—around the Huai, Liao, and Hai rivers—and a 37 percent decline in the country's wheat, rice, and corn yields in the second half of the century. It also predicted that the Yangtze and Yellow rivers, which derive much of their water from glaciers in Tibet, would overflow as the glaciers melted and then dry up. And both Chinese and international scientists now warn that due to rising sea levels, Shanghai could be submerged by 2050.

Collateral Damage

China's environmental problems are already affecting the rest of the world. Japan and South Korea have long suffered from the acid rain produced by China's coal-fired power plants and from the eastbound dust storms that sweep across the Gobi Desert in the spring and dump toxic yellow dust on their land. Researchers in the United States are tracking dust, sulfur, soot, and trace metals as these travel across the Pacific from China. The U.S. Environmental Protection Agency estimates that on some days, 25 percent of the particulates in the atmosphere in Los Angeles originated in China.[1] Scientists have also traced rising levels of mercury deposits on U.S. soil back to coal-fired power plants and cement factories in China. (When ingested in significant quantities, mercury can cause birth defects and developmental problems.) Reportedly, 25–40 percent of all mercury emissions in the world come from China.

What China dumps into its waters is also polluting the rest of the world. According to the international NGO the World Wildlife Fund, China is now the largest polluter of the Pacific Ocean. As Liu Quangfeng, an adviser to the National People's Congress, put it, "Almost no river that flows into the Bo Hai [a sea along China's northern coast] is clean." China releases about 2.8 billion tons of contaminated water into the Bo Hai annually, and the content of heavy metal in the mud at the bottom of it is now 2,000 times as high as China's own official safety standard. The prawn catch has dropped by 90 percent over the past 15 years. In 2006, in the heavily industrialized southeastern provinces of Guangdong and Fujian, almost 8.3 billion tons of sewage were discharged into the ocean without treatment, a 60 percent increase from 2001. More than 80 percent of the East China Sea, one of the world's largest fisheries, is now rated unsuitable for fishing, up from 53 percent in 2000.

Furthermore, China is already attracting international attention for its rapidly growing contribution to climate change. According to a 2007 report from the Netherlands Environmental Assessment Agency, it has already surpassed the United States as the world's largest contributor of carbon dioxide, a leading greenhouse gas, to the atmosphere. Unless China rethinks its use of various sources of energy and adopts cutting-edge environmentally friendly technologies, warned Fatih Birol, the chief economist of the International Energy Agency, last April, in 25 years China will emit twice as much carbon dioxide as all the countries of the Organization for Economic Cooperation and Development combined.

China's close economic partners in the developing world face additional environmental burdens from China's economic activities. Chinese multinationals, which are exploiting natural resources in Africa, Latin America, and Southeast Asia in order to fuel China's continued economic rise, are devastating these regions' habitats in the process. China's hunger for timber has exploded over the past decade and a half, and particularly since 1998, when devastating floods led Beijing to crack down on domestic logging. China's timber imports more than tripled between 1993 and 2005. According to the World Wildlife Fund, China's demand for timber, paper, and pulp will likely increase by 33 percent between 2005 and 2010.

China is already the largest importer of illegally logged timber in the world: an estimated 50 percent of its timber imports are reportedly illegal. Illegal logging is especially damaging to the environment because it often targets rare old-growth forests, endangers biodiversity, and ignores sustainable forestry practices. In 2006, the government of Cambodia, for example, ignored its own laws and awarded China's Wuzhishan LS Group a 99-year concession that was 20 times as large as the size permitted by Cambodian law. The company's practices, including the spraying of large amounts of herbicides, have prompted repeated protests by local Cambodians. According to the international NGO Global Witness, Chinese companies have destroyed large parts of the forests along the Chinese-Myanmar border and are now moving deeper into Myanmar's forests in their search for timber. In many instances, illicit logging activity takes place with the active support of corrupt local officials. Central government officials in Myanmar and Indonesia, countries where China's loggers are active, have protested such arrangements to Beijing, but relief has been limited. These activities, along with those of Chinese mining and energy companies, raise serious environmental concerns for many local populations in the developing world.

Spoiling the Party

In the view of China's leaders, however, damage to the environment itself is a secondary problem. Of greater concern to them are its indirect effects: the threat it poses to the continuation of the Chinese economic miracle and to public health, social stability, and the country's international reputation. Taken together, these challenges could undermine the authority of the Communist Party.

China's leaders are worried about the environment's impact on the economy. Several studies conducted both inside and outside China estimate that environmental degradation and pollution cost the Chinese economy between 8 percent and 12 percent of GDP annually. The Chinese media frequently publish the results of studies on the impact of pollution on agriculture, industrial output, or public health: water pollution costs of $35.8 billion one year, air pollution costs of $27.5 billion another, and on and on with weather disasters ($26.5 billion), acid rain ($13.3 billion), desertification ($6 billion), or crop damage from soil pollution ($2.5 billion). The city of Chongqing, which sits on the banks of the Yangtze River, estimates that dealing with the effects of water pollution on its agriculture and public health costs as much as 4.3 percent of the city's annual gross product. Shanxi Province has watched its coal resources fuel the rest of the country while it pays the price in withered trees, contaminated air and water, and land subsidence. Local authorities there estimate the costs of environmental degradation and pollution at 10.9 percent of the province's annual gross product and have called on Beijing to compensate the province for its "contribution and sacrifice."

China's Ministry of Public Health is also sounding the alarm with increasing urgency. In a survey of 30 cities and 78 counties released in the spring, the ministry blamed worsening air and water pollution for dramatic increases in the incidence of cancer throughout the country: a 19 percent rise in urban areas and a 23 percent rise in rural areas since 2005. One research institute affiliated with SEPA has put the total number of premature deaths in China caused by respiratory diseases related to air pollution at 400,000 a year. But this may be a conservative estimate: according to a joint research project by the World Bank and the Chinese government released this year, the total number of such deaths is 750,000 a year. (Beijing is said not to have wanted to release the latter figure for fear of inciting social unrest.) Less well documented but potentially even more devastating is the health impact of China's polluted water. Today, fully 190 million Chinese are sick from drinking contaminated water. All along China's major rivers, villages report skyrocketing rates of diarrheal diseases, cancer, tumors, leukemia, and stunted growth.

Social unrest over these issues is rising. In the spring of 2006, China's top environmental official, Zhou Shengxian, announced that there had been 51,000 pollution-related protests in 2005, which amounts to almost 1,000 protests each week. Citizen complaints about the environment, expressed on official hotlines and in letters to local officials, are increasing at a rate of 30 percent a year; they will likely top 450,000 in 2007. But few of them are resolved satisfactorily, and so people throughout the country are increasingly taking to the streets. For several months in 2006, for example, the residents of six neighboring villages in Gansu Province held repeated protests against zinc and iron smelters that they believed were poisoning them. Fully half of the 4,000–5,000 villagers exhibited lead-related illnesses, ranging from vitamin D deficiency to neurological problems.

Many pollution-related marches are relatively small and peaceful. But when such demonstrations fail, the protesters sometimes resort to violence. After trying for two years to get redress by petitioning local, provincial, and even central government officials for spoiled crops and poisoned air, in the spring of 2005, 30,000–40,000 villagers from Zhejiang Province swarmed 13 chemical plants, broke windows and overturned buses, attacked government officials, and torched police cars. The government sent in 10,000 members of the People's Armed Police in response. The plants were ordered to close down, and several environmental activists who attempted to monitor the plants' compliance with these orders were later arrested. China's leaders have generally managed to prevent—if sometimes violently—discontent over environmental issues from spreading across provincial boundaries or morphing into calls for broader political reform.

In the face of such problems, China's leaders have recently injected a new urgency into their rhetoric concerning the need to protect the country's environment. On paper, this has translated into an aggressive strategy to increase investment in environmental protection, set ambitious targets for the reduction of pollution and energy intensity (the amount of energy used to produce a unit of GDP), and introduce new environmentally friendly technologies. In 2005, Beijing set out a number of impressive targets for its next five-year plan: by 2010, it wants 10 percent of the nation's power to come from renewable energy sources, energy intensity to have been reduced by 20 percent and key pollutants such as sulfur dioxide by 10 percent, water consumption to have decreased by 30 percent, and investment in environmental protection to have increased from 1.3 percent to 1.6 percent of GDP. Premier Wen Jiabao has issued a stern warning to local officials to shut down some of the plants in the most energy-intensive industries—power generation and aluminum, copper, steel, coke and coal, and cement production—and to slow the growth of other industries by denying them tax breaks and other production incentives.

These goals are laudable—even breathtaking in some respects—but history suggests that only limited optimism is warranted; achieving such targets has proved elusive in the past. In 2001, the Chinese government pledged to cut sulfur dioxide emissions by 10 percent between 2002 and 2005. Instead, emissions rose by 27 percent. Beijing is already encountering difficulties reaching its latest goals: for instance, it has failed to meet its first target for reducing energy intensity and pollution. Despite warnings from Premier Wen, the six industries that were slated to slow down posted a 20.6 percent increase in output during the first quarter of 2007—a 6.6 percent jump from the same period last year. According to one senior executive with the Indian wind-power firm Suzlon Energy, only 37 percent of the wind-power projects the Chinese government approved in 2004 have been built. Perhaps worried that yet another target would fall by the wayside, in early 2007, Beijing revised its announced goal of reducing the country's water consumption by 30 percent by 2010 to just 20 percent.

Even the Olympics are proving to be a challenge. Since Beijing promised in 2001 to hold a "green Olympics" in 2008, the International Olympic Committee has pulled out all the stops. Beijing is now ringed with rows of newly planted trees, hybrid taxis and buses are roaming its streets (some of which are soon to be lined with solar-powered lamps), the most heavily polluting factories have been pushed outside the city limits, and the Olympic dormitories are models of energy efficiency. Yet in key respects, Beijing has failed to deliver. City officials are backtracking from their pledge to provide safe tap water to all of Beijing for the Olympics; they now say that they will provide it only for residents of the Olympic Village. They have announced drastic stopgap measures for the duration of the games, such as banning one million of the city's three million cars from the city's streets and halting production at factories in and around Beijing (some of them are resisting). Whatever progress city authorities have managed over the past six years—such as increasing the number of days per year that the city's air is deemed to be clean—is not enough to ensure that the air will be clean for the Olympic Games. Preparing for the Olympics has come to symbolize the intractability of China's environmental challenges and the limits of Beijing's approach to addressing them.

Problems with the Locals

Clearly, something has got to give. The costs of inaction to China's economy, public health, and international reputation are growing. And perhaps more important, social discontent is rising. The Chinese people have clearly run out of patience with the government's inability or unwillingness to turn the environmental situation around. And the government is well aware of the increasing potential for environmental protest to ignite broader social unrest.

One event this spring particularly alarmed China's leaders. For several days in May in the coastal city of Xiamen, after months of mounting opposition to the planned construction of a $1.4 billion petrochemical plant nearby, students and professors at Xiamen University, among others, are said to have sent out a million mobile-phone text messages calling on their fellow citizens to take to the streets on June 1. That day, and the following, protesters reportedly numbering between 7,000 and 20,000 marched peacefully through the city, some defying threats of expulsion from school or from the Communist Party. The protest was captured on video and uploaded to YouTube. One video featured a haunting voice-over that linked the Xiamen demonstration to an ongoing environmental crisis near Tai Hu, a lake some 400 miles away (a large bloom of blue-green algae caused by industrial wastewater and sewage dumped in the lake had contaminated the water supply of the city of Wuxi). It also referred to the Tiananmen Square protest of 1989. The Xiamen march, the narrator said, was perhaps "the first genuine parade since Tiananmen."

In response, city authorities did stay the construction of the plant, but they also launched an all-out campaign to discredit the protesters and their videos. Still, more comments about the protest and calls not to forget Tiananmen appeared on various Web sites. Such messages, posted openly and accessible to all Chinese, represent the Chinese leadership's greatest fear, namely, that its failure to protect the environment may someday serve as the catalyst for broad-based demands for political change.

Such public demonstrations are also evidence that China's environmental challenges cannot be met with only impressive targets and more investment. They must be tackled with a fundamental reform of how the country does business and protects the environment. So far, Beijing has structured its environmental protection efforts in much the same way that it has pursued economic growth: by granting local authorities and factory owners wide decision-making power and by actively courting the international community and Chinese NGOs for their expertise while carefully monitoring their activities.

Consider, for example, China's most important environmental authority, SEPA, in Beijing. SEPA has become a wellspring of China's most innovative environmental policies: it has promoted an environmental impact assessment law; a law requiring local officials to release information about environmental disasters, pollution statistics, and the names of known polluters to the public; an experiment to calculate the costs of environ-

mental degradation and pollution to the country's GDP; and an all-out effort to halt over 100 large-scale infrastructure projects that had proceeded without proper environmental impact assessments. But SEPA operates with barely 300 full-time professional staff in the capital and only a few hundred employees spread throughout the country. (The U.S. Environmental Protection Agency has a staff of almost 9,000 in Washington, D.C., alone.) And authority for enforcing SEPA's mandates rests overwhelmingly with local officials and the local environmental protection officials they oversee. In some cases, this has allowed for exciting experimentation. In the eastern province of Jiangsu, for instance, the World Bank and the Natural Resources Defense Council have launched the Greenwatch program, which grades 12,000 factories according to their compliance with standards for industrial wastewater treatment and discloses both the ratings and the reasons for them. More often, however, China's highly decentralized system has meant limited progress: only seven to ten percent of China's more than 660 cities meet the standards required to receive the designation of National Model Environmental City from SEPA. According to Wang Canfa, one of China's top environmental lawyers, barely ten percent of China's environmental laws and regulations are actually enforced.

One of the problems is that local officials have few incentives to place a priority on environmental protection. Even as Beijing touts the need to protect the environment, Premier Wen has called for quadrupling the Chinese economy by 2020. The price of water is rising in some cities, such as Beijing, but in many others it remains as low as 20 percent of the replacement cost. That ensures that factories and municipalities have little reason to invest in wastewater treatment or other water-conservation efforts. Fines for polluting are so low that factory managers often prefer to pay them rather than adopt costlier pollution-control technologies. One manager of a coal-fired power plant explained to a Chinese reporter in 2005 that he was ignoring a recent edict mandating that all new power plants use desulfurization equipment because the technology cost as much as would 15 years' worth of fines.

Local governments also turn a blind eye to serious pollution problems out of self-interest. Officials sometimes have a direct financial stake in factories or personal relationships with their owners. And the local environmental protection bureaus tasked with guarding against such corruption must report to the local governments, making them easy targets for political pressure. In recent years, the Chinese media have uncovered cases in which local officials have put pressure on the courts, the press, or even hospitals to prevent the wrongdoings of factories from coming to light. (Just this year, in the province of Zhejiang, officials reportedly promised factories with an output of $1.2 million or more that they would not be subjected to government inspections without the factories' prior approval.)

Moreover, local officials frequently divert environmental protection funds and spend them on unrelated or ancillary endeavors. The Chinese Academy for Environmental Planning, which reports to SEPA, disclosed this year that only half of the 1.3 percent of the country's annual GDP dedicated to environmental protection between 2001 and 2005 had found its way to legitimate projects. According to the study, about 60 percent of the environmental protection funds spent in urban areas during that period went into the creation of, among other things, parks, factory production lines, gas stations, and sewage-treatment plants rather than into waste- or wastewater-treatment facilities.

Many local officials also thwart efforts to hold them accountable for their failure to protect the environment. In 2005, SEPA launched the "Green GDP" campaign, a project designed to calculate the costs of environmental degradation and pollution to local economies and provide a basis for evaluating the performance of local officials both according to their economic stewardship and according to how well they protect the environment. Several provinces balked, however, worried that the numbers would reveal the extent of the damage suffered by the environment. SEPA's partner in the campaign, the National Bureau of Statistics of China, also undermined the effort by announcing that it did not possess the tools to do Green GDP accounting accurately and that in any case it did not believe officials should be evaluated on such a basis. After releasing a partial report in September 2006, the NBS has refused to release this year's findings to the public.

Another problem is that many Chinese companies see little direct value in ratcheting up their environmental protection efforts. The computer manufacturer Lenovo and the appliance manufacturer Haier have received high marks for taking creative environmental measures, and the solar energy company Suntech has become a leading exporter of solar cells. But a recent poll found that only 18 percent of Chinese companies believed that they could thrive economically while doing the right thing environmentally. Another poll of business executives found that an overwhelming proportion of them do not understand the benefits of responsible corporate behavior, such as environmental protection, or consider the requirements too burdensome.

Not Good Enough

The limitations of the formal authorities tasked with environmental protection in China have led the country's leaders to seek assistance from others outside the bureaucracy. Over the past 15 years or so, China's NGOs, the Chinese media, and the international community have become central actors in the country's bid to rescue its environment. But the Chinese government remains wary of them.

China's homegrown environmental activists and their allies in the media have become the most potent—and potentially explosive—force for environmental change in China. From four or five NGOs devoted primarily to environmental education and biodiversity protection in the mid-1990s, the Chinese environmental movement has grown to include thousands of NGOs, run primarily by dynamic Chinese in their 30s and 40s. These groups now routinely expose polluting factories to the central government, sue for the rights of villagers poisoned by contaminated water or air, give seed money to small newer NGOs throughout the country, and go undercover to expose multinationals that ignore international environmental standards. They often protest via letters to the government, campaigns on the Internet, and editorials in Chinese newspapers. The media are an important ally in this fight: they shame polluters, uncover environmental abuse, and highlight environmental protection successes.

Beijing has come to tolerate NGOs and media outlets that play environmental watchdog at the local level, but it remains vigilant in making sure that certain limits are not crossed, and especially that the central government is not directly criticized. The penalties for misjudging these boundaries can be severe. Wu Lihong worked for 16 years to address the pollution in Tai Hu (which recently spawned blue-green algae), gathering evidence that has forced almost 200 factories to close. Although in 2005 Beijing honored Wu as one of the country's top environmentalists, he was beaten by local thugs several times during the course of his investigations, and in 2006 the government of the town of Yixing arrested him on dubious charges of blackmail. And Yu Xiaogang, the 2006 winner of the prestigious Goldman Environmental Prize, honoring grass-roots environmentalists, was forbidden to travel abroad in retaliation for educating villagers about the potential downsides of a proposed dam relocation in Yunnan Province.

The Chinese government's openness to environmental cooperation with the international community is also fraught. Beijing has welcomed bilateral agreements for technology development or financial assistance for demonstration projects, but it is concerned about other endeavors. On the one hand, it lauds international environmental NGOs for their contributions to China's environmental protection efforts. On the other hand, it fears that some of them will become advocates for democratization.

The government also subjects MNCs to an uncertain operating environment. Many corporations have responded to the government's calls that they assume a leading role in the country's environmental protection efforts by deploying top-of-the-line environmental technologies, financing environmental education in Chinese schools, undertaking community-based efforts, and raising operating standards in their industries. Coca-Cola, for example, recently pledged to become a net-zero consumer of water, and Wal-Mart is set to launch a nationwide education and sales initiative to promote the use of energy-efficient compact fluorescent bulbs. Sometimes, MNCs have been rewarded with awards or significant publicity. But in the past two years, Chinese officials (as well as local NGOs) have adopted a much tougher stance toward them, arguing at times that MNCs have turned China into the pollution capital of the world. On issues such as electronic waste, the detractors have a point. But China's attacks, with Internet postings accusing MNCs of practicing "eco-colonialism," have become unjustifiably broad. Such antiforeign sentiment spiked in late 2006, after the release of a pollution map listing more than 3,000 factories that were violating water pollution standards. The 33 among them that supplied MNCs were immediately targeted in the media, while the other few thousand Chinese factories cited somehow escaped the frenzy. A few Chinese officials and activists privately acknowledge that domestic Chinese companies pollute far more than foreign companies, but it seems unlikely that the spotlight will move off MNCs in the near future. For now, it is simply more expedient to let international corporations bear the bulk of the blame.

From Red to Green

Why is China unable to get its environmental house in order? Its top officials want what the United States, Europe, and Japan have: thriving economies with manageable environmental problems. But they are unwilling to pay the political and economic price to get there. Beijing's message to local officials continues to be that economic growth cannot be sacrificed to environmental protection—that the two objectives must go hand in hand.

This, however, only works sometimes. Greater energy efficiency can bring economic benefits, and investments to reduce pollution, such as in building wastewater-treatment plants, are expenses that can be balanced against the costs of losing crops to contaminated soil and having a sickly work force. Yet much of the time, charting a new environmental course comes with serious economic costs up front. Growth slows down in some industries or some regions. Some businesses are forced to close down. Developing pollution-treatment and pollution-prevention technologies requires serious investment. In fact, it is because they recognize these costs that local officials in China pursue their short-term economic interests first and for the most part ignore Beijing's directives to change their ways.

This is not an unusual problem. All countries suffer internal tugs of war over how to balance the short-term costs of improving environmental protection with the long-term costs of failing to do so. But China faces an additional burden. Its environmental problems stem as much from China's corrupt and undemocratic political system as from Beijing's continued focus on economic growth. Local officials and business leaders routinely—and with impunity—ignore environmental laws and regulations, abscond with environmental protection funds, and silence those who challenge them. Thus, improving the environment in China is not simply a matter of mandating pollution-control technologies; it is also a matter of reforming the country's political culture. Effective environmental protection requires transparent information, official accountability, and an independent legal system. But these features are the building blocks of a political system fundamentally different from that of China today, and so far there is little indication that China's leaders will risk the authority of the Communist Party on charting a new environmental course. Until the party is willing to open the door to such reform, it will not have the wherewithal to meet its ambitious environmental targets and lead a growing economy with manageable environmental problems.

Given this reality, the United States—and the rest of the world—will have to get much smarter about how to cooperate with China in order to assist its environmental protection efforts. Above all, the United States must devise a limited and coherent set of priorities. China's needs are vast, but its capacity is poor; therefore, launching one or two significant initiatives over the next five to ten years would do more good than a vast array of uncoordinated projects. These endeavors could focus on discrete issues, such as climate change or the illegal timber trade; institutional changes, such as strengthening the legal system in regard to China's environmental protection efforts; or broad reforms, such as promoting energy efficiency throughout the Chinese economy. Another key to an effective U.S.-Chinese partnership is U.S. leadership. Although U.S. NGOs and U.S.-based MNCs are often at the forefront of environmental policy and technological innovation, the U.S. government itself is not a world leader on key environmental concerns. Unless the United States improves its own policies and practices on, for example, climate change, the illegal timber trade, and energy efficiency, it will have little credibility or leverage to push China.

China, for its part, will undoubtedly continue to place a priority on gaining easy access to financial and technological assistance. Granting this, however, would be the wrong way to go. Joint efforts between the United States and China, such as the recently announced project to capture methane from 15 Chinese coal mines, are important, of course. But the systemic changes needed to set China on a new environmental trajectory necessitate a bottom-up overhaul. One way to start would be to promote energy efficiency in Chinese factories and buildings. Simply bringing these up to world standards would bring vast gains. International and Chinese NGOs, Chinese environmental protection bureaus, and MNCs could audit and rate Chinese factories based on how well their manufacturing processes and building standards met a set of energy-efficiency targets. Their scores (and the factors that determined them) could then be disclosed to the public via the Internet and the print media, and factories with subpar performances could be given the means to improve their practices.

A pilot program in Guangdong Province, which is run under the auspices of the U.S. consulate in Hong Kong, provides just such a mechanism. Factories that apply for energy audits can take out loans from participating banks to pay for efficiency upgrades, with the expectation that they will pay the loans back over time out of the savings they will realize from using fewer materials or conserving energy. Such programs should be encouraged and could be reinforced by requiring, for example, that the U.S.-based MNCs that worked with the participating factories rewarded those that met or exceeded the standards and penalized those that did not (the MNCs could either expand or reduce their orders, for example). NGOs and the media in China could also publicize the names of the factories that refused to cooperate. These initiatives would have the advantages of operating within the realities of China's environmental protection system, providing both incentives and disincentives to encourage factories to comply; strengthening the role of key actors such as NGOs, the media, and local environmental protection bureaus; and engaging new actors such as Chinese banks. It is likely that as with the Greenwatch program, factory owners and local officials not used to transparency would oppose such efforts, but if they were persuaded that full participation would bring more sales to MNCs and grow local economies, many of them would be more open to public disclosure.

Of course, much of the burden and the opportunity for China to revolutionize the way it reconciles environmental protection and economic development rests with the Chinese government itself. No amount of international assistance can transform China's domestic environment or its contribution to global environmental challenges. Real change will arise only from strong central leadership and the development of a system of incentives that make it easier for local officials and the Chinese people to embrace environmental protection. This will sometimes mean making tough economic choices.

Improvements to energy efficiency, of the type promoted by the program in Guangdong, are reforms of the low-hanging-fruit variety: they promise both economic gains and benefits to the environment. It will be more difficult to implement reforms that are economically costly (such as reforms that raise the costs of manufacturing in order to encourage conservation and recycling and those that impose higher fines against polluters), are likely to be unpopular (such as reforms that hike the price of water), or could undermine the Communist Party's authority (such as reforms that open up the media or give freer rein to civil society). But such measures are also necessary. And their high up-front costs must be weighed against the long-term costs to economic growth, public health, and social stability in which the Chinese government's continued inaction would result. The government must ensure greater accountability among local officials by promoting greater grass-roots oversight, greater transparency via the media or other outlets, and greater independence in the legal system.

China's leaders have shown themselves capable of bold reform in the past. Two and half decades ago, Deng Xiaoping and his supporters launched a set of ambitious reforms despite stiff political resistance and set the current economic miracle in motion. In order to continue on its extraordinary trajectory, China needs leaders with the vision to introduce a new set of economic and political initiatives that will transform the way the country does business. Without such measures, China will not return to global preeminence in the twenty-first century. Instead, it will suffer stagnation or regression—and all because leaders who recognized the challenge before them were unwilling to do what was necessary to surmount it.

Note

1. The original Associated Press story that was the source for the statement was mistaken and has been corrected. In fact, the EPA, citing a model saying that Asia contributes about 30 percent of the background sulfate particulate matter in the western United States, estimates that Asia contributes about one percent of all particulate matter in Los Angeles.

Elizabeth C. Economy is C. V. Starr Senior Fellow and Director for Asia Studies at the Council on Foreign Relations and the author of *The River Runs Black: The Environmental Challenges to China's Future.*

Water Is Running Out
How Inevitable Are International Conflicts?

MOUREEN LAMONGE

The world's population is growing and water consumption is increasing, but water resources are decreasing. "The world is running out of water," stated Tony Clarke and Maude Barlow, activists and experts on water issues, in their article "Water Wars," published by the Polaris Institute in 2003. They said that by 2025, world population would increase to 2.6 billion more than the present day and water demands would exceed availability by 56 percent. People will live in water-scarcity areas, and disputes over resources are inevitable.

There are currently 263 rivers and countless aquifers that either cross or demarcate international political boundaries, according to the Atlas of International Freshwater Agreement, and 90 percent of countries in the world must share these water basins with at least one or two other states.

The Global Policy Forum, a United States-based nonprofit organization with consultative status at the United Nations, uses the term "water stress" to describe situations in which each person in a country has access to less than 1,500 cubic meters of water each year. The term "water scarcity" refers to situations in which each person in a country has access to less than 1,000 cubic meters of water per year. It is estimated that two-thirds of the world's population will live in areas of acute water stress or water scarcity by 2025.

Nowadays, tensions and disputes between countries are rising due to increasing problems of water scarcity, rapid population growth, degradation in water quality, and uneven economic growth.

"If current trends continue, we could be faced with a very grave situation," said former Soviet Union President Mikhail Gorbachev, who is now president of the Green Cross International, an organization that provides analysis and expertise in environmental and economic issues.

The issue of water and the sharing of water has always been a key concern in the Middle East. Across watersheds of Jordan to the Tigris and Euphrates rivers, the potential for strife today is even higher than before, as the regions are running out of water as political insecurities increase. Since 1950, approximately 80 percent of all violent disputes over water resources globally have occurred in the Middle East. According to Aaron Wolf of the Transboundry Freshwater Dispute Database at Oregon University in the U.S., people living in the region for generations have taken for granted the availability of water. Only recently have they started to realize the shortage of this vital resource. He warned that this diminishing supply could further weaken the fragile relationships between nations, between economic sectors, and between individuals and their environment in the region.

Armed conflict between Israel and Palestine over the Jordan River has been going on for more than 50 years, and it is getting worse. This sacred river for Christians, Muslims, and Jews is now facing a serious problem, as it carries not only less water each year but the water itself is increasingly unclean.

An Israeli "kibbutznik" said, "It's hard to believe now, but we used to actually drink the water and go swimming with the children without worrying."

Friends of Earth Israeli director Gidon Bromberg said the Israeli government needs to act immediately to solve the problem of the Jordan River.

"The river's ecosystem has been so badly compromised that the damage may be irreversible," he said.

In Southeast Asia, the nations of Bangladesh, India, and Nepal dispute the best uses of water from the Ganges-Brahmaputra Basin. Tensions and disagreements over water are also erupting along the Mekong River in Indochina as well as around the Aral Sea in Eastern Europe. There have been longstanding disputes between Ethiopia, Sudan, and Egypt over the Nile River: The vast majority of the river's flows are used by Egypt, even though it originates in Ethiopia.

"We generate about 85 percent of the total Nile waters," said Misfinta Genny, Ethiopia's deputy minister of water. "We have not utilized this resource at all so far . . . We must develop these resources, basically for the benefit of our people."

Egypt's main concern is that Ethiopia would deplete the water supply before it reached Egypt, with serious implications for agriculture and small industries along the banks of the Nile. Competition for water is also on the rise within countries.

Increasingly, experts have cautioned that if certain countries do not improve water management and cooperation in the future, water wars are inevitable. Former U.N. Secretary General Boutros Boutros Ghali threatened that, "The next war among countries will not be for oil or territorial borders, but only for the problem of water."

Background on International Water

Globally, there are some 263 river basins that span across international borders. Europe has the greatest number of international basins (67), followed by Africa (59), Asia (57), North America (40), and South America (38). These international river basins cover almost one-half of the earth's land surface and are also home to approximately 40 percent of the world's population. These rivers generate 60 percent of freshwater flows around the globe.

Most of these basins cross two or more political borders. The Danube, for instance, has 17 riparian states. The Congo, Nile, Niger, and Rhine are all located in nine different countries. The Amazon, the Mekong River, the Euphrates, the Tigris, the Aral Sea, the Ganges, the Jordan, and La Plata in South America are situated in or flow through at least five sovereign states. The third international World Water Forum in Kyotoa, Japan, in 2003 emphasized the critical and urgent need of water management and cooperation between riparian states in order to preserve water supply and prevent disputes.

Gorbachev, representing Green Cross International, said, "Water management can only be effective based on the basin approach. All countries involved—the entire basin—have to be considered together."

Basis of Conflict

According to the World Water Organization, a humanitarian network based in Montreal, Canada, there is a lengthy history of conflicts and tensions over water resources. The Pacific Institute for Studies in Development, Environment, and Security began a project in the 1980's to trace all incidents and tensions originating from water issues. Water-related conflicts are chronologically presented from 3,000 B.C. until the present day. The different categories and types of conflict based on the severity of the event include:

- Control of water resources (state and non-state actors): where water supplies or access to water is at the root of tensions.
- Military tool (state actors): where water resources or water systems themselves are used by a nation or a state as a weapon during a military action.
- Political tool (state and non-state actors): where water resources or water systems themselves are used by a nation, state, or non-state actor for a political goal.
- Terrorism (non-state actors): where water resources or water systems are either targets or tools of violence or coercion by non-state actors.
- Military target (state actors): where water resources or systems are targets of military actions by nations or states.
- Development disputes (state and non-state actors): where water resources or water systems are a major source of contention and dispute in the context of economic and social development.

Water resources are crucial for domestic, industrial, agricultural, and environmental use. By controlling water resources, a country has the ability to control the economy and population. For instance, upstream regions or countries enjoy the benefit of using water flows firsthand, while downstream areas might receive lesser amounts of many watersheds across state borders. Cooperation between riparian states can be highly problematic.

Industrial development or the expansion of agriculture can also cause water conflicts when the excessive use of water by one state affects the water supply of another. In India and China in particular, the massive and unregulated use of private pumps is depleting underground aquifers at unsustainable and unprecedented rates.

Urbanization has also disproportionately increased the demand for water for urban populations, when it is arguably their rural counterparts, with farms and livestock, who need more water. The problem of uneven water distribution and the deterioration in water quality due to pollution and chemical contamination all contribute to the emergence of tensions and conflicts both within and between states.

Water and Civil Conflict

On July 6, 2000, thousands of farmers in the Yellow River basin in China clashed with police over a government plan to relocate excess water from a local reservoir to cities and industries. The farmers had been expecting to use the reservoir to irrigate their crops following a bad drought that dried up the usual river flows that fed their fields. The incident took place downstream in Shandong, the last province the Yellow River runs through before reaching the sea. China's Yellow River has run dry before reaching the sea several times since 1972. The longest record, for 226 days, was recorded in 1997.

In the same year, water disputes also occurred between northern and southern provinces in Thailand, where the water level of the Chao Phraya River had markedly decreased. Tensions have also simmered for years in the downstream areas of the Indus River, where Pakistan's Punjab and Sind provinces fight over water use. In April 2001, desperate demonstrators shouting, "Give us water!" clashed violently with police in Karachi.

Typically, tensions erupt into violent conflict when access to resources is tightened due to exceptional factors such as drought. In southern India in 2002, clashes broke out between two southern Indian states, Karnataka and Tamil Nadu, over access to the Chauvery River, which flows from Karnataka to Tamil Nadu. Karnataka accused Tamil Nadu of wasting water and greedily expanding its irrigated land. Tamil Nadu said its neighbor had forgotten the principle of sharing and suggested the farmers there concentrate on crops other than rice. Farmers and local youths blocked roads with burning tires and shouted slogans against Tamil Nadu. When the Indian Supreme Court ordered Karnataka to release more water from its dams, public anger in Karnataka worsened. Similar water-related violence occurred in 1991 in Bangalore, where 25 people died.

In Kenya in January 2005, thousands of people fled their homes due to clashes over water in Kenya's Rift Valley, northwest of the capital, Nairobi. Youths from the Maasai and Kikuyu communities fought using machetes, spears, bows and arrows, and clubs. At least 15 people were killed.

In late July 2006, a headline from one newspaper in Sri Lanka shouted, "Water War Has Begun!" Violent conflicts were reported between the government armies and the Liberation Tigers of Tamil Eelam. The government accused the rebels of shutting the Maavilaru sluice gate in northeast Sri Lanka. The Tigers defended themselves by saying they had closed the gate in protest over government delays in improving the water system in the region. This conflict affected 50,000 people, who have limited alternative drinking-water supplies and no access to water to irrigate their farms as a result of the closure.

Another critical concern for southern Sri Lanka is a lack of sufficient groundwater. The Maavilaru waterway is the region's main water supplier, but because it has been blocked, the area has become more vulnerable. It is reported that tractors have been used to transport water to the region. The conflict has directly affected farmers, who for five of the last six seasons have had difficult times, experiencing water shortages, low prices for rice, and high costs of fuel, labors, and pesticide. Only a few have made any profit and surplus.

Palitha Kohona, Sri Lanka's head secretary for peace, told Reuters, "Water is critical to human existence. Our objective is to secure the water, and we will get it [back]".

Sri Lanka government has stated that the Tamil Tigers have breached the laws of war by blocking the water supply. These events are the latest in hostilities between the government and the Tamil Tigers rebels that have led to the deaths of at least 800 people this year and more than 85,000 people since 1983.

Water expert Aaron T. Wolf stated that by 2015, nearly three billion people, or 40 percent of the expected world population, will be living in countries that have difficulty mobilizing enough water to meet their industrial and domestic needs. Competition for water between cities and farms, between neighboring states and provinces, will be intense. Tensions at the regional or intra-national level can eventually intrigue conflict across borders. As water quantity decreases every year and water quality worsens in many parts of the world, national, regional and international stability are at stake. Internal water stresses will also shift international political alliances and create more humanitarian crises.

Water and International Conflict

Increasingly, politicians and experts in water-related issues believe that nations will go to war over water and not oil in the 21st century. It is calculated that at least 90 percent of water resources are situated under several sovereign nations.

Riparian states have natural advantages or disadvantages. Downstream states face potentially nightmare situations of having little if any control over the quantity of water flowing into their land. The vulnerability of states further away from the source of any river is naturally increased. Egypt and the Nile basin illustrate the problems this can cause. Egypt lives in fear of its upstream neighbor, Sudan, in terms of water consumption.

In a similar case, Turkey, which profits from the headwaters of the Tigris and the Euphrates, has developed 19 hydroelectric power stations and 22 dams as part of their Southeastern Anatolia Project, which is commonly known by its Turkish acronym GAP. The project is intended to increase the quantity of irrigated water available to Turkish farmers. A side effect, however, is that downstream Iraq and Syria have seen a decline of approximately 50 percent of water from both rivers since the 1990's—and the project is still four years from its planned completion date in 2010. Syria obtains around 80 percent of its water supply from these rivers, while Iraq is 100 percent dependent.

In February 1992, at the opening of the Ataturk Dam, Turkey's former President Suleyman Demirel said, "Neither Syria nor Iraq can lay claim to Turkey's rivers any more than Ankara could claim their oil. This is a matter of sovereignty. We have a right to do anything we like. The water resources are Turkey's; the oil resources are theirs. We don't say we share their oil resources, and they can't say they share our water resources."

This plan almost caused military conflict between Turkey and Syria later in 1998. Damascus accused Ankara of restraining water supply to downstream countries, while Ankara accused Syria of protecting Kurdish separatist leaders. The implications of less water are massive for predominantly agrarian societies that depend on river water in their agriculture and for their nascent industries.

In 2000, a dispute between China and India arose over the Brahmaputra River. India accused China of not sharing any information on water pressure and heavy rainfall in the upstream countries. Excess water caused a landslide and collapsed dam in Tibet, which unleashed a 26-meter wall of water that rushed into India and Bangladesh, causing flooding, destroying properties, and claiming lives. Further concern emerged when China was reported to be planning to divert the river's water for building dams and hydropower potential.

Several water experts said that heavily populated countries would likely feel the greatest impact from water scarcity. The Global Policy Forum said that India, a country with one of the lowest water-resource levels in the world, would become severely starved for water by 2015.

The Okavango is the fourth-largest river in southern Africa. Its basin spans Angola, Botswana, Namibia, and Zimbabwe. In 1996, Namibia planned to divert the river's water to its capital city, Windhoek. Angola and Botswana protested Namibia's plan, saying it would harm people and the river's ecosystem. Even though the Okavango Commission was formed in 1994 to manage disputes in the area, water rivalries continue.

Who Owns Water?

Sovereignty over water flows is hard to define and enforce, even though agreements between some riparian states have been reached. Clear identification of "ownership" of water resources is problematic but necessary in order to enhance political stability and international relations. Negotiation of agreements can take years. In the meantime, the ecosystem of a river may continue to be harmed or even destroyed, with the accompanying deterioration of the quality and quantity of water impacting the local population. The Indus treaty took 10 years of negotiations, while the agreements dealing with the Ganges took 30 years, and the Jordan 40 years.

According to the Pacific Institute for Studies in Development, Environment, and Security, there have been 507 international disputes concerning water resources in the last 50 years. Only 37 of these have become violent, the majority involving Israel and its neighbors. Nevertheless, analysts warn that with ever-diminishing resources, overuse and exploitation of water, and rapidly rising populations, the threat of violence becomes even more serious.

Peter Gleick, an international water expert and president of the Pacific Institute, told IRIN, "There is long history of water conflict, and as water becomes more scarce, it will, indeed, lead to violent conflict in the future."

Plastic Bags Are Killing Us

The most ubiquitous consumer item on Earth, the lowly plastic bag is an environmental scourge like none other, sapping the life out of our oceans and thwarting our attempts to recycle it.

KATHARINE MIESZKOWSKI

On a foggy Tuesday morning, kids out of school for summer break are learning to sail on the waters of Lake Merritt. A great egret hunts for fish, while dozens of cormorants perch, drying their wings. But we're not here to bird-watch or go boating. Twice a week volunteers with the Lake Merritt Institute gather on these shores of the nation's oldest national wildlife refuge to fish trash out of the water, and one of their prime targets is plastic bags. Armed with gloves and nets with long handles, like the kind you'd use to fish leaves out of a backyard swimming pool, we take to the shores to seek our watery prey.

Dr. Richard Bailey, executive director of the institute, is most concerned about the bags that get waterlogged and sink to the bottom. "We have a lot of animals that live on the bottom: shrimp, shellfish, sponges," he says. "It's like you're eating at your dinner table and somebody comes along and throws a plastic tarp over your dinner table and you."

This morning, a turtle feeds serenely next to a half submerged Walgreens bag. The bag looks ghostly, ethereal even, floating, as if in some kind of purgatory suspended between its briefly useful past and its none-too-promising future. A bright blue bags floats just out of reach, while a duck cruises by. Here's a Ziploc bag, there a Safeway bag. In a couple of hours, I fish more than two dozen plastic bags out of the lake with my net, along with cigarette butts, candy wrappers and a soccer ball. As we work, numerous passersby on the popular trail that circles the urban lake shout their thanks, which is an undeniable boost. Yet I can't help being struck that our efforts represent a tiny drop in the ocean. If there's one thing we know about these plastic bags, it's that there are billions and billions more where they came from.

The plastic bag is an icon of convenience culture, by some estimates the single most ubiquitous consumer item on Earth, numbering in the trillions. They're made from petroleum or natural gas with all the attendant environmental impacts of harvesting fossil fuels. One recent study found that the inks and colorants used on some bags contain lead, a toxin. Every year, Americans throw away some 100 billion plastic bags after

they've been used to transport a prescription home from the drugstore or a quart of milk from the grocery store. It's equivalent to dumping nearly 12 million barrels of oil.

Only 1 percent of plastic bags are recycled worldwide—about 2 percent in the U.S.—and the rest, when discarded, can persist for centuries. They can spend eternity in landfills, but that's not always the case. "They're so aerodynamic that even when they're properly disposed of in a trash can they can still blow away and become litter," says Mark Murray, executive director of Californians Against Waste. It's as litter that plastic bags have the most baleful effect. And we're not talking about your everyday eyesore.

Once aloft, stray bags cartwheel down city streets, alight in trees, billow from fences like flags, clog storm drains, wash into rivers and bays and even end up in the ocean, washed out to sea. Bits of plastic bags have been found in the nests of albatrosses in the remote Midway Islands. Floating bags can look all too much like tasty jellyfish to hungry marine critters. According to the Blue Ocean Society for Marine Conservation, more than a million birds and 100,000 marine mammals and sea turtles die every year from eating or getting entangled in plastic. The conservation group estimates that 50 percent of all marine litter is some form of plastic. There are 46,000 pieces of plastic litter floating in every square mile of ocean, according to the United Nations Environment Programme. In the Northern Pacific Gyre, a great vortex of ocean currents, there's now a swirling mass of plastic trash about 1,000 miles off the coast of California, which spans an area that's twice the size of Texas, including fragments of plastic bags. There's six times as much plastic as biomass, including plankton and jellyfish, in the gyre. "It's an endless stream of incessant plastic particles everywhere you look," says Dr. Marcus Eriksen, director of education and research for the Algalita Marine Research Foundation, which studies plastics in the marine environment. "Fifty or 60 years ago, there was no plastic out there."

Following the lead of countries like Ireland, Bangladesh, South Africa, Thailand and Taiwan, some U.S. cities are striking back against what they see as an expensive, wasteful and unnecessary mess. This year, San Francisco and Oakland outlawed the use of plastic bags in large grocery stores and pharmacies, permitting only paper bags with at least 40 percent recycled content or otherwise compostable bags. The bans have not taken effect yet, but already the city of Oakland is being sued by an association of plastic bag manufacturers calling itself the Coalition to Support Plastic Bag Recycling. Meanwhile, other communities across the country, including Santa Monica, Calif., New Haven, Conn., Annapolis, Md., and Portland, Ore., are considering taking drastic legislative action against the bags. In Ireland, a now 22-cent tax on plastic bags has slashed their use by more than 90 percent since 2002. In flood-prone Bangladesh, where plastic bags choked drainage systems, the bags have been banned since 2002.

The problem with plastic bags isn't just where they end up, it's that they never seem to end. "All the plastic that has been made is still around in smaller and smaller pieces," says Stephanie Barger, executive director of the Earth Resource Foundation, which has undertaken a Campaign Against the Plastic Plague. Plastic doesn't biodegrade. That means unless they've been incinerated—a noxious proposition—every plastic bag you've ever used in your entire life, including all those bags that the newspaper arrives in on your doorstep, even on cloudless days when there isn't a sliver of a chance of rain, still exists in some form, even fragmented bits, and will exist long after you're dead.

Grand efforts are under way to recycle plastic bags, but so far those efforts have resulted mostly in a mass of confusion. A tour of Recycle Central in San Francisco makes it easy to see why. The plant is a Willie Wonka factory of refuse. Located on a bay pier with a stunning view of the downtown skyline, some 700 tons of discarded annual reports, Rolling Rock bottles, Diet Coke cans, Amazon.com cardboard boxes, Tide plastic detergent bottles and StarKist tuna fish cans surge into this warehouse every weekday, dumped from trucks into a great clattering, shifting mound. The building tinkles and thumps with the sound of thousands of pounds of glass, aluminum, paper, plastic and cardboard knocking together, as all this detritus passes through a dizzying network of conveyor belts, spinning disks, magnets and gloved human hands to emerge as 16 different sorted, recyclable commodities, baled up by the ton to be shipped or trucked away and made into something new again. It's one way that the city of San Francisco manages to divert some 69 percent of its waste from landfills. But this city's vaunted recycling program, which is so advanced that it can collect coffee grounds and banana peels from urbanites' apartment kitchens and transform them into compost used to grow grapes in Napa Valley vineyards, simply cannot master the plastic bag.

Ask John Jurinek, the plant manager at Recycle Central, what's wrong with plastic bags and he has a one-word answer: "Everything." Plastic bags, of which San Franciscans use some 180 million per year, cannot be recycled here. Yet the hopeful arrow symbol emblazoned on the bags no doubt inspires lots of residents to toss their used ones into the blue recycling bin, feeling good that they've done the right thing. But that symbol on all kinds of plastic items by no means guarantees they can be recycled curbside. (The plastic bags collected at the recycling plant are trucked to the regular dump.) By chucking their plastic

bags in the recycling, what those well-meaning San Franciscans have done is throw a plastic wrench into the city's grand recycling factory. If you want to recycle a plastic bag it's better to bring it back to the store where you got it.

As the great mass of recyclables moves past the initial sort deck on a series of spinning disks, stray plastic bags clog the machinery. It's such a problem that one machine is shut down while a worker wearing kneepads and armed with a knife spends an hour climbing precariously on the disks to cut the bags out, yielding a Medusa's hair-mass of wrenched and twisted plastic. In the middle of the night, when the vast sorting operation grinds to a halt to prepare for the next 700-ton day, two workers will spend hours at this dirty job.

Some states are attacking the recycling problem by trying to encourage shoppers to take the bags back to grocery stores. California requires large grocery stores and pharmacies that distribute the bags known in the trade as T-shirt bags—those common polyethylene bags with two handles, usually made from petroleum or natural gas—to take them back for recycling, and to print instructions on the bags to encourage shoppers to return them to the stores. San Francisco Environment Department spokesperson Mark Westlund, who can see plastic bags lodged in the trees on Market Street from his second-story office window, is skeptical about the state's ability to get shoppers to take back their bags. "We've had in store recycling in San Francisco for over 10 years, and it's never really been successful," says Westlund, who estimates that the city achieved only a 1 percent recycling rate of plastic bags at the stores. "People have to pack up the bags, bring them into the store and drop them off. I think you'd be more inclined to bring your own bag than do that."

Regardless, polyethylene plastic bags are recyclable, says Howie Fendley, a senior environmental chemist for MBDC, an ecological design firm. "It's a matter of getting the feedstock to the point where a recycler can economically justify taking those bags and recycling them. The problem is they're mostly air. There has to be a system in place where they get a nice big chunk of polyethylene that can be mechanically ground, melted and then re-extruded."

So far that system nationwide consists mainly of supermarkets and superstores like Wal-Mart voluntarily stockpiling the bags brought back in by conscientious shoppers, and selling them to recyclers or plastic brokers, who in turn sell them to recyclers. In the U.S., one company buys half of the used plastic bags available on the open market in the United States, using about 1.5 billion plastic bags per year. That's Trex, based in Winchester, Va., which makes composite decking out of the bags and recycled wood. It takes some 2,250 plastic bags to make a single 16-foot-long, 2-inch-by-6-inch plank. It might feel good to buy decking made out of something that otherwise could have choked a sea turtle, but not so fast. That use is not an example of true recycling, points out Carol Misseldine, sustainability coordinator for the city of Oakland. "We're not recycling plastic bags into plastic bags," she says. "They're being downcycled, meaning that they're being put into another product that itself can never be recycled."

Unlike a glass beer bottle or an aluminum can, it's unusual that a plastic bag is made back into another plastic bag, because it's typically more expensive than just making a new plastic bag. After all, the major appeal of plastic bags to stores is that they're much cheaper than paper. Plastic bags cost grocery stores under 2 cents per bag, while paper goes for 4 to 6 cents and compostable bags 9 to 14 cents. However, says Eriksen from the Algalita Marine Research Foundation, "The long-term cost of having these plastic bags blowing across our landscape, across our beaches and accumulating in the northern Pacific far outweighs the short-term loss to a few."

Of course, shoppers could just bring their own canvas bags, and avoid the debate altogether. The California bag recycling law also requires stores to sell reusable bags. Yet it will be a sad irony if outlawing the bags, as San Francisco and Oakland have, doesn't inspire shoppers to bring their own canvas bags, but simply sends them to paper bags, which come with their own environmental baggage. In fact, plastic bags were once thought to be an ecologically friendly alternative to cutting down trees to make paper ones. It takes 14 million trees to produce the 10 billion paper grocery bags used every year by Americans, according to the Natural Resources Defense Council. Yet suggesting that plastic bags made out of petroleum are a better choice burns up Barger from the Earth Resources Foundation. "People say, 'I'm using plastic. I'm saving trees,'" he says. "But have you ever seen what Shell, Mobil and Chevron are doing down in the rain forests to get oil?"

Gordon Bennett, an executive in the San Francisco Bay chapter of the Sierra Club, agrees. "The fundamental thing about trees is that if you manage them properly they're a renewable resource," he says. "I haven't heard about the oil guys growing more oil lately." Still, as the plastic bag industry never tires of pointing out, paper bags are heavier than plastic bags, so they take more fossil fuels to transport. Some life cycle assessments have put plastic bags out ahead of paper, when it comes to energy and waste in the manufacturing process. But paper bags with recycled content, like those soon to be required in San Francisco and Oakland, use less energy and produce less waste than those made from virgin paper.

The only salient answer to paper or plastic is neither. Bring a reusable canvas bag, says Darby Hoover, a senior resource specialist for the Natural Resources Defense Council. However, if you have to make a choice between the two, she recommends taking whichever bag you're more likely to reuse the most times, since, like many products, the production of plastic or paper bags has the biggest environmental impact, not the disposal of them. "Reusing is a better option because it avoids the purchase of another product."

Some stores, like IKEA, have started trying to get customers to bring their own bags by charging them 5 cents per plastic bag. The Swedish furniture company donates the proceeds from the bag sales to a conservation group. Another solution just might be fashion. Bringing your own bag—or BYOB as Whole Foods dubs it—is the latest eco-chic statement. When designer Anya Hindmarch's "I am not a plastic bag" bag hit stores in Taiwan, there was so much demand for the limited-edition bag that the riot police had to be called in to control a stampede, which sent 30 people to the hospital.

Cry of the Wild

Last week four gorillas were slaughtered in Congo. With hunting on the rise, our most majestic animals are facing a new extinction crisis.

SHARON BEGLEY

On the lush plains of Congo's Virunga National Park last week, the convoy of porters rounded the final hill and trooped into camp. They gently set down the wooden frame they had carried for miles, and with it the very symbol of the African jungle: a 600-pound silverback mountain gorilla. A leader of a troop often visited by tourists, his arms and legs were lashed to the wood, his head hanging low and spots of blood speckling his fur. The barefoot porters, shirts torn and pants caked with dust from their trek, lay him beside three smaller gorillas, all females, who had also been killed, then silently formed a semicircle around the bodies. As the stench of death wafted across the camp in the waning afternoon light, a park warden stepped forward. "What man would do this?" he thundered. He answered himself: "Not even a beast would do this."

Park rangers don't know who killed the four mountain gorillas found shot to death in Virunga, but it was the seventh killing of the critically endangered primates in two months. Authorities doubt the killers are poachers, since the gorillas' bodies were left behind and an infant—who could bring thousands of dollars from a collector—was found clinging to its dead mother in one of the earlier murders. The brutality and senselessness of the crime had conservation experts concerned that the most dangerous animal in the world had found yet another excuse to slaughter the creatures with whom we share the planet. "This area must be immediately secured," said Deo Kujirakwinja of the Wildlife Conservation Society's Congo Program, "or we stand to lose an entire population of these endangered animals."

Back when the Amazon was aflame and the forests of Southeast Asia were being systematically clear-cut, biologists were clear about what posed the greatest threat to the world's wildlife, and it wasn't men with guns. For decades, the chief threat was habitat destruction. Whether it was from impoverished locals burning a forest to raise cattle or a multinational denuding a tree-covered Malaysian hillside, wildlife was dying because species were being driven from their homes. Yes, poachers killed tigers and other trophy animals—as they had since before Theodore Roosevelt—and subsistence hunters took monkeys for bushmeat to put on their tables, but they were not a primary danger.

That has changed. "Hunting, especially in Central and West Africa, is much more serious than we imagined," says Russell Mittermeier, president of Conservation International. "It's huge," with the result that hunting now constitutes the pre-eminent threat to some species. That threat has been escalating over the past decade largely because the opening of forests to logging and mining means that roads connect once impenetrable places to towns. "It's easier to get to where the wildlife is and then to have access to markets," says conservation biologist Elizabeth Bennett of the Wildlife Conservation Society. Economic forces are also at play. Thanks to globalization, meat, fur, skins and other animal parts "are sold on an increasingly massive scale across the world," she says. Smoked monkey carcasses travel from Ghana to New York and London, while gourmets in Hanoi and Guangzhou feast on turtles and pangolins (scaly anteaters) from Indonesia. There is a thriving market for bushmeat among immigrants in Paris, New York, Montreal, Chicago and other points in the African diaspora, with an estimated 13,000 pounds of bushmeat—much of it primates—arriving every month in seven European and North American cities alone. "Hunting and trade have already resulted in widespread local extinctions in Asia and West Africa," says Bennett. "The world's wild places are falling silent."

When a company wins a logging or mining concession, it immediately builds roads wide enough for massive trucks where the principal access routes had been dirt paths no wider than a jaguar. "Almost no tropical forests remain across Africa and Asia which are not penetrated by logging or other roads," says Bennett. Hunters and weapons follow, she notes, "and wildlife flows cheaply and rapidly down to distant towns where it is either sold directly or links in to global markets." How quickly can opening a forest ravage the resident wildlife? Three weeks after a logging company opened up one Congo forest, the density of animals fell more than 25 percent; a year after a logging road went into forest areas in Sarawak, Malaysia, in 2001, not a single large mammal remained.

A big reason why hunting used to pale next to habitat destruction is that as recently as the 1990s animals were killed mostly for subsistence, with locals taking only what they needed to live. Governments and conservation groups helped reduce even that through innovative programs giving locals an economic stake in the preservation of forests and the survival of wildlife. In the mountains of Rwanda, for instance, tourists pay $500 to spend an hour with the majestic mountain gorillas, bolstering the economy of the surrounding region. But recent years have brought a more dangerous kind of hunter, and not only because they use AK-47s and even land mines to hunt.

The problem now is that hunting, even of supposedly protected animals, is a global, multimillion-dollar business. Eating bushmeat "is now a status symbol," says Thomas Brooks of Conservation International. "It's not a subsistence issue. It's not a poverty issue. It's considered supersexy to eat bushmeat." Exact figures are hard to come by, but what conservation groups know about is sobering. Every year a single province in Laos exports $3.6 million worth of wildlife, including pangolins, cats, bears and primates. In Sumatra, about 51 tigers were killed each year between 1998 and 2002; there are currently an estimated 350 tigers left on the island (down from 1,000 or so in the 1980s) and fewer than 5,000 in the world.

If a wild population is large enough, it can withstand hunting. But for many species that "if" has not existed for decades. As a result, hunting in Kilum-Ijim, Cameroon, has pushed local elephants, buffalo, bushbuck, chimpanzees, leopards and lions to the brink of extinction. The common hippopotamus, which in 1996 was classified as of "least concern" because its numbers seemed to be healthy, is now "vulnerable": over the past 10 years its numbers have fallen as much as 20 percent, largely because the hippos are illegally hunted for meat and ivory. Pygmy hippos, classified as "vulnerable" in 2000, by last year had become endangered, at risk of going extinct. Logging has allowed bushmeat hunters to reach the West African forests where the hippos live; fewer than 3,000 remain.

Setting aside parks and other conservation areas is only as good as local enforcement. "Half of the major protected areas in Southeast Asia have lost at least one species of large mammal due to hunting, and most have lost many more," says Bennett. In Thailand's Doi Inthanon and Doi Suthep National Parks, for instance, elephants, tigers and wild cattle have been hunted into oblivion, as has been every primate and hornbill in Sarawak's Kubah National Park. The world-famous Project Tiger site in India's Sariska National Park has no tigers, biologists announced in 2005. Governments cannot afford to pay as many rangers as are needed to patrol huge regions, and corruption is rife. The result is "empty-forest syndrome": majestic landscapes where flora and small fauna thrive, but where larger wildlife has been hunted out.

Which is not to say the situation is hopeless. With governments and conservationists recognizing the extinction threat posed by logging and mining, they are taking steps to ensure that animals do not come out along with the wood and minerals. In one collaboration, the government of Congo and the WCS work with a Swiss company, Congolaise Industrielle des Bois—which has a logging concession near Nouabalé-Ndoki National Park—to ensure that employees and their families hunt only for their own food needs; the company also makes sure that bushmeat does not get stowed away on logging trucks as illegal hunters try to take their haul to market. Despite the logging, gorillas, chimps, forest elephants and bongos are thriving in the park.

Anyone who thrills at the sight of man's distant cousins staring silently through the bush can only hope that the executions of Virunga's gorillas is an aberration. At the end of the week, UNESCO announced that it was sending a team to investigate the slaughter.

UNIT 4

Political Economy

Unit Selections

Key Points to Consider

- Are those who argue that globalization is inevitable overly optimistic? Why or why not?

- What are some of the impediments to a truly global political economy?

- How has globalization accelerated the growth of criminal behavior?

- What transformations will societies that are heavy users of fossil fuels undergo in order to meet future energy needs?

- How are the political economies of traditional societies different from those of the consumer-oriented societies?

- What are some of the barriers that make it difficult for non-industrial countries to develop?

- How are China and other emerging countries trying to alter their ways of doing business in order to meet the challenges of globalization? Are they likely to succeed?

- What economic challenges do countries like Japan and the United States face in the years to come?

Student Web Site

www.mhcls.com/online

Internet References

Further information regarding these Web sites may be found in this book's preface or online.

Belfer Center for Science and International Affairs (BCSIA)
http://ksgwww.harvard.edu/csia/

U.S. Agency for International Development
http://www.usaid.gov

The World Bank Group
http://www.worldbank.org

A defining characteristic of the twentieth century was the intense struggle between proponents of two economic ideologies. At the heart of the conflict was the question of what role government should play in the management of a country's economy. For some, the dominant capitalist economic system appeared to be organized primarily for the benefit of a few wealthy people. From their perspective, the masses were trapped in poverty, supplying cheap labor to further enrich the privileged elite. These critics argued that the capitalist system could be changed only by gaining control of the political system and radically changing the ownership of the means of production. In striking contrast to this perspective, others argued that the best way to create wealth and eliminate poverty was through the profit motive, which encouraged entrepreneurs to create new products and businesses. An open and competitive marketplace, from this point of view, minimized government interference was the best system for making decisions about production, wages, and the distribution of goods and services.

Violent conflict at times characterized the contest between capitalism and socialism/communism. The Russian and Chinese revolutions overthrew the old social order and created radical changes in the political and economic systems in these two important countries. The political structures that were created to support new systems of agricultural and industrial production (along with the centralized planning of virtually all aspects of economic activity) eliminated most private ownership of property. These two revolutions were, in short, unparalleled experiments in social engineering.

The collapse of the Soviet Union and the dramatic economic reforms in China have recast the debate about how to best structure contemporary economic systems. Some believe, that with the end of communism and the resulting participation of hundreds of millions of new consumers in the global market, an unprecedented new era has been entered. Many have noted that this process of "globalization" is being accelerated by a revolution in communication and computer technologies. Proponents of this view argue that a new global economy is emerging that will ultimately eliminate national economic systems.

Others are less optimistic about the prospects of globalization. They argue that the creation of a single economic system where there are no boundaries to impede the flow of both capital and goods and services does not mean a closing of the gap between the world's rich and poor. Rather, they argue that giant corporations will have fewer legal constraints on their behavior, and this will lead to greater exploitation of workers and the accelerated destruction of the environment. Further, these critics point out that the unintended globalization of drug trafficking and other criminal behaviors is developing more rapidly than appropriate remedies can be developed.

The use of the term "political economy" for the title of this unit recognizes that economic and political systems are not separate. All economic systems have some type of marketplace where goods and services are bought and sold. Government (either national or international) regulates these transactions to some degree; that is, government sets the rules that regulate the marketplace.

Publication of the National Oceanic and Atmospheric Administration (NOAA)

One of the most important concepts in assessing the contemporary political economy is "development." For the purposes of this unit, the term "development" is defined as an improvement in the basic aspects of life: lower infant mortality rates, longer life expectancy, lower disease rates, higher rates of literacy, healthier diets, and improved sanitation. Judged by these standards, some countries are more "developed" than others. A fundamental question that a thoughtful reader must consider is whether globalization is resulting in increased development not only for a few people but also for all of those participating in the global political economy.

The unit is organized into three sections. The first is a general discussion of the concept of globalization. How is it defined, and what are some of the differing perspectives on this process? For example, is the idea of a global economy merely wishful thinking by those who sit on top of the power hierarchy, self-deluded into believing that globalization is an inexorable force that will evolve in its own way, following its own rules? Or will there continue to be the traditional tensions of nation-state power politics that transcend global economic processes, that is, conflict between the powerful and those who are either ascending or descending in power?

Following the first section are two sets of case studies. The first focuses on specific countries and/or economic sectors. The second set of case studies examines the global energy sector. All of the case studies have been selected to challenge the reader to develop his or her own conclusions about the positive and negative consequences of the globalization process. Does the contemporary global political economy result in increasing the gap between economic winners and losers, or can everyone positively benefit from its system of wealth creation and distribution?

Globalization and Its Contents

Peter Marber

Ask ten different people to define the term "globalization" and you are likely to receive ten different answers. For many, the meaning of globalization has been shaped largely by media coverage of an angry opposition: from right-wing nationalist xenophobes and left-wing labor leaders who fear rampant economic competition from low-wage countries to social activists who see a conspiracy on the part of multinational corporations to seek profits no matter what the cost to local cultures and economic equality to environmentalists who believe the earth is being systematically ravaged by capitalism run amok. "Globalization"—as if it were a machine that could be turned off—has been presented as fundamentally flawed and dangerous. But "globalization" is a term that encompasses all cross-border interactions, whether economic, political, or cultural. And behind the negative headlines lies a story of human progress and promise that should make even the most pessimistic analysts view globalization in an entirely different light.

Two decades ago, globalization was hardly discussed. At the time, less than 15 percent of the world's population participated in true global trade. Pessimism colored discussions of the Third World, of "lesser developed" or "backward" countries. Pawns in the Cold War's global chess game, these countries conjured images of famine, overpopulation, military dictatorship, and general chaos. At the time, the prospect of the Soviet Union or Communist China integrating economically with the West, or of strongman regimes in Latin America or Asia abandoning central planning, seemed farfetched. The possibility of these countries making meaningful socioeconomic progress and attaining Western standards of living appeared utterly unrealistic. Yet the forces of globalization were already at work.

On average, people are living twice as long as they did a century ago. Moreover, the world's aggregate material infrastructure and productive capabilities are hundreds—if not thousands—of times greater than they were a hundred years ago.[1] Much of this acceleration has occurred since 1950, with a powerful upsurge in the last 25 years. No matter how one measures wealth—whether by means of economic, bio-social, or financial indicators—there have been gains in virtually every meaningful aspect of life in the last two generations, and the trend should continue upward at least through the middle of the twenty-first century.

Most people are living longer, healthier, fuller lives. This is most evident in poor parts of the world. For example, since 1950, life expectancy in emerging markets (countries with less than one-third the per capita income of the United States, or nearly 85 percent of the world's population) has increased by more than 50 percent, reaching levels the West enjoyed only two generations ago. These longevity gains are linked to lower infant mortality, better nutrition (including an 85 percent increase in daily caloric intake), improved sanitation, immunizations, and other public health advances.

Literacy rates in developing countries have also risen dramatically in the last 50 years. In 1950, only a third of the people in Eastern Europe and in parts of Latin [America] living in these countries (roughly 800 million) could read or write; today nearly two-thirds—more than 3.2 billion people—are literate. And while it took the United States and Great Britain more than 120 years to increase average formal education from 2 years in the early nineteenth century to 12 years by the mid-twentieth century, some fast-growing developing countries, like South Korea, have accomplished this feat in fewer than 40 years.

The world now has a far more educated population with greater intellectual capacity than at any other time in history. This is particularly clear in much of Asia, where mass public education has allowed billions of people to increase their productivity and integrate in the global economy as workers and consumers. Similar trends can be seen in Eastern Europe and in parts of Latin America. This increase in human capital has led to historic highs in economic output and financial assets per capita (see chart).

During the twentieth century, economic output in the United States and other West European countries often doubled in less than 30 years, and Japan's postwar economy doubled in less than 16 years. In recent decades, developing country economies have surged so quickly that some—like South Korea in the 1960s and 1970s, or China in recent years—have often doubled productive output in just 7 to 10 years.

We often forget that poverty was the human living standard for most of recorded history. Until approximately two hundred years ago, virtually everyone lived at a subsistence level. As the economist John Maynard Keynes wrote in 1931 in *Essays in Persuasion*: "From the earliest times of which we have record—back, say, to two thousand years before Christ—down to the beginning of the eighteenth century, there was no very great change in the standard life of the average man living in civilized centers of the earth. Ups and downs certainly. Visitation

	1950	2000	2050
Global Output, Per Capita ($)	586	6,666	15,155
Global Financial Market			
Capitalization, Per Capita ($)	158	13,333	75,000
Percent of Global GDP			
Emerging Markets	5	50	55
Industrial Countries	95	75	45
Life Expectancy (years)			
Emerging Markets	41	64	76
Industrial Countries	65	77	82
Daily Caloric Intake			
Emerging Markets	1200	2600	3000
Industrial Countries	2200	3100	3200
Infant Mortality (per 1000)			
Emerging Markets	140	65	10
Industrial Countries	30	8	4
Literacy Rate (per 100)			
Emerging Markets	33	64	90
Industrial Countries	95	98	99

*Sources: Bloomberg, World Bank, United Nations, and author's estimates.
Output and financial market capitalization figures are inflation-adjusted.*

Figure 1   Measured Global Progress, 1950–2050E.

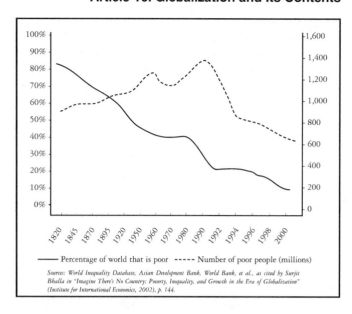

— Percentage of world that is poor   ----- Number of poor people (millions)

Sources: World Inequality Database, Asian Development Bank, World Bank, et al., as cited by Surjit Bhalla in "Imagine There's No Country: Poverty, Inequality, and Growth in the Era of Globalization" (Institute for International Economics, 2002), p. 144.

Figure 2   Historic World Poverty Levels, 1820–2000.

of plague, famine, and war. Golden intervals. But no progressive violent change. This slow rate of progress was due to two reasons—to the remarkable absence of technical improvements and the failure of capital to accumulate." Beginning in the early nineteenth century, this picture began to change. The proportion of the world's population living in poverty declined from over 80 percent in 1820 to under 15 percent in 2000; moreover, the actual number of people living in poverty over that period declined, even as the world's population exploded from something over 1 billion to more than 6 billion.

The application of mass production technology, together with excess capital (or "profit") and a free market technologies—is at the root of our modern prosperity. Upon further examination, one can see the virtuous cycle that connects human progress, technology, and globalization. Let's take two countries, one being richer than the other. The richer country has a more educated workforce, with nearly 99 percent literacy, while the poor one has only 50 percent literacy. Due to its less educated workforce and lack of infrastructure, the poor country might only be able to participate in global trade through exporting commodities—let's say fruits and vegetables. The rich country grows fruits and vegetables as well, but it also produces clothing and light manufactured goods such as radios. In the classic Ricardo/Smith models of comparative advantage and free trade, the wealthy country should utilize its skilled workforce to produce more clothing and radios for domestic consumption and export, and it should import more fruits and vegetables from the poorer country. This would, in turn, provide the poorer country with capital to improve education and infrastructure.

As this trade pattern creates profits for both countries, human capital can be mutually developed. Eventually, the poorer country (by boosting literacy and education) should develop its own ability to produce clothes and radios. Over time, the wealthier country—having reinvested profits in higher education, research and development, etc.—will begin to produce higher-tech goods rather than clothes and radios, perhaps televisions and cars. At this stage, the wealthy country would export its cars and televisions, and import clothes and radios. In turn, the poorer country begins to import agricultural products from an even poorer third country while exporting clothing and radios to both countries. As participating countries make progress through crossborder trade and the continuous upgrading of their workforces, it follows naturally that patterns of labor and employment will evolve over time.

It is sometimes argued that free trade harms economic growth and the poor by causing job losses, particularly in wealthier countries. But trade liberalization works by encouraging a shift of labor and capital from import-competitive sectors to more dynamic export industries where comparative advantages lie. Therefore, the unemployment caused by open trade can be expected to be temporary, being offset by job creation in other export sectors (which often requires some transition time). Output losses due to this transitional unemployment should also be small relative to long-term gains in national income (and lower prices) due to production increases elsewhere. In other words, these short-term labor adjustments should be seen as lesser evils when compared to the costs of continued economic stagnation and isolation that occur without open trade.

The shifting U.S. labor pattern from low-wage agricultural labor to manufacturing to higher-paid office and service employment during the nineteenth and twentieth centuries resulted largely from trade. Similar shifts are now seen all over the globe. In the 1950 and 1960s, the United States imported electronics from Japan, and exported cars and other heavy goods. In the 1970s, we began importing small cars from Japan. In the last 30-odd years, Japan has seen its dominance in electronics and economy cars wither amid competition from China and South

Korea. But Japan has made a successful push upmarket into larger, pricier luxury cars and sport utility vehicles. While these markets were shifting over the last three decades, jobs were lost, gained, and relocated in the United States and abroad. But living standards in America, Japan, South Korea, and China have all improved dramatically over that same time.

Working Less, Producing More

There is a growing consensus that international trade has a positive effect on per capita income. A 1999 World Bank study estimates that increasing the ratio of trade to national output by one percentage point raises per capita income by between 0.5 and 2 percent.[2] But the most dramatic illustration of how greater prosperity is spread through globalization is by our increased purchasing power. Ultimately, what determines wealth is the ability to work less and consume more. The time needed for an average American worker to earn the purchase price of various goods and services decreased dramatically during the twentieth century.

In 1919, it took an American worker 30 minutes of labor to earn enough to buy a pound of ground beef. This number dropped to 23 minutes in 1950, 11 minutes in 1975, and 6 minutes in 1997.[3] But this downward trend is even more impressive with respect to manufactured goods and services. For example, in 1895 the list price for an American-made bicycle in the Montgomery Ward catalog was $65. Today an American can buy a Chinese-manufactured 21-speed bike at any mass retailer for the same amount. But an average American needed to work some 260 hours in 1895 to earn the purchase price of the old bicycle, whereas it would take the average worker less than 5 hours to earn enough to buy today's bicycle.[4] In our own lifetimes, the costs of goods and services, everything from televisions to household appliances to telephone calls, computers, and airplane travel have plummeted relative to income—and not just in the United States.

Around the world, both basic commodities and items once considered luxury items now fill store shelves and pantries as increasing output and income have lifted most people above the subsistence level. The 50 most populous countries average more than 95 televisions per 100 households. In the 25 wealthiest countries, there are approximately 450 automobiles per 1,000 people, and China is now among the fastest-growing markets for cars, clothes, computers, cellular phones, and hundreds of household items.

This deflationary effect has also led to a radically improved quality of life. In 1870, the average American worker labored 3,069 hours per year—or six 10-hour days a week. By 1950, the average hours worked had fallen to 2,075.[5] Today, that number is closer to 1,730.[6] This pattern has been repeated around the world. In 1960, the average Japanese worker toiled 2,432 hours a year over a six-day work week; by 1988, this figure had dropped to 2,111 hours a year, and by 2000 it was down to 1,878 hours. There were even more dramatic reductions in European countries like France, Germany, and Sweden.[7] The Nobel Prize–winning economist Robert William Fogel estimates that the average American's lifetime working hours will have declined from 182,100 in 1880 to a projected 75,900 by 2040, with similar trends in other wealthy industrial countries. Fogel notes that while work took up 60 percent of an American's life in 1870, by 1990 it only took up about 30 percent. Between 1880 and 1990, the average American's cumulative lifetime leisure time swelled from 48,300 hours to a remarkable 246,000 hours, or 22 years.[8] This is a pattern of improvement in the human condition that we first saw in the industrialized West and then in Japan, and which is now spreading to dozens of developing countries that are integrating into the global economy.

A Thriving Middle Class

The recent surge in progress is certainly tied to technological advances, but it is also due to the adoption of free-market practices. Cross-border trade has ballooned by a factor of 20 over the past 50 years and now accounts for more than 20 percent of global output, according to the World Bank. Indeed, trade—which grew twice as fast as global output in the 1990s—will continue to drive economic specialization and growth. The global economy is becoming more sophisticated, segmented, and diversified.

The adoption of free-market practices has gone hand-in-hand with greater political freedoms. At the beginning of the twentieth century, less than 10 percent of the world's population had the right to vote, according to Freedom House. By 1950, approximately 35 percent of the global population in less than a quarter of the world's countries enjoyed this right. By 2000, more than two-thirds of the world's countries had implemented universal suffrage.

These symbiotic developments have helped completely recompose the world's "middle class"—those with a per capita income of roughly $10–40 per day, adjusted for inflation and purchasing power parity (PPP). According to the United Nations, in 1960 two-thirds of the world's middle-class citizens lived in the industrialized world—that is, in the United States, Canada, Western Europe, Japan, and Australia. By 1980, over 60 percent of the global middle class lived in developing countries, and by 2000 this number had reached a remarkable 83 percent. It is anticipated that India and China combined could easily produce middle classes of 400–800 million people over the next two generations—roughly the size of the current middle-class populations of the United States, Western Europe, and Japan combined.

A thriving middle class is an important component of economic, political, and social stability that comes with globalization. According to the World Bank, a higher share of income for the middle class is associated with increased national income and growth, improved health, better infrastructure, sounder economic policies, less instability and civil war, and more social modernization and democracy. There are numerous studies that also suggest that increasing wealth promotes gender equality, greater voter participation, income equality, greater concern for the environment, and more transparency in the business and political arenas, all of the quality-of-life issues that concern globalization skeptics.[9]

Measuring Inequality

Even if they concede that the world is wealthier overall, many critics of globalization cite the dangers of growing income inequality. Although the science of analyzing such long-term trends is far from perfect, there are indicators that point toward measurable progress even on this front.[10] The preoccupation with income or gross national product (GNP) as the sole measure of progress is unfortunate. Income is one measure of wealth, but not the only one. And income comparisons do not always reflect informal or unreported economic activity, which tends to be more prevalent in poor countries.

Many social scientists use Gini coefficients (a measure of income dispersion between and within countries) to bolster their arguments about inequality. The lower the Gini figure (between one and zero), the more equal income distribution tends to be. Unfortunately, the Gini index does not take into consideration purchasing power parity, the age dispersion of a population, and other variables that affect the overall picture. When adjusted for PPP, the Gini index for world income distribution decreased from 0.59 to 0.52 between 1965 and 1997, an improvement of nearly 12 percent.[11] Poverty rate trends are also cited by condemners of globalization, but this approach is problematic as well. The impoverished are often defined as those who earn 50 percent less than the median income in a country. But because 50 percent of median American income is very different than 50 percent of median income in Bangladesh, poverty rates may not tell us as much about human progress as we might think.

We can better gauge human progress by examining broader trends in bio-social development than income-centered analyses. A yardstick like the United Nations Development Program's human development index (HDI), for example, which looks at not only income but also life expectancy and education (including literacy and school enrollment), with the higher numbers denoting greater development, provides a clearer picture of global well-being:

	1960	1993	2002
OECD Countries	.80	.91	.91
Developing Countries	.26	.56	.70
Least Developed Countries	.16	.33	.44

What these numbers show is not only that human development has improved overall but that differentials between rich and poor countries are closing. While the HDI figure for wealthy oecd countries in 1960 was five times greater than that for the least developed countries (and three times higher than that for developing countries), those gaps were nearly halved by 1993. And in the most intense period of recent globalization, from 1993 to 2002, these gaps closed even further.

This by no means negates the reality of poverty in many parts of the world. There are still an estimated 1 billion people living in "abject" poverty today, but the World Bank estimates that this number should decline by 50 percent by 2015, if current growth trends hold.

Potholes on the Road to Globalization

The great gains and momentum of the last 25 years should not be seen as sufficient or irreversible. There are still formidable impediments to continued progress, the four most serious being protectionism, armed conflict, environmental stress, and demographic imbalances.

- *Protectionism.* One of the responses to globalization has been the attempt to pull inward, to save traditional industries and cultures, and to expel foreigners and foreign ideas. In India, consumers have protested against McDonald's restaurants for violating Hindu dietary laws. In France, angry farmers have uprooted genetically engineered crops, saying they threatened domestic control over food production.

  Possibly the most harmful protectionism today relates to global agricultural policy. Farming subsidies in wealthy countries now total approximately $350 billion a year, or seven times the $50 billion that such countries provide annually in foreign aid to the developing world.[12] Global trade policies may exclude developing countries from $700 billion in commerce annually, denying them not only needed foreign currency but also the commercial and social interaction necessary to bio-social progress.[13]

  Protectionism in the form of tariffs, rigid labor and immigration laws, capital controls, and regressive tax structures also should be resisted. Wealthy countries should not cling to old industries like apparel or agriculture; it is far more profitable, economically and socially, to look forward and outward, to focus on growing higher-skill industries—like aviation, pharmaceuticals, and entertainment—and to embrace new markets. In turn, poorer countries have generally grown richer through economic interaction with foreign countries, by refocusing nationalistic energies and policies toward future-oriented, internationally engaged commercial activity. The late-twentieth-century march away from closed economies has improved the lives of billions of people. To bow to nationalistic calls for protectionist policies could slow and even reverse this momentum.

- *Armed Conflict.* Countries cannot compete economically, cultivate human capital, or develop financial markets in the midst of armed conflict. According to the Stockholm International Peace Research Institute, there were 57 major armed conflicts in 45 different locations between 1990 and 2001; all but 3 of these were civil wars, which inflict deep economic damage and stunt development. In addition to ongoing civil wars, there are a number of potential cross-border powder kegs (beyond the recent U.S. invasions of Afghanistan and Iraq): Kashmir, over which nuclearized India and Pakistan have been at odds for decades; Taiwan, over which China claims sovereignty; Israel and its Arab neighbors; and the Korean peninsula. The economic, political, and cultural uncertainty surrounding these areas of potential conflict restricts the flow of capital, and paralyzes businesses, investors, and consumers.

To the extent that defense budgets continue to grow in tandem with global tensions and economic resources are used for military purposes, there will be fewer resources devoted to the development of human capital and economic competitiveness.

- *Environmental Stress.* There is no getting around the fact that the success of globalization is underscored by dramatic increases in consumption. With increased consumption comes environmental degradation. Damage to the environment, current or projected, can impede economic progress in many ways. Climatic changes attributed to greenhouse gas emissions and pressure on natural resources are serious problems. Resource scarcity is only one issue we will have to confront as 2–3 billion more people consume like middle-class Americans over the next 50 years. In the face of these environmental dangers, a host of new regulations may be enacted locally or globally. Increased environmental awareness among wealthier populations may lead to domestic policies that will raise costs to businesses and consumers, which in turn could curb economic expansion.

One step in the right direction would be increased public spending on alternative and renewable energy sources in the wealthier countries. The world is clearly underpowered, and the need for diversified energy grows as we speak. The benefits of a burgeoning alternative energy sector could be multiplicative. First, it might spur new economic growth areas for employment in rich countries, supplying them with potential technologies for export while reducing their reliance on foreign oil. Second, it might encourage developing countries that are over-reliant on oil exports to develop and modernize their economies and societies. Third, it would allow developing countries to build their infrastructures with a more diversified, sustainable energy approach than the first wave of industrializing countries.

- *Demographic Imbalances.* There are sharply contrasting population trends around the globe: developing nations are experiencing a youth bulge while industrialized countries are aging rapidly. This divergence may present a variety of challenges to globalization. In poorer developing countries, the youth bulge equals economic opportunity but is also potentially disruptive. In more than 50 of these countries, 50 percent of the population is under the age of 25. In some cases, half the population is under 20, and in extreme cases, even younger. These developing nations are also among the poorest, the fastest urbanizing, and the least politically or institutionally developed, making them susceptible to violence and instability. The large number of unemployed, disenfranchised young men in these countries may explain the growth of Islamic fundamentalism and the existence of pillaging bands of armed warriors in sub-Saharan Africa. Large young populations may also lead to unregulated, unlawful migration that can create long-lasting instability.[14]

While the youth bulge can cause problems that derail global progress, the richest countries may fall victim to their past success. Prosperity, while providing more lifestyle choices and wellness, also results in lower birth rates and increasing longevity which could dampen long-term economic demand. The aging of wealthier populations also stresses public pension schemes that were conceived under different demographic circumstances—eras of robust population and consumption growth. In economies where populations are stagnant or shrinking, the specter of lengthy "aging recessions"—characterized by vicious cycles of falling demand for consumer goods (and deflation), collapsing asset values (including real estate), shrinking corporate profits, deteriorating household and financial institution balance sheets, weakening currencies, and soaring budget pressures—looms large.

Preparing for the Best, Not the Worst

Globalization and its major engines—burgeoning human capital, freer markets, increasing cross-border interaction—have created a new world order that has incited passionate debate, pro and con. However, both sides have more in common than one might imagine.

First, if human capital is a key component of improved living standards, it is arguable that increased spending on education should become a priority in rich and poor countries alike. Wealthier nations continually need to boost productivity and comparative advantage, while poorer countries need to develop skills to compete in the global economy. By adding to the numbers of the educated, there will be a wider base of workers and consumers to contribute to the virtuous cycle of prosperity we have witnessed in the last 50 years.

Second, boosting human capital in poor countries through increased financial and technical aid should also help broaden the marketplace in terms of workers and consumers. Appropriating an extra $100 billion in aid each year—a drop in the bucket for the 20 richest countries—could help some 2 billion people overcome their daily struggles with malnutrition, HIV/AIDS, malaria, and dirty drinking water, thereby increasing the number of healthy, productive workers and consumers.

Third, reorienting wealthy country subsidies away from low-tech areas like agriculture and mining toward higher-tech industries (including alternative energy development) would accelerate comparative advantage and stimulate greater trade. With wealthy countries focusing on higher-value-added industries for domestic consumption and export, poorer countries could pick up the slack in lower-skilled sectors where they can begin to engage the global economy. Over time, the poorer countries would become larger markets for goods and services. This, along with the two attitudinal and policy shifts mentioned above, could have a positive effect on the well-being of the world's population.

Even with its positive trends, globalization is not a perfect process. It is not a panacea for every problem for every person at every moment in time. It is a messy, complicated web of interdependent relationships, some long-term, some fleeting. But globalization is too often cited as creating a variety of human miseries such as sweatshop labor, civil war, and corruption—as if such ills never existed before 1980. Poverty is more at the root of such miseries. That is why the wholesale rejection of globalization—without acknowledging its tremendously positive record in alleviating poverty—is shortsighted. Indeed, one could see how simply embracing globalization as inevitable—rather than debating its definition and purported shortcomings—could potentially foster more cross-border coordination on a variety of issues such as drug trafficking, ethnic cleansing, illegal immigration, famine, epidemic disease, environmental stress, and terrorism.

Emotion and confusion have unfortunately tainted the globalization debate both in the United States and abroad, and the focus is often on anecdotal successes or failures. Anxieties and economies may ebb and flow in the short run, but the responsibility to manage these progressive evolutions and revolutions—with worldwide human prosperity as the goal—should be our consistent aim in both government and the marketplace.

Notes

Many of the issues and arguments presented here in abbreviated form are examined at greater length in my book, *Money Changes Everything: How Global Prosperity Is Reshaping Our Needs, Values, and Lifestyles* (Upper Saddle River, NJ: FT Prentice Hall, 2003).

1. See Angus Maddison, *Monitoring the World Economy: 1820–1992* (Paris: OECD, 1995).
2. Jeffrey A. Frankel and David Romer, "Does Trade Growth Cause Growth?" *American Economic Review,* vol. 89 (June 1999), pp. 379–99.
3. W. Michael Cox and Richard Alm, *Time Well Spent: The Declining Real Cost of Living in America*, annual report (Dallas: Federal Reserve Bank, 1997), p. 4.
4. Based on average U.S. industrial wages of approximately $15 per hour in 2000.
5. W. Michael Cox and Richard Alm, *These Are the Good Old Days: A Report on US Living Standards*, annual report (Dallas: Federal Reserve Bank, 1994), p. 7.
6. Robert William Fogel, *The Fourth Great Awakening and the Future of Egalitarianism* (Chicago: University of Chicago Press, 2000), p. 185.
7. Ibid., p. 186.
8. Ibid., pp. 184–90.
9. See Marber, *Money Changes Everything*. For more on specific shifts in attitudes and values relative to economic development, the University of Michigan's Ron Inglehart's seminal Human Values Surveys are an invaluable resource.
10. For a balanced study of this subject, see Arne Mechoir, Kjetil Telle, and Henrik Wiig, *Globalisation and Inequality: World Income and Living Standards, 1960–1998*, Norwegian Ministry of Foreign Affairs, Report 6B:2000, October 2000, available at http://odin.dep.no/archive/udvedlegg/01/01/rev_016.pdf.
11. Ibid., p. 14.
12. James Wolfensohn, "How Rich Countries Keep the Rest of the World in Poverty," *Irish Independent*, September 30, 2002.
13. Ibid.
14. See Michael Teitelbaum, "Are North/South Population Growth Differentials a Prelude to Conflict?" at http://www.csis.org/gai/Graying/speeches/teitelbaum.html.

PETER MARBER is an author, professional money manager, and faculty member at the School of International and Public Affairs at Columbia University.

From *World Policy Journal,* Winter 2004/2005, pp. 29–30, 33–37. Copyright © 2005 by World Policy Institute. Reprinted by permission.

Why the World Isn't Flat

Globalization has bound people, countries, and markets closer than ever, rendering national borders relics of a bygone era—or so we're told. But a close look at the data reveals a world that's just a fraction as integrated as the one we thought we knew. In fact, more than 90 percent of all phone calls, Web traffic, and investment is local. What's more, even this small level of globalization could still slip away.

PANKAJ GHEMAWAT

Ideas will spread faster, leaping borders. Poor countries will have immediate access to information that was once restricted to the industrial world and traveled only slowly, if at all, beyond it. Entire electorates will learn things that once only a few bureaucrats knew. Small companies will offer services that previously only giants could provide. In all these ways, the communications revolution is profoundly democratic and liberating, leveling the imbalance between large and small, rich and poor." The global vision that Frances Cairncross predicted in her *Death of Distance* appears to be upon us. We seem to live in a world that is no longer a collection of isolated, "local" nations, effectively separated by high tariff walls, poor communications networks, and mutual suspicion. It's a world that, if you believe the most prominent proponents of globalization, is increasingly wired, informed, and, well, "flat."

It's an attractive idea. And if publishing trends are any indication, globalization is more than just a powerful economic and political transformation; it's a booming cottage industry. According to the U.S. Library of Congress's catalog, in the 1990s, about 500 books were published on globalization. Between 2000 and 2004, there were more than 4,000. In fact, between the mid-1990s and 2003, the rate of increase in globalization-related titles more than doubled every 18 months.

Amid all this clutter, several books on the subject have managed to attract significant attention. During a recent TV interview, the first question I was asked—quite earnestly—was why I still thought the world was round. The interviewer was referring of course to the thesis of *New York Times* columnist Thomas L. Friedman's bestselling book *The World Is Flat*. Friedman asserts that 10 forces—most of which enable connectivity and collaboration at a distance—are "flattening" the Earth and leveling a playing field of global competitiveness, the likes of which the world has never before seen.

It sounds compelling enough. But Friedman's assertions are simply the latest in a series of exaggerated visions that also include the "end of history" and the "convergence of tastes." Some writers in this vein view globalization as a good thing—an escape from the ancient tribal rifts that have divided humans, or an opportunity to sell the same thing to everyone on Earth. Others lament its cancerous spread, a process at the end of which everyone will be eating the same fast food. Their arguments are mostly characterized by emotional rather than cerebral appeals, a reliance on prophecy, semiotic arousal (that is, treating everything as a sign), a focus on technology as the driver of change, an emphasis on education that creates "new" people, and perhaps above all, a clamor for attention. But they all have one thing in common: They're wrong.

In truth, the world is not nearly as connected as these writers would have us believe. Despite talk of a new, wired world where information, ideas, money, and people can move around the planet faster than ever before, just a fraction of what we consider globalization actually exists. The portrait that emerges from a hard look at the way companies, people, and states interact is a world that's only beginning to realize the potential of true global integration. And what these trend's backers won't tell you is that globalization's future is more fragile than you know.

The 10 Percent Presumption

The few cities that dominate international financial activity—Frankfurt, Hong Kong, London, New York—are at the height of modern global integration; which is to say, they are all relatively well connected with one another. But when you examine the numbers, the picture is one of extreme connectivity at the local level, not a flat world. What do such statistics reveal? Most types of economic activity that could be conducted either within or across borders turn out to still be quite domestically concentrated.

One favorite mantra from globalization champions is how "investment knows no boundaries." But how much of all the capital being invested around the world is conducted by companies outside of their home countries? The fact is, the total amount of the world's capital formation that is generated from foreign direct investment (FDI) has been less than 10 percent for the last three years for which data are available (2003–05). In other words, more than 90 percent of the fixed investment around the world is still domestic. And though merger waves can push the ratio higher, it has never reached 20 percent. In a thoroughly globalized environment, one would expect this number to be much higher—about 90 percent, by my calculation. And FDI isn't an odd or unrepresentative example.

The levels of internationalization associated with cross-border migration, telephone calls, management research and education, private charitable giving, patenting, stock investment, and trade, as a fraction of gross domestic product (GDP), all stand much closer to 10 percent than 100 percent. The biggest exception in absolute terms—the trade-to-GDP—recedes most of the way back down toward 20 percent if you adjust for certain kinds of double-counting. So if someone asked me to guess the internationalization level of some activity about which I had no particular information, I would guess it to be much closer to 10 percent—than to 100 percent. I call this the "10 Percent Presumption."

More broadly, these and other data on cross-border integration suggest a semiglobalized world, in which neither the bridges nor the barriers between countries can be ignored. From this perspective, the most astonishing aspect of various writings on globalization is the extent of exaggeration involved. In short, the levels of internationalization in the world today are roughly an order of magnitude lower than those implied by globalization proponents.

A Strong National Defense

If you buy into the more extreme views of the globalization triumphalists, you would expect to see a world where national borders are irrelevant, and where citizens increasingly view themselves as members of ever broader political entities. True, communications technologies have improved dramatically during the past 100 years. The cost of a three-minute telephone call from New York to London fell from $350 in 1930 to about 40 cents in 1999, and it is now approaching zero for voice-over-Internet telephony. And the Internet itself is just one of many newer forms of connectivity that have progressed several times faster than plain old telephone service. This pace of improvement has inspired excited proclamations about the pace of global integration. But it's a huge leap to go from predicting such changes to asserting that declining communication costs will obliterate the effects of distance. Although the barriers at borders have declined significantly, they haven't disappeared.

To see why, consider the Indian software industry—a favorite of Friedman and others. Friedman cites Nandan Nilekani, the CEO of the second-largest such firm, Infosys, as his muse for the notion of a flat world. But what Nilekani has pointed out privately is that while Indian software programmers can now serve the United States from India, access is assured, in part, by U.S. capital being invested—quite literally—in that outcome. In other words, the success of the Indian IT industry is not exempt from political and geographic constraints. The country of origin matters—even for capital, which is often considered stateless.

Or consider the largest Indian software firm, Tata Consultancy Services (TCS). Friedman has written at least two columns in the *New York Times* on TCS's Latin American operations: "[I]n today's world, having an Indian company led by a Hungarian-Uruguayan servicing American banks with Montevidean engineers managed by Indian technologists who have learned to eat Uruguayan veggie is just the new normal," Friedman writes. Perhaps. But the real question is why the company established those operations in the first place. Having worked as a strategy advisor to TCS since 2000, I can testify that reasons related to the tyranny of time zones, languages, and the need for proximity to clients' local operations loomed large in that decision. This is a far cry from globalization proponents' oft-cited world in which geography, language, and distance don't matter.

Trade flows certainly bear that theory out. Consider Canadian-U.S. trade, the largest bilateral relationship of its kind in the world. In 1988, before the North American Free Trade Agreement (NAFTA) took effect, merchandise trade levels between Canadian provinces—that is, within the country—were estimated to be 20 times as large as their trade with similarly sized and similarly distant U.S. states. In other words, there was a built-in "home bias." Although NAFTA helped reduce this ratio of domestic to international trade—the home bias—to 10 to 1 by the mid-1990s, it still exceeds 5 to 1 today. And these ratios are just for merchandise; for services, the ratio is still several times larger. Clearly, the borders in our seemingly "borderless world" still matter to most people.

Geographical boundaries are so pervasive, they even extend to cyberspace. If there were one realm in which borders should be rendered meaningless and the globalization proponents should be correct in their overly optimistic models, it should be the Internet. Yet Web traffic within countries and regions has increased far faster than traffic between them. Just as in the real world, Internet links decay with distance. People across the world may be getting more connected, but they aren't connecting with each other. The average South Korean Web user may be spending several hours a day online—connected to the rest of the world in theory—but he is probably chatting with friends across town and e-mailing family across the country rather than meeting a fellow surfer in Los Angeles. We're more wired, but no more "global."

Just look at Google, which boasts of supporting more than 100 languages and, partly as a result, has recently been rated the most globalized Web site. But Google's operation in Russia (cofounder Sergey Brin's native country) reaches only 28 percent of the market there, versus 64 percent for the Russian market leader in search services, Yandex, and 53 percent for Rambler.

Indeed, these two local competitors account for 91 percent of the Russian market for online ads linked to Web searches. What has stymied Google's expansion into the Russian market? The biggest reason is the difficulty of designing a search engine to handle the linguistic complexities of the Russian language. In addition, these local competitors are more in tune with the Russian market, for example, developing payment methods through traditional banks to compensate for the dearth of credit cards. And, though Google has doubled its reach since 2003, it's had to set up a Moscow office in Russia and hire Russian software engineers, underlining the continued importance of physical location. Even now, borders between countries define—and constrain—our movements more than globalization breaks them down.

Turning Back the Clock

If globalization is an inadequate term for the current state of integration, there's an obvious rejoinder: Even if the world isn't quite flat today, it will be tomorrow. To respond, we have to look at trends, rather than levels of integration at one point in time. The results are telling. Along a few dimensions, integration reached its all-time high many years ago. For example, rough calculations suggest that the number of long-term international migrants amounted to 3 percent of the world's population in 1900—the high-water mark of an earlier era of migration—versus 2.9 percent in 2005.

Along other dimensions, it's true that new records are being set. But this growth has happened only relatively recently, and only after long periods of stagnation and reversal. For example, FDI stocks divided by GDP peaked before World War I and didn't return to that level until the 1990s. Several economists have argued that the most remarkable development over the long term was the declining level of internationalization between the two World Wars. And despite the records being set, the current level of trade intensity falls far short of completeness, as the Canadian-U.S. trade data suggest. In fact, when trade economists look at these figures, they are amazed not at how much trade there is, but how little.

It's also useful to examine the considerable momentum that globalization proponents attribute to the constellation of policy changes that led many countries—particularly China, India, and the former Soviet Union—to engage more extensively with the international economy. One of the better-researched descriptions of these policy changes and their implications is provided by economists Jeffrey Sachs and Andrew Warner:

"The years between 1970 and 1995, and especially the last decade, have witnessed the most remarkable institutional harmonization and economic integration among nations in world history. While economic integration was increasing throughout the 1970s and 1980s, the extent of integration has come sharply into focus only since the collapse of communism in 1989. In 1995, one dominant global economic system is emerging."

Yes, such policy openings are important. But to paint them as a sea change is inaccurate at best. Remember the 10 Percent Presumption, and that integration is only beginning. The policies that we fickle humans enact are surprisingly reversible. Thus, Francis Fukuyama's *The End of History,* in which liberal democracy and technologically driven capitalism were supposed to have triumphed over other ideologies, seems quite quaint today. In the wake of Sept. 11, 2001, Samuel Huntington's *Clash of Civilizations* looks at least a bit more prescient. But even if you stay on the economic plane, as Sachs and Warner mostly do, you quickly see counterevidence to the supposed decisiveness of policy openings. The so-called Washington Consensus around market-friendly policies ran up against the 1997 Asian currency crisis and has since frayed substantially—for example, in the swing toward neopopulism across much of Latin America. In terms of economic outcomes, the number of countries—in Latin America, coastal Africa, and the former Soviet Union—that have dropped out of the "convergence club" (defined in terms of narrowing productivity and structural gaps vis-à-vis the advanced industrialized countries) is at least as impressive as the number of countries that have joined the club. At a multilateral level, the suspension of the Doha round of trade talks in the summer of 2006—prompting *The Economist* to run a cover titled "The Future of Globalization" and depicting a beached wreck—is no promising omen. In addition, the recent wave of cross-border mergers and acquisitions seems to be encountering more protectionism, in a broader range of countries, than did the previous wave in the late 1990s.

Of course, given that sentiments in these respects have shifted in the past 10 years or so, there is a fair chance that they may shift yet again in the next decade. The point is, it's not only possible to turn back the clock on globalization-friendly policies, it's relatively easy to imagine it happening. Specifically, we have to entertain the possibility that deep international economic integration may be inherently incompatible with national sovereignty—especially given the tendency of voters in many countries, including advanced ones, to support more protectionism, rather than less. As Jeff Immelt, CEO of GE, put it in late 2006, "If you put globalization to a popular vote in the U.S., it would lose." And even if cross-border integration continues on its upward path, the road from here to there is unlikely to be either smooth or straight. There will be shocks and cycles, in all likelihood, and maybe even another period of stagnation or reversal that will endure for decades. It wouldn't be unprecedented.

The champions of globalization are describing a world that doesn't exist. It's a fine strategy to sell books and even describe a potential environment that may someday exist. Because such episodes of mass delusion tend to be relatively short-lived even when they do achieve broad currency, one might simply be tempted to wait this one out as well. But the stakes are far too high for that. Governments that buy into the flat world are likely to pay too much attention to the "golden straitjacket" that Friedman emphasized in his earlier book, *The Lexus and the Olive Tree,* which is supposed to ensure that economics matters more and more and politics less and less. Buying into this version of an integrated world—or worse, using it as a basis for policy-making—is not only unproductive. It is dangerous.

PANKAJ GHEMAWAT is the Anselmo Rubiralta professor of global strategy at IESE Business School and the Jaime and Josefina Chua Tiampo professor of business administration at Harvard Business School. His new book is *Redefining Global Strategy* (Boston: Harvard Business School Press, September 2007).

From *Foreign Policy,* March/April 2007. Copyright © 2007 by the Carnegie Endowment for International Peace. Reprinted with permission. www.foreignpolicy.com

The Lost Continent

For decades, Latin America's weight in the world has been shrinking. It is not an economic powerhouse, a security threat, or a population bomb. Even its tragedies pale in comparison to Africa's. The region will not rise until it ends its search for magic formulas. It may not make for a good sound bite, but patience is Latin America's biggest deficit of all.

Moisés Naím

L atin America has grown used to living in the backyard of the United States. For decades, it has been a region where the U.S. government meddled in local politics, fought communists, and promoted its business interests. Even if the rest of the world wasn't paying attention to Latin America, the United States occasionally was. Then came September 11, and even the United States seemed to tune out. Naturally, the world's attention centered almost exclusively on terrorism, the wars in Afghanistan, Iraq, and Lebanon, and on the nuclear ambitions of North Korea and Iran. Latin America became Atlantis—the lost continent. Almost overnight, it disappeared from the maps of investors, generals, diplomats, and journalists.

Indeed, as one commentator recently quipped, Latin America can't compete on the world stage in any aspect, even as a threat. Unlike anti-Americans elsewhere, Latin Americans are not willing to die for the sake of their geopolitical hatreds. Latin America is a nuclear-weapons free zone. Its only weapon of mass destruction is cocaine. In contrast to emerging markets like India and China, Latin America is a minor economic player whose global significance is declining. Sure, a few countries export oil and gas, but only Venezuela is in the top league of the world's energy market.

Not even Latin America's disasters seem to elicit global concern anymore. Argentina experienced a massive financial stroke in 2001, and no one abroad seemed to care. Unlike prior crashes, no government or international financial institution rushed to bail it out. Latin America doesn't have Africa's famines, genocides, an HIV/AIDS pandemic, wholesale state failures, or rock stars who routinely adopt its tragedies. Bono, Bill Gates, and Angelina Jolie worry about Botswana, not Brazil.

But just as the five-year-old war on terror pronounced the necessity of confronting threats where they linger, it also underscored the dangers of neglect. Like Afghanistan, Latin America shows how quickly and easy it is for the United States to lose its influence when Washington is distracted by other priorities.

In both places, Washington's disinterest produced a vacuum that was filled by political groups and leaders hostile to the United States.

No, Latin America is not churning out Islamic terrorists as Afghanistan was during the days of the Taliban. In Latin America, the power gap is being filled by a group of disparate leaders often lumped together under the banner of populism. On the rare occasions that Latin American countries do make international news, it's the election of a so-called populist, an apparently anti-American, anti-market leader, that raises hackles. However, Latin America's populists aren't a monolith. Some are worse for international stability than is usually reported. But some have the potential to chart a new, positive course for the region. Underlying the ascent of these new leaders are several real, stubborn threads running through Latin Americans' frustration with the status quo in their countries. Unfortunately, the United States'—and the rest of the world's—lack of interest in that region means that the forces that are shaping disparate political movements in Latin America are often glossed over, misinterpreted, or ignored. Ultimately, though, what matters most is not what the northern giant thinks or does as much as what half a billion Latin Americans think and do. And in the last couple of decades, the wild swings in their political behavior have created a highly unstable terrain where building the institutions indispensable for progress or for fighting poverty has become increasingly difficult. There is a way out. But it's not the quick fix that too many of Latin America's leaders have promised and that an impatient population demands.

The Left Turn that Wasn't

In the 1990s, politicians throughout Latin America won elections by promising economic reforms inspired by the "Washington Consensus" and closer ties to the United States. The Free Trade Area of the Americas offered hope for a better economic future for all. The United States could count on its neighbors to the south as reliable international allies. In Argentina, for example, the country's political and military links with the United States were so strong that in 1998, it was invited to become part of a select group of "major non-NATO allies." Today, however, President Néstor Kirchner nurtures a 70-percent approval rating by lobbing derision and invective against the "empire" up north. His main ally abroad is Venezuelan President Hugo Chávez, not George W. Bush. Nowadays, running for political office in Latin America openly advocating privatization, free trade, or claiming the support of the U.S. government is political suicide. Denouncing the corruption and inequality spurred by the "savage capitalism" of the 1990s, promising to help the poor and battle the rich, and disparaging the abusive international behavior of the American superpower and what is seen as its "globalization" ruse is a political platform that has acquired renewed potency throughout the region. In nearly every country, these ideas have helped new political leaders gain a national following and in Argentina, Bolivia, and Venezuela, even to win the presidency. In most other countries, notably in Mexico, Peru, Ecuador, and Nicaragua, proponents of these views enjoy wide popular support and are a fundamental factor in their countries' politics.

Latin America can't compete on the world stage in any way, not even as a threat.

So what happened? The first alarm bells sounded with the election in rapid succession of Chávez in Venezuela in 1998, Luiz Inácio "Lula" da Silva in Brazil in 2002, Kirchner in Argentina in 2003, and Tabaré Vázquez in Uruguay in 2004. All of them represented left-of-center coalitions and all promised to undo the "neoliberal excesses" of their predecessors. All of them also stressed the need to reassert their nations' independence from the United States and limit the superpower's influence.

Yet, none of these new presidents really delivered on their more extreme campaign promises, especially their plans to roll back the economic reforms of the 1990s. Brazil's Lula has followed an orthodox economic policy, anchored in painfully high interest rates and the active promotion of foreign investments. In Argentina, the only significant departure from the economic orthodoxy of the 1990s has been the adoption of widespread price controls and a disdainful attitude toward foreign investors.

In Venezuela, the rhetoric (and sometimes the deeds) are more in line with rabid anti-American, anti-free trade, and anti-market postures. Chávez routinely denounces free-trade agreements with the United States: He has been known to say that "[c]apitalism will lead to the destruction of humanity," and that the United States is the "devil that represents capitalism." Chávez's anti-trade posture conveniently glosses over the reality that Venezuela enjoys a de facto free trade agreement with the United States. In fact, America is the top market for Venezuela's oil. During Chávez's tenure, Venezuela has become one of the world's fastest-growing markets for manufactured American

products. And even the capitalist devils that are the objects of Chávez's wrath aren't suffering as much as might be expected. As the *Financial Times* reported in August, "Bankers traditionally face firing squads in times of revolution. But in Venezuela, they are having a party." Local bankers close to the regime are reaping huge profits. Foreign bankers who cater to the wealthy return from trips to Caracas with long lists of newly acquired clients in need of discreet "asset management" abroad.

Although some of these populist leaders have so far failed to live up to the radical economic changes they promised on the campaign trail, the gaps between incendiary rhetoric and actual practice have been far narrower in the region's foreign policies—especially in Venezuela and its relations with the United States. President Chávez, easily the world's most vocal anti-American leader, has called President George W. Bush, among other things, a "donkey," "a drunkard," and "an assassin." Not even Osama bin Laden has spouted such vitriol. Chávez has embraced Cuban leader Fidel Castro as his mentor and comrade-in-arms, and in so doing, he has become the region's most visible leader since Che Guevara. Like Che, Chávez often seems hellbent on sparking an armed confrontation to further his revolution; he calls Saddam Hussein a "brother," and is arming new local militias with 100,000 AK-47s to repel the "imminent" U.S. invasion. His international activism now routinely takes him around the world. In Damascus this summer, Chávez and Syrian President Bashar Assad issued a joint declaration stating that they were "firmly united against imperialist aggression and the hegemonic intentions of the U.S. Empire."

The main concern is not just that Chávez is developing close ties with prominent U.S. foes worldwide, but rather his efforts to refashion the domestic politics of his neighboring countries. His persona and his message are certainly attractive to large blocs of voters in other countries. Politicians elsewhere in Latin America who emulate him and his platforms are gaining popularity, and it's hard to imagine that Chávez is refraining from using his enormous oil wealth to support their political ascendancy. The international concern about trends in Latin America peaked in late 2005, as 12 presidential elections were scheduled for the ensuing months. In several countries—Bolivia, Costa Rica, Ecuador, Mexico, Nicaragua, and Peru—leftist candidates with Chávez-sounding platforms stood a good chance of winning.

Yet that expectation did not come to pass. So far, the only election where a Chávez ally has won is Bolivia. There, Evo Morales, the leader of the coca growers, announced that he would become "the United States' worst nightmare," and quickly proceeded to enter into a close alliance with Venezuela and Cuba. But the election of Chávez-backed candidates turned out to be more the exception than the rule. Surprisingly, running for office with too close an identification with Chávez or his policies has become an electoral kiss of death. Not even his promises of supplying cheap oil and financial aid if his candidate won were enough to compensate for the strong voter backlash against a foreign president openly trying to influence the outcome of national elections.

But the electoral defeat of candidates running on platforms perceived to be too extreme or too close to Chávez does not mean that the ideas they represent are unappealing. Latin

American voters are aggrieved, impatient, and eager to vote for new candidates who offer a break with the past and who promise a way out of the dire present.

If Not Left, Then Where?

Since the late 1990s, Latin American political systems have been rocked by a wide variety of frustrations. Therefore lumping the different types of discontent under generic "leftist" or "populist" monikers is misleading. Indeed, in today's Latin America, some of the grievances are clearly anti-market, while others are rooted in dissatisfactions caused not by overreliance on the market but by governmental overreach. Curbing corruption, for example, is a strong political demand that is unlikely to be satisfied by increasing the economic activities controlled by an already overwhelmed and corrupt public sector. Other grievances unite the far left and the far right. Economic nationalists who resent the market-opening reforms that allow foreign products to displace locally made ones include both right-wing business groups who profited handsomely from the protectionism, as well as leftist labor leaders who have seen their ranks shrink as local factories went out of business, unable to compete with foreign imports.

The responses to these political demands have also been varied. Some leaders, like Chávez and Kirchner, are behaving in a traditional, populist fashion, relying on massive and often wasteful public spending, on prices kept artificially low through governmental controls, or the scapegoating of the private sector to cement their popularity. Many others, however, like Lula in Brazil, Vicente Fox in Mexico, Alvaro Uribe in Colombia, or Ricardo Lagos in Chile have been models of more responsible economic governance and have shown a willingness to absorb the costs of unpopular but necessary economic policies.

What unites almost all Latin American countries, however, are two long-standing trends that multiply and deepen the variety of the grievances that are sprouting throughout the region: Prolonged mediocre economic performance, and the decay of traditional forms of political organization, and political parties in particular.

Latin America has suffered from slow economic growth for more than a quarter-century. Episodes of rapid growth have been short lived and often ended in painful financial crashes with devastating effects on the poor and the middle class. Economic growth in Latin America has been slower than it was in the 1960s and 70s, worse relative to all other emerging markets in the world, and unremittingly less than what the region itself needs to lift the poor standard of living of most of the population. This economic disappointment has become increasingly unacceptable to voters who have been promised much and gotten little and who have become better informed than ever about the standards of living of others at home and abroad. Latin Americans are fed up. Naturally, the frustrations produced by the wide gap between expectations and reality and between the living standards of the few who have so much and the many who have almost nothing create fertile ground for the fractious politics that make governing so difficult. Inevitably, political parties,

Latin American Merchandise Exports
(as a percentage of world total)

Foreign Direct Investment into Latin America
(as a percentage of world total)

Figure 1 Shrinking Share. Latin America's economic clout continues to slide.

and especially those in power, have suffered tremendous losses in loyalty, credibility, and legitimacy. Some of this disrepute is well deserved and often self-inflicted, as most political parties have failed to modernize their thinking or replace their ineffectual leaders. Corruption, patronage, and the use of politics as the fastest route for personal wealth are also rampant.

But it is also true that governing in a region where the political attitudes of large swaths of the population are imbued with rage, revenge, and impatience, and where the machinery of the public sector is often broken, is bound to end in failure. Because the region is resource-rich, the most common explanation for poverty amid so much imagined wealth is corruption. End the corruption and the standard of living of the poor will more or less automatically improve, goes the thinking. This assumption of course ignores the fact that a nation's prosperity depends more on being rich in competent public institutions, rule of law, and a well-educated population than in exportable raw materials.

Moreover, while the widespread presence and ravaging effects of corruption are indisputable, the reality is that poverty in Latin America owes as much, if not more, to the region's inability to find ways to compete more effectively in a globalized economy than to the pervasive thievery of those in power. It is hard to argue that China or India or the fast-growing economies of East Asia are substantially less corrupt than Latin America. Yet their growth rates and their ability to lift their populations out of poverty have been better than those of Latin America. Why? The fact is that the region's democracy and activist politics make its wages too high to compete with the low-wage Asian economies. Latin America's poor educational systems and low level of technological development make it unable to compete effectively in most international markets where success is driven by know-how and innovation. With its high wages and low technology, Latin America is having a hard time fitting into the hypercompetitive global economy. That fact gets far less attention than others that are more urgent, visible, or politically popular. Yet many of these problems—unemployment, poverty, slow economic growth—are manifestations of national economies that are ill-suited to prosper under the conditions prevalent in today's world.

The Waiting Game

Like all fundamental development problems, Latin America's global competitive shortcomings cannot be reduced simply or quickly. The specific reasons behind a country's disadvantageous position in the global economy vary. Alleviating them requires simultaneous efforts on many fronts by different actors over a long period. And herein lies a central difficulty besetting all attempts to create positive, sustained change in Latin America: They all take more time than voters, politicians, investors, social activists, and journalists are willing to wait before moving on to another idea or another leader.

Latin America's most important deficit is patience. Unless the patience of all influential actors is raised, efforts will continue to fail before they are fully tested or executed. Investors will continue to ignore good projects that cannot offer quick returns, governments will only pick policies that can generate rapid, visible results even if they are unsustainable or mostly cosmetic, and voters will continue to shed leaders that don't deliver soon enough.

Reducing the patience deficit is impossible without alleviating Latin America's most immediate and urgent needs. But it is a mistake to assume that sustainable improvements will only occur as a result of radical, emergency measures. Large-scale social progress will require years of sustained efforts that are not prematurely terminated and replaced by a new, "big-bang" solution. Continuous progress demands the stability created by agreement on a set of basic shared goals and ideas among major political players. In the past, this patience was either ruthlessly forced on the population by military governments or induced by the adoption of a similar ideology shared by influential social groups. Both approaches are highly problematic and not viable in the long run.

Therefore, rather than seeking ideological consensus or forcing ideological hegemony, Latin Americans should build from what exists and seems to be working, rather than dismiss what already exists just because its champions are political competitors. Only those individuals and organizations who are able to bridge ideological divides and bring together different approaches will fix Latin America's long-standing problems. And give them time.

It's not as though there's no precedent for this kind of progressive governance. Former Presidents Fernando Henrique Cardoso in Brazil and Lagos in Chile integrated different ideological perspectives and developed pragmatic approaches to balance conflicting demands. Both came from socialist backgrounds and while in office made enormous and often successful efforts to fight poverty and improve social conditions. But they were also quite sensitive about the need to maintain economic stability—which often meant painful cuts in public spending—and to foster an attractive business environment for investors. Although neither Cardoso nor Lagos was able to drastically overhaul his nation's poor social conditions, both easily rank among the most effective and successful presidents of the last decade—anywhere. They made far more progress in alleviating poverty in their countries than any of the more strident Latin American revolutionaries whose radical efforts on behalf of the poor so often ended up creating only more poverty and inequality.

With its high wages and low technology, Latin America is having a hard time fitting into the global economy.

It is natural for Latin American citizens and politicians to be captivated by promises that seem too good to be true. People who find themselves in dire straits naturally want extreme, quick solutions. Latin Americans have been experimenting with brutal, heavy-handed swings in their political economies since the 1970s. Yet, this search for silver-bullet solutions, though understandable given the grave problems of the region, is mistaken. Latin Americans must learn that, precisely because their illnesses are so acute, the solutions must be, paradoxically, more tempered. It might seem counterintuitive to reject the promises of the men and women offering radical change for a region so used to failure and neglect. But it may be the only way to lift millions out of poverty. And in the process, get Latin America back on the map.

Moisés Naím is editor in chief of *Foreign Policy*.

Political Graft: The Russian Way

"While we normally think of corruption as attempts by government officials to extort money from private sector businessmen, Russia offers increasingly numerous examples in which government officials go further and actually attempt to take over a business for the state or, recently, for themselves."

MARSHALL I. GOLDMAN

Russia is traditionally classified as one of the most corrupt countries in the world, and certainly the most corrupt among economically developed countries. The question thus arises: What is there in present-day Russia's history, culture, and endowment that has made it so corrupt? Addressing this question may help us to assess the prospects of undoing or offsetting the forces of corruption that continue to impede Russia's political and economic development.

For countries seeking to eliminate official bribery, influence peddling, and other corrupt activities, the longer and more deeply ingrained the corruption in the culture, the more difficult it is to eradicate. For corruption fighters in Africa and Latin America, this observation is nothing new. It takes on a different perspective, however, when a country undergoes a fundamental transformation of its economic system, as Russia did after the demise of the Communist Party system and central planning in 1991. An underlying assumption during this process was that with a newly adopted democracy and a market system would come transparency and Western market-system mores (mostly positive ones, though a few Enronlike values could be expected as well).

That corruption was so deeply entrenched in Russian history and culture did not seem to matter. True, the philosopher Nikolai Berdyaev had noted that in the czarist era "bribery is the only constitution in our life." Short stories by Nikolai Gogol, "The Inspector General" and "Dead Souls," as well as Leo Tolstoy's novels, also reflected this reality. Russia in general provides an excellent sense of how deeply ingrained corruption was in nineteenth-century autocracies. Corruption flourished under twentieth-century communist states as well. Yet, with the collapse of the Soviet Union in Russia, there was to be a new beginning and a new mentality. Unfortunately, that has not happened. Without a transformation in the underlying conditions that nurture corrupt behavior, there is no reason to expect any real change.

The Perfect Climate

In both the czarist and Soviet eras, the state was all-powerful. In the late nineteenth century, after the emancipation of the serfs and the substantial growth of semi-private industries, hints emerged of a growing business sector that on occasion proved somewhat independent of the state. However, the absence in Russia of the Renaissance and Reformation as well as a commercial or industrial awakening meant there was almost no legitimate force willing or able to challenge the absolute power of the czar or affect the czar's ability to dictate land use and resource distribution. This provided a perfect climate for influence peddling and bribery.

Moreover, with the exception of St. Petersburg and Moscow, Russian cities remained for the most part administrative, not commercial or manufacturing centers, and thus the country lacked a growing bourgeois class large enough, or angry and bold enough, to impose restraints on the rulers. There was nothing comparable to the Magna Carta, which imposed limits on the British monarch's ability to tax and spend. In Russia, only belatedly and weakly did legislatures and judicial institutions with their checks and balances take root, an essential prerequisite for a corruption-free environment.

Absent, too, until the late 1980s were an independent press and nongovernment watchdogs, also prerequisites for corruption-free government. True to its conspiratorial nature, the Soviet Union had no interest in transparency. In fact, during the Soviet period it was taken for granted that government authorities would insist on secrecy in their dealings not only with foreigners but often with their own citizens. Officials did all they could, for example, to obscure the true owners of the corporations they set up overseas. Thus it was typically the case that a Soviet machine-importing company operating in Belgium would be owned by the Foreign Trade Organization headquartered in the Ministry of Foreign Trade in Moscow as well as by a sister Soviet-owned machinery importing company in Finland, which in turn was owned by the Russian machine importing company operating in Belgium. This was done intentionally to mask ownership and make it a bit easier for the KGB to send its spies to "work" in such outposts. The use of commercial entities for espionage inevitably tainted even legitimate business operations in the Soviet Union, a legacy that continues since the Soviet system's disintegration.

While these overseas Soviet business operations contributed to the notion that there was nothing wrong with deceiving foreigners, there was also a longstanding acceptance of the idea that there was nothing wrong when Russians cheated and deceived themselves and their own country. Prince Gregory Potemkin went so far as to build an eighteenth-century stage set in Ukraine filled with smiling peasants to show Czarina Catherine the Great how happy he had made his serfs. Russians even had a word for it—*pokazukha,* to pull the wool over someone's eyes. After all, they were only stealing from the czar, which meant that since the czar ultimately owned all the country's land, they were only stealing from themselves.

Some trace these sentiments back to attempts to deceive the tax collection efforts of Mongol invaders and the various Russian princes who served as their agents. With the advent of the Soviet system and the complete nationalization of all means of production in both agriculture and industry, the sense of entitlement and the belief that it was appropriate to defraud the state all but destroyed whatever feelings of integrity and fair play might have endured or developed in the latter days of the czarist system.

Extortion, a Right of Office

It was not only the past that postcommunist reforms had to contend with, but also the present. Even if the czars or Soviet officials had been models of probity, those in authority when Boris Yeltsin came to power would have been sorely tested when hit with the hyperinflation that marked the early years of the Yeltsin administration. Prices in 1992 alone rose twenty-six-fold. This not only destroyed whatever savings the Russian public may have held; it also meant that government salaries that are slower to respond to inflation than those in the private sector no longer sufficed to buy the necessities of life. In self-defense, government officials throughout the country began to demand bribes in lieu of higher salaries. Extortion became a right of office.

This was as true on the streets as it was in government ministries and city halls. It became commonplace to see traffic police stop every tenth car to find some minor infraction of the law. Today this is considered the most common form of corruption. A survey conducted in 2002 by INDEM, a Russian think tank, found that 7 out of every 10 encounters with traffic police resulted in a bribe. According to one estimate, in 2001 drivers paid the traffic police $368 million. For those who on a rare occasion might decide to contest their violation, the police would frequently add a charge of being drunk. This charge in turn would require a blood test with a common needle. Rather than risk AIDS, drivers usually ended the argument.

Justice for Sale

Extortion is not limited to so-called traffic violations. An estimated $449 million was paid in 2004 as bribes to university officials by those seeking admission. Similarly, those in need of medical care in 2004 paid an estimated $401 million under the table. It also has become standard practice to bribe judges. The same INDEM study concluded that $275 million was paid in bribes to "win justice in court." (A joke is told about two judges who were each handed an envelope with $100,000 by the defendant only to see the next day that the plaintiff had left each of them $150,000. When meeting to discuss how to handle the situation, the judges decided to return $50,000 to the plaintiff and then decide the case on its merits.)

In August 2003, the Ethics Committee of the Russian Union of Industrialists and Entrepreneurs (RSPP) reported that in its view court judgments lack independence and are instead swayed by local authorities, governments, and businesses "just paying" for their decisions. So discredited is the court system that a new phrase has entered the Russian language: court auction, or "whoever pays more, wins." Given the circumstances, members of the RSPP agreed that henceforth, when disputes arose between them, they would avoid the courts and instead seek help from a pre-approved list of independent arbitrators.

Reflecting how widespread bribery has become, Russian journalists openly charge for writing both negative and laudatory articles. Boris Fedorov, a former finance minister, found himself under attack in the press from senior officials of Gazprom, Russia's natural gas monopoly. Fedorov had challenged the integrity of the company's leadership. At the height of the campaign, more than 50 newspapers published negative articles about him. Deciding to investigate this coordinated attack, Fedorov was able to compile the going rate for critical articles, including one by *Vedomosti,* one of the country's most respected newspapers.

Openings for Bureaucrats

The post-Soviet public's acceptance of bribe taking, to a degree that seems to exceed behavior during the czarist or Soviet eras, has been very much influenced by the realization that so much wealth is there for the taking. The privatization of what were once state-owned assets resulted in one of the greatest transfers of wealth in world history. As a few formerly ordinary citizens became millionaires and even billionaires overnight, it was easy to understand why envious government officials from the ordinary traffic police to senior government bureaucrats felt they were entitled to at least some of this new wealth. Certainly the new private owners were well equipped to buy off any official troublemakers. Graft would have been less tempting if Russia had not been so well endowed with raw materials, particularly oil and gas.

A survey found that 7 out of every 10 encounters with traffic police resulted in a bribe.

82

And as if the sudden acquisition of all that wealth did not make the newly rich tempting targets on their own, in almost every instance these new owners found themselves in need of some government permit. This could be nothing more than a license from the government to operate an elevator or a sewer, or to pass a fire inspection. In one of the more lucrative cases, because of limited oil pipeline capacity, oil companies wishing to sell their product abroad have to apply for a permit. This often proves to be the most expensive part of the transaction.

Government bureaucrats have not been slow to appreciate the opportunities open to them. Since oil prices outside of Russia are significantly higher than prices inside Russia, determining pipeline access generally is worth a lot of money. Because of physical limitations (not enough pipeline), someone has to decide who will be allowed access; government bureaucrats, not impartial or computer auctioneers, have taken the job. In other cases, where no economic or scarcity constraint already exists, bureaucrats have done all they can to create artificial limitations that can then be resolved only with the aid of some bureaucratic intervention. For example, police regulations require that all jewelry stores have bars on their windows. However, the fire laws require there be no bars on the windows. This is nirvana for the bureaucrats.

Such contradictions in the law as well as scarcity of resources occur in all societies, and there are few if any places in the world where no official has ever taken a bribe. Deciding on the allocation of scarce resources is part of the job description of most government employees. And sometimes there is a fine line between bribery and impartial rationing. For example, what happens when two or more highway contractors submit the same contract bid? Should a bureaucrat be authorized to choose between them? If so, on what basis? And is it corruption when a VIP lounge is opened at Sheremetevo Airport not only to government officials but also to private individuals who offer to pay an extra fee?

It is generally agreed that the more bureaucrats there are, the more cumbersome and time consuming the task of obtaining regulatory approval. To his credit, President Vladimir Putin and his economic advisers recognize this and have embarked on several campaigns to shrink the bureaucracy as well as the number of regulatory requirements and permissions needed. Putin announced in April 2004 that he intended to shrink the bureaucracy by 20 percent. A flow chart of the steps that had to be taken in the year 2000 by anyone seeking to open a new business looks like the back of a transistor. One store operator reported he needs 100 approvals from government authorities before he could open a retail outlet. Against this background, it is understandable why only 10 to 15 percent of Russia's gross domestic product originates in the small and medium business sectors. In contrast, small and medium businesses generate over 50 percent of GDP in Western Europe and the United States.

There are many reports that Putin's efforts have been successful. He has tried to create a one-stop system of registration as opposed to the all but impenetrable bureaucratic maze that was previously in place. The problem, however, is that bureaucrats and bureaucracies are not easily discouraged. This was the essence of what the historian Cyril Northcote Parkinson found in Great Britain after the collapse of the British empire. Russia is not much different. An article in the May 25, 2005, issue of the journal *Argumenti I Fakty* reported that, despite the fact that Russia is smaller than the Soviet Union, the number of bureaucrats and state officials has doubled to over 1 million since the Soviet Union dissolved in 1991. It also reported that corruption under Putin has worsened.

Overhaul, Anyone?

Given how deeply rooted corruption is in Russian culture and history, cleaning it up will not be easy. Indeed, it is hard to think of what else could have been done in the aftermath of centuries of czarism and decades of communism to embed corruption any more deeply in Russian culture than it already is. When Vladimir Rushaylo, the minister of interior, attempted in 2001 to refute the allegation that 70 percent of all Russian officials are corrupt by insisting that it is wrong "to mistake bribe taking for corruption," you know you have a problem. (For Rushaylo, corruption occurs only when those taking bribes have links to organized criminal gangs.) This means that to be effective, any effort now to eliminate corruption would probably require nothing less than a complete cultural overhaul. Piecemeal ad hoc measures are unlikely to be effective.

It is just such reckoning that led Victor Yushchenko, the new president of Ukraine, to decide to abolish the Ukrainian traffic police force with all of its 23,000 members. In this way, he hoped it would be possible for Ukrainian drivers to travel a few blocks without having to pay a bribe. His counterpart, Mikhail Saakashvili, did much the same thing earlier in Georgia. As we saw, Russian drivers have a similar problem. Numerous attempts have been made to clean up the existing system to no avail. If Yushchenko is successful, the Russians may also reconsider and ultimately decide to take drastic action.

When corruption is not so completely woven into a country's daily life, less draconian measures may work. Japan and West Germany managed to recover after World War II in a relatively corruption-free fashion. Of course it helped that US Army occupation forces pushed both countries in that direction (something that the Russians probably would not regard as an attractive option). However, both countries were relatively corruption-free before their defeat (which may explain why the US Army in postwar Italy, where there was a very different culture, was less successful).

This is not to say that businesses in Russia can do nothing to protect themselves. But it is risky and it takes determination. Managers of the furniture chain Ikea simply refused to go along when local authorities north of Moscow declined to issue an operating license for a just-constructed store. This forced Ikea to cancel its opening day ceremonies.

Though he feared for his safety, Lennart Dahlgren, an Ikea executive, would not pay the bribes that he said were demanded of him for the issuance of the license. Most foreign businesses fear going public this way, but in the end local officials were so embarrassed they conceded and the Ikea store opened without paying a bribe.

The Russia Disease

Such behavior by officials in Russia does not go unnoticed. Inevitably there is a cost; investors hold back or direct their investment to other countries. The reaction of the petroleum industry to what was viewed as the political trial of Mikhail Khodorkovsky, the former chief of Yukos Oil, is perhaps one of the easiest cases to document. In the early years of his business life, Khodorkovsky engaged in many questionable practices that even impartial judges and juries would have found troubling. But it also was fairly clear that political pressure from the Kremlin led to his arrest in October 2003 and his eventual trial and conviction. Observers at the trial were dismayed to see how dependent the judges were on minute-by-minute instructions from the Kremlin. If that were not enough, large portions of the verdict were taken word for word and in some cases mistake by mistake from the prosecutors' arguments. This can be considered an extreme form of corruption.

Not surprisingly, as it became a foregone conclusion that Khodorkovsky would be found guilty, oligarchs in some of the other petroleum companies began to fear something comparable might happen to them. Indeed, other businessmen began to find new demands from the tax authorities in their mailboxes. These were not as large as those sent to Yukos, but in the case of BP/TNK the taxes owed came to almost $1 billion (this was later reduced to about $300 million). Under these circumstances, some oil companies began to cut back on their investments. Sibneft, for example, which also reported it was being audited by Russian tax authorities, cut back its investment in new oil fields from $57 million in 2003 to zero in 2004.

Even though the oil sector has been the main target under attack by the Putin administration, other parts of the economy have suffered as well. Andrei Illarionov, despite being an economic adviser to Putin, has likened the harassment of Russia's energy sector by the Russian government to what he calls the "Venezuela disease." (I call it the Russia disease.) The more the state interferes in the operation of the country's oil-producing companies, the more pressure there is to make appointments based on political patronage and less on technical skill and experience. In Illarionov's words, "bureaucrats tend to make decisions that have a higher rate of return for themselves, not for the country." That is, they redistribute payoffs rather than implement responsible economic policies. The inevitable results include waste, misuse of resources, and falling production.

As Illarionov sees it, political interference along with higher world oil prices shows up in a lower rate of overall industrial growth. Corruption and bureaucratic intransigence are but one factor, but Illarionov argues that they are one reason why Russia's annual economic growth has been 2 percentage points lower than it otherwise would have been. As in the petroleum industry, overall investment suffers. Potential investors worry that without objective courts, honest judges, and a noncorrupt civil service, their investments will not be safe. This does not mean there will be no investment, only that Russia will attract less than it other-wise would have. Since the Yukos affair, overall investment has not been increasing as fast as it did a year or two earlier.

So discredited is the court system that a new phrase has entered the Russian language: court auction, or "whoever pays more, wins."

Enter the Siloviki

While we normally think of corruption as attempts by government officials to extort money from private sector businessmen, Russia offers an increasing number of examples in which government officials go further and actually attempt to take over a business for the state or, recently, for themselves. Of course, in the extreme case a socialist government will nationalize an entire industry or, as in 1917, the entire private sector. But what has been happening in Russia these past few years seems different from nationalization, in part because it is being done without calling it that. Nor is socialist ideology invoked to rationalize takeovers. It is more a reaction to greed—the greed of the oligarchs and a reactive form of greed by government officials who now seek to push out the original oligarchs and insert themselves as the new chairmen and CEOs in their place. Russia is not the only country where this has happened, but the frequency with which it has occurred and the size of the companies being seized make Russia special.

From the beginning of the Russian privatization process, some government officials managed to secure control of a few important companies for themselves. Vagit Alekperov, at the time the deputy minister of petroleum, was able to carve out three lucrative oil fields for himself, which became the core of Lukoil, now one of the country's largest oil companies. Similarly, Vladimir Bogdanov, a regional oil executive in Siberia, privatized many of the oil-producing assets under his jurisdiction and formed Surgutneftegaz, a large private entity. Rem Vyakhirev went them one better. With the help of his former boss, Viktor Chernomyrdin, he privatized Gazprom, which had been the entire natural gas ministry. They did not end up owning the majority of the stock. But until 2001, when the state stepped in and used its 38 percent of the shares to push Vyakhirev out, he ran Gazprom as if it were his own personal asset.

The latest encroachment on private ownership in Russia is very different in nature. A product of the period from 2002 to 2005, it involves a select group of officials, many of them alumni of the KGB whom the Russians refer to as *siloviki*, or law and order types. Ostensibly, they have stepped in to remove some of the original private oligarchs on charges of tax evasion, fraud, embezzlement, and, on occasion, murder. Undoubtedly many such charges have merit, but why they go after one oligarch and not another is often determined by

Siloviki in Business

Name	Title	Business	Concentration	Kremlin job
Sergei Chemezov*	CEO	Rosoboronexport	Arms exports	Former Kremlin aide
Viktor Ivanov*	Chairman	Aeroflot	Airline	Putin aide
Dmitry Medvedev	Chairman	Gazprom	Natural gas	Putin Chief of Staff
Sergei Prikhodko	Chairman	Tvel	Nuclear fuel trading	Foreign affairs adviser to Putin
Igor Sechin*	Chairman	Rosneft	Oil	Kremlin staff
Yevgeny Shkolov	Vice President	Transneft	Oil pipeline	Presidential aide
Igor Shuvalov	Board of Directors	Russia Railways	Railway	Presidential economic adviser
Vladislav Surkov	Chairman	Transnefteprodukt	Pipeline hardware	Kremlin staff
Vladimir Yakunin*	President	Russia Railways Co.	Transportation	Former aide

*Former KGB member

whether the intended target controls an asset that is particularly attractive to a particular silovik. Some of the targeted oligarchs such as Khodorkovsky may also have had political ambitions that were viewed as a threat by some in the siloviki. Even more intriguing, many of the siloviki also have jobs as officials in the Kremlin (see the table).

As they push out the old oligarchs, the siloviki slip themselves into the vacated positions. Thus Igor Sechin, the deputy chief of administration in the Kremlin under Putin, has made himself chairman of Rosneft, the state-owned company that seized Yukos's most productive and valuable subsidiary. It would be surprising if, after a few years, Sechin's income and net worth were not considerably higher. In the case of the new siloviki oligarchs, the sums they seize will be measured not in thousands of dollars, but in millions if not hundreds of millions. Only in Africa and Latin America, regions also rich in valuable raw materials, can corruption of such magnitude be found.

As political scientist Yan Sun noted in the September 2005 issue of *Current History,* the transition from a communist society to a market-based system is fraught with temptations. So far neither China nor Russia has been able to resist. But there do seem to be important differences. There have been significant scandals associated with some land transfers in China, but again nothing like what the siloviki are doing in Russia. And as Yan Sun notes, the Chinese see more power for the central government as the cure for their corruption problem. Only in this way can the local authorities be held back. By comparison, in Russia there appears to be a preference for less central control and by extension more restraint and less leeway for the siloviki. This is not to say the Russian provinces are devoid of corruption—only that by comparison with the massive theft in Moscow, corruption in the regions seems more manageable.

The Culture of Corruption

Is there any hope that transition countries like Russia and China will be able to rein in the corruption they are experiencing? So far, the trend is not very promising. Of course, as Yan Sun points out, Chinese-dominated societies such as Hong Kong and Singapore are among the most corruption-free areas of the world. But they did not evolve out of a communist system, they are much smaller in size, and their corruption-free culture is largely an inheritance of British imperialism. It is unlikely that China will ever break up again into city-states, much less invite the British in to run their governmental operations.

As for the former Soviet Union, almost none of its republic constituents have navigated the transition well. Georgia and Ukraine are making a try but the odds are not in their favor. If there is an exception to the pitfall of corruption, it may be some of the Baltic countries, such as Latvia and Estonia. They are not free of corruption, but it certainly is less of a problem. But again, both countries are small in size and population, and they historically are products of the Hanseatic League—not quite as effective as British imperialism but certainly very different from the legacy of czarism. It also helped that neither came to accept communism or Russian dominance. Against this perspective, until there is a fundamental change in Russia's underlying culture, efforts to curb corruption hold little promise.

MARSHALL I. GOLDMAN, a *Current History* contributing editor, is a professor emeritus at Wellesley College and associate director of the Davis Center for Russian and Eurasian Studies at Harvard University. His most recent book is *The Piratization of Russia: Russian Reform Goes Awry* (Routledge, 2003).

Reprinted from *Current History,* October 2005, pp. 313–318. Copyright © 2005 by Current History, Inc. Reprinted with permission.

Promises and Poverty

Starbucks calls its coffee worker-friendly— but in Ethiopia, a day's pay is a dollar.

Tom Knudson

Gemadro, Ethiopia—Tucked inside a fancy black box, the $26-a-pound Starbucks Black Apron Exclusives coffee promised to be more than just another bag of beans.

Not only was the premium coffee from a remote plantation in Ethiopia "rare, exotic, cherished," according to Starbucks advertising, it was grown in ways that were good for the environment—and for local people, too.

Companies routinely boast about what they're doing for the planet, in part because guilt-ridden consumers expect as much—and are willing to pay extra for it. But, in this case, Starbucks' eco-friendly sales pitch does not begin to reflect the complex story of coffee in East Africa.

Inside the front flap of Starbucks' box are African arabica beans grown on a plantation in a threatened mountain rain forest. Behind the lofty phrases on the back label are coffee workers who make less than a dollar a day and a dispute between plantation officials and neighboring tribal people, who accuse the plantation of using their ancestral land and jeopardizing their way of life.

"We used to hunt and fish in there, and also we used to have honeybee hives in trees," one tribal member, Mikael Yatola, said through a translator. "But now we can't do that. . . . When we were told to remove our beehives from there, we felt deep sorrow, deep sadness."

25 New U.S. Stores per Week

Few companies have so dramatically conquered the American retail landscape as Starbucks. Last year, the $7.8 billion company opened an average of 25 new stores a week in the United States alone. Nowhere is Starbucks a more common sight than in environmentally conscious California, which has 2,350 outlets, more than New York, Massachusetts, Florida, Oregon and Washington—Starbucks' home state—combined.

No coffee company claims to do more for the environment and Third World farmers than Starbucks either. In full-page ads in *The New York Times,* in brochures and on its Web page, Starbucks says that it pays premium prices for premium beans, protects tropical forests and enhances the lives of farmers by building schools, clinics and other projects.

In places, Starbucks delivers on those promises, certainly more so than other multinational coffee companies. In parts of Latin America, for instance, its work has helped improve water quality, educate children and protect biodiversity.

Inside many Starbucks outlets across America, the African décor is hard to miss. There are photographs and watercolors of quaint coffee-growing scenes from Ethiopia to Tanzania to Zimbabwe. Yet such images clash with the reality of African life.

They don't show the industrial arm of coffee—the large farms and estates that encroach on wild forest regions. They don't reveal that even in the best of times in Ethiopia, the birthplace of wild coffee and the source of some of Starbucks' priciest offerings, there is barely enough for the peasant coffee farmers who still grow most of the nation's beans.

Even where Starbucks has built its bricks-and-mortar projects in Ethiopia, poverty remains a cornerstone of life, visible in the soot-stained cooking pots, spindly legs and ragged T-shirts, in the mad scramble of children for a visitor's cookie or empty water bottle.

"We plant coffee, harvest coffee but we never get anything out of it," said Muel Alema, a rail-thin coffee farmer who lives near a Starbucks-funded footbridge spanning a narrow chasm in Ethiopia's famous Sidamo coffee-growing region.

Alema's tattered shirt looked years old. So did his mud-splattered thongs. The red coffee berries he sold to a local buyer last fall were mixed with mountains of others, stripped of their pulp and sold as beans to distant companies—like other farmers, he did not know which ones—that made millions selling Sidamo coffee. Only $220 dribbled back to him.

This February, after Alema paid workers to pick the beans and bought grain for his family, just $110 remained—not enough, he said, to feed his wife and three children, to buy them clothes until the crop ripens again.

'A Marketing Genius'

Starbucks conveys a different image on the white foil bags of Ethiopia Sidamo whole bean coffee it sells for $10.45 a pound. "Good coffee, doing good," says lettering on the side.

"We believe there's a connection between the farmers who grow our coffees, us and you. That's why we work together with coffee-growing communities—paying prices that help farmers support their families . . . and funding projects like building a bridge in Ethiopia's Sidamo region to help farmers get to market safely. . . . By drinking this coffee, you're helping to make a difference."

And while the Sidamo footbridge does make travel safer, it is but a simple yellow-brown concrete slab, 10 paces long.

Dean Cycon, founder of Dean's Beans, an organic coffee company in Massachusetts, calls Starbucks "a marketing genius."

"They put out cleverly crafted material that makes the consumer feel they are doing everything possible," Cycon said. "But there is no institutional commitment. They do it to capture a market and shut up the activists."

Starbucks officials insist such critics have it wrong. As proof, they point to Latin America, the source of the bulk of the company's beans.

"You go to Nariño, Colombia. We built 1,800 (coffee) washing stations and sanitation facilities and homes," said Dub Hay, Starbucks senior vice president for global coffee procurement. "It's literally changed the face of that whole area."

"The same is true throughout Latin America," Hay added. "They call it the Starbucks effect."

Starbucks' dealings in Latin America have drawn some fire. Near the El Triunfo Biosphere Reserve in Chiapas, Mexico, for instance, farmers cut off relations about three years ago over a dispute about selling to an exporter instead of directly to Starbucks. The new arrangement, farmers said, would drain profits from peasant growers.

Starbucks, the farmers charged in a memo to coffee buyers, was supporting "a pseudo-fair trade system, adapted to their own neo-liberal interests, to dismantle structures and advances that we have made."

In an e-mailed response to The Bee, Starbucks vice president for global communications, Frank Kern, wrote that the Chiapas farmers were ultimately "given the opportunity to ship directly to us as they requested, but they were unable to manage it."

Sharper Focus on Africa

In Ethiopia, Starbucks says, it spent $25,000 on three footbridges in 2004. The company estimates the structures are used by 70,000 farmers and family members—about 1 percent of those who depend upon coffee for income. Some Ethiopian coffee leaders say there is a better way to help.

"If we are paid a (coffee) price which is decent, the people can make the bridge on their own," said Tadesse Meskela, general manager of the Oromia Coffee Farmers' Cooperative Union of 100,000 farmers, which has sold to Starbucks. "We don't have to be always beggars."

Starbucks won't disclose what it pays for Ethiopian coffee. Instead, it lumps its purchases together into a global average, which last year was $1.42 a pound, 16 cents more than the Fair Trade minimum. Much of that money, though, never makes it into the pockets of farmers but instead is siphoned off by buyers, processors and other middlemen.

Starbucks executives say they want to shrink that supply chain. "You end up at least five levels removed from the farmer and that's where the money goes," said Hay. "And that's a shame." Hay said that as the company buys more coffee from Africa—it plans to double its purchases there to 36 million pounds by 2009—the commerce will spur more progress.

"That's our goal," Hay said. "Africa is 6 percent of our purchases. . . . Seventy percent is from Latin America. So that's where our money has gone."

Making an impact in Ethiopia is undeniably a challenge. Good roads, electricity, potable water don't exist in many places. The climate is often hostile. There are ethnic conflicts, border disputes and rebel movements, and a sea of young faces that gather every time a car stops.

Since 1990, Ethiopia's population has jumped from 52 million to about 80 million: two new Los Angeleses. The more people, the less there is to go around. Ethiopia's per capita annual income is only $180, one of the lowest on Earth.

The environment is hurting, too, as coffee and tea plantations—as well as peasant farmers—spread into once wild areas, raising concern about the demise of one of the country's natural treasures: its biologically rich southwestern rain forest.

However, Samuel Assefa, the Ethiopian ambassador to the United States, said human suffering must be taken into consideration, too.

"We have a population of more than 80 million people, many of them living in rural and impoverished circumstances," he wrote in an e-mail. "Returning all cleared land to rain forest might be a victory for some extreme environmentalists, but it would condemn millions of my fellow citizens to starvation."

Atonement in a Cup

Starbucks has bought coffee from Africa for years. But now it is expanding rapidly there because it wants more of the continent's high-quality arabica beans. In Ethiopia alone, Starbucks purchases jumped 400 percent between 2002 and 2006.

While Starbucks is rapidly cloning retail outlets globally, 79 percent of its revenue last year was made in one caffeine-crazed country: the United States. With just 5 percent of the world's people, the United States drinks one-fifth of its coffee, more than any other nation.

Thanks largely to Starbucks, coffee is no longer just coffee. Now it is a vanilla soy latte, a java chip Frappuccino, a grande zebra mocha or—if you're feeling guilty— a Fair Trade-certified, bird-friendly, shade-grown caramel macchiato.

Starbucks did not pioneer the push for more equitable, conservation-based coffee. But it has woven the theme into everything from the earthy feel of its stores to its own certification program—called Coffee and Farmer Equity practices, or C.A.F.E.—that rewards farmers for meeting social and environmental goals.

"Social justice is becoming increasingly important to consumers," said industry analyst Judith Ganes-Chase as she flashed slides across a screen at a Long Beach coffee conference. One slide read: "Fair Trade is absolution in a cup."

Atonement, though, is not as simple as it may seem.

"It's very comfortable to believe Starbucks is doing the right thing—and to some degree, they are," said Eric Perkunder, a Seattle resident who worked as a Starbucks environmental manager in the 1980s and '90s. "They lull us into complacency. The stores are comfortable. You see pictures of people from origin countries. You believe

certain things they are telling you. But there's more to the story."

Dirt Road, Stick Huts

Part of that story lies in the southwestern corner of Ethiopia, in a swath of mountains not far from the Sudan border. There, a dirt road snakes through one of the country's largest coffee plantations—the Ethiopia Gemadro Estate—and comes to a halt in a dense mat of reeds and grasses.

A narrow path winds through the thicket and spills out into a clearing of stick huts. This is the home of an African Sheka tribe that for generations has lived off the land— catching fish, gathering wild honey and trapping animals in the forest. They call themselves the Shabuyye.

"The land over there used to belong to our forefathers," said Yatola, the tribal member in his 20s, as he nodded toward the plantation.

Conflict with local people and tribes is growing across southwest Ethiopia as coffee and tea plantations spread into the region under the government's effort to sow more development. At Gemadro, 2,496 acres of coffee were planted from 1998 to 2001 on land the company obtained from the government in a countylike jurisdiction called the Sheka Zone.

"One of Ethiopia's last remaining forests, Sheka Forest, is under huge pressure. . . . The rate of deforestation is now increasing and threatens the forest biodiversity . . . and the very livelihood" of forest-dwelling tribes, says the 2006 annual report of Melca Mahiber, an environmental group in the nation's capital, Addis Ababa.

However, Haile Michael Shiferaw, the plantation's manager—who attended the Long Beach coffee conference—said the Gemadro Estate had not displaced any tribe members.

"Before our farm was started," he said, "very few people were living in Gemadro."

Last year, Starbucks bought about 75,000 pounds of coffee from the Gemadro plantation and sold it as one of its "Black Apron Exclusives." At the time, the purchase was the 12th in the series of vintage offerings, six of which originated in Africa.

Starbucks packaged the beans in the fancy black box and inserted a flier touting the plantation's environmental and social track record. It also donated $15,000 to the Gemadro Estate for a school and health clinic.

"With its pure water supply, near pristine growing environment and dedication to conservation-based farming methods, this 2,300-hectare (5,700-acre) farm . . . is setting new standards for progressive, sustainable coffee farming," the flier said. "Gemadro workers and their families enjoy access to clean water, health care, housing and schools, all in keeping with the estate's commitment to maintain the highest standards of social and environmental stewardship."

Family's Income: 66 Cents a Day

Hailu is one of those workers. He stood outside his one-room, dirt-floor home, folded his arms across his chest and said that while he was happy to have a job, he was struggling to support his wife and family on just 6 Ethiopian birr per day—66 cents.

"Life is expensive," he said. "We have to go all the way to the town of Tepi (about 35 miles) for supplies." The round-trip bus ticket costs him four days' pay.

Plantation manager Shiferaw said Gemadro Estate wages are higher than the 55 cents a day workers earn at a government plantation near Tepi. Gemadro workers—most of whom are classified as temporary—also subsequently received a raise to between 77 cents and $1.10 a day, he said, adding, "We pay more than the minimum wage of the country."

That's still not a livable wage, according to the U.S. State Department. In a 2006 report on human rights in Ethiopia, the agency said that "there is no national minimum wage" and that public employees earn about $23 a month; private workers, $27. Those wages, it said, do "not provide a decent standard of living."

The Gemadro Estate is owned by Ethiopian-born Saudi Sheik Mohammed Al Amoudi, ranked by Forbes magazine as one of the world's 100 wealthiest individuals, with a net worth of $8 billion.

Al Amoudi owns many businesses in Ethiopia, from the posh Sheraton Hotel in Addis Ababa where rooms start at $270 a night—about a year's wages on the coffee plantation—to Ethio Agri-CEFT Plc, the farm management company that oversees the plantation.

Asked about the contrast between the sheik's wealth and the plantation wages, Assefa Tekle, Ethio Agri-CEFT's commercial manager, said, "There is no additional income that has been given from Sheik Al Amoudi. So what can you do? You have to be profitable to exist."

Ethiopian Ecology Suffers

Plantation wages are only one issue for workers and neighbors, however. The health care partially supported by Starbucks is another.

"When the estate came, they said they were going to give us adequate health service," said Geremew Gelito, an elder in the tiny village of Gemadro, where many estate workers live. He called the clinic bureaucratic and ineffective.

"As far as the promise of adequate health service, we have not received it," Gelito said. Shiferaw—the farm manager—said there are plans to improve the care. "It is not a very big clinic," he said, "but now we are increasing."

In his office above a furniture store in Addis Ababa, 2½ days' drive to the northeast, the agricultural manager for Ethio Agri-CEFT, Biru Abebe, said he was unaware of any complaints.

"Everybody goes and gets treatment," he said.

That even includes the native tribe, said Tekle, the commercial manager, a claim that exceeds that of Starbucks. "They are people of the environment so the farm has to give assistance."

But tribal member Yatola said the Shabuyye who live just downstream cannot get health care. "The company just gives medical attention to people who work for the company," he charged. Sitting in a stick hut, Yatola looked pensive. "We were isolated before. We didn't interact with anyone," he said as women outside pounded grain into mash with heavy wooden sticks. "But since the company has come, the road has acquainted us with the outside world."

Outsiders show up along the river, catching fish that feed the tribe, Yatola said. "There are less fish—and more people fishing," he said. "When we hear that the company, the way they have operated, they have created a nice relationship with the community, we know it's not true."

What's unfolding in the Gemadro region is not unique. An article in the April 2007 Journal of Agrarian Change points out that as coffee growing expands in southwest Ethiopia, the ecology can suffer.

"Environmental degradation is a serious concern with rates of deforestation estimated at 10,000 hectares per year (25,000 acres) in the coffee growing areas," the article said. "High levels of river pollution are also a major problem near coffee pulping and washing stations."

During the fall harvest, Yatola said, coffee processing pulp appears in the river from somewhere upstream. "The river becomes black, almost like oil," he said. "It smells like a dead horse."

Abebe, Ethio Agri-CEFT's agricultural manager, said the plantation has a lagoon to control pollution, that no waste flows from the Gemadro Estate. "The river is clean throughout the year. There is no pollution from our farm," he said. "Zero."

However, plantation manager Shiferaw said that not long ago valuable coffee beans did show up in the estate's wastewater lagoon, where a handful of workers and area farmers had dumped them in a failed theft attempt. "They are in prison now," he said.

In late February, four months after the bustling coffee harvest season, the Gemadro River looked clean. But in one of the ankle-deep side streams flowing into it, a white truck used to haul coffee was parked in the silvery water, being scrubbed of dirt and grease—a different but obvious pollution source.

"Sometimes it happens," acknowledged Tekle, the commercial manager.

"We don't have any control over that," Abebe said. "That road, though we made it, is a public road, so any truck can go and come."

Deforestation Takes a Toll

Although public, the road into the Gemadro Estate felt private. Armed guards checked vehicles entering or leaving to prevent coffee smuggling.

A row of rusty metal shacks looked like tool sheds, but were in fact worker housing. Even Shiferaw, the plantation manager, acknowledged they were not adequate.

"Yes, some is not. OK?" he said. "But we have a program to improve. When you see the standards of the country, it is better than most."

Along the bumpy dirt road, waxy green rows of coffee trees sprouted in rows, shaded by clumps of taller trees that not long ago were part of a denser, more diverse forest.

To Tadesse Gole—an ecologist in Addis Ababa and a native Ethiopian whose doctoral thesis at the University of Bonn, Germany, focused on preservation of wild arabica coffee—that manicured landscape is a biological calamity.

"This is an Afromontane rain forest—an area of high plant diversity, of unique epiphytic plants that grow on the branches of trees," Gole said. "We lose those plant species. And we lose many of the animals, birds and insects dependent on them."

Gole is the author of a recent study about the environmental and cultural impacts of coffee and tea plantations in Ethiopia, including the Gemadro Estate. The estate has spawned a wave of imitators, Gole said: smaller coffee and tea farms that are toppling more trees.

The estate itself is growing, too.

Last year, the Ethiopian Herald cited the plantation's project manager, Asenake Nigatu, telling the Ethiopian News Agency that Gemadro had "developed coffee on 1,000 hectares (about 2,470 acres) of land" it had obtained from the state investment bureau and had begun "activities to develop additional coffee on 1,500 hectares (about 3,700 acres) of land."

Gole tapped the touchpad on his laptop. An image based on satellite photography popped up showing land use changes in the Gemadro region from 1973 to 1987. A small puddle of red blotches appeared, indicating deforested areas. Gole tapped again, bringing up an image

through 2001—three years after the plantation started. The red blotches had spread across the map, like measles. His eyes widened.

"This is quite big," he said.

In his study, prepared for a future book, Gole analyzed coffee planting and forest change across two woredas—local districts—in the Sheka Zone. "The area under forest cover has dropped significantly in all parts," he wrote in the study. One area in particular stood out.

"The highest deforestation rate was observed in Gemadro, with (an) annual deforestation rate of 12.2 percent," he wrote.

But Abebe, the Ethio-Agri CEFT agricultural manager, said Gole's statements are misleading because the region was partially settled and cleared before the plantation came.

Ambassador Assefa agreed. "As I understand it, the land was largely cleared before Gemadro acquired the property," he said.

In addition, Abebe said, Gemadro is helping the land recover by incorporating conservation principles into its practices. To bolster his point, he pointed to an award the estate recently received from the Southern Nations, Nationalities and Peoples' Regional State for, he said, "being a model coffee farm."

Those model practices include planting grasses and reeds to slow erosion, planting shade trees for coffee and leaving 3,200 acres untouched for wildlife, Abebe said, adding that they "have even planted indigenous trees in the appropriate areas."

Gole, however, said such practices come up short. Many trees are non-native, he said, changing the composition of the forests. The plantation's Web site says cover crops planted there include some from South America, Mexico and India.

Struggle over Trademarks

The Ethiopian government's advocacy for its coffee industry—as well as for tea and other rural developments—has drawn international concern about the fate of its highland rain forests. A 2007 article by two German scientists blamed a lack of consistent forest policies.

"Ethiopia's montane rain forests are declining at an alarming rate," scientists Carmen Richerzhagen and Detlef Virchow wrote in the International Journal of Biotechnology. "The absence of a land use policy in Ethiopia creates spontaneous decisions on land allocations in a disorganized manner—therefore the forest is always the one to suffer."

But Ethiopia's push to grow more coffee drew plenty of encouragement at a conference in Addis Ababa in

February attended by representatives of the world's leading coffee companies, including Starbucks.

At the time, Starbucks and Ethiopia were locked in a struggle over the government's effort to trademark its famous coffee names—including Muel Alema's Sidamo—to create a distinctive brand that could funnel more profits back to the countryside.

Starbucks fought the effort, saying geographical certification programs, such as those in place for Colombian coffees, keep prices higher by guaranteeing that coffee from Colombia really is from Colombia.

"A trademark does not do that," said Hay, the Starbucks vice president, in a February interview in Addis Ababa. "It could be Sidamo and toilet paper. It doesn't mean anything about the region or the quality."

At times, the dispute turned bitter.

"What I don't understand is why Starbucks is resisting this," said Getachew Mengistie, director general of Ethiopia's Intellectual Property Office. "They are for improving the lives of the farmers. We are for improving the lives of the farmers. Where is the problem?"

In May, the issue was resolved in the government's favor, a positive step, said the ambassador.

"Starbucks is an important supporter of Ethiopia's efforts to control our specialty coffee brands, and it is critical that our relationship isn't about charity but about sound business," Ambassador Assefa said. "While the company only buys a small fraction of Ethiopia's coffee, our agreement will encourage market forces to allow Ethiopian farmers to capture a greater share of retail prices. This broad effort already has benefited thousands of poor farmers and could potentially benefit millions more."

Who Checked the Plantation?

Improving the lives of farmers and the environment is the goal of many coffee certification systems, such as Fair Trade, Rain Forest Alliance and Smithsonian Bird-Friendly. The Gemadro Estate has been approved by the European-based Utz Certified, an organization started by a Dutch coffee roaster and Guatemalan growers.

"It's good," said Yehasab Aschale, Utz's field representative in Ethiopia who said he toured the Gemadro plantation last year. "They are environmentally friendly. They are planting shade trees of the indigenous types. And they are improving the working conditions of the workers."

Starbucks also gave the estate's beans its own C.A.F.E. practices approval last year, signifying that the plantation protected the environment, paid workers fairly and provided them with decent housing.

Yet no one from Starbucks ever inspected the Gemadro plantation for C.A.F.E. certification. Dub Hay—the Starbucks global purchasing executive—said he knew little about the plantation because he hadn't been there. Starbucks bought the coffee after tasting it in Europe, Hay said, adding that a coffee buyer from Switzerland visited at some point.

No one from the company Starbucks pays to oversee C.A.F.E. verification, Scientific Certification Systems of Emeryville, inspected Gemadro either. Instead, the plantation hired and paid an Africa-based company to do the job—a common industry practice.

Then, something out of the ordinary happened: The African company's inspector was fired for doing a poor job, a fact that emerged only after The Bee asked about the verification process.

"Clearly, the inspector didn't do as good, or as thorough, a job as is to be expected in C.A.F.E. practices," said Ted Howes, vice president of corporate social responsibility for Scientific Certification Systems.

Howes declined to release a copy of the inspection report, but he said his company would visit the plantation this year. "There are issues we want to look at more closely," he said.

Dennis Macray, Starbucks' director of corporate responsibility, added that such problems "can happen in any kind of a system. . . . You can have something go wrong."

If the C.A.F.E. certification process was flawed, why did Starbucks certify the beans?

"I can't tell you," Macray said at the Long Beach conference. With that, the trail went cold. Macray did not return follow-up calls. Starbucks spokeswoman Stacey Krum said details are confidential.

Krum, however, defended C.A.F.E. practices in general.

"There isn't a standard code for the coffee industry; this is something we are learning as we go along," she said. "And we are proud of it and confident it is achieving results."

Bee reporter **TOM KNUDSON** spent three weeks in Ethiopia during his four months of reporting this story, including journeys to the Gemadro Estate, the Sidamo and Yirgacheffe regions, and an international coffee conference in Addis Ababa. He interviewed coffee farmers, plantation workers, tribal people, scientists and coffee industry leaders in Africa and the United States. And he reviewed dozens of studies, reports, books and scientific journal articles about coffee growing and marketing. Travel and research were underwritten by a grant from the Alicia Patterson Foundation in Washington, D.C.

Where the Money Went

How did developing countries wind up owing $2.5 trillion?
Hint: Western institutions haven't exactly been innocent bystanders.

JAMES S. HENRY

By the dawn of the 21st century, after 30 years of development strategies that were designed in Washington, New York, London, Frankfurt, Paris, and Tokyo, and trillions of dollars in foreign loans, aid, and investment, more than half of the world's population still finds daily life a struggle, surviving on less than $2 a day—about the same level of real income they had 30 years ago. More than two billion people still lack access to basic amenities like electricity, clean water, sanitation, land titles, police and fire protection, and paved roads, let alone their own phones, bank accounts, or medical care.

And despite years of rhetoric about debt relief and dozens of structural adjustment plans, the real value of Third World debt has continued to grow, to more than $2.5 trillion. The cost of servicing that debt now exceeds $375 billion a year—more than all Third World spending on health or education, almost 20 times what developing countries receive each year in foreign aid, and more than twice as much as they have recently received annually in foreign direct investment.

How did 30 years of greatly expanded international lending, investment, aid, and development efforts end up producing such a fiasco? Where did all that money actually go? And what can we do, if anything, to undo all the damage that has been done?

There is no shortage of armchair analyses of the so-called Third World debt crisis, or even of the globalization crisis that succeeded it and continues to this day. The 1980s debt crisis became visible as early as August 1982, when Mexico, Argentina, and 26 other countries suddenly rescheduled their debts at once. Our disappointments with globalization have been a popular subject for economists and development policy-makers at least since the Mexico crunch of January 1995, as amplified by the East Asian and Russian crises in 1997–98, and in Turkey, Ecuador, Bolivia, Argentina, Venezuela, and other countries since then.

But there has been no detailed account of the *structural roots* of this prolonged development crisis. Among orthodox economists, the conventional wisdom is that the crisis originated in a combination of unpredictable shocks and Third World policies that were either stupid or corrupt, on top of factors like bad geographic luck. In other words, we have a slightly more sophisticated version of the same blame-the-victim ideology that ruling elites have used for centuries to explain poverty and wealth: It is either "tough luck" or "their own damn fault."

For example, the conventional view of the 1980s debt crisis is that, in response to the 1973 oil-price rise, Western banks recycled oil deposits from the Middle East back to the Third World, lending to finance oil imports and development projects. Independently, a huge tidal wave of capital flight sprang up alongside all this lending. Then an unfortunate combination of events—rising interest rates, recession, and the 1982 Falklands conflict—supposedly took everyone by surprise. In this version of the crisis, no one was responsible for it. There were no villains or victims—just innocent bystanders.

Conventional portraits of the global development crisis are fairy tales.

Similarly, in the case of more recent debacles in submerging markets like Indonesia and Thailand, the official story is that these resulted almost entirely from Third World mistakes and market imperfections; poorly designed bank regulations, faulty accounting, inexplicable failures to privatize and liberalize fast enough, or indigenous "corruption, cronyism, and collusion." The notion that there might be serious oversimplifications in the development paradigms themselves, that Western banks, investors, policy-makers, and the structure of international capital markets might have aggravated such problems—or that they might have conspired with local elites and even taught them a thing or two about "clever chicanery"—has received much less attention. And while numerous globalization critics have recently emerged, including some prominent economists and international investors as well as a rising tide of mass protesters, much of this criticism has dealt in generalities, lacking the gory investigative details needed to drive the points home and do justice to the problem's global scale.

Behind the Official Story

The fact is that conventional portraits of the global development crisis are economists' fairy tales. They leave out the blood and guts of what really happened—all the payoffs for privatizations, fraudulent loans, intentionally wasteful projects, black market "round-trip" transfers, arms deals, insider deals, and the behind-the-scenes operation of the global-haven banking network that has facilitated all this and more. They ignore the fact that in the mid-1970s, and again in the mid-1990s, repeated warnings of deep trouble were ignored: Irresponsible overlending, poorly conceived projects and privatizations, phony back-to-back loans, outright looting of central-bank reserves, and massive capital flight continued right under the noses of Western bankers and government officials who were in a position to do something about the problems but chose not to.

This begs the question of why some developing countries and banks got into so much more trouble than others, and why certain bankers, investors, and officials got rich. Standard analyses focus on uncontrollable shocks to the system, skate far too quickly over the structure of that system itself, and ignore the systematic role of specific global interests in shaping this structure.

Most importantly, the official story of shocks, surprises, and indigenous corruption ignores the pivotal role that was often played by sophisticated banks and multinationals. They were aided by their governments and the local elites in pressing countries first to overborrow, then to overservice their debts—to honor their overpriced privatization contracts—and then to liberalize and privatize far too quickly. Many of these players were also aggressively recruiting flight capital and investment deals from these very same countries and teaching their clients the basics of how to launder, plunder, and conceal.

The conventional fairy tales gloss over many key questions. What really became of all the loans and investments? Why did foreign banks lend so much money to these governments, even while their private banking arms knew full well that they were financing a massive capital-flight exodus? Who ended up owning all the juicy assets? How much did the IMF and the World Bank know about all these shenanigans, and why didn't they do more to stop them?

It is not easy to give precise answers to such questions. Studying the global underground economy is an exercise in night vision, not double-entry accounting or armchair analysis. One actually has to get up out of the armchair and do some investigative reporting. And the patterns that become visible turn out to be full of villains and victims.

Unfortunately, it has taken years to uncover the truth about such matters, and we've really only begun to scratch the surface. In the last decade, bits and pieces of this story have become more accessible. The demise of "kleptocracies" like those of Abacha, Andres Perez, Collor, Duvalier, Marcos, Mobuto, Milosevic, Salinas, Suharto, and Stroessner focused attention on the billions that such nefarious regimes managed to steal and stash abroad. The collapse of leading money-laundering banks like BCCI and BNL, and the corrupt regimes of Salinas in Mexico, Menem in Argentina, the ruling cliques in Turkey, and Suharto in Indonesia demonstrated the risks that corrupt banking poses to the entire global financial system.

However, partly because this kind of investigative research is so difficult, there are only a few rather armchairish studies of the global underground economy and the "real-economique" of underdevelopment. And these have also usually treated the subjects of irresponsible lending, wasteful projects, capital flight, corruption, money laundering, and havens separately, In fact, they go hand in hand. The rise of Third World lending in the 1970s and 1980s laid the foundations for the haven network that now shelters the wealth of the world's most venal citizens. And the corruption that this network facilitated was just a special case of a much more general phenomenon—the export of vast quantities of capital and tax-free incomes by the elites of poor countries, even as their countries were incurring vast debts and struggling to service them. Individual kleptocratic regimes and evil dictators come and go, but this sophisticated transnational system is more vibrant than ever.

A Marshall Plan in Reverse

This haven network has matured in the last 30 years, coinciding with the rise of global lending, the liberalization of capital markets, and the development crisis. Of course, "private banking" is hardly new. Except for electronic transfers and airplanes, most of its paraphernalia—secret accounts, shell companies, black-market exchanges, mis-invoicing, back-to-back loans, and backdated transactions—were very important early innovations in the history of capitalism. They helped to bring "mattress money" out into the open so that it could be productively invested.

For decades, these tools were underutilized. Then, from the 1970s through the 1990s, their use expanded tremendously under the impact of the greatest torrent of loose lending in history. This torrent was driven by a coalition of influential interests that included leading Western private banks, equipment vendors, and construction companies—plus their allies among aid donors, export finance agencies, the multilateral banks, and local elites. It drove a hole in developing-country defenses against overborrowing and created a source of fundamental instability in the world's financial system that continues to this day.

It is possible to estimate the volume and composition of the flight capital that was financed by all this lending. Sag Harbor Group estimates rely on a combination of statistical methods and interviews with more than 100 private bankers and their wealthy clients. They show that at least *half* the funds borrowed by the largest "debtor" countries flowed right out the back door, usually the same year or even the same month that the loans arrived. For the developing world as a whole, this amounted to a huge Marshall Plan in reverse.

The corresponding stock of unrecorded foreign wealth owned by Third World elites is even larger than these outflows, since the outflows were typically invested in tax havens where—unlike the earnings of low-income "guest workers"—they accumulate tax-free interest, dividends, and capital gains. By the late 1980s, there was already enough anonymous Third World flight wealth on hand in Europe and the United States that the income it generated would have been able to service the *entire* Third World debt—if only this stock of "anonymous capital" had been subjected to a modest global tax. By the late 1990s, the market value of private wealth accumulated outside developing countries by their resident elites totaled at least $1.5 trillion. As one Federal Reserve official chuckled at the time, "The problem is not that these countries don't have any assets. The problem is, they're in Miami."

Most of the resulting flight wealth—defined simply as foreign capital whose true ownership is concealed—ended up in just a handful of First World havens. Their identity may surprise those who usually associate "tax havens" and money laundering with obscure nameplate banks in sultry tropical paradises. BCCI's exceptional case notwithstanding, shady banks have never been very important in the flight market—most rich people would never trust them. Rather, Third World decapitalization has taken place with the active aid of pre-eminent global financial institutions, including Citigroup, JP Morgan Chase (Chemical MHT), UBS, Barclays, Credit Suisse First Boston, ABN-AMRO Merrill Lynch, ING Bank, the Bank of New York, American Express Bank, and two dozen other leading Swiss, British, Dutch, French, German, and Austrian banks. These august institutions led the way in knowingly facilitating these perverse capital flows. In fact, despite their reputations as lenders, many of these institutions were actually net borrowers from poor countries for most of the last 30 years. International private banking—a large share of which was for Third World elites—thus became one of their most profitable lines of business.

The leading global banks were successful at profiting from Third World grief.

Because their leading global banks were so successful at profiting from Third World grief, the United States, the United Kingdom, and Switzerland were also—despite their reputations as major capital providers and aid donors—net debtors with respect to the Third World throughout the last 30 years. It is really misleading to speak of a "Third World debt" crisis—for developing countries, it has really been an *assets* crisis, while for these key First World countries and their banks, it was an incredibly profitable *global bleed-out*.

The upshot is that ownership of Third Wealth onshore and offshore wealth is even more concentrated than it was before the 1980s debt crisis and the 1990s privatization wave. Depending on the country, the top 1 percent of households now accounts for 70 to 90 percent of all private financial wealth and real estate. We are not talking about millions of diligent middle-class savers. These are the 700 members of the Rio Country Club, the 1,000 top landowners of Argentina, El Salvador's *catorce*, the 50 top families of Caracas, the 300 top families of Mexico City, and so on. These are not people who merely observe the rules of the game. When a minister builds a dam, nationalizes a private

company or its debts, privatizes a state enterprise, and floats a currency or manipulates tax provisions, these folks have the inside track. This is not to say that there are no new self-made Third World elites, or that the top tier is limited to capitalists—there are also quite a few politicians, generals, diplomats, union bosses, and even a bishop or cardinal.

Conventional explanations ignore the international community's responsibility.

But the overall system is beautifully symbiotic. On the one hand, havens provide an ideal way to launder loot. On the other, in the long run, corruption, insider deals, and the inequalities they generate encourage still more disinvestments and emigration. For individuals living in these countries, of course, the incentives for engaging in money laundering were often so powerful that it would have been quixotic not to do so. At the macroeconomic level, however, conventional explanations of capital flight, overborrowing, and mismanaged privatizations, which focus on technical policy errors and the "riskiness" of Third World markets, ignore these systemic factors. They also ignore the international community's collective responsibility for perpetuating a system that encourages noneconomic lending, tax evasion, flight-prone speculative investments, and perverse privatizations.

The Borderline of Existence

Other key ingredients in the "money trail" puzzle, in addition to capital flight, were wasteful projects and arms purchases. Hundreds of billions of Third World loans were devoted to nonproductive projects and the corruption that encouraged them. Many of these debt-financed projects also had harmful long-term consequences. In some cases, there was novel chicanery on a purely local level. But what is most striking are the global patterns—overpricing, rigged bids, endless delays, loans to front companies with close ties to the government, investments in dubious technologies and excessively capital-intensive projects, "public" projects undertaken for private motives, and private debts assumed by the state.

Over and over again, the handiwork of the very same international banks, contractors, equipment vendors, and export credit agencies grew fat while the countries grew poorer. These were not ideological errors—regimes of different ideological hues proved equally vulnerable. Nor were they due to random policy mistakes or indigenous corruption. A sophisticated *transnational system* of influential institutions contrived to produce similar mistakes over and over again, in every region of the world. Corruption has always existed, but without this global system, the abuses simply could not have been generalized on such a massive scale.

Recently, some of the leading players in the global haven industry, Citigroup and JP Morgan Chase, had also applied their "haveneering" skills to help Enron, WorldCom, and Global Crossing, using Panama and Cayman Islands shell companies to conceal billions in off-balance-sheet loans from their stockholders. When this scandal surfaced in 2001–02, the resulting bankruptcies cost investors several hundred billion dollars. Analysts who had not followed the history of these banks in the Third World were shocked . . . shocked! Those who knew them better were just reminded that "character is destiny" and that "what goes around comes around." As a wise, rather ethical business colleague of mine once said, "The problem with a rat race is that, even if you win, you are still a rat."

The emphasis on these darker details is not meant to imply that every banker was a briber, or every public official a crook. But dirty money, bad banking, money laundering, and self-seeking chicanery were not incidental to the development crisis. As a governor of the Bank of International Settlements admitted privately in the late 1980s, "If Latin America's corrupt politicians simply gave back all the money they've stolen from their own countries, the debt problem could be solved. And most of that thievery simply could not have occurred without the active assistance of leading First World banks, contractors, vendors, multilateral lenders, advisors, and governments. This was not a natural catastrophe but a *manmade* one. For the developing world to overcome it, it is not only the developing world that will have to be reformed."

Today, despite decades of official development efforts and trillions in foreign loans, bonds, and investments, the vast majority of the world's residents are living on the borderline of existence. Yet the "developing countries" they inhabit are not really poor at all, in terms of natural resources, technical know-how, and raw human talent.

Some have searched for the explanation among the natural disadvantages of climate, pestilence, and topography that many of these countries experience. Some have pointed toward cultural deficiencies—for example, a purported lack of trust outside the family in some countries, or an unusual propensity for corruption at all levels of society in others. Some have invoked the *deus ex machina* of "policy errors" like overvalued exchange rates, excessive borrowing, and weak security laws, as if these were uncaused causes and as if policy was made in a disinterested vacuum, where ministers don't own bank accounts and everything would have worked out fine if only they'd been Ivy-educated. Still others have emphasized the ill winds of misfortune to which developing countries are subject—the HIV/AIDS epidemic in Africa, China, India, and Russia; Indonesia's bad luck in having Thailand as a neighbor when its currency plummeted in July 1997, Brazil's bad luck in having Russia's 1998 crisis compound Indonesia's, Argentina's in having Brazil as a neighbor, and so on.

These explanations are all the profound contribution that First World countries and their global agents have made, not only in the last 30 years but for much longer, in tolerating, contributing to, and profiting from the immiseration around them.

If one really looks objectively at why countries like the Philippines, Guatemala, Indonesia, the Congo, South Africa, Argentina, Venezuela, Brazil, Mexico, Haiti, and India have ended up as they have in the world economy, one cannot ignore the negative influence of First World corporations, governments, and financial institutions. As a rule, the closer and more unequal those relationships have been, the worse things have turned out for developing countries.

Today, the developing world is in its deepest crisis in a half-century. The First World, now so concerned about security, needs to place these security concerns and the "war on terrorism" in the context of an even more global war—underdevelopment. The world is simply getting too rickety, too interdependent, for us to ignore this other war any longer. Forest fires in the Amazon or Kalimantan set by poor people clearing land because they can't find jobs threaten the whole world's air supply. Epidemics left untreated in Africa or Russia threaten to create drug-resistant diseases that could sweep the planet. And the hatred bred by the real "weapons of mass destruction"—outrageous poverty and inequality—are only a plane or boat ride away in Port-au-Prince, Jakarta, Cairo, Kabul, and Karachi.

The first step is understanding. First Worlders, in particular, are living in a bubble—only about 20 percent of Americans have passports, just 21 percent of non-Hispanic Americans speak a second language, less than a fifth of adults have traveled abroad, and a poll taken in late 2002 showed that only 13 percent of 18-to-24-year-olds in the United States could even find Iraq on a map, 14 percent could find Israel, 31 percent could find the United Kingdom, and 42 percent could find Japan, and only two-thirds could even find the Pacific Ocean. This kind of ignorance is not just unfortunate. It is dangerous. It is especially menacing to the citizens of the Third World, because the First World now has more political, economic, and military hegemony than ever before. It is also a menace to ourselves, because if this power is not used wisely, a growing portion of the Third World will simply disappear into "the Fourth World," a vast, impoverished, hostile labor camp without visitors or investments. And that, in turn, will only heighten our insecurities, raise the drawbridge even higher, and increase hostilities.

Those who wish to alter these current trends toward immiseration and anti-development may choose to put their faith in the global economy, free trade, investment, technology, and entrepreneurship. But these market-based nostrums have not been sufficient. To go beyond them, people will need to invest in their own globalization, their own practical education about how the world really works.

Today, the developing world is in its deepest crisis in a half-century.

This kind of education is not available in university economics courses. People need to understand why political parties, the police, the military, the media, the courts, and the church are often so unresponsive to popular demands, even in nominal "democracies"; why senior officials, banks, corporations, and the elite continue to prefer monster projects to schools and clinics; why courts rarely enforce laws against people of means, let alone global companies like Freeport McMoran or Citigroup; why the radical liberalization of global capital markets and trade has taken precedence over the enforcement of tax codes, labor laws, health codes, security regulation, environmental laws, education rights, pension reform, and property rights for ordinary people; and why the poor are subject to unavoidable excise taxes while the elite are encouraged to invest, tax-free, at home and abroad.

They also need to ask why developed and developing countries alike, after 50 years of malpractice, still permit First World bankers, corporations, and investors to engage in business practices in the Third World that are grossly illegal; why the anti-foreign bribery statutes of the United States and the OECD countries are so underenforced; why undocumented capital is recruited so aggressively from developing countries while undocumented labor is increasingly harassed; and why the huge proportion of the Third World's $2.5 trillion debt that was contracted illegally and spent on failed projects and elite bank accounts deserve to be serviced at all.

But first, they may want to start with the question of where the money went.

JAMES S. HENRY is founder and managing director of the Sag Harbor Group, a strategy consulting firm, former chief economist for McKinsey & Co., and former vice president of strategy for IBM/Lotus. From *The Blood Bankers: Tales From the Underground Global Economy* (Four Walls Eight Windows). © 2003

Ensuring Energy Security

Daniel Yergin

Old Questions, New Answers

On the eve of World War I, First Lord of the Admiralty Winston Churchill made a historic decision: to shift the power source of the British navy's ships from coal to oil. He intended to make the fleet faster than its German counterpart. But the switch also meant that the Royal Navy would rely not on coal from Wales but on insecure oil supplies from what was then Persia. Energy security thus became a question of national strategy. Churchill's answer? "Safety and certainty in oil," he said, "lie in variety and variety alone."

Since Churchill's decision, energy security has repeatedly emerged as an issue of great importance, and it is so once again today. But the subject now needs to be rethought, for what has been the paradigm of energy security for the past three decades is too limited and must be expanded to include many new factors. Moreover, it must be recognized that energy security does not stand by itself but is lodged in the larger relations among nations and how they interact with one another.

Energy security will be the number one topic on the agenda when the group of eight highly industrialized countries (G-8) meets in St. Petersburg in July. The renewed focus on energy security is driven in part by an exceedingly tight oil market and by high oil prices, which have doubled over the past three years. But it is also fueled by the threat of terrorism, instability in some exporting nations, a nationalist backlash, fears of a scramble for supplies, geopolitical rivalries, and countries' fundamental need for energy to power their economic growth. In the background—but not too far back—is renewed anxiety over whether there will be sufficient resources to meet the world's energy requirements in the decades ahead.

Concerns over energy security are not limited to oil. Power blackouts on both the East and West Coasts of the United States, in Europe, and in Russia, as well as chronic shortages of electric power in China, India, and other developing countries, have raised worries about the reliability of electricity supply systems. When it comes to natural gas, rising demand and constrained supplies mean that North America can no longer be self-reliant, and so the United States is joining the new global market in natural gas that will link countries, continents, and prices together in an unprecedented way.

At the same time, a new range of vulnerabilities has become more evident. Al Qaeda has threatened to attack what Osama bin Laden calls the "hinges" of the world's economy, that is, its critical infrastructure—of which energy is among the most crucial elements. The world will increasingly depend on new sources of supply from places where security systems are still being developed, such as the oil and natural gas fields offshore of West Africa and in the Caspian Sea. And the vulnerabilities are not limited to threats of terrorism, political turmoil, armed conflict, and piracy. In August and September 2005, Hurricanes Katrina and Rita delivered the world's first integrated energy shock, simultaneously disrupting flows of oil, natural gas, and electric power.

Events since the beginning of this year have underlined the significance of the issue. The Russian-Ukrainian natural gas dispute temporarily cut supplies to Europe. Rising tensions over Tehran's nuclear program brought threats from Iran, the second-largest OPEC producer, to "unleash an oil crisis." And scattered attacks on some oil facilities reduced exports from Nigeria, which is a major supplier to the United States.

Since Churchill's day, the key to energy security has been diversification. This remains true, but a wider approach is now required that takes into account the rapid evolution of the global energy trade, supply-chain vulnerabilities, terrorism, and the integration of major new economies into the world market.

Although in the developed world the usual definition of energy security is simply the availability of sufficient supplies at affordable prices, different countries interpret what the concept means for them differently. Energy-exporting countries focus on maintaining the "security of demand" for their exports, which after all generate the overwhelming share of their government revenues. For Russia, the aim is to reassert state control over "strategic resources" and gain primacy over the main pipelines and market channels through which it ships its hydrocarbons to international markets. The concern for developing countries is how changes in energy prices affect their balance of payments. For China and India, energy security now lies in their ability to rapidly adjust to their new dependence on global markets, which represents a major shift away from their former commitments to self-sufficiency. For Japan, it means offsetting its stark scarcity of domestic resources through diversification, trade, and investment. In Europe, the major debate centers on how to manage dependence on imported natural gas—and in most countries, aside from France and Finland, whether to build new nuclear power plants and perhaps to return to (clean) coal. And the United States must face the uncomfortable fact that its goal of "energy independence"—a phrase that has become a mantra since it was first articulated by Richard Nixon four weeks after the 1973 embargo was put in place—is increasingly at odds with reality.

Shocks to Supply and Demand

After the Persian Gulf War, concerns over energy security seemed to recede. Saddam Hussein's bid to dominate the Persian Gulf had been foiled, and it appeared that the world oil market would remain a market (rather than becoming Saddam's instrument of political manipulation) and that supplies would be abundant at prices that would not impede the global economy. But 15 years later, prices are high, and fears of shortages dominate energy markets. What happened? The answer is to be found in both markets and politics.

The last decade has witnessed a substantial increase in the world's demand for oil, primarily because of the dramatic economic growth in developing countries, in particular China and India. As late as 1993, China was self-sufficient in oil. Since then, its GDP has almost tripled and its demand for oil has more than doubled. Today, China imports 3 million barrels of oil per day, which accounts for almost half of its total consumption. China's share of the world oil market is about 8 percent, but its share of total growth in demand since 2000 has been 30 percent. World oil demand has grown by 7 million barrels per day since 2000; of this growth, 2 million barrels each day have gone to China. India's oil consumption is currently less than 40 percent of China's, but because India has now embarked on what the economist Vijay Kelkar calls the "growth turnpike," its demand for oil will accelerate. (Ironically, India's current high growth rates were partly triggered by the spike in oil prices during the 1990–91 Persian Gulf crisis. The resulting balance-of-payments shock left India with almost no foreign currency reserves, opening the door to the reforms initiated by then Finance Minister Manmohan Singh, now India's prime minister.)

The impact of growth in China, India, and elsewhere on the global demand for energy has been far-reaching. In the 1970s, North America consumed twice as much oil as Asia. Last year, for the first time ever, Asia's oil consumption exceeded North America's. The trend will continue: half of the total growth in oil consumption in the next 15 years will come from Asia, according to projections by Cambridge Energy Research Associates (CERA). However, Asia's growing impact became widely apparent only in 2004, when the best global economic performance in a generation translated into a "demand shock"—that is, unexpected worldwide growth in petroleum consumption that represented a rate of growth that was more than double the annual average growth rates of the preceding decade. China's demand in 2004 rose by an extraordinary 16 percent compared to 2003, driven partly by electricity bottlenecks that led to a surge in oil use for improvised electric generation. U.S. consumption also grew strongly in 2004, as did that of other countries. The result was the tightest oil market in three decades (except for the first couple of months after Saddam's invasion of Kuwait in 1990). Hardly any wells were available to produce

additional oil. That remains the case today, and there is a further catch. What additional oil might be produced cannot be easily sold because it would not be of sufficiently good quality to be used in the world's available oil refineries.

Refining capacity is a major constraint on supply, because there is a significant mismatch between the product requirements of the world's consumers and refineries' capabilities. Although often presented solely as a U.S. problem, inadequate refining capacity is in fact a global phenomenon. The biggest growth in demand worldwide has been for what are called "middle distillates": diesel, jet fuel, and heating oil. Diesel is a favorite fuel of European motorists, half of whom now buy diesel cars, and it is increasingly used to power economic growth in Asia, where it is utilized not just for transportation but also to generate electricity. But the global refining system does not have enough so-called deep conversion capacity to turn heavier crudes into middle distillates. This shortfall in capacity has created additional demand for the lighter grades of crude, such as the benchmark WTI (West Texas Intermediate), further boosting prices.

Last year, for the first time ever, Asia's oil consumption exceeded North America's.

Other factors, including problems in several major energy-exporting countries, have also contributed to high prices. Indeed, the current era of high oil prices really began in late 2002 and early 2003, just before the start of the Iraq war, when President Hugo Chavez's drive to consolidate his control over Venezuela's political system, state-owned oil company, and oil revenues sparked strikes and protests. This shut down oil production in Venezuela, which had been among the most reliable of oil exporters since World War II. The loss of oil to the world market from the strikes was significant, greater than the impact of the war in Iraq on supplies. Venezuela's output has never fully recovered, and it is currently running about 500,000 barrels per day below the prestrike level.

Saddam's failing regime in Iraq did not torch oil facilities during the 2003 war, as many had feared, but the large postwar surge in Iraqi output that some had expected has certainly not occurred. The tens of billions of dollars required to bring the industry's output back up to its 1978 peak of 3.5 million barrels per day have not been invested both because of the continuing attacks on the country's infrastructure and work force and because of uncertainty about Iraq's political and legal structures and the contractual framework for investment. As a result, Iraqi oil exports are 30 to 40 percent below prewar levels.

Over the past five years, by contrast, Russia's oil fields have been central to the growth of worldwide supply, providing almost 40 percent of the world's total production increase since 2000. But the growth of Russia's output slowed substantially last year because of political risks, insufficient investment, uncertainties over government policy, regulatory obstacles, and, in some regions, geological challenges. Meanwhile, despite such problems in some major supplier countries, other sources that get less attention, such as Brazil's and Angola's offshore fields, were increasing their output—until Hurricanes Katrina and Rita shut down 27 percent of U.S. oil production (as well as 21 percent of U.S. refining capacity). As late as January 2006, U.S. facilities that before the hurricanes had produced 400,000 barrels of oil a day were still out of operation. Altogether, the experience of the last couple of years confirms the maxim that a tight market is a market vulnerable to events.

All of these problems have provoked a new round of fears that the world is running out of oil. Such bouts of anxiety have recurred since as far back as the 1880s. But global output has actually increased by 60 percent since the 1970s, the last time the world was supposedly running out of oil. (The demand shock of 2004 attracted more notice than the cooling off of the growth in demand that occurred in 2005, when Chinese consumption did not grow at all and world demand returned to the average growth rates of 1994–2003.) Although talk about an imminent peak in oil output followed by a rapid decline has become common in some circles, CERA's field-by-field analysis of projects and development plans indicates that net productive capacity could increase by as much as 20 to 25 percent over the next decade. Despite the current pessimism, higher oil prices will do what higher prices usually do: fuel growth in new supplies by significantly increasing investment and by turning marginal opportunities into commercial prospects (as well as, of course, moderating demand and stimulating the development of alternatives).

A good part of this capacity growth is already in the works. A substantial part of it will come from the exploitation of nontraditional supplies, ranging from Canadian oil sands (also known as tar sands) to deposits in ultradeep water to a very high-quality diesel-like fuel derived from natural gas—all made possible by continuing advances in technology. But conventional supplies will grow as well: Saudi Arabia is on track to increase its capacity by about 15 percent, to over 12 million barrels per day, by 2009, and other projects are under way elsewhere, such as in the Caspian Sea and even in the United States' offshore fields. Although energy companies will be prospecting in more difficult environments, the major obstacle to the development of new supplies is not geology but what happens above ground: namely, international affairs, politics, decision-making by governments, and energy investment and new technological development. It should be noted, however, that current projections do show that after 2010 the major growth in supplies will come from fewer countries than it comes from today, which could accentuate security concerns.

A New Framework

The current energy security system was created in response to the 1973 Arab oil embargo to ensure coordination among the industrialized countries in the event of a disruption in supply, encourage collaboration on energy policies, avoid bruising scrambles for supplies, and deter any future use of an "oil weapon" by exporters. Its key elements are the Paris-based International Energy Agency (IEA), whose members are the industrialized countries; strategic stockpiles of oil, including the U.S. Strategic Petroleum Reserve; continued monitoring and analysis of energy markets and policies; and energy conservation and coordinated emergency sharing of supplies in the event of a disruption. The emergency system was set up to offset major disruptions that threatened the global economy and stability, not to manage prices and the commodity cycle. Since the system's inception in the 1970s, a coordinated emergency drawdown of strategic stockpiles has occurred only twice: on the eve of the Gulf War in 1991 and in the autumn of 2005 after Hurricane Katrina. (The system was also readied in anticipation of possible use before January 1, 2000, because of concerns over the potential problems arising from the Y2K computer bug, during the shutdown of production in Venezuela in 2002–3, and in the spring of 2003, before the invasion of Iraq.)

Experience has shown that to maintain energy security countries must abide by several principles. The first and most familiar is what Churchill urged more than 90 years ago: diversification of supply. Multiplying one's supply sources reduces the impact of a disruption in supply from one source by providing alternatives, serving the interests of both consumers and producers, for whom stable markets are a prime concern. But diversification is not enough. A second principle is resilience, a "security margin" in the energy supply system that provides a buffer against shocks and facilitates recovery after disruptions. Resilience can come from many factors, including sufficient spare production capacity, strategic reserves, backup supplies of equipment, adequate storage capacity along the supply chain, and the stockpiling of critical parts for electric power production and distribution, as well as carefully conceived plans for responding to disruptions that may affect large regions. Hence the third principle: recognizing the reality of integration. There is only one oil market, a complex and worldwide system that moves and consumes about 86 million barrels of oil every day. For all consumers, security resides in the stability of this market. Secession is not an option.

A fourth principle is the importance of information. High-quality information underpins well-functioning markets. On an international level, the IEA has led the way in improving the flow of information about world markets and energy prospects. That work is being complemented by the new International Energy Forum, which will seek to integrate information from producers and consumers. Information is no less crucial in a crisis, when consumer panics can be instigated by a mixture of actual disruptions, rumors, and fear. Reality can be obscured by accusations, acrimony, outrage, and a fevered hunt for conspiracies, transforming a difficult situation into something much worse. In such situations, governments and the private sector should collaborate to counter panics with high-quality, timely information. The U.S. government can promote flexibility and market adjustments by expediting its communication with companies and permitting the exchange of information among them, with appropriate antitrust safeguards, when necessary.

As important as these principles are, the past several years have highlighted the need to expand the concept of energy security in two critical dimensions: the recognition of the globalization of the energy security system, which can be achieved especially by engaging China and India, and the acknowledgment of the fact that the entire energy supply chain needs to be protected.

China's thirst for energy has become a decisive plot element in suspense novels and films. Even in the real world there is no shortage of suspicion: some in the United States see a Chinese grand strategy to preempt the United States and the West when it comes to new oil and gas supplies, and some strategists in Beijing fear that the United States may someday try to interdict China's foreign energy supplies. But the actual situation is less dramatic. Despite all the attention being paid to China's efforts to secure international petroleum reserves, for example, the entire amount that China currently produces per day outside of its own borders is equivalent to just 10 percent of the daily production of one of the supermajor oil companies. If there were a serious controversy between the United States and China involving oil or gas, it would likely arise not because of a competition for the resources themselves, but rather because they had become part of larger foreign policy issues (such as a clash over a specific regime or over how to respond to Iran's nuclear program). Indeed, from the viewpoint of consumers in North America, Europe, and Japan, Chinese and Indian investment in the development of new energy supplies around the world is not a threat but something to be desired, because it means there will be more energy available for everyone in the years ahead as India's and China's demand grows.

It would be wiser—and indeed it is urgent—to engage these two giants in the global network of trade and investment rather than see them tilt toward a mercantilist, state-to-state approach. Engaging India and China will require understanding what energy security means for them. Both countries are rapidly moving from self-sufficiency to integration into the world economy, which means they will grow increasingly dependent on global markets even as they are under tremendous pressure to deliver economic growth for their huge populations, which cope with energy shortages and blackouts on a daily basis. Thus, the primary concern for both China and India is to ensure that they have sufficient energy to support economic growth and prevent debilitating energy shortfalls that could trigger social and political turbulence. For India, where the balance-of-payments crisis of 1990 is still on policymakers' minds, international production is also a way to hedge against high oil prices. And so India and China, and other key countries such as Brazil, should be brought into coordination with the existing IEA energy security system to assure them that their interests will be protected in the event of turbulence and to ensure that the system works more effectively.

Security and Flexibility

The current model of energy security, which was born of the 1973 crisis, focuses primarily on how to handle any disruption of oil supplies from producing countries. Today, the concept of energy security needs to be expanded to include the protection of the entire energy supply chain and infrastructure—an awesome task. In the United States alone, there are more than 150 refineries, 4,000 offshore platforms, 160,000 miles of oil pipelines, facilities to handle 15 million barrels of oil a day of imports and exports, 10,400 power plants, 160,000 miles of high-voltage electric power transmission lines and millions of miles of electric power distribution wires, 410 underground gas storage fields, and 1.4 million miles of natural gas pipelines. None of the world's complex, integrated supply chains were built with security, defined in this broad way, in mind. Hurricanes Katrina and Rita brought a new perspective to the security question by demonstrating how fundamental the electric grid is to everything else. After the storms, the Gulf Coast refineries and the big U.S. pipelines were unable to operate—not because they were damaged, but because they could not get power.

Energy interdependence and the growing scale of energy trade require continuing collaboration among both producers and consumers to ensure the security of the entire supply chain. Long-distance, cross-border pipelines are becoming an ever-larger fixture in the global energy trade. There are also many chokepoints along the transportation routes of seaborne oil and, in many cases, liquefied natural gas (LNG) that create particular vulnerabilities: the Strait of Hormuz, which lies at the entrance to the Persian Gulf; the Suez Canal, which connects the Red Sea and the Mediterranean; the Bab el Mandeb strait, which provides entrance to the Red Sea; the Bosporus strait, which is a major export channel for Russian and Caspian oil; and the Strait of Malacca, through which passes 80 percent of Japan's and South Korea's oil and about half of China's. Ships commandeered and scuttled in these strategic waterways could disrupt supply lines for extended periods. Securing pipelines and chokepoints will require augmented monitoring as well as the development of multilateral rapid-response capabilities.

The challenge of energy security will grow more urgent in the years ahead, because the scale of the global trade in energy will grow substantially as world markets become more integrated. Currently, every day some 40 million barrels of oil cross oceans on tankers; by 2020, that number could jump to 67 million. By then, the United States could be importing 70 percent of its oil (compared to 58 percent today and 33 percent in 1973), and so could China. The amount of natural gas crossing oceans as LNG will triple to 460 million tons by 2020. The United States will be an important part of that market: although LNG meets only about 3 percent of U.S. demand today, its share could reach more than 25 percent by 2020. Assuring the security of global energy markets will require coordination on both an international and a national basis among companies and governments, including energy, environmental, military, law enforcement, and intelligence agencies.

But in the United States, as in other countries, the lines of responsibility—and the sources of funding—for protecting critical infrastructures, such as energy, are far from clear. The private sector, the federal government, and state and local agencies need to take steps to better coordinate their activities. Maintaining the commitment to do so during periods of low or moderate prices will require discipline as well as vigilance. As Stephen Flynn, a homeland security expert at the Council on Foreign Relations, observes, "Security is not free." Both the public and private sectors need to invest in building a higher degree of security into the energy system—meaning that energy security will be part of both the price of energy and the cost of homeland security.

Markets need to be recognized as a source of security in themselves. The energy security system was created when energy prices were regulated in the United States, energy trading was only just beginning, and futures markets were several years away. Today, large, flexible, and well-functioning energy markets provide security by absorbing shocks and allowing supply and demand to respond more quickly and with greater ingenuity than a controlled system could. Such markets will guarantee security for the growing LNG market and thereby boost the confidence of the countries that import it. Thus, governments must resist the temptation to bow to political pressure and micromanage markets. Intervention and controls, however well meaning, can backfire, slowing and even preventing the movement of supplies to respond to disruptions. At least in the United States, any price spike or disruption evokes the memory of the infamous gas lines of the 1970s—even for those who were only toddlers then (and perhaps even for those not yet born at the time). Yet those lines were to a considerable degree self-inflicted—the consequence of price controls and a heavy-handed allocation system that sent gasoline where it was not needed and denied its being sent where it was.

Contrast that to what happened immediately after Hurricane Katrina. A major disruption to the U.S. oil supply was compounded by reports of price gouging and of stations running out of gasoline, which together could have created new gas lines along the East Coast. Yet the markets were back in balance sooner and prices came down more quickly than almost anyone had expected. Emergency supplies from the U.S. Strategic Petroleum Reserve and other IEA reserves were released, sending a "do not panic" message to the market. At the same time, two critical regulatory restrictions were eased. One was the Jones Act (which bars non-U.S.-flagged ships from carrying cargo between U.S. ports), which was waived to allow non-U.S. tankers to ship supplies bottlenecked on the Gulf Coast around Florida to the East Coast, where they were needed. The other was the set of "boutique gasoline" regulations that require different qualities of gasoline for different cities, which were temporarily lifted to permit supplies from other parts of the country to move into the Southeast. The experience highlights the need to incorporate regulatory and environmental flexibility—and a clear understanding of the impediments to adjustment—into the energy security machinery in order to cope as effectively as possible with disruptions and emergencies.

The U.S. government and the private sector should also make a renewed commitment to energy efficiency and conservation. Although often underrated, the impact of conservation on the economy has been enormous over the past several decades. Over the past 30 years, U.S. GDP has grown by 150 percent, while U.S.

energy consumption has grown by only 25 percent. In the 1970s and 1980s, many considered that kind of decoupling impossible, or at least certain to be economically ruinous. True, many of the gains in energy efficiency have come because the U.S. economy is "lighter," as former Federal Reserve Chair Alan Greenspan has put it, than it was three decades ago—that is, GDP today is composed of less manufacturing and more services (especially information technology) than could have been imagined in the 1970s. But the basic point remains: conservation has worked. Current and future advances in technology could permit very large additional gains, which would be highly beneficial not only for advanced economies such as that of the United States, but also for the economies of countries such as India and China (in fact, China has recently made conservation a priority).

Finally, the investment climate itself must become a key concern in energy security. There needs to be a continual flow of investment and technology in order for new resources to be developed. The IEA recently estimated that as much as $17 trillion will be required for new energy development over the next 25 years. These capital flows will not materialize without reasonable and stable investment frameworks, timely decision-making by governments, and open markets. How to facilitate energy investment will be one of the critical questions on the G-8's energy security agenda in 2006.

Future Shocks

Inevitably, there will be shocks to energy markets in the future. Some of the possible causes may be roughly foreseeable, such as coordinated attacks by terrorists, disruptions in the Middle East and Africa, or turmoil in Latin America that affects output in Venezuela, the third-largest OPEC producer. Other possible causes, however, may come as a surprise. The offshore oil industry has long built facilities to withstand a "hundred-year storm"—but nobody anticipated that two such devastating storms would strike the energy complex in the Gulf of Mexico within a matter of weeks. And the creators of the IEA emergency sharing system in the 1970s never for a moment considered that it might have to be activated to blunt the effects of a disruption in the United States.

Diversification will remain the fundamental starting principle of energy security for both oil and gas. Today, however, it will likely also require developing a new generation of nuclear power and "clean coal" technologies and encouraging a growing role for a variety of renewable energy sources as they become more competitive. It will also require investing in new technologies, ranging from near-term ones, such as the conversion of natural gas into a liquid fuel, to ones that are still in the lab, such as the biological engineering of energy supplies. Investment in technology all along the energy spectrum is surging today, and this will have a positive effect not only on the future energy picture but also on the environment.

Yet energy security also exists in a larger context. In a world of increasing interdependence, energy security will depend much on how countries manage their relations with one another, whether bilaterally or within multilateral frameworks. That is why energy security will be one of the main challenges for U.S. foreign policy in the years ahead. Part of that challenge will be anticipating and assessing the "what ifs." And that requires looking not only around the corner, but also beyond the ups and downs of cycles to both the reality of an ever more complex and integrated global energy system and the relations among the countries that participate in it.

DANIEL YERGIN is Chair of Cambridge Energy Research Associates and the author of *The Prize: The Epic Quest for Oil, Money, and Power*. He is currently writing a new book on oil and geopolitics.

Reprinted by permission of *Foreign Affairs*, Vol. 85, no. 2, March/April 2006, pp. 69–82. Copyright © 2006 by the Council on Foreign Relations, Inc.

Nuclear Now!

How Clean, Green Atomic Energy Can Stop Global Warming

PETER SCHWARTZ AND SPENCER REISS

On a cool spring morning a quarter century ago, a place in Pennsylvania called Three Mile Island exploded into the headlines and stopped the US nuclear power industry in its tracks. What had been billed as the clean, cheap, limitless energy source for a shining future was suddenly too hot to handle.

In the years since, we've searched for alternatives, pouring billions of dollars into windmills, solar panels, and biofuels. We've designed fantastically efficient lightbulbs, air conditioners, and refrigerators. We've built enough gas-fired generators to bankrupt California. But mainly, each year we hack 400 million more tons of coal out of Earth's crust than we did a quarter century before, light it on fire, and shoot the proceeds into the atmosphere.

The consequences aren't pretty. Burning coal and other fossil fuels is driving climate change, which is blamed for everything from western forest fires and Florida hurricanes to melting polar ice sheets and flooded Himalayan hamlets. On top of that, coal-burning electric power plants have fouled the air with enough heavy metals and other noxious pollutants to cause 15,000 premature deaths annually in the US alone, according to a Harvard School of Public Health study. Believe it or not, a coal-fired plant releases 100 times more radioactive material than an equivalent nuclear reactor—right into the air, too, not into some carefully guarded storage site. (And, by the way, more than 5,200 Chinese coal miners perished in accidents last year.)

Burning hydrocarbons is a luxury that a planet with 6 billion energy-hungry souls can't afford. There's only one sane, practical alternative: nuclear power.

We now know that the risks of splitting atoms pale beside the dreadful toll exacted by fossil fuels. Radiation containment, waste disposal, and nuclear weapons proliferation are manageable problems in a way that global warming is not. Unlike the usual green alternatives—water, wind, solar, and biomass—nuclear energy is here, now, in industrial quantities. Sure, nuke plants are expensive to build—upward of $2 billion apiece—but they start to look cheap when you factor in the true cost to people and the planet of burning fossil fuels. And nuclear is our best hope for cleanly and efficiently generating hydrogen, which would end our other ugly hydrocarbon addiction—dependence on gasoline and diesel for transport.

Some of the world's most thoughtful greens have discovered the logic of nuclear power, including Gaia theorist James Lovelock, Greenpeace cofounder Patrick Moore, and Britain's Bishop Hugh Montefiore, a longtime board member of Friends of the Earth. Western Europe is quietly backing away from planned nuclear phaseouts. Finland has ordered a big reactor specifically to meet the terms of the Kyoto Protocol on climate change. China's new nuke plants—26 by 2025—are part of a desperate effort at smog control.

Even the shell-shocked US nuclear industry is coming out of its stupor. The 2001 report of Vice President Cheney's energy task force was only the most high profile in a series of pro-nuke developments. Nuke boosters are especially buoyed by more efficient plant designs, streamlined licensing procedures, and the prospect of federal subsidies.

In fact, new plants are on the way, however tentatively. Three groups of generating companies have entered a bureaucratic maze expected to lead to formal applications for plants by 2008. If everything breaks right, the first new reactors in decades will be online by 2014. If this seems ambitious, it's not; the industry hopes merely to hold on to nuclear's current 20 percent of the rapidly growing US electric power market.

That's not nearly enough. We should be shooting to match France, which gets 77 percent of its electricity from nukes. It's past time for a decisive leap out of the hydrocarbon era, time to send King Coal and, soon after, Big Oil shambling off to their well-deserved final resting places—maybe on a nostalgic old steam locomotive.

Besides, wouldn't it be a blast to barrel down the freeway in a hydrogen Hummer with a clean conscience as your copilot? Or not to feel like a planet killer every time you flick on the A/C? That's how the future could be, if only we would get over our fear of the nuclear bogeyman and forge ahead—for real this time—into the atomic age.

The granola crowd likes to talk about conservation and efficiency, and surely substantial gains can be made in those areas. But energy is not a luxury people can do without, like a gym membership or hair gel. The developed world built its wealth on cheap power—burning firewood, coal, petroleum, and natural gas, with carbon emissions the inevitable byproduct.

Indeed, material progress can be tracked in what gets pumped out of smokestacks. An hour of coal-generated 100-watt electric light creates 0.05 pounds of atmospheric carbon, a bucket of ice makes 0.3 pounds, an hour's car ride 5. The average American sends nearly half a ton of carbon spewing into the atmosphere every month. Europe and Japan are a little more economical, but even the most remote forest-burning peasants happily do their part.

And the worst—by far—is yet to come. An MIT study forecasts that worldwide energy demand could triple by 2050. China could build a Three Gorges Dam every year forever and still not meet its growing demand for electricity. Even the carbon reductions required by the Kyoto Protocol—which pointedly exempts developing countries like China—will be a drop in the atmospheric sewer.

What is a rapidly carbonizing world to do? The high-minded answer, of course, is renewables. But the notion that wind, water, solar, or biomass will save the day is at least as fanciful as the once-popular idea that nuclear energy would be too cheap to meter. Jesse Ausubel, director of the human environment program at New York's Rockefeller University, calls renewable energy sources "false gods"—attractive but powerless. They're capital- and land-intensive, and solar is not yet remotely cost-competitive. Despite all the hype, tax breaks, and incentives, the proportion of US electricity production from renewables has actually fallen in the past 15 years, from 11.0 percent to 9.1 percent.

The decline would be even worse without hydropower, which accounts for 92 percent of the world's renewable electricity. While dams in the US are under attack from environmentalists trying to protect wild fish populations, the Chinese are building them on an ever grander scale. But even China's autocrats can't get past Nimby. Stung by criticism of the monumental Three Gorges project—which required the forcible relocation of 1 million people—officials have suspended an even bigger project on the Nu Jiang River in the country's remote southwest. Or maybe someone in Beijing questioned the wisdom of reacting to climate change with a multibillion-dollar bet on rainfall.

Solar power doesn't look much better. Its number-one problem is cost: While the price of photovoltaic cells has been slowly dropping, solar-generated electricity is still four times more expensive than nuclear (and more than five times the cost of coal). Maybe someday we'll all live in houses with photovoltaic roof tiles, but in the real world, a run-of-the-mill 1,000-megawatt photovoltaic plant will require about 60 square miles of panes alone. In other words, the largest industrial structure ever built.

Wind is more promising, which is one reason it's the lone renewable attracting serious interest from big-time equipment manufacturers like General Electric. But even though price and performance are expected to improve, wind, like solar, is inherently fickle, hard to capture, and widely dispersed. And wind turbines take up a lot of space; Ausubel points out that the wind equivalent of a typical utility plant would require 300 square miles of turbines plus costly transmission lines from the wind-scoured fields of, say, North Dakota. Alternatively, there's California's Altamont Pass, where 5,400 windmills slice and dice some 1,300 birds of prey annually.

What about biomass? Ethanol is clean, but growing the amount of cellulose required to shift US electricity production to biomass would require farming—no wilting organics, please—an area the size of 10 Iowas.

Among fossil fuels, natural gas holds some allure; it emits a third as much carbon as coal. That's an improvement but not enough if you're serious about rolling back carbon levels. Washington's favorite solution is so-called clean coal, ballyhooed in stump speeches by both President Bush (who offered a $2 billion research program) and challenger John Kerry (who upped the ante to $10 billion). But most of the work so far has been aimed at reducing acid rain by cutting sulphur dioxide and nitrogen oxide emissions, and more recently gasifying coal to make it burn cleaner. Actual zero-emissions coal is still a lab experiment that even fans say could double or triple generating costs. It would also leave the question of what to do with 1 million tons of extracted [Sulphur] each year.

By contrast, nuclear power is thriving around the world despite decades of obituaries. Belgium derives 58 percent of its electricity from nukes, Sweden 45 percent, South Korea 40, Switzerland 37 percent, Japan 31 percent, Spain 27 percent, and the UK 23 percent. Turkey plans to build three plants over the next several years. South Korea has eight more reactors coming, Japan 13, China at least 20. France, where nukes generate more than three-quarters of the country's electricity, is privatizing a third of its state-owned nuclear energy group, Areva, to deal with the rush of new business.

The last US nuke plant to be built was ordered in 1973, yet nuclear power is growing here as well. With clever engineering and smart management, nukes have steadily increased their share of generating capacity in the US. The 103 reactors operating in the US pump out electricity at more than 90 percent of capacity, up from 60 percent when Three Mile Island made headlines. That increase is the equivalent of adding 40 new reactors, without bothering anyone's backyard or spewing any more carbon into the air.

So atomic power is less expensive than it used to be—but could it possibly be cost-effective? Even before Three Mile Island sank, the US nuclear industry was foundering on the shoals of economics. Regulatory delays and billion-dollar construction-cost overruns turned the business into a financial nightmare. But increasing experience and efficiency gains have changed all that. Current operating costs are the lowest ever—1.82 cents per kilowatt-hour versus 2.13 cents for coal-fired plants and 3.69 cents for natural gas. The ultimate vindication of nuclear economics is playing out in the stock market: Over the past five years, the stocks of leading nuclear generating companies such as Exelon and Entergy have more than doubled. Indeed, Exelon is feeling so flush that it bought New Jersey's Public Service Enterprise Group in December, adding four reactors to its former roster of 17.

This remarkable success suggests that nuclear energy realistically could replace coal in the US without a cost increase and ultimately lead the way to a clean, green future. The trick is to start building nuke plants and keep building them at a furious pace. Anything less leaves carbon in the climatic driver's seat.

A decade ago, anyone thinking about constructing nuclear plants in the US would have been dismissed as out of touch with reality. But today, for the first time since the building of Three Mile Island, new nukes in the US seem possible. Thanks to improvements in reactor design and increasing encouragement from Washington, DC, the nuclear industry is posed for unlikely revival. "All the planets seem to be coming into alignment," says David Brown, VP for congressional affairs at Exelon.

The original US nuclear plants, built during the 1950s and '60s, were descended from propulsion units in 1950s-vintage nuclear submarines, now known as generation I. During the '80s and '90s, when new construction halted in the US, the major reactor makers—GE Power Systems, British-owned Westinghouse, France's Framatome (part of Areva), and Canada's AECL—went after customers in Europe. This new round of business led to system improvements that could eventually, after some prototyping, be deployed back in the US.

By all accounts, the latest reactors, generation III+, are a big improvement. They're fuel-efficient. They employ passive safety technologies, such as gravity-fed emergency cooling rather than pumps. Thanks to standardized construction, they may even be cost-competitive to build—$1,200 per kilowatt-hour of generating capacity versus more than $1,300 for the latest low-emission (which is not to say low-carbon) coal plants. But there's no way to know for sure until someone actually builds one. And even then, the first few will almost certainly cost more.

Prodded by the Cheney report, the US Department of Energy agreed in 2002 to pick up the tab of the first hurdle—getting from engineering design to working blueprints. Three groups of utility companies and reactor makers have stepped up for the program, optimistically dubbed Nuclear Power 2010. The government's bill to taxpayers for this stage of development could top $500 million, but at least we'll get working reactors rather than "promising technologies."

But newer, better designs don't free the industry from the intense public oversight that has been nuclear power's special burden from the start. Believe it or not, Three Mile Island wasn't the ultimate nightmare; that would be Shoreham, the Long Island power plant shuttered in 1994 after a nine-year legal battle, without ever having sold a single electron. Construction was already complete when opponents challenged the plant's application for an operating license. Wall Street won't invest billions in new plants ($5.5 billion in Shoreham's case) without a clear path through the maze of judges and regulators.

Shoreham didn't die completely in vain. The 1992 Energy Policy Act aims to forestall such debacles by authorizing the Nuclear Regulatory Commission to issue combined construction and operating licenses. It also allows the NRC to pre-certify specific reactor models and the energy companies to bank preapproved sites. Utility executives fret that no one has ever road-tested the new process, which still requires public hearings and shelves of supporting documents. An idle reactor site at Browns Ferry, Alabama, could be an early test case; the Tennessee Valley Authority is exploring options to refurbish it rather than start from scratch.

Meanwhile, Congress looks ready to provide a boost to the nuclear energy industry. Pete Domenici (R-New Mexico), chair of the Senate's energy committee and the patron saint of nuclear power in Washington, has vowed to revive last year's energy bill, which died in the Senate. Earlier versions included a 1.85 cent per-kilowatt-hour production tax credit for the first half-dozen nuke plants to come online. That could add up to as much as $8 billion in federal outlays and should go a long way toward luring Wall Street back into the fray. As pork goes, the provision is easy to defend. Nuclear power's extraordinary startup costs and safety risks make it a special case for government intervention. And the amount is precisely the same bounty Washington spends annually in tax credits for wind, biomass, and other zero-emission kilowattage.

Safer plants, more sensible regulation, and even a helping hand from Congress—all are on the way. What's still missing is a place to put radioactive waste. By law, US companies that generate nuclear power pay the Feds a tenth of a cent per kilowatt-hour to dispose of their spent fuel. The fund—currently $24 billion and counting—is supposed to finance a permanent waste repository, the ill-fated Yucca Mountain in Nevada. Two decades ago when the payments started, opening day was scheduled for January 31, 1998. But the Nevada facility remains embroiled in hearings, debates, and studies, and waste is piling up at 30-odd sites around the country. Nobody will build a nuke plant until Washington offers a better answer than "keep piling."

At Yucca Mountain, perfection has been the enemy of adequacy. It's fun to discuss what the design life of an underground nuclear waste facility ought to be. One hundred years? Two hundred years? How about 100,000? A quarter of a million? Science fiction meets the US government budgeting process. In court!

But throwing waste into a black hole at Yucca Mountain isn't such a great idea anyway. For one thing, in coming decades we might devise better disposal methods, such as corrosion-proof containers that can withstand millennia of heat and moisture. For another, used nuclear fuel can be recycled as a source for the production of more energy. Either way, it's clear that the whole waste disposal problem has been misconstrued. We don't need a million-year solution. A hundred years will do just fine—long enough to let the stuff cool down and allow us to decide what to do with it.

The name for this approach is interim storage: Find a few patches of isolated real estate—we're not talking about taking it over for eternity—and pour nice big concrete pads; add floodlights, motion detectors, and razor wire; truck in nuclear waste in bombproof 20-foot-high concrete casks. Voilà: safe storage while you wait for either Yucca Mountain or plan B.

Two dozen reactor sites around the country already have their own interim facilities; a private company has applied with the NRC to open one on the Goshute Indian reservation in Skull Valley, Utah. Establishing a half-dozen federally managed sites is closer to the right idea. Domenici says he'll introduce legislation this year for a national interim storage system.

A handful of new US plants will be a fine start, but the real goal has to be dethroning King Coal and—until something better comes along—pushing nuclear power out front as the world's default energy source. Kicking carbon cold turkey won't be easy, but it can be done. Four crucial steps can help increase the momentum: Regulate carbon emissions, revamp the fuel cycle, rekindle innovation in nuclear technology, and, finally, replace gasoline with hydrogen.

- **Regulate carbon emissions.** Nuclear plants have to account for every radioactive atom of waste. Meanwhile, coal-fired plants dump tons of deadly refuse into the atmosphere at zero cost. It's time for that free ride to end, but only the government can make it happen.

The industry seems ready to pay up. Andy White, CEO of GE Energy's nuclear division, recently asked a roomful of US utility executives what they thought about the possibility of regulating carbon emissions. The idea didn't faze them. "The only question any of them had," he says, "was when and how much."

A flat-out carbon tax is almost certainly a nonstarter in Washington. But an arrangement in which all energy producers are allowed a limited number of carbon pollution credits to use or sell could pass muster; after all, this kind of cap-and-trade scheme is already a fact of life for US utilities with a variety of other pollutants. Senators John McCain and Joe Lieberman have been pushing legislation [for] such a system. This would send a clear message to utility executives that fossil energy's free pass is over.

- **Recycle nuclear fuel.** Here's a fun fact: Spent nuclear fuel—the stuff intended for permanent disposal at Yucca Mountain—retains 95 percent of its energy content. Imagine what Toyota could do for fuel efficiency if 95 percent of the average car's gasoline passed through the engine and out the tailpipe. In France, Japan, and Britain, nuclear engineers do the sensible thing: recycle. Alone among the nuclear powers, the US doesn't, for reasons that have nothing to do with nuclear power.

Recycling spent fuel—the technical word is reprocessing—is one way to make the key ingredient of a nuclear bomb, enriched uranium. In 1977, Jimmy Carter, the only nuclear engineer ever to occupy the White House, banned reprocessing in the US in favor of a so-called once-through fuel cycle. Four decades later, more than a dozen countries reprocess or enrich uranium, including North Korea and Iran. At this point, hanging onto spent fuel from US reactors does little good abroad and real mischief at home.

The Bush administration has reopened the door with modest funding to resume research into the nuclear fuel cycle. The president himself has floated a proposal to provide all comers with a guaranteed supply of reactor fuel in exchange for a promise not to reprocess spent fuel themselves. Other proposals would create a global nuclear fuel company, possibly under the auspices of the International Atomic Energy Agency. This company would collect, reprocess, and distribute fuel to every nation in the world, thus keeping potential bomb fixings out of circulation.

In the short term, reprocessing would maximize resources and minimize the problem of how to dispose of radioactive waste. In fact, it would eliminate most of the waste from nuclear power

production. Over decades, it could also ease pressure on uranium supplies. The world's existing reserves are generally reckoned sufficient to withstand 50 years of rapid nuclear expansion without a significant price increase. In a pinch, there's always the ocean, whose 4.5 billion tons of dissolved uranium can be extracted today at 5 to 10 times the cost of conventional mining.

Uranium is so cheap today that reprocessing is more about reducing waste than stretching the fuel supply. But advanced breeder reactors, which create more fuel as they generate power, could well be the economically competitive choice—and renewable as well.

- **Rekindle innovation.** Although nuclear technology has come a long way since Three Mile Island, the field is hardly a hotbed of innovation. Government-funded research—such as the DOE's Next Generation Nuclear Plant program—is aimed at designing advanced reactors, including high temperature, gas-cooled plants of the kind being built in China and South Africa and fast-breeder reactors that will use uranium 60 times more efficiently than today's reactors. Still, the nuclear industry suffers from its legacy of having been born under a mushroom cloud and raised by your local electric company. A tight leash on nuclear R&D may be good, even necessary. But there's nothing like a little competition to spur creativity. That's reason enough to want to see US companies squarely back on the nuclear power field—research is great, but more and smarter buyers ultimately drive quality up and prices down.

In fact, the possibility of a nuclear gold rush—not just a modest rebirth—depends on economics as much as technology. The generation IV pebble-bed reactors being developed in China and South Africa get attention for their meltdown-proof designs. . . . But it's their low capital cost and potential for fast, modular construction that could blow the game open, as surely as the PC did for computing. As long as investments come in $2 billion increments, purchase orders will be few and far between. At $300 million a pop for safe, clean energy, watch the floodgates open around the world.

- **Replace gasoline with hydrogen.** If a single change could truly ignite nuclear power, it's the grab bag of technologies and wishful schemes traveling under the rubric of the hydrogen economy. Leaving behind petroleum is as important to the planet's future as eliminating coal. The hitch is that it takes energy to extract hydrogen from substances like methane and water. Where will it come from?

Today, the most common energy source for producing hydrogen is natural gas, followed by oil. It's conceivable that renewables could do it in limited quantities. By the luck of physics, though, two things nuclear reactors do best—generate both electricity and very high temperatures—are exactly what it takes to produce hydrogen most efficiently. Last November, the DOE's Idaho National Engineering and Environmental Laboratory showed how a single next-gen nuke could produce the hydrogen equivalent of 400,000 gallons of gasoline every day. Nuclear energy's potential for freeing us not only from coal but also oil holds the promise of a bright green future for the US and the world at large.

The more seriously you take the idea of global warming, the more seriously you have to take nuclear power. Clean coal, solar-powered roof tiles, wind farms in North Dakota—they're all pie in the emissions-free sky. Sure, give them a shot. But zero-carbon reactors are here and now. We know we can build them. Their price tag is no mystery. They fit into the existing electric grid without a hitch. Flannel-shirted environmentalists who fight these realities run the risk of ending up with as much soot on their hands as the slickest coal-mining CEO.

America's voracious energy appetite doesn't have to be a bug—it can be a feature. Shanghai, Seoul, and São Paolo are more likely to look to Los Angeles or Houston as a model than to some solar-powered idyll. Energy technology is no different than any other; innovation can change all the rules. But if

the best we can offer the developing world is bromides about energy independence, we'll deserve the carbon-choked nightmare of a planet we get.

Nuclear energy is the big bang still reverberating. It's the power to light a city in a lump the size of a soda can. Peter Huber and Mark Mills have written an iconoclastic new book on energy, *The Bottomless Well*. They see nuclear power as merely the latest in a series of technologies that will gradually eliminate our need to carve up huge swaths of the planet. "Energy isn't the problem. Energy is the solution," they write. "Energy begets more energy. The more of it we capture and put to use, the more readily we will capture still more."

The best way to avoid running out of fossil fuels is to switch to something better. The Stone Age famously did not end for lack of stones, and neither should we wait for the last chunk of anthracite to flicker out before we kiss hydrocarbons good-bye. Especially not when something cleaner, safer, more efficient, and more abundant is ready to roll. It's time to get real.

Looking into the Sun

If David Slawson is right about solar power, our days of oil dependency are numbered.

DAVID H. FREEDMAN

A relentlessly blue sky stretches over the sparse, nappy scrub and cacti in the desert several miles outside Albuquerque. Here, where there is otherwise little in any direction to suggest human existence, a lone, dusty road has led to a few unremarkable bungalows. Alongside them is a less unremarkable sight: a cluster of a half-dozen satellite-style dishes that look big enough to pick up programs from the outer planets. But these house-size dishes don't traffic in television. Their mirrored surfaces are aimed directly at the sun, twisting a few inches every six seconds to track it across the sky. Each dish focuses the equivalent of 10,000 suns' worth of heat on an eight-inch-wide maze of thin metal tubing perched above the dish's center.

Admiring one of the contraptions from below is David Slawson, a somewhat diminutive fellow in a leather jacket and slacks. Slawson may not cut an impressive figure, but he makes up for it with ambition. His dishes are self-contained, electricity-generating plants, fueled by the particles of energy hurled across 93 million miles of space by the nuclear reactor sitting at the center of our solar system—that is, the sun. Slawson's quixotic plan: to cover large swaths of the earth's desert regions with emissionless solar farms. "A farm 100 miles by 100 miles would be enough to displace the fossil-fuel consumption of the U.S.," he says, sweeping his hand as if this vast installation already lies just off to the side. The dishes, he adds, will also help bring cheap electricity to the planet's 1.5 billion rural poor currently living without it.

Heady stuff, to be sure, and easy to dismiss. On the other hand, Slawson's company, Stirling Energy Systems, has some interesting credentials, including ownership of technology developed by McDonnell Douglas, Southern California Edison, and others at a cost of $400 million; $3 million in grants from the Department of Energy; a steady flow of angel investment that he says has averaged $2 million a year for nine years; a preliminary agreement to provide a major utility with up to $2.7 billion worth of electricity over 20 years; and another $1.3 billion deal on tap with another utility.

Slawson, 57, came to the unlikely role of would-be slayer of the world's monster oil habit through an even more unlikely route. He was running an alternative health care school in Portland, Oreg., in 1989 and had just moved to an apartment downtown. On his first night there, he opened his window before going to bed—and got a faceful of vehicle exhaust. What, he wheezed to himself, is this world coming to? And more important, what was he, David Slawson, going to do about it? Charging across the street to a library first thing in the morning, he found his answer.

Solar energy seems like a no-brainer—hey, free energy from the sky, what's not to like?—but on closer inspection some thorny issues pop up. The biggest one is the "conversion efficiency" issue. Sunlight is energy, all right, but it needs to be converted to a form that can be used to run cars, heat homes, and display Leno. Electricity fills the bill, but a funny thing happens when you enlist sunlight to create electricity: Most of the energy flits away uselessly. The most common approach is to use sunlight to knock electrons out of a semiconducting material like silicon, creating an electric current. But the efficiency of even the very best photovoltaic systems, as the approach is called, tops out around 15%—in other words, 85% of the sunlight's energy is wasted. Big, expensive solar panels in very sunny areas produce relatively little power, which winds up costing about 25 cents per kilowatt hour of electricity. (A kilowatt is about enough to power 14 75-watt bulbs.) Electricity from a conventional natural-gas-burning power station, by contrast, costs about seven cents per kilowatt hour.

Slawson's library raid turned up a book that detailed a different approach: a thermoelectric solar dish system developed by McDonnell Douglas (later absorbed into Boeing) with a Swedish firm called Kockums, technology that was later sold to and tested by Southern California Edison. Instead of using rays of sunlight to knock out electrons, the dish reflects and concentrates the rays in order to heat and thus expand a gas. That expansion is then put to work by a device called a Stirling engine to turn a conventional electric generator. The approach is nearly twice as efficient as most photovoltaic systems—while doing away with semiconductors and other expensive materials.

"A solar farm 100 miles by 100 miles would be enough to displace the fossil-fuel consumption of the U.S."

These solar dishes are the world's great hope for renewable energy, says Slawson. Sure, there's hydropower, but there are only so many Niagara Falls. Drilling and other operating costs limit geothermal power, which taps heat energy trapped below ground. There's wind, but finding frequently windy sites where windmills don't spoil scenic vistas is a challenge—and even then, the wind tends to die down during the summer and in the daytime, when demand is highest. And forget fuel cells—they generate electricity, but the hydrogen they run on comes either from fossil fuels or by zapping water with electricity that still needs to come from somewhere else. "If you're an electric utility that wants renewable energy and you can get hold of a big plot of desert land, you're going to look at solar thermoelectric," says Michael Eckhart, a former General Electric and power industry executive who now heads the American Council on Renewable Energy in Washington, D.C.

Stirling Energy's technology isn't the only thermoelectric approach, but so far the others can't match its efficiency. In any case, the real competition to any renewable energy source is not other new technologies but conventional power generation. And the energy industry is notoriously resistant to change. "This is not a go-fast industry, like telecommunications or computers," says Eckhart. Unless regulation or customer preferences force utilities to go whole hog into renewable energy, Slawson will have to get his dishes to produce energy reliably at pennies per kilowatt. That means finding ways to manufacture the systems more cheaply and get more electricity out of each dish.

The company is working furiously on both goals in facilities set up in the desert bungalows outside Albuquerque. Slawson employs some 30 people, many from the teams that first developed the technology, and they are engaged in an endless game of tweaking. The original prototype dish and engine would have cost $300,000 each to manufacture in quantity. That would have led to a $6 billion price tag for setting up the 20,000 dishes required to put out the 500 megawatts of a typical generating station, about enough to light a medium-size city.

To slash costs, the engineers replaced Boeing's airplane-style, customized, sheet-metal-and-rivets approach to the dish frame with a mass-producible, bolted, rolled-steel design. A custom heat exchanger was replaced with off-the-shelf race car radiators, and the 82 three- by four-foot mirrors that cover each dish's surface, which originally cost hundreds of dollars apiece, are now producible for less than $30 each by the same process used to create makeup compacts. Slawson says he can build a dish system for about $25,000—bringing the total price of a 500-megawatt installation to about $600 million, about the same as a conventional generating station. The bottom line: Slawson claims he's already capable of turning out electricity at less than eight cents per kilowatt, making it competitive with a gas-fired plant. "I don't want to say how much less than eight cents it costs me because I

don't want to have to sell it too cheaply," he says. "Just cheaply enough to win contracts."

Slawson says he's close to signing a contract for a 500-megawatt solar farm with a major California utility (which he declined to identify); another utility has placed Stirling on a short list for a second 500-megawatt farm. In early 2007, he plans to manufacture 300 dishes a month; he'll bump that up to 1,000 a month by 2009. Unlike a conventional power station, which doesn't produce any juice until it's completed, a solar farm can in theory begin financing itself long before the last dish is up. "We can generate revenue as soon as we start putting dishes in," says Slawson. By 2010, he predicts, Stirling Energy will be pulling in $300 million a year.

That's a pretty bold business plan for a fellow who started out flipping burgers at a Portland Bun 'N Burger he bought with a friend in 1971, shortly after college. Slawson sold the restaurant after a few years and became a massage therapist; by 1978 his practice had become an extensive alternative health care facility that eventually employed 70 professionals. In 1981 he acquired a small alternative health care school and built it into one of the largest such schools in the country—the East-West College of the Healing Arts. Then came the move to downtown Portland in 1989 and the awakening of his solar consciousness.

Following a stint living in Maui, Slawson returned to Portland. In 1996, he learned that Southern California Edison had been cutting back on R&D and was looking for a buyer for the solar dish technology. The price tag, Slawson says, was "hundreds of thousands of dollars." Slawson raised the money from family, friends, and various well-heeled green contacts he had made over the years—there's overlap between the massage-homeopathy crowd and clean-air enthusiasts—and founded Stirling Energy Systems in Phoenix, the unofficial capital of the desert Southwest. By February of 1996, Slawson was in the solar energy business.

His scrappy, New Age background may turn out to be an important strength. The Renewable Energy Council's Eckhart says that when it comes to new sources of power, utilities aren't concerned just with kilowatt pricing—they also want to be sure the company that's providing it will survive to make sure the juice keeps flowing. In the end, he says, it may be Slawson's unwavering, decadelong commitment that clinches the sale. If Stirling Energy can parlay that passion into a big utility sale, Eckhart adds, other utilities are likely to follow "as a herd." If that happens, says Slawson, he expects buyout offers to come flying in from utilities, oil companies, and other big players. But he's not interested in selling. His goal is to go public and partner with established giants on some really, really big solar farms planted on sun-scorched land that now mostly goes to waste. "If we can cover 1% of the world's deserts," he says, "we can produce 100% of the world's energy needs."

Contributing editor **DAVID H. FREEDMAN** writes the "What's Next" column.

UNIT 5
Conflict

Unit Selections

Key Points to Consider

- Are violent conflicts and warfare increasing or decreasing?

- Where are the major hot spots in the world where conflict is taking place?

- What changes have taken place in recent years in the types of conflicts and who participates?

- How is military doctrine changing to reflect new political realities?

- How is the nature of terrorism different than conventional warfare? What new threats do terrorists pose?

- What are the motivations and attitudes of those who use terror as a political tool?

- What challenges does nuclear proliferation pose to the United States?

- How is the national security policy of the United States likely to change? What about Russia, India, and China?

Student Web Site
www.mhcls.com/online

Internet References
Further information regarding these Web sites may be found in this book's preface or online.

DefenseLINK
http://www.defenselink.mil
Federation of American Scientists (FAS)
http://www.fas.org
ISN International Relations and Security Network
http://www.isn.ethz.ch
The NATO Integrated Data Service (NIDS)
http://www.nato.int/structur/nids/nids.htm

Digital Vision/Getty Images

Do you lock your doors at night? Do you secure your personal property to avoid theft? These are basic questions that have to do with your sense of personal security. Most individuals take steps to protect what they have, including their lives. The same is true for groups of people, including countries.

In the international arena, governments frequently pursue their national interest by entering into mutually agreeable "deals" with other governments. Social scientists call these types of arrangements "exchanges" (i.e., each side gives up something it values in order to gain something in return that it values even more). On an economic level, it functions like this: "I have the oil that you need and am willing to sell it. In return I want to buy from you the agricultural products that I lack". Whether on the governmental level or the personal level ("If you help me with my homework, then I will drive you home this weekend"), exchanges are the process used by most individuals and groups to obtain and protect what is of value. The exchange process, however, can break down. When threats and punishments replace mutual exchanges, conflict ensues. Neither side benefits and there are costs to both. Further, each may use threats with the expectation that the other will capitulate. But if efforts at intimidation and coercion fail, the conflict may escalate into violent confrontation.

With the end of the cold war, issues of national security and the nature of international conflict have changed. In the late 1980s agreements between the former Soviet Union and the United States led to the elimination of superpower support for participants in low-intensity conflicts in Central America, Africa, and Southeast Asia. Fighting the cold war by proxy is now a thing of the past. In addition, cold war military alliances have either collapsed or have been significantly redefined. Despite these historic changes, there is no shortage of conflicts in the world today.

Many experts initially predicted that the collapse of the Soviet Union would decrease the arms race and diminish the threat of nuclear war. However, some analysts now believe that the threat of nuclear war has in fact increased as control of nuclear weapons has become less centralized and the command structure less reliable. In addition, the proliferation of nuclear weapons into North Korea and South Asia (India and Pakistan) is a growing security issue. Further, there are concerns about both dictatorial governments and terrorist organizations obtaining weapons of mass destruction. What these changing circumstances mean for U.S. policy is a topic of considerable debate.

The unit focuses on two general issues. The first is the changing nature of conflict and traditional measures of power and influence, including the role of nuclear weapons. The second are case studies that provide insights into the roots of terrorism and armed conflicts in the Middle East, North Africa, and Asia.

As in the case of the other global issues described in this anthology, international conflict is a dynamic problem. It is important to understand that conflicts are not random events,

but follow patterns and trends. Forty-five years of cold war established discernable patterns of international conflict as the superpowers deterred each other with vast expenditures of money and technological know-how. The consequence of this stalemate was often a shift to the developing world for conflict by superpower proxy.

The changing circumstances of the post–cold war era generate a series of important new policy questions: Will there be more nuclear proliferation? Is there an increased danger of so-called "rogue" states destabilizing the international arena? Is the threat of terror a temporary or permanent feature of world affairs? Will there be a growing emphasis on low-intensity conflicts related to the interdiction of drugs, or will some other unforeseen issue determine the world's hot spots? Will the United States and its European allies lose interest in security issues that do not directly involve their economic interests and simply look the other way, for example, as age-old ethnic conflicts become brutally violent? Can the international community develop viable institutions to mediate and resolve disputes before they become violent? The answers to these and related questions will determine the patterns of conflict in the twenty-first century.

Terrorist Rivals
Beyond the State-Centric Model

LOUISE RICHARDSON

B y any standard measure, the United States is currently the most powerful country in the history of the world. Its defense budget of US$440 billion in 2007 (US$560 billion if one includes the budgets for the wars in Iraq and Afghanistan) is greater than the combined military expenditure of the rest of the world. In 2003 the International Institute for Strategic Studies calculated that the US defense budget was greater than the combined budgets of the next 13 countries and more than double the combination of the remaining 158 countries. Potential challengers cannot even begin to rival this power. The European Union can compete with the United States in terms of population and GNP, but it does not have the will or the institutional ability to act in concert on foreign or security initiatives. Russia, which until relatively recently was considered the closest challenger, retains vast armies but lags dramatically in military spending and technological development. The United States even outspends China, the nation most often mentioned as a challenger, by about seven to one. China is a formidable economic powerhouse, but only spends 3.9 percent of its GDP on defense, whereas it would have to spend about 25 percent to begin to rival the United States.

Yet in spite of this extraordinary and quite unprecedented preeminence, the United States has been unable to impose its will on the impoverished state of Afghanistan, on the sectarian chaos that is Iraq, or even on an organization, Al Qaeda, which is led by a few men believed to be hiding in caves in remote parts of Afghanistan and Pakistan. What does it say about traditional conceptions of the balance of power when the most powerful country on the planet cannot effectively apply its power to achieve its objectives?

The inability of the United States to achieve its security objectives is not due to the fact that other countries have balanced or "bandwagoned" against it, as traditional conceptions of a balance of power mechanism would have claimed. On the contrary, most of our would-be rivals share the United States' desire to destroy Al Qaeda, have supported its efforts to rebuild Afghanistan, and have acquiesced, albeit reluctantly, to its operations in Iraq. Indeed the United States has failed to achieve its security objectives because it has failed to appreciate the nature of the adversaries it faces and because of its inability to transform its military might into an effective arsenal against these adversaries.

Military Strength Misapplied

On September 11, 2001, a small substate group inflicted greater casualties on US civilians than any enemy government had ever inflicted on the United States before. The Japanese attack on Pearl Harbor killed 2,403 servicemen and 68 civilians, and vastly more US citizens were killed by fellow countrymen in the course of the Civil War, but an attack from an enemy state of this scale was simply unprecedented. In the words of President George W. Bush, "September 11 changed our world." Vice President Dick Cheney was more specific, commenting on NBC News that "9/11 changed everything. It changed the way we think about threats to the United States. It changed our recognition of our vulnerabilities. It changed in terms of the kind of national security strategy we need to pursue, in terms of guaranteeing the safety and security of the American people."

The US government nevertheless responded in an entirely traditional way: it declared war. However, rather than declaring war on an enemy state, it declared war first on the tactic of terrorism and later, and even less sensibly, on the emotion of terror. As a practical matter, however, it waged a conventional war—first against Afghanistan, whose government had harbored the terrorists who committed the attacks on New York and Washington, and later against Iraq, whose government had no connection to these same attacks. Its overwhelming military force brought down both governments in short order and with little cost in terms of US lives.

More than five years after the attack, however, the leaders of Al Qaeda, Osama bin Laden and Ayman Al Zawahiri, as well as the head of the government that supported them, Mullah Mohammed Omar, remain at large. A new government was democratically elected in Afghanistan, but within six months of the US invasion more civilians had been killed than on September 11, the security situation had deteriorated significantly, and opium production had spiralled out of control. Meanwhile more US citizens have been killed in Iraq than on September 11, and tens of thousands of Iraqis have been killed in sectarian violence as the country slips into a bloody civil war. For all its preeminent power, the United States has manifestly failed to capture its greatest enemies or to impose its will, much less its democratic principles, on two infinitely weaker polities.

The fact that the Taliban were defeated while Al Qaeda remained at large should have demonstrated to the Bush administration that it was not facing a traditional state adversary. Instead, however, it insisted on attributing Al Qaeda's strength to state support and, in flagrant denial of all available evidence, insisted on fabricating a link between the government of Iraq and Al Qaeda. Indeed, the current military occupation has only succeeded in allowing for the rise of an Al Qaeda faction in Iraq. Like the drunk who searches for his car keys under the street lamp, not because he lost them there but because the light is better, the United States used its military might against two countries simply because this might is formidable, and not because military force is the most effective means to defeat terrorism. Indeed, it is not.

A New Brand of Enemy

It can certainly be argued that the threat the United States faces in the 21st century is from terrorism itself, rather than from a rising power. The Bush administration came into office convinced that China would soon become the new Soviet Union, but it has since substituted terrorism as the principal threat to the American way of life. Many of the behavior patterns seen in the Cold War are beginning to re-emerge. In that era, attitudes toward communism were the litmus test for alliance with the United States. Indeed, the US government found itself in alliance with a great many unsavory states that in no way shared its commitment to liberal democratic principles but rather its abhorrence of communism. Today, it is similarly prepared to overlook the domestic abuses of regimes that are willing to join in the war against terror.

During the Cold War, this approach severely undermined the United States' moral authority in the world by suggesting that its commitment to human and civil rights reached only as far as its borders. It also precluded the possibility of the United States allying itself with those seeking legitimate democratic change in their societies and caused it to neglect the domestic forces at play in countries for which the bipolar distribution of power was largely irrelevant. Today the pattern seems to be repeating itself. The difference, of course, is that during the Cold War the United States did have a major state rival that was prepared to play a game of deterrence and balance. However, there is now no state basis to the forces currently emerging to oppose US power: these actors have no interest in interstate rivalry and play by an entirely different set of rules.

Terrorism itself is not a threat. It is a tactic used by the weak in an effort to exact vengeance against the strong, to acquire glory for oneself and to provoke one's adversaries into overreaction. It is a tactic used in many parts of the world by many different groups seeking many different political objectives. The particular terrorists who pose a threat to the United States today are jihadis rebelling against the pervasiveness of US culture and the projection of US power throughout the world. They completely reject the notion of a balance of power, which they see as an entirely Western construct. They mobilized to attack the United States only after they had successfully defeated the Soviet Union in Afghanistan, which convinced them that having defeated one superpower, they could take on another. Their ultimate goal is to eliminate Western influence in the region entirely and to restore the empire of the caliphate, with borders stretching from Spain to Indonesia.

There is obviously no way of computing terrorists' actual military strength or financial resources, but, as they freely admit, they are infinitely weaker than their adversaries. In the words of their chief strategist, Ayman Al Zawahiri: "However far our capabilities reach, they will never be equal to one thousandth of the capabilities of the kingdom of Satan that is waging war on us." Their strength derives not from traditional military calculations but instead from the popularity of their ideology and their unwavering fanaticism, which manifests itself in a disregard for personal survival and a willingness to act outside the norms of behavior by killing as many civilians and spreading as much fear as is possible. Nevertheless, US citizens feel more vulnerable today than they did when facing 10,000 strategic and 30,000 non-strategic nuclear warheads directed at them from the Soviet Union.

The potential of militant Islam posing a greater threat to the United States than any rising power is a real one. This is not because these groups can rival US power or resources. However, given that a fifth of the world's population is Muslim, if the United States were to define itself as an enemy of Islam or to act in such a way that Muslims come to believe the small number of extremists in their midst who insist that the West wishes to wage war on them, then the United States would indeed be facing a real threat. The realist response to this security dilemma would be to form alliances with as many moderate Muslim states as possible in order to balance against Muslim extremists. But the problem with this approach is that many of these moderate Muslim leaders do not share Western values, do not represent their citizens, and do not have the popular support of their resident populations.

In a feat of astonishing naivety, the Bush administration believed that it could bring democracy to the Middle East and recreate the region in the United States' image. The belief was that democracy would bring prosperity, stability, trade, and a secure supply of oil, which would serve both US and regional interests. From the hegemonic point of view, this was an entirely reasonable way to extend one's influence and power without acquiring the formal trappings of empire. The problem, of course, is that local citizens often have their own ideas. Many citizens in the Middle East seek to counter pervasive US influence in the region. When given a choice, many have not voted for democrats, claiming instead that the groups that provide most effectively for their social needs-Hamas, Hezbollah, and the Muslim Brotherhood, for example—deserve representation, regardless of their views on democracy. Confronted with the election of those we consider enemies, US enthusiasm for democracy in the Middle East has waned significantly.

An Obsolete Framework

The successful functioning of the balance of power mechanism requires the predictable behavior of a small group of leaders who understand the rules of the game and pursue their states' interests within a set of predetermined boundaries. But today's leaders no longer have the requisite monopoly on information or on power. While the West might see globalization as a means of spreading its wealth around the world and contributing to the development of all, for others, that wealth appears to be distributed very inequitably and is acquired only with considerable cost. Indeed many see globalization as little more than a latter-day version of US imperialism. Photographs of US soldiers abusing Muslim prisoners in Iraq undermine national leaders' ability to claim that it is in their country's interest to be allied with the United States. These images also make it immeasurably more difficult for the US government to persuade the world that the United States is a power with which they should wish to be aligned.

Terrorist groups have no interest in balancing or bandwagoning against US power.

The balance of power as traditionally practiced was based on the state as the fundamental unit in the international order. The difference today is that due to technological developments, smaller and smaller groups are now able to acquire weapons of ever greater lethality. Moreover, through effective use of the Internet, these groups can coordinate actions across borders, recruit followers, plan complex attacks, and generate support from all over the world. Indeed, terrorist groups have no interest in balancing or bandwagoning against US power; they wish simply to expel the United States from the Middle East altogether.

That a country with secure borders, a formidable nuclear deterrent, and no military rivals in sight nevertheless feels vulnerable speaks to the inadequacies of the traditional formulation of the balance of power. This is not the first time in history in which military preeminence has bred hubris, as evinced by the casual deployment of 5,000 US troops to Saudi Arabia following the first Gulf War despite the action's local unpopularity. A similar miscalculation was the decision to launch a military invasion of Iraq without first taking the trouble to understand the nature of the task ahead.

Indeed, the weakness of the world's sole remaining superpower is not the result of any bandwagoning of rivals against it, but of deficiencies within its own borders. Ironically, increased military expenditures are undermining US security by contributing to federal deficits and reliance on foreign creditors, particularly China, to keep the economy afloat. Moreover, the projection of its power abroad is serving to ignite emnity against the United States. And meanwhile, confidence in US military superiority is diverting attention away from other important vulnerabilities, most crucially US dependence on foreign oil. But the vagaries of electoral politics guarantee that efforts to enhance US security through developing societal resilience to terrorism, or through questioning the appropriateness of spiraling defense expenditures, will never be successful.

Principles for the Future

The forces emerging against the United States are not being recruited, organized, or mobilized by any single state, but rather by loose networks of individuals with an appealing ideology disseminated by means of recent technological developments. With the United States' wealth, technological advantages, and attractive national ideology, it is in a unique position to confront this threat. To do so effectively, however, requires appealing not to the heads of other governments, but also to their populations and the potential recruits of terrorist adversaries.

The six principles that should guide US actions are first, the development of a defensible and achievable goal, second, a commitment to live by US principles, third, acquiring intelligence about the enemy, fourth, a separation of terrorists from their

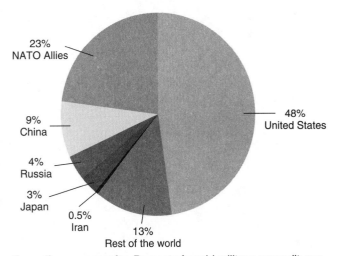

23%
NATO Allies

9%
China

4%
Russia

3%
Japan

0.5%
Iran

13%
Rest of the world

48%
United States

Spending on security. Percent of world military expenditures.

This pie chart shows the relative sizes of military budgets among several world powers. Total world military spending is estimated at $ 1.36 trillion USD, and the US budget for 2008 is almost half of this total, at $644 billion. Iran, despite its role in the "Axis of Evil" and as a security threat to the United States, spends a meager $6.6 billion annually on its military.

Source: International Institute for Strategic Studies, U.S. Department of Defense

communities, fifth, a willingness to engage others in countering terrorism, and sixth, a commitment to patience and maintaining perspective. Such a strategy requires recognition of the limits of the traditional state-centric approach and an appreciation of the ever growing importance of substate and trans-state actors in international relations. If the United States continues to rely on its military and diplomacy, it will find itself quite unprepared to take on the adversary that it currently faces—an adversary that does not play by the rules and does not consider itself in any sort of balance of power arrangement.

LOUISE RICHARDSON is Executive Dean of the Radcliffe Institute for Advanced Study, Senior Lecturer in Government at Harvard University, and Lecturer on Law at Harvard Law School.

State of Denial

BOB WOODWARD

Former Secretary of State Henry Kissinger had a powerful, largely invisible influence on the foreign policy of the Bush administration.

"Of the outside people that I talk to in this job," Vice President Cheney told me in the summer of 2005, "I probably talk to Henry Kissinger more than I talk to anybody else. He just comes by and I guess at least once a month, Scooter and I sit down with him."

Cheney had worked closely with Kissinger in the Ford administration, when Cheney was deputy and later chief of staff. Kissinger at first had been both secretary of state and national security adviser, an arrangement that every subsequent secretary of state had envied. Kissinger's ego was monumental, but Cheney found his hard-line advice useful after 9/11. They shared a worldview that international relations were a matter of military and economic power. Diplomatic power derived from threatening to and then actually using that power. In its rawest form, using the military sent a useful message to the world: It's dangerous to be an enemy of the United States.

The president also met privately with Kissinger every couple of months, making the former secretary the most regular and frequent outside adviser to Bush on foreign affairs. Bush, according to Cheney, was "a big fan" of Kissinger. Of the Bush-Kissinger meetings, Rumsfeld said, "I helped set it up." The president, who generally discounts the importance of outside advisers, found his discussions with Kissinger important, according to Cheney, Rumsfeld and others in the White House.

Card and the president's personal office staff knew that Kissinger was one of the few nonfamily outsiders with a standing invitation to call whenever he was coming to Washington to see if the president was available. By Card's calculation about half the meetings were just the president and Kissinger. Either he or Rice attended the other half.

No one in the American foreign policy establishment was more controversial or carried more baggage than Kissinger, then 82 years old.

Vietnam was like a stone around his neck and the prism through which he saw the world. After Lyndon Johnson, Richard Nixon and Robert McNamara, probably nobody else was so associated with that war. He had been the architect with Nixon, and later Ford, of U.S. foreign policy from 1969 to 1975. In his writing, speeches and private comments, Kissinger claimed that the United States had essentially won the war in 1972, only to lose it because of weakened resolve by the public and Congress.

If Kissinger felt he had something to say, he generally wrote about it, often in opinion pieces in *The Washington Post.* He had lots of thoughts about Iraq and Bush. He supported the war. Though he had little problem with Bush's second inaugural urging the spread of democracy and the end of tyranny, Kissinger would have been more modest in applying it. "We cannot abandon national security in pursuit of virtue," he had written in his 1999 book, *Years of Renewal,* on the Ford presidency. The United States "must temper its missionary spirit with a concept of national interest and rely on its head as well as its heart in defining its duty to the world."

In a practical sense, Kissinger was not at all certain that Iraq was ready for democracy, and he had reservations about using American combat troops in a massive effort to train a foreign military. In addition, since most Iraqis identified first and foremost with their tribal or religious sectarian background—Sunni, Shiite or Kurd—the question was how to encourage the development of a national Iraqi identity. Closely related was the crucial question of who the Iraqi army would fight for.

Kissinger liked Bush personally, though he told colleagues that it was not clear to him that the president really knew how to run the government. One of the big problems, he felt, was that Bush did not have the people or a system of national security policy decision making that ensured careful examination of the downsides of major decisions.

Kissinger sensed wobbliness everywhere on Iraq, and he increasingly saw it through his Vietnam prism. For Kissinger, the overriding lesson of Vietnam is to stick it out.

His column in the *Post* on August 12, 2005, was entitled "Lessons for an Exit Strategy." It was almost as long as Bush's second inaugural address. In the key line, Kissinger wrote, *"Victory over the insurgency is the only meaningful exit strategy."* He then made the rounds at the White House with Bush, Cheney and Hadley. Victory had to be the goal, he told all. Don't let it happen again. Don't give an inch, or else the media, the Congress and the American culture of avoiding hardship will walk you back. He also said that the eventual outcome in Iraq was more important than Vietnam had been. A radical Islamic or Taliban-style government in Iraq would be a model that could challenge the internal stability of the key countries in the Middle East and elsewhere.

Kissinger told Rice that in Vietnam they didn't have the time, focus, energy or support at home to get the politics in place. That's why it had collapsed like a house of cards. He urged that the Bush administration get the politics right, both in Iraq and on the home front. Partially withdrawing troops had its own dangers. Even entertaining the idea of withdrawing any troops could create momentum for an exit that was less than victory.

Rice understood that Kissinger's message reinforced a conviction that the president already held.

In early September 2005, Mike Gerson went to see Kissinger in New York City.

"Why did you support the Iraq War?" Gerson asked him.

"Because Afghanistan wasn't enough," Kissinger answered. In the conflict with radical Islam, he said, they want to humiliate us. "And we need to humiliate them." The American response to 9/11 had essentially to be more than proportionate—on a larger scale than simply invading Afghanistan and overthrowing the Taliban. Something else was needed. The Iraq War was essential to send a larger message, "in order to make a point that we're not going to live in this world that they want for us." He said he had defended the war ever since. In Manhattan, this position got him in trouble, particularly at cocktail parties, he noted with a smile.

Gerson understood that Kissinger viewed Iraq purely in the context of power politics. It was not idealism. He didn't seem to connect with Bush's goal of promoting democracy. "What did you think of the second inaugural?" Gerson asked him.

"At first I was appalled," Kissinger said, carefully covering himself because that was what he had told others, and continued to say in private. On reflection, he claimed, he now believed the speech served a purpose and was a very smart move, setting the war on terror and overall U.S. foreign policy in the context of American values. That would help sustain a long campaign.

On Iran, Kissinger said it was absolutely critical that Iran not be allowed to gain nuclear capability and nuclear weapons. If it does, he said, all the powers in the region—Turkey, Egypt, Saudi Arabia and the others—would go nuclear. "That would be one of the worst strategic nightmares that America could imagine," he said. That could dwarf the uncertainties of the Cold War.

Returning to Iraq, Kissinger told Gerson that Bush needed to resist the pressure to withdraw American troops, repeating his axiom that the only meaningful exit strategy was victory. "The president can't be talking about troop reductions as a centerpiece," Kissinger said. "You may want to reduce troops." But troop reduction should not be the objective. "This is not where you put the emphasis."

He then gave Gerson a copy of his so-called salted peanut memo, written during the first year of the Nixon administration. In the memo to President Nixon, dated September 10, 1969, Kissinger warned, "Withdrawal of U.S. troops will become like salted peanuts to the American public; the more U.S. troops come home, the more will be demanded." The policy of "Vietnamization," turning the fight over to the South Vietnamese military, Kissinger wrote, might increase pressure to end the war because the American public wanted a quick resolution. Troop withdrawals would only encourage the enemy. "It will become harder and harder to maintain the morale of those who remain, not to speak of their mothers."

For Kissinger, Iraq was the Vietnam sequel. He replayed for Gerson his version of the end of the Vietnam War. The public, the Congress, the Defense Department and the military had all lost their will. At one point, he said, he had proposed to President Nixon a major ultimatum to the North Vietnamese with dire consequences if they did not negotiate peace. But it didn't happen, the former national security adviser said wistfully. "I didn't have enough power."

The Long March to Be a Superpower

The People's Liberation Army is investing heavily to give China the military muscle to match its economic power. But can it begin to rival America?

The sight is as odd as its surroundings are bleak. Where a flat expanse of mud flats, salt pans and fish farms reaches the Bohai Gulf, a vast ship looms through the polluted haze. It is an aircraft-carrier, the *Kiev,* once the proud possession of the Soviet Union. Now it is a tourist attraction. Chinese visitors sit on the flight deck under Pepsi umbrellas, reflecting perhaps on a great power that was and another, theirs, that is fast in the making.

Inside the *Kiev,* the hangar bay is divided into two. On one side, bored-looking visitors watch an assortment of dance routines featuring performers in ethnic-minority costumes. On the other side is a full-size model of China's new J-10, a plane unveiled with great fanfare in January as the most advanced fighter built by the Chinese themselves (except for the Ukrainian or Russian turbofan engines—but officials prefer not to advertise this). A version of this, some military analysts believe, could one day be deployed on a Chinese ship.

The Pentagon is watching China's aircraft-carrier ambitions with bemused interest. Since the 1980s, China has bought four of them (three from the former Soviet Union and an Australian one whose construction began in Britain during the second world war). Like the *Kiev,* the *Minsk* (berthed near Hong Kong) has been turned into a tourist attraction having first been studied closely by Chinese naval engineers. Australia's carrier, the *Melbourne,* has been scrapped. The biggest and most modern one, the *Varyag,* is in the northern port city of Dalian, where it is being refurbished. Its destiny is uncertain. The Pentagon says it might be put into service, used for training carrier crews, or become yet another floating theme-park.

American global supremacy is not about to be challenged by China's tinkering with aircraft-carriers. Even if China were to commission one—which analysts think unlikely before at least 2015—it would be useless in the most probable area of potential conflict between China and America, the Taiwan Strait. China could far more easily launch its jets from shore. But it would be widely seen as a potent symbol of China's rise as a military power. Some Chinese officers want to fly the flag ever farther afield as a demonstration of China's rise. As China emerges as a trading giant (one increasingly dependent on imported oil), a few of its military analysts talk about the need to protect distant sea lanes in the Malacca Strait and beyond.

This week China's People's Liberation Army (PLA), as the armed forces are known, is celebrating the 80th year since it was born as a group of ragtag rebels against China's then rulers. Today it is vying to become one of the world's most capable forces: one that could, if necessary, keep even the Americans at bay. The PLA has little urge to confront America head-on, but plenty to deter it from protecting Taiwan.

The pace of China's military upgrading is causing concern in the Pentagon. Eric McVadon, a retired rear admiral, told a congressional commission in 2005 that China had achieved a "remarkable leap" in the modernisation of forces needed to overwhelm Taiwan and deter or confront any American intervention. And the pace of this, he said, was "urgently continuing". By Pentagon standards, Admiral McVadon is doveish.

In its annual report to Congress on China's military strength, published in May, the Pentagon said China's "expanding military capabilities" were a "major factor" in altering military balances in East Asia. It said China's ability to project power over long distances remained limited. But it repeated its observation, made in 2006, that among "major and emerging powers" China had the "greatest potential to compete militarily" with America.

Since the mid-1990s China has become increasingly worried that Taiwan might cut its national ties with the mainland. To instil fear into any Taiwanese leader so inclined, it has been deploying short-range ballistic missiles (SRBMs) on the coast facing the island as fast as it can produce them—about 100 a year. The Pentagon says there are now about 900 of these DF-11s (CSS-7) and DF-15s (CSS-6). They are getting more accurate. Salvoes of them might devastate Taiwan's military infrastructure so quickly that any war would be over before America could respond.

Much has changed since 1995 and 1996, when China's weakness in the face of American power was put on stunning display. In a fit of anger over America's decision in 1995 to allow Lee Teng-hui, then Taiwan's president, to make a high-profile trip to his alma mater, Cornell University, China fired ten unarmed DF-15s into waters off Taiwan. The Americans, confident that China would quickly back off, sent two aircraft-carrier battle groups to the region as a warning. The tactic worked. Today America would have to think twice. Douglas Paal, America's unofficial ambassador to Taiwan from 2002 to 2006, says the "cost of conflict has certainly gone up."

The Chinese are now trying to make sure that American aircraft-carriers cannot get anywhere near. Admiral McVadon worries about their development of DF-21 (CSS-5) medium-range ballistic missiles. With their far higher re-entry velocities than the SRBMs, they would be much harder for Taiwan's missile defences to cope with. They could even be launched far beyond Taiwan into the Pacific to hit aircraft-carriers. This would be a big technical challenge. But Admiral McVadon says America "might have to worry" about such a possibility within a couple of years.

Once the missiles have done their job, China's armed forces could (so they hope) follow up with a panoply of advanced Russian weaponry—mostly amassed in the past decade. Last year the Pentagon said China had imported around $11 billion of weapons between 2000 and 2005, mainly from Russia.

China knows it has a lot of catching up to do. Many Americans may be unenthusiastic about America's military excursions in recent years, particularly about the war in Iraq. But Chinese military authors, in numerous books and articles, see much to be inspired by.

On paper at least, China's gains have been impressive. Even into the 1990s China had little more than a conscript army of ill-educated peasants using equipment based largely on obsolete Soviet designs of the 1950s and outdated cold-war (or even guerrilla-war) doctrine. Now the emphasis has shifted from ground troops to the navy and air force, which would spearhead any attack on Taiwan. China has bought 12 Russian Kilo-class diesel attack submarines. The newest of these are equipped with supersonic Sizzler cruise missiles that America's carriers, many analysts believe, would find hard to stop.

There are supersonic cruise missiles too aboard China's four new Sovremenny-class destroyers, made to order by the Russians and designed to attack aircraft-carriers and their escorts. And China's own shipbuilders have not been idle. In an exhibition marking the 80th anniversary, Beijing's Military Museum displays what Chinese official websites say is a model of a new nuclear-powered attack submarine, the *Shang*. These submarines would allow the navy to push deep into the Pacific, well beyond Taiwan, and, China hopes, help defeat American carriers long before they get close. Last year, much to America's embarrassment, a newly developed Chinese diesel submarine for shorter-range missions surfaced close to the American carrier *Kitty Hawk* near Okinawa without being detected beforehand.

American air superiority in the region is now challenged by more than 200 advanced Russian Su-27 and Su-30 fighters China has acquired since the 1990s. Some of these have been made under licence in China itself. The Pentagon thinks China is also interested in buying Su-33s, which would be useful for deployment on an aircraft-carrier, if China decides to build one.

During the Taiwan Strait crisis of 1995–96, America could be reasonably sure that, even if war did break out (few seriously thought it would), it could cope with any threat from China's nuclear arsenal. China's handful of strategic missiles capable of hitting mainland America were based in silos, whose positions the Americans most probably knew. Launch preparations would take so long that the Americans would have plenty of time to knock them out. China has been working hard to remedy this. It is deploying six road-mobile, solid-fuelled (which means quick to launch) intercontinental DF-31s and is believed to be developing

DF-31As with a longer range that could hit anywhere in America, as well as submarine-launched (so more concealable) JL-2s that could threaten much of America too.

All Dressed up and Ready to Fight?

But how much use is all this hardware? Not a great deal is known about the PLA's fighting capability. It is by far the most secretive of the world's big armies. One of the few titbits it has been truly open about in the build-up to the celebrations is the introduction of new uniforms to mark the occasion: more body-hugging and, to howls of criticism from some users of popular Chinese internet sites, more American-looking.

As Chinese military analysts are well aware, America's military strength is not just about technology. It also involves training, co-ordination between different branches of the military ("jointness", in the jargon), gathering and processing intelligence, experience and morale. China is struggling to catch up in these areas too. But it has had next to no combat experience since a brief and undistinguished foray into Vietnam in 1979 and a huge deployment to crush pro-democracy unrest ten years later.

China is even coyer about its war-fighting capabilities than it is about its weaponry. It has not rehearsed deep-sea drills against aircraft-carriers. It does not want to create alarm in the region, nor to rile America. There is also a problem of making all this Russian equipment work. Some analysts say the Chinese have not been entirely pleased with their Su-27 and Su-30 fighters. Keeping them maintained and supplied with spare parts (from Russia) has not been easy. A Western diplomat says China is also struggling to keep its Russian destroyers and submarines in good working order. "We have to be cautious about saying 'wow'," he suggests of the new equipment.

China is making some progress in its efforts to wean itself off dependence on the Russians. After decades of effort, some analysts believe, China is finally beginning to use its own turbofan engines, an essential technology for advanced fighters. But self-sufficiency is still a long way off. The Russians are sometimes still reluctant to hand over their most sophisticated technologies. "The only trustworthy thing [the Chinese] have is missiles," says Andrew Yang of the Chinese Council of Advanced Policy Studies in Taiwan.

The Pentagon, for all its fretting, is trying to keep channels open to the Chinese. Military exchanges have been slowly reviving since their nadir of April 2001, when a Chinese fighter jet hit an American spy plane close to China. Last year, for the first time, the two sides conducted joint exercises—search-and-rescue missions off the coasts of America and China. But these were simple manoeuvres and the Americans learned little from them. The Chinese remain reluctant to engage in anything more complex, perhaps for fear of revealing their weaknesses.

The Russians have gained deeper insights. Two years ago the PLA staged large-scale exercises with them, the first with a foreign army. Although not advertised as such, these were partly aimed at scaring the Taiwanese. The two countries practised blockades, capturing airfields and amphibious landings. The

Russians showed off some of the weaponry they hope to sell to the big-spending Chinese.

Another large joint exercise is due to be held on August 9th–17th in the Urals (a few troops from other members of the Shanghai Co-operation Organisation, a six-nation group including Central Asian states, will also take part). But David Shambaugh of George Washington University says the Russians have not been very impressed by China's skills. After the joint exercise of 2005, Russians muttered about the PLA's lack of "jointness", its poor communications and the slowness of its tanks.

China has won much praise in the West for its increasing involvement in United Nations peacekeeping operations. But this engagement has revealed little of China's combat capability. Almost all of the 1,600 Chinese peacekeepers deployed (including in Lebanon, Congo and Liberia) are engineers, transport troops or medical staff.

A series of "white papers" published by the Chinese government since 1998 on its military developments have shed little light either, particularly on how much the PLA is spending and on what. By China's opaque calculations, the PLA enjoyed an average annual budget increase of more than 15% between 1990 and 2005 (nearly 10% in real terms). This year the budget was increased by nearly 18%. But this appears not to include arms imports, spending on strategic missile forces and research and development. The International Institute for Strategic Studies in London says the real level of spending in 2004 could have been about 1.7 times higher than the officially declared budget of 220 billion yuan ($26.5 billion at then exchange rates).

This estimate would make China's spending roughly the same as that of France in 2004. But the different purchasing power of the dollar in the two countries—as well as China's double-digit spending increases since then—push the Chinese total far higher. China is struggling hard to make its army more professional—keeping servicemen for longer and attracting better-educated recruits. This is tough at a time when the civilian economy is booming and wages are climbing. The PLA is having to spend much more on pay and conditions for its 2.3m people.

Keeping the army happy is a preoccupation of China's leaders, mindful of how the PLA saved the party from probable destruction during the unrest of 1989. In the 1990s they encouraged military units to run businesses to make more money for themselves. At the end of the decade, seeing that this was fuelling corruption, they ordered the PLA to hand over its business to civilian control. Bigger budgets are now helping the PLA to make up for some of those lost earnings.

The party still sees the army as a bulwark against the kind of upheaval that has toppled communist regimes elsewhere. Chinese leaders lash out at suggestions (believed to be supported by some officers) that the PLA should be put under the state's control instead of the party's. The PLA is riddled with party spies who monitor officers' loyalty. But the party also gives the army considerable leeway to manage its own affairs. It worries about military corruption but seldom moves against it, at least openly (in a rare exception to this, a deputy chief of the navy was dismissed last year for taking bribes and "loose morals"). The PLA's culture of secrecy allowed the unmonitored spread of SARS, an often fatal respiratory ailment, in the army's medical system in 2003.

Carrier Trade

The PLA knows its weaknesses. It has few illusions that China can compete head-on with the Americans militarily. The Soviet Union's determination to do so is widely seen in China as the cause of its collapse. Instead China emphasises weaponry and doctrine that could be used to defeat a far more powerful enemy using "asymmetric capabilities".

The idea is to exploit America's perceived weak points such as its dependence on satellites and information networks. China's successful (if messy and diplomatically damaging) destruction in January of one of its own ageing satellites with a rocket was clearly intended as a demonstration of such power. Some analysts believe Chinese people with state backing have been trying to hack into Pentagon computers. Richard Lawless, a Pentagon official, recently said China had developed a "very sophisticated" ability to attack American computer and internet systems.

The Pentagon's fear is that military leaders enamoured of new technology may underestimate the diplomatic consequences of trying it out. Some Chinese see a problem here too. The antisatellite test has revived academic discussion in China of the need for setting up an American-style national security council that would help military planners co-ordinate more effectively with foreign-policy makers.

But the Americans find it difficult to tell China bluntly to stop doing what others are doing too (including India, which has aircraft-carriers and Russian fighter planes). In May Admiral Timothy Keating, the chief of America's Pacific Command, said China's interest in aircraft-carriers was "understandable". He even said that if China chose to develop them, America would "help them to the degree that they seek and the degree that we're capable." But, he noted, "it ain't as easy as it looks."

A senior Pentagon official later suggested Admiral Keating had been misunderstood. Building a carrier for the Chinese armed forces would be going a bit far. But the two sides are now talking about setting up a military hotline. The Americans want to stay cautiously friendly as the dragon grows stronger.

North Korea Takes on the World

"The road ahead for Korean denuclearization and the normalization of US-North Korean relations promises to be bumpy and unpredictable."

CHARLES K. ARMSTRONG

Since the early 1990s, the main U.S. policy concern and the bulk of Western media attention regarding North Korea (officially the Democratic People's Republic of Korea, or DPRK) have focused on the "nuclear issue"—North Korea's potential, or actual, production of nuclear weapons. A confrontation over North Korea's diversion of spent fuel from its Yongbyon nuclear power plant, possibly to produce weapons, led the United States and North Korea to the brink of war in June 1994.

Last October, the nuclear issue reached a new level of crisis when North Korea tested a nuclear device, three months after it had tested a half dozen medium- and long-range missiles. The nuclear test was almost universally condemned. It prompted a harsh United Nations sanctions resolution. Even China, North Korea's strongest ally and largest source of economic aid, joined in criticizing North Korea's actions. For Bush administration hard-liners, the nuclear test and the resulting sanctions offered an opportunity to discard the diplomatic approach it had reluctantly pursued since April 2003. North Korea had defied the world, it seemed, and would have to suffer the consequences.

Yet, in the end, the world and North Korea reached a compromise. The United States and North Korea, along with the other participants in six-party talks—South Korea, China, Russia, and Japan—returned to negotiations in February 2007. For all the rhetoric about coercion and regime change coming from the Bush administration's sidelines, Washington has reconfirmed its desire for a diplomatic solution.

The six-party agreement of February 13, 2007, brings us more or less back to where we were when the earlier nuclear crisis was defused in October 1994, with North Korea promising to cease its nuclear program in exchange for energy assistance and movement toward normalization of relations with the United States and Japan. The hard-line approach of the first six years of the Bush administration proved to be a failure, resulting in little more than lost time and missed opportunities.

North Korea this summer shut down its Yongbyon plant, as the February agreement required. Even so, the road ahead for Korean denuclearization and the normalization of US-North Korean relations promises to be bumpy and unpredictable. This is especially so in the context of a North Korea that is changing domestically in ways that are not yet entirely clear, and given the changing dynamic of relations among the other countries involved in the six-party process.

The Genie is Out

North Korea has several motivations for developing nuclear weapons. One is security, in particular security against the United States. North Korea has long been vulnerable to US nuclear weapons based in East Asia and the Pacific, including South Korea. This sense of vulnerability was heightened significantly after the Soviet Union collapsed in 1991 and China recognized South Korea in 1992, removing most of what remained of the Russian-Chinese nuclear umbrella over the North. That is why, at that time, Pyongyang accelerated its nuclear program.

The US invasion of Iraq in 2003 was intended to "shock and awe" North Koreans as well as Iraqis into capitulating to America. For North Korea, the invasion probably had the opposite effect: encouraging Pyongyang to build up a nuclear deterrent against US attack should North Korea find itself next on the list for coercive "regime change." With a nuclear deterrent now in place, Pyongyang believes it is able to negotiate with the United States from a much stronger position than before.

Nuclear brinkmanship is a dangerous game, but North Korea has played it with some skill over the past 15 years, using the threat of producing atomic weapons to gain economic and political concessions from the United States and other countries. Now that North Korea has removed the "strategic ambiguity" about its possession of nuclear arms, the regime may feel it can extract an even higher price for their removal. This could very well be correct.

Nuclear arms also carry high prestige both domestically and abroad. The military sector, which currently dominates the country's leadership, can be satisfied that its interests are being met and that North Korean leader Kim Jong Il has put the regime's security above all else. In the North Korean media, the October 2006 nuclear test was announced as a "historic event that brought happiness to our military and people." Having little else to brag about, given its dismal economy and international marginalization, North Korea can present its admission into the elite nuclear weapons club as a source of pride—including, not least, to the people of South Korea.

Given the value of nuclear weapons to the current North Korean leadership, what are the chances that they are likely to give them up? It remains to be seen whether the agreements of recent months will lead to a complete denuclearization of North Korea, as the United States and other participants in the six-party talks have demanded. No doubt Pyongyang would prefer to have its cake and eat it too—gain the economic benefits, diplomatic recognition, and security assurance that it seeks while maintaining a nuclear deterrent "just in case." It may be that North Korea can never feel entirely secure without having nuclear weapons in reserve, in which case the current talks have little hope of success.

But if the North Korean leadership is persuaded that the benefits of denuclearization outweigh the benefits of nuclear deterrence, especially within the context of a more stable and integrated Northeast Asian security environment, then Pyongyang may eventually dismantle the nuclear program completely. Only time will tell. Unfortunately, much time has already been lost. The Bush administration's six-year refusal to engage directly and bilaterally with North Korea not only failed to resolve the nuclear issue—it left the world in a much more difficult situation than before.

Last year North Korea withdrew from the nuclear Non-Proliferation Treaty—something it had only threatened to do before. The February 2007 agreement is indeed similar to the Framework Agreement of 1994—except that now North Korea has proved its ability to produce a nuclear weapon. In essence, Pyongyang stared down the world, and the world blinked. The genie has been let out the bottle, and it will take skillful diplomacy and strong nerves on all sides to put it back in.

Change in the North

An important assumption underlying the hard-line approach toward Pyongyang that characterized the Bush administration until recently (a view still embraced by some, but no longer the dominant paradigm) is that the North Korean regime is weak, possibly on the verge of collapse, and that economic pressure can bring it to its knees or perhaps eliminate it altogether.

In fact, the regime was probably more secure when George W. Bush entered office than it had been a few years earlier, and is more stable today than it was a decade ago. If there was any time when North Korea was on the verge of collapse, it was during the famine years of the 1990s—although it is not certain the regime was mortally vulnerable even then. During that disastrous decade, North Korea lost most of its communist allies, its founding leader, and hundreds of thousands of its people. But by the early 2000s, economic aid from China, South Korea, and Western donors had staved off the worst of the economic crisis. The regime had begun tinkering with economic reform. And Kim was leading his country toward a cautious but significant opening to the outside world.

North Koreans have been saying recently that the United States can serve as a counterweight to the growing influence of China.

Long before the famine of 1995–1999, there were signs of liberalization and the growth of local markets in the North Korean economy. In recent years, however, Pyongyang has officially acknowledged and sanctioned such markets. In July 2002, the DPRK instituted far-reaching changes in currency exchange rates, the setting of wages and prices, the distribution of food, and other aspects of the economy. Although far short of the reforms introduced by China in the 1980s, much less the quasi-capitalism of contemporary China and Vietnam, collectively the 2002 reforms represented the single biggest set of economic changes since the DPRK's founding in 1948.

The results of this economic restructuring have been mixed. Inflation and other by-products of the reforms have made life more difficult for some North Koreans, while benefiting others; the social effect of this growing economic divide remains to be seen. A model "special administrative district" established in the city of Sinuiju on the Sino–North Korean border, reminiscent of China's Special Economic Zones, failed to take off when Chinese authorities arrested the man personally appointed by Kim to run the project—a wealthy Chinese-born Dutch citizen named Yang Bin. On the other hand, the special economic zone in Kae-song, near the border with South Korea, has drawn in a considerable amount of South Korean capital, especially small- and medium-sized businesses.

Concurrent with these economic reforms, beginning in 2003, North Korea promoted a new slogan, "Military-First Politics" *(Songun chongch'i)*. The military was declared the vanguard of North Korean society, ahead of the Communist Party and even the working class itself. North Korea was not about to let the pernicious influences of capitalism undermine its socialist system; the DPRK seemed determined to continue with economic reform only under the control of the party-military apparatus, maintaining a firm defense against both external threats and any potential internal subversion.

Yet signs were strong that North Korea had made the strategic choice to open its economy, albeit in a highly controlled fashion, to the outside "capitalist" world, including—perhaps especially—Japan and the United States. If this was, in fact, the strategy, it has fallen far short of success. The September 2002 summit meeting between Kim and then-Prime Minister Junichiro Koizumi of Japan, during which Kim admitted that North Korean agents had kidnapped Japanese citizens to train North Korean spies in the 1970s and 1980s, led to outrage in Japan and a fixation on the "abduction issue" that has blocked improvement in North Korea–Japan relations to this day.

The Return to Diplomacy

The situation with the United States has been even worse. In his first term, President Bush made no secret of his disdain for the North Korean regime and Kim personally. He famously labeled North Korea a member of an "Axis of Evil," along with Iran and Saddam Hussein's Iraq. Neoconservatives in the administration saw Clinton-era engagement as nothing but appeasement.

The remnants of the engagement policy were themselves shattered in October 2002 when Assistant Secretary of State James Kelly confronted North Korean officials in Pyongyang with "incontrovertible evidence" that North Korea had been engaged in a highly enriched uranium (HEU) program to develop nuclear weapons. More recent US intelligence reports have cast some doubt on how far such a program had actually developed. In any case, the HEU accusation brought negotiations to a screeching halt, and the second US–North Korean nuclear crisis soon followed—in some ways an accelerated version of the 1994 crisis.

The Bush administration countered North Korea's demand for bilateral talks to resolve the crisis by insisting on multilateral negotiations that involved North Korea's regional neighbors. In particular, the United States wanted to involve China, seen to have special leverage over North Korea because of their long history of relations and China's indispensable role as supplier of oil and food. In April 2003, North Korean, American, and Chinese officials met in Beijing to discuss a way out of the impasse. Still, the United States, while stating it did not intend to attack the DPRK, acted as if coercion and pressure alone would resolve the problem—with North Korea either giving in to US demands or collapsing.

In the end, Washington had little choice but to return to diplomacy, in effect bringing US-DPRK relations back to 1994. War was simply not a viable option if the United States wanted to avoid disaster. Meanwhile, however, many things had changed in North Korea, on the Korean peninsula, and in Northeast Asia. The countries in the region, including Russia, China, and even Japan (which hewed closest to the US position, in part because of its security dependence on Washington) were willing to be more flexible and accommodating toward the DPRK than the United States was.

Equally if not more important, inter-Korean relations had changed significantly since the days when South Korean President Kim Young Sam feared that a US-DPRK agreement would harm South Korean interests. The engagement policies of President Kim Dae Jung and his successor, Roh Moo Hyun, had created a new dynamic on the Korean peninsula that ran counter to the hard-line US approach. In this context, the six-party process became a complex multilateral dialogue.

Crossing the Threshold

The complexity of the six-party process was not helped by the mixed signals given by the United States itself. A fourth round of talks finally yielded an agreement signed on September 19, 2005. This pact was vague in its details but offered each side what it had demanded: North Korea promised to dismantle its nuclear program; Japan and the United States agreed to take steps toward normalizing relations with the DPRK; and China, Japan, Russia, the United States, and South Korea agreed to provide the North with energy assistance.

The problem was that at the same time the September agreement was being finalized, the US Department of Treasury, under Article 311 of the Patriot Act, impounded North Korean bank accounts held in Banco Delta Asia in Macau, accusing the bank of laundering money for illicit activities of the DPRK government and members of the North Korean elite. Pyongyang condemned the action and demanded the North Korean accounts be unfrozen. The Treasury Department refused. North Korea then refused to return to the six-party talks until the issue was resolved.

In the early morning of July 5, 2006—the Fourth of July in the United States—North Korea tested seven ballistic missiles,

breaking its self-imposed missile-testing moratorium from 1999. Although the tests were not terribly successful—the one long-range missile tested exploded within seconds of launch—they certainly brought the world's attention to North Korea, which was no doubt Pyongyang's intention. Japan brought a resolution condemning the tests to the UN Security Council. A somewhat softer version of the Japanese proposal, addressing Chinese and Russian concerns that the UN not authorize the use of force against North Korea, was passed unanimously by the Security Council on July 15. This was the first time the Security Council had so forcefully condemned a North Korean act since it authorized military action in the Korean War (in the absence of the Soviet Union) in June 1950. China's support for such a strongly worded resolution was particularly striking, since Beijing had previously been cautious in its criticism of North Korea and preferred to apply quiet pressure behind the scenes.

Even so, the sanctions did not force North Korea back to the negotiating table. Pyongyang's game of brinkmanship had escalated since the second nuclear crisis began at the end of 2002. North Korea's announcement that it had exploded a nuclear device on October 9, 2006, was the logical culmination of this process. The explosion itself was probably quite small. But North Korea had crossed the nuclear threshold, most likely using plutonium extracted from the Yongbyon reactor. The October test brought to an end 15 years of speculation that the DPRK might have a nuclear weapon, and led immediately to more international condemnation of North Korea and a second Security Council resolution calling for sanctions.

The fallout, so to speak, was less than many expected. UN Resolution 1718 called for bans on travel to and from the DPRK, inspection of cargo, and regular monitoring of North Korea's activities. It called for preventing transfers of all weapons as well as luxury goods, and the freezing of any funds related to the production of weapons of mass destruction.

Yet no major incident over inspection of North Korean cargo ensued, and North Korea did not react as if the sanctions were an "act of war," as it had threatened to do when the United States first proposed UN sanctions in 1993. Neither has the nuclear test provoked Japan into developing its own nuclear deterrent, or set off a nuclear arms race in East Asia—so far, at least. And, in fact, North Korea did return to the talks. Washington, for its part, seemed finally willing to put serious effort into diplomacy.

There is reason to doubt that North Korea will ever give up nuclear weapons completely.

The China Factor

The United States has demonstrated considerable faith in China's ability to influence North Korea. China's role in the North Korean nuclear crisis has been important, but ambiguous. To be sure, Beijing's decision to join in the condemnation of North Korea's missile and nuclear tests was essential for the Security Council resolutions to pass. And it is true that China is North Korea's largest trading partner and main source of foreign aid. Overall, however, it seems fair to say that China's leverage over North Korea is greater than the Chinese claim, but less than others (especially the Americans) tend to think.

Theoretically, China could cut off oil supplies and bring North Korea's fragile economy to a halt. But as much as China fears a nuclear North Korea, it is even more concerned about a chaotic and disintegrating North Korea that could destabilize the region and disrupt China's robust economic development. Nor is Beijing keen on a US-allied South Korea absorbing the North and bringing US troops to China's borders. Therefore, China is very unlikely to use its economic leverage in a forceful and overt way.

North Korea, for its part, is unlikely to trust China and follow its lead, notwithstanding the fading Korean War rhetoric of "blood-cemented friendship" and a relationship "as close as lips and teeth." Distrust of China's designs on the Korean peninsula runs deep in highly nationalistic North Korea. Indeed, North Koreans have been saying recently that the United States can serve as a counterweight to the growing influence of China in East Asia. A North Korean official suggested to no less a foreign policy personage than Henry Kissinger, America's grand master of *realpolitik,* that North Korea and the United States should cooperate to prevent Chinese hegemony in the region. That might be a stretch even for Kissingerian strategic thinking, but it should not be taken for granted that North Korea necessarily sees China as a permanent friend and America as a permanent enemy.

A similar ambivalence underlies the US posture toward North Korea. In some respects, North Korea has long played as a substitute for China in US policy. For both the United States and Japan, North Korean nuclear weapons offer an ideal rationalization for the development of a missile defense that is in reality directed against China. Some Chinese military leaders seem to believe that the United States actually wanted North Korea to go nuclear precisely to provide such cover for anti-Chinese measures. At the same time, the Banco Delta Asia sanctions may have had as their real target (at least in part) the Chinese banks that hold much larger North Korean assets than the measly $25 million held in Banco Delta Asia—"killing the chickens to scare the monkeys," to use the Chinese proverb.

The February 13 Agreement

The fifth round of the six-party talks concluded on February 13, 2007, with the new agreement reaffirming the principles of the September 2005 statement, and including a few more details. North Korea agreed to shut down its Yongbyon nuclear facility, and invite International Atomic Energy Agency inspectors to monitor and verify its actions, within 60 days. In the same period,

the United States and Japan would begin talks with the DPRK aimed at resolving their respective bilateral issues and normalizing diplomatic relations. Energy and humanitarian assistance to North Korea would resume, including an initial shipment of 50,000 tons of fuel oil. In a second phase, according to the agreement, the DPRK would dismantle all its existing nuclear facilities, and the six parties would explore ways to promote security cooperation and mutual trust in Northeast Asia, including a possible peace agreement to replace the Korean War armistice.

It is an ambitious agenda with many potential pitfalls, not all of them predictable. The six parties reconvened in Beijing on March 19, and—apparently to the surprise of the chief US negotiator Christopher Hill—the issue of the Banco Delta Asia funds, which the North Koreans insisted had to be unfrozen, could not be immediately settled. The North Koreans refused to proceed until the issue was resolved, and the 60-day deadline for shutting down Yongbyon came and went. Eventually, the funds were released and North Korea shut down its reactor in July 2007.

The February 13 agreement is an important step toward resolving the nuclear issue, but still only one step in a potentially long and difficult path. There is reason to doubt that North Korea will ever give up nuclear weapons completely. Pyongyang, for its part, may have reason to question the reliability of a US government that has flipped from active engagement under Bill Clinton, to coercion under the first Bush administration, to a newfound enthusiasm for diplomacy in Bush's second term.

Nevertheless, the step-by-step, action-for-action outline of the agreement offers a chance to test each side's intentions at every stage, even if many of the important details remain to be worked out. It is possible that North Korea will not abide by the terms of the agreement, in which case sanctions should again come into play. But it is also possible, and certainly preferable for all parties concerned, that under the right conditions North Korea will be induced to give up its nuclear capability.

More is at stake than the nuclear issue alone. If successful, the six-party process could establish the framework for both a peace agreement to finally end the Korean War and a long-term security mechanism for maintaining the peace within a more integrated, more peaceful Northeast Asia. The world has come to the brink of disaster twice over Pyongyang's nuclear program, in 1994 and again in 2006. Now, after confronting the world, North Korea may be ready to join it.

CHARLES K. ARMSTRONG is an associate professor of history and director of the Center for Korean Research at Columbia University. His books include *The North Korean Revolution, 1945–1950* (Cornell University Press, 2003).

Reprinted from *Current History,* September 2007, pp. 263–267. Copyright © 2007 by Current History, Inc. Reprinted with permission.

Lifting the Veil
Understanding the Roots of Islamic Militancy

HENRY MUNSON

In the wake of the attacks of September 11, 2001, many intellectuals have argued that Muslim extremists like Osama bin Laden despise the United States primarily because of its foreign policy. Conversely, US President George Bush's administration and its supporters have insisted that extremists loathe the United States simply because they are religious fanatics who "hate our freedoms." These conflicting views of the roots of militant Islamic hostility toward the United States lead to very different policy prescriptions. If US policies have caused much of this hostility, it would make sense to change those policies, if possible, to dilute the rage that fuels Islamic militancy. If, on the other hand, the hostility is the result of religious fanaticism, then the use of brute force to suppress fanaticism would appear to be a sensible course of action.

Groundings for Animosity

Public opinion polls taken in the Islamic world in recent years provide considerable insight into the roots of Muslim hostility toward the United States, indicating that for the most part, this hostility has less to do with cultural or religious differences than with US policies in the Arab world. In February and March 2003, Zogby International conducted a survey on behalf of Professor Shibley Telhami of the University of Maryland involving 2,620 men and women in Egypt, Jordan, Lebanon, Morocco, and Saudi Arabia. Most of those surveyed had "unfavorable attitudes" toward the United States and said that their hostility to the United States was based primarily on US policy rather than on their values. This was true of 67 percent of the Saudis surveyed. In Egypt, however, only 46 percent said their hostility resulted from US policy, while 43 percent attributed their attitudes to their values as Arabs. This is surprising given that the prevailing religious values in Saudi Arabia are more conservative than in Egypt. Be that as it may, a plurality of people in all the countries surveyed said that their hostility toward the United States was primarily based on their opposition to US policy.

The issue that arouses the most hostility in the Middle East toward the United States is the Israeli-Palestinian conflict and what Muslims perceive as US responsibility for the suffering of the Palestinians. A similar Zogby International survey from the summer of 2001 found that more than 80 percent of the respondents in Egypt, Kuwait, Lebanon, and Saudi Arabia ranked the Palestinian issue as one of the three issues of greatest importance to them. A survey of Muslim "opinion leaders" released by the Pew Research Center for the People and the Press in December 2001 also found that the US position on the Israeli-Palestinian conflict was the main source of hostility toward the United States.

It is true that Muslim hostility toward Israel is often expressed in terms of anti-Semitic stereotypes and conspiracy theories—think, for example, of the belief widely-held in the Islamic world that Jews were responsible for the terrorists attacks of September 11, 2001. Muslim governments and educators need to further eliminate anti-Semitic bias in the Islamic world. However, it would be a serious mistake to dismiss Muslim and Arab hostility toward Israel as simply a matter of anti-Semitism. In the context of Jewish history, Israel represents liberation. In the context of Palestinian history, it represents subjugation. There will always be a gap between how the West and how the Muslim societies perceive Israel. There will also always be some Muslims (like Osama bin Laden) who will refuse to accept any solution to the Israeli-Palestinian conflict other than the destruction of the state of Israel. That said, if the United States is serious about winning the so-called "war on terror," then resolution of the Israeli-Palestinian conflict should be among its top priorities in the Middle East.

Eradicating, or at least curbing, Palestinian terrorism entails reducing the humiliation, despair, and rage that drive many Palestinians to support militant Islamic groups like Hamas and Islamic Jihad. When soldiers at an Israeli checkpoint prevented Ahmad Qurei (Abu al Ala), one of the principal negotiators of the Oslo accords and president of the Palestinian Authority's parliament, from traveling from Gaza to his home on the West Bank, he declared, "Soon, I too will join Hamas." Qurei's words reflected his outrage at the subjugation of his people and the humiliation that Palestinians experience every day at the checkpoints that surround their homes. Defeating groups like Hamas requires diluting the rage that fuels them. Relying on force alone tends to increase rather than weaken their appeal. This is demonstrated by some of the unintended consequences of the US-led invasion and occupation of Iraq in the spring of 2003.

On June 3, 2003, the Pew Research Center for the People and the Press released a report entitled *Views of a Changing World*

June 2003. This study was primarily based on a survey of nearly 16,000 people in 21 countries (including the Palestinian Authority) from April 28 to May 15, 2003, shortly after the fall of Saddam Hussein's regime. The survey results were supplemented by data from earlier polls, especially a survey of 38,000 people in 44 countries in 2002. The study found a marked increase in Muslim hostility toward the United States from 2002 to 2003. In the summer of 2002, 61 percent of Indonesians held a favorable view of the United States. By May of 2003, only 15 percent did. During the same period of time, the decline in Turkey was from 30 percent to 15 percent, and in Jordan it was from 25 percent to one percent.

Indeed, the Bush administration's war on terror has been a major reason for the increased hostility toward the United States. The Pew Center's 2003 survey found that few Muslims support this war. Only 23 percent of Indonesians did so in May of 2003, down from 31 percent in the summer of 2002. In Turkey, support dropped from 30 percent to 22 percent. In Pakistan, support dropped from 30 percent to 16 percent, and in Jordan from 13 percent to two percent. These decreases reflect overwhelming Muslim opposition to the war in Iraq, which most Muslims saw as yet another act of imperial subjugation of Muslims by the West.

The 2003 Zogby International poll found that most Arabs believe that the United States attacked Iraq to gain control of Iraqi oil and to help Israel. Over three-fourths of all those surveyed felt that oil was a major reason for the war. More than three-fourths of the Saudis and Jordanians said that helping Israel was a major reason, as did 72 percent of the Moroccans and over 50 percent of the Egyptians and Lebanese. Most Arabs clearly do not believe that the United States overthrew Saddam Hussein out of humanita1rian motives. Even in Iraq itself, where there was considerable support for the war, most people attribute the war to the US desire to gain control of Iraqi oil and help Israel.

Not only has the Bush administration failed to win much Muslim support for its war on terrorism, its conduct of the war has generated a dangerous backlash. Most Muslims see the US fight against terror as a war against the Islamic world. The 2003 Pew survey found that over 70 percent of Indonesians, Pakistanis, and Turks were either somewhat or very worried about a potential US threat to their countries, as were over half of Jordanians and Kuwaitis.

This sense of a US threat is linked to the 2003 Pew report's finding of widespread support for Osama bin Laden. The survey of April and May 2003 found that over half those surveyed in Indonesia, Jordan, and the Palestinian Authority, and almost half those surveyed in Morocco and Pakistan, listed bin Laden as one of the three world figures in whom they had the most confidence "to do the right thing." For most US citizens, this admiration for the man responsible for the attacks of September 11, 2001, is incomprehensible. But no matter how outrageous this widespread belief may be, it is vitally important to understand its origins. If one does not understand why people think the way they do, one cannot induce them to think differently. Similarly, if one does not understand why people act as they do, one cannot hope to induce them to act differently.

The Appeal of Osama bin Laden

Osama bin Laden first engaged in violence because of the occupation of a Muslim country by an "infidel" superpower. He did not fight the Russians in Afghanistan because he hated their values or their freedoms, but because they had occupied a Muslim land. He participated in and supported the Afghan resistance to the Soviet occupation from 1979 to 1989, which ended with the withdrawal of the Russians. Bin Laden saw this war as legitimate resistance to foreign occupation. At the same time, he saw it as a *jihad*, or holy war, on behalf of Muslims oppressed by infidels.

When Saddam Hussein invaded Kuwait in August 1990, bin Laden offered to lead an army to defend Saudi Arabia. The Saudis rejected this offer and instead allowed the United States to establish bases in their kingdom, leading to bin Laden's active opposition to the United States. One can only speculate what bin Laden would have done for the rest of his life if the United States had not stationed hundreds of thousands of US troops in Saudi Arabia in 1990. Conceivably, bin Laden's hostility toward the United States might have remained passive and verbal instead of active and violent. All we can say with certainty is that the presence of US troops in Saudi Arabia did trigger bin Laden's holy war against the United States. It was no accident that the bombing of two US embassies in Africa on August 7, 1998, marked the eighth anniversary of the introduction of US forces into Saudi Arabia as part of Operation Desert Storm.

Part of bin Laden's opposition to the presence of US military presence in Saudi Arabia resulted from the fact that US troops were infidels on or near holy Islamic ground. Non-Muslims are not allowed to enter Mecca and Medina, the two holiest places in Islam, and they are allowed to live in Saudi Arabia only as temporary residents. Bin Laden is a reactionary Wahhabi Muslim who undoubtedly does hate all non-Muslims. But that hatred was not in itself enough to trigger his *jihad* against the United States.

Indeed, bin Laden's opposition to the presence of US troops in Saudi Arabia had a nationalistic and anti-imperialist tone. In 1996, he declared that Saudi Arabia had become an American colony. There is nothing specifically religious or fundamentalist about this assertion. In his book *Chronique d'une Guerre d'Orient*, Gilles Kepel describes a wealthy whiskey-drinking Saudi who left part of his fortune to bin Laden because he alone "was defending the honor of the country, reduced in his eyes to a simple American protectorate."

In 1996, bin Laden issued his first major manifesto, entitled a "Declaration of Jihad against the Americans Occupying the Land of the Two Holy Places." The very title focuses on the presence of US troops in Saudi Arabia, which bin Laden calls an "occupation." But this manifesto also refers to other examples of what bin Laden sees as the oppression of Muslims by infidels. "It is no secret that the people of Islam have suffered from the oppression, injustice, and aggression of the alliance of Jews and Christians and their collaborators to the point that the blood of the Muslims became the cheapest and their wealth was loot in the hands of the enemies," he writes. "Their blood was spilled in Palestine and Iraq."

Bin Laden has referred to the suffering of the Palestinians and the Iraqis (especially with respect to the deaths caused by sanctions) in all of his public statements since at least the mid-1990s. His 1996 "Declaration of Jihad" is no exception. Nonetheless, it primarily focuses on the idea that the Saudi regime has "lost all legitimacy" because it "has permitted the enemies of the Islamic community, the Crusader American forces, to occupy our land for many years." In this 1996 text, bin Laden even contends that the members of the Saudi royal family are apostates because they helped infidels fight the Muslim Iraqis in the Persian Gulf War of 1991.

A number of neo-conservatives have advocated the overthrow of the Saudi regime because of its support for terrorism. It is true that the Saudis have funded militant Islamic movements. It is also true that Saudi textbooks and teachers often encourage hatred of infidels and allow the extremist views of bin Laden to thrive. It is also probably true that members of the Saudi royal family have financially supported terrorist groups. The fact remains, however, that bin Laden and his followers in Al Qaeda have themselves repeatedly called for the overthrow of the Saudi regime, saying that it has turned Saudi Arabia into "an American colony."

If the United States were to send troops to Saudi Arabia once again, this time to overthrow the Saudi regime itself, the main beneficiaries would be bin Laden and those who think like him. On January 27, 2002, a *New York Times* article referenced a Saudi intelligence survey conducted in October 2001 that showed that 95 percent of educated Saudis between the ages of 25 and 41 supported bin Laden. If the United States were to overthrow the Saudi regime, such people would lead a guerrilla war that US forces would inevitably find themselves fighting. This war would attract recruits from all over the Islamic world outraged by the desecration of "the land of the two holy places." Given that US forces are already fighting protracted guerrilla wars in Iraq and Afghanistan, starting a third one in Saudi Arabia would not be the most effective way of eradicating terror in the Middle East.

Those who would advocate the overthrow of the Saudi regime by US troops seem to forget why bin Laden began his holy war against the United States in the first place. They also seem to forget that no one is more committed to the overthrow of the Saudi regime than bin Laden himself. Saudi Arabia is in dire need of reform, but yet another US occupation of a Muslim country is not the way to make it happen.

In December 1998, Palestinian journalist Jamal Abd al Latif Isma'il asked bin Laden, "Who is Osama bin Laden, and what does he want?" After providing a brief history of his life, bin Laden responded to the second part of the question, "We demand that our land be liberated from the enemies, that our land be liberated from the Americans. God almighty, may He be praised, gave all living beings a natural desire to reject external intruders. Take chickens, for example. If an armed soldier enters a chicken's home wanting to attack it, it fights him even though it is just a chicken." For bin Laden and millions of other Muslims, the Afghans, the Chechens, the Iraqis, the Kashmiris, and the Palestinians are all just "chickens" defending their homes against the attacks of foreign soldiers.

In his videotaped message of October 7, 2001, after the attacks of September 11, 2001, bin Laden declared, "What America is tasting now is nothing compared to what we have been tasting for decades. For over 80 years our *umma* has been tasting this humiliation and this degradation. Its sons are killed, its blood is shed, its holy places are violated, and it is ruled by other than that which God has revealed. Yet no one hears. No one responds."

Bin Laden's defiance of the United States and his criticism of Muslim governments who ignore what most Muslims see as the oppression of the Palestinians, Iraqis, Chechens, and others, have made him a hero of Muslims who do not agree with his goal of a strictly Islamic state and society. Even young Arab girls in tight jeans praise bin Laden as an anti-imperialist hero. A young Iraqi woman and her Palestinian friends told Gilles Kepel in the fall of 2001, "He stood up to defend us. He is the only one."

Looking Ahead

Feelings of impotence, humiliation, and rage currently pervade the Islamic world, especially the Muslim Middle East. The invasion and occupation of Iraq has exacerbated Muslim concerns about the United States. In this context, bin Laden is seen as a heroic Osama Maccabeus descending from his mountain cave to fight the infidel oppressors to whom the worldly rulers of the Islamic world bow and scrape.

The violent actions of Osama bin Laden and those who share his views are not simply caused by "hatred of Western freedoms." They result, in part at least, from US policies that have enraged the Muslim world. Certainly, Islamic zealots like bin Laden do despise many aspects of Western culture. They do hate "infidels" in general, and Jews in particular. Muslims do need to seriously examine the existence and perpetuation of such hatred in their societies and cultures. But invading and occupying their countries simply exacerbates the sense of impotence, humiliation, and rage that induce them to support people like bin Laden. Defeating terror entails diluting the rage that fuels it.

HENRY MUNSON is Chair of the Department of Anthropology at the University of Maine.

From *Harvard International Review*, Winter 2004, pp. 20–23. Copyright © 2004 by the President of Harvard College. Reprinted by permission.

A Farewell to Arms Control?

Changing Course on Nuclear Talks

Philip E. Coyle

North Korea's detonation of a nuclear bomb at the beginning of October, now confirmed by seismic and radioactive air sample measurements, has many Americans wondering if other countries will embark on a nuclear arms race. And many people are asking, "Whatever happened to arms control?"

Conservative politicians in Japan have started calling for the country to arm itself with nuclear weapons, which Japan has resisted since World War II. Japanese citizens remember the death and destruction from atomic bombs that fell on Hiroshima and Nagasaki and have vowed to keep Japan free from nuclear weapons. But with neighboring North Korea rattling its nuclear sword, will Japanese conservatives gain the political leverage they need to change this long-standing policy?

If Japan develops nuclear weapons, will South Korea, which has relied greatly upon the United States for its defense, go nuclear? Such a chain reaction could extend to Taiwan, further exacerbating tensions with China.

A nuclear arms race in Asia is the last thing the world needs, and the United States has an opportunity to demonstrate new leadership in arms control that could change the course of nuclear proliferation. However, perhaps due to the war in Iraq and the preoccupation with terrorism, the United States has not devoted the kind of effort it did in the past to arms control.

As Max Kampelman, President Ronald Reagan's chief arms control negotiator put it recently, "Unfortunately, the goal of globally eliminating all weapons of mass destruction—nuclear, chemical and biological arms—is today not an integral part of American foreign policy; it needs to be put back at the top of our agenda." (OpEd, April 24, 2006, *New York Times*).

To complicate matters further, the United States has been pursuing new nuclear weapons initiatives and funding a program so as to be able to resume nuclear testing in 18 months, if deemed necessary, to address future concerns over the dependability of the U.S. nuclear weapons stockpile. If the United States decides to resume nuclear testing, it would violate the Comprehensive Nuclear Test Ban Treaty signed in New York a decade ago but still not ratified by the U.S. Congress.

The new nuclear weapons initiatives have included the development of new "Reliable Replacement Warheads" that provide better performance for the existing U.S. nuclear stockpile, revitalizing the U.S. nuclear weapons manufacturing complex and a program to develop a new nuclear earth-penetrating weapon to attack underground enemy facilities. While there are legitimate arguments for each of these programs, in the absence of balancing a high-level effort toward arms control by the United States, these initiatives can be viewed by other nations as dangerous and provocative.

One of the foremost experts on nuclear weapons in Congress, Rep. David Hobson, R-Ohio, summarized the situation in remarks to the U.S. National Academy of Sciences two years ago. "I view the Advanced (nuclear weapons) Concepts research proposal, the Robust Nuclear Earth Penetrator study, and the effort to reduce the nuclear test readiness posture to 18 months as very provocative and overly aggressive policies that undermine our moral authority to argue that other nations should forgo nuclear weapons. We cannot advocate for nuclear nonproliferation around the globe and pursue more usable nuclear weapon options here at home. That inconsistency is not lost on anyone in the international community."

In effect, the United States is saying to North Korea and Iran, "Do as I say, not as I do." This doesn't wash with countries that feel threatened by the United States, especially when the United States is not taking a more active role in arms control. Increasingly, the special rights and privileges accorded to the five original nuclear weapons states—the United States, Russia, China, France and the United Kingdom—by the nuclear Non-Proliferation Treaty are being challenged by other states. These same five nuclear weapons states are also the five permanent members of the UN Security Council, each of which has veto power over any UN resolution. Thus, by failing to lead in arms control, the United States is jeopardizing its role in the international community and in the United Nations.

In June, Russian President Vladimir Putin called for "renewed dialogue on the main disarmament issues," and proposed talks with the United States on renewing or replacing the Strategic Arms Reduction Treaty, START-1, which is set to expire in 2009. Initially proposed by Reagan, and finally signed by the United States and the Soviet Union in 1991, the treaty limits each side to 1,600 delivery systems—Intercontinental Ballistic Missiles, Submarine Launched Ballistic Missiles and bombers—and 6,000 nuclear warheads.

Considering the upcoming U.S. presidential elections in 2008, Putin's call deserves a vigorous U.S. response. It will be unlikely that START-1 can be extended or renegotiated before it expires if we wait until after the 2008 presidential elections, no matter who wins. The first year of every U.S. presidency is consumed with filling cabinet positions, new federal budget formulations and reorganization. Considering how long arms control agreements can take to be renegotiated, if START-1 is to be saved, we must begin now.

However, the tepid U.S. response so far tells Russia that we don't see START-1 as an urgent matter.

More is at stake than simply the future of START-1. The United States, Russia and China enjoy positions of authority in the international community and in the UN Security Council, which can be squandered if the three countries do not continue to show leadership in arms control.

In 2002, Russia and the United States reached agreement on the Strategic Offensive Reductions Treaty, better known as the Moscow Treaty. This agreement achieves important and significant reductions in nuclear weapons, at least on paper. But there are no verification provisions in this treaty, the reductions are not required to be permanent—warheads may be placed in storage and later redeployed—and the reductions are required to be completed only by the time the treaty expires Dec. 31, 2012, and can be reversed the very next day. While the Moscow Treaty is perhaps better than nothing, it is not in itself enough to sustain America's traditional role of leadership in arms control.

Nuclear weapons, which were a source of strength to the United States in World War II, and one of deterrence for the world's major powers during the Cold War, are becoming the trademark of smaller and weaker states that claim to be threatened, such as North Korea and Iran.

It is not necessary that countries must have nuclear weapons, and many countries have willingly given up their nuclear weapons programs. For example, Argentina, Brazil, the Ukraine, Belarus, Kazakhstan, South Africa (which reportedly had six nuclear weapons), Iraq (after the 1991 Gulf War and UN actions) and Libya in 2003 (thanks to effective European diplomacy) all gave up active or contemplated nuclear weapons development programs.

But for other countries, such as Iran or North Korea to give up their nuclear programs, the United States must do more than call for sanctions; it also must be visible as an honest broker for arms control. How the United States, Russia and China behave with respect to their own nuclear policies will be key in joint efforts to achieve arms reductions worldwide.

The United States faces an analogous situation in the Middle East. The United States has lost its role as an honest broker between Islam and Judaism. The United States was credible in 1947 at the time of the United Nations' Partition Plan when Israel was formed, and in 1978 at the Camp David Accords, and still later in 1993 with the Oslo Peace Accords. Today, however, the United States is the focus of the debate between Islam and the West, and no longer has the standing for effective arms-length diplomacy.

To control nuclear weapons, and the nuclear materials from which they can be made, requires strong international leadership and consistent actions. By failing to stop or slow the spread of nuclear weapons in Asia, we could compound the already murky situation in the Middle East. Real arms control must be put back at the top of the agenda.

Because of the poor esteem in which the United States is held in many parts of the world today, the United States must work with Russia and China to change the landscape of arms control. A strong effort by the United States to renew the START-1 agreement is a way to begin. Such efforts cannot only serve to reduce the threat from nuclear weapons, but also restore America's image as a country committed to peace.

	First test	Last test	Treaty signed	Ratified	Number of tests, by country
U.S.	1945	1992	Yes	**No**	**1,030**
Russia	1949	1990	Yes	**Yes**	715
France	1960	1996	Yes	**Yes**	210
U.K.	1952	1991	Yes	**Yes**	45
China	1964	1996	Yes	**No**	45
India	1974	1998	No	**No**	3
Pakistan	1998	1998	No	**No**	2
N. Korea	2006	2006	No	**No**	1

Figure 1 Nuclear Testing Tally. These countries are known to have conducted nuclear tests since 1945.

Source: Arms Control Association (U.S).

PHILIP E. COYLE, who lives in Sacramento, is a senior adviser at the Center for Defense Information and a former Assistant Secretary of Defense for Test and Evaluation from 1994 to 2001.

The Politics of Death in Darfur

"'Genocide' is big because it carries the Nazi label, which sells well. . . . But simply killing is boring, especially in Africa."

GÉRARD PRUNIER

For the world at large Darfur has been and remains the quintessential "African crisis": distant, esoteric, extremely violent, rooted in complex ethnic and historical factors that few understand, and devoid of any identifiable practical interest for the rich countries.

Since the international media got hold of it in 2004, Darfur has become not a political or military crisis but a "humanitarian crisis"—in other words, something that many "realist" politicians see (without saying so) as just another insoluble problem. In the post–cold war world such problems have been passed on to the United Nations. But the UN has not known what to do with this one, especially since the possibility emerged that this was another genocide.

Fearing that it would have to intervene and that the developed world would encourage it to act without giving it the means to do so, the UN passed the catastrophe on to the care of the newly reborn African Union, formerly the Organization of African Unity. For a continental organization wanting a new start, this was a dangerous gift. "African solutions to African problems" had become the politically correct way of saying "We do not really care."

Thus, in many ways, the hard reality of Darfur has been kept at arm's length, while statistics, press releases, UN resolutions, and photo opportunities have taken center stage. As in all globalized world crises, this recreation of the situation resulting from media attention and UN discussion has acquired as much importance as the reality it has been applied to, if not more, because whether real or not, it has deeply affected the initial reality. The result is continued talk and hand-wringing in the face of a crisis that, even now, grows worse.

Arabs and Africans

Darfur was for several hundred years an independent Islamic sultanate, with a population of both Arabs and black African tribes. As a result of intermarriage, the "Arabs" are all quite

black, and the distinction between the two groups—since both are Muslim—has been based on their respective native tongues. Annexed to Sudan by the British in 1916 (because London feared that the sultanate might enter the war on the side of Turkey and Germany), Darfur was thereafter completely neglected by the colonial power. When Sudan became independent in 1956, the new government continued this policy of neglect.

This was far from exceptional. Sudan is both enormous and overcentralized. The core area, centered around Khartoum and inhabited by riverine Arabs, has largely ignored the country's peripheral areas, though they represent the greatest part both of the territory and the population. The south, being Negro-African in culture and Christian religiously, was the first to rebel. The Muslim areas, blinded by the illusory "common bond" of Islam, took much longer to realize that they were no better off than the Christian south.

In February 2003, the Darfuri realized that the southern Christians were about to sign a peace agreement with the Islamist government in Khartoum and that they, the Muslims, would most likely be completely excluded from the new power- and wealth-sharing arrangements. After years of marginalization, resentment, frustration, and increasing social troubles, the Darfuri revolted in their turn.

Since they made up a large chunk of the army, Khartoum could not ask Darfuri soldiers to go home and shoot their own relatives. So, because the insurgents were mostly blacks, the government tapped the Darfuri Arab tribes for militiamen, telling them that the *abid* (slaves) were about to take over. The strategy worked wonderfully. Soon the Darfuri Arab militias, known as the *janjaweed* (which can be loosely translated as "the evil horsemen"), were looting, burning, raping, and killing entire black villages.

The Killer Story

At first the Darfur crisis went almost unnoticed by the media. For a year there was hardly any reaction on the part of the international community, which had always misunderstood the Sudanese civil war, taking it to be a religious conflict and not a racial one. The logic explaining why Muslims were now killing Muslims was not part of the international community's available conceptual equipment.

The focus remained instead on peace negotiations in Naivasha, Kenya, between the Sudanese government and a rebel group in the south, the Sudan People's Liberation Army (SPLA). Even in Khartoum, Sudan's capital, a few nomads shooting up villages in distant Darfur did not draw much attention. After all, had not these people devoted themselves to fighting each other for as long as anyone could remember?

The school of explaining conflicts by "ancient tribal hatreds" is not the sole preserve of Western journalists. It has many adherents in Africa itself. An unconscious form of Sudanese cultural racism enabled the government (which in some ways believed its own propaganda) to dismiss the whole thing as "another instance of tribal conflict."

The deteriorating situation in Darfur had been known to the wider world since about 1999, but only through specialized publications such as *Africa Confidential* or the *Indian Ocean Newsletter*. In Sudan itself the national press began to give some space to the activities of the "bandits" around the middle of 2003, and the word "janjaweed" first appeared in September of that year when an attack on the small town of Kadnir in Jebel Marra was reported.

Everyone knew that a military operation was the only form of intervention that could have any drastic effect.

But the international media did not pick up on "evil horsemen" who had attacked yet another African village in a God-forsaken province at the center of the continent. It was nongovernmental organizations that began noting Darfur, first Amnesty International and then the International Crisis Group, and it is largely through them that the crisis began to emerge from the shadows.

Given their interest in Chad, the French media were among the first to give attention to the Darfur situation. The first US article on the subject appeared in *The New York Times*. It focused immediately on the "black versus Arab" side of the problem, an aspect that, even if justified, was going to obscure rather than clarify the essential elements

in the following months. By then the Voice of America had followed the BBC in covering the growing crisis, and press agencies had begun sending reporters to eastern Chad.

What actually "blew the ratings," however, was an interview given by the UN Human Rights Coordinator for Sudan, Mukesh Kapila, to the UN's own IRIN network in March 2004. Kapila declared that Darfur was "the world's greatest humanitarian crisis" and that "the only difference between Rwanda and Darfur is now the numbers involved." He cited a tentative figure of 10,000 casualties. Having worked in Rwanda at the time of the genocide there, he knew what he was talking about. And although Rwanda itself had been neglected in its hour of need 10 years before, it had by then become the baseline reference for absolute evil and the need to care.

Newspapers went wild, and *The New York Times* started to write about "genocide." The "angle" had been found: Darfur was a genocide and the Arabs were killing the blacks. The journalists did not seem unduly concerned by the fact that the Arabs were often black, or that the "genocide" was strangely timed given Khartoum's goal of reaching a peace accord in Naivasha. Few people had ever heard of Darfur before; its history was a mystery that nobody particularly wanted to plumb. But now there was a good story: the first genocide of the twenty-first century.

Suddenly it was the Naivasha talks in which interest seemed to slacken. Here was something really serious and happening *now,* not like the peace negotiations, which had been dragging on for two years. Heart-wrenching images of children, rapes, and horsemen appeared, and suddenly everyone was interested, from the quality press to the mass media by way of the intellectual publications. What is conventionally known as "world opinion" finally cared about Darfur, even if the actual mechanics of what was happening remained obscure.

Delayed Reaction

The moral outrage that was felt tended to overshadow, if not hide completely, the political nature of the problem. Some specialized articles started to disentangle the various lines of causality, but they soon were lost amid the loud humanitarian demands for action. "Action" was a big word, although no one went so far to as to demand military intervention. Iraq and its image of easy military success leading to political discomfiture were still too present on television screens.

Moral indignation and its attendant media coverage kept rolling on until the end of 2004. Darfur was *the* humanitarian crisis and horror story of the year and writing about it was now obligatory. Then came the Asian tsunami on December 26, and Darfur instantly vanished from television screens and newspaper pages. The media could handle only one emotion-laden story at a time.

Darfur had enjoyed its famous 15 minutes of Warholian celebrity. It had even remained in the limelight for over six months, which for an African horror story is a considerable amount of time. And if it was true that some sort of "peace" had been signed in Nairobi on January 9, 2005, surely the show was over.

But before we move back to reality as opposed to its media image, we have to answer one question about the Darfur coverage: Why so much so late? The lateness is probably easiest to explain. Darfur was not expected to happen when it did, and it did not fit the common patterns of thinking about Sudan. Everyone knew Sudan's north-south conflict was a religious war in which wicked Muslims killed desperately struggling Christians. There had been over a million casualties, perhaps as many as a million and a half, and we had accepted that. Peace was at last about to be achieved now that the evil Hassan al-Turabi had been replaced as Sudan's leader by the far from virtuous but acceptable Omar Hassan al-Beshir. Yet this sudden Muslim-on-Muslim violence had surged to the forefront of world attention in a way that was completely unexpected and hardly explicable.

This violation of settled understanding also helps to explain the intensity of the media coverage once it finally took off. There was a kind of delayed reaction, a substitute for disappointment. The media were preparing for a nice story: peace at last, returning refugees, selfless NGO and UN workers helping the destitute, Muslim-Christian coexistence and perhaps even reconciliation, a farewell to arms. In other words, an African success story.

Now everything, even the way of interpreting the situation, had turned topsy-turvy, which is why the "genocide" angle soon became so important. No one denied that an enormous quantity of human beings had been killed, but was it or was it not genocide? Although it made little difference to the interested parties who continued to die without recourse to international legal concepts, the word became a question of the utmost relevance in the media.

Meanwhile humanitarian action was trying, as so often before in similar circumstances, to fill the gap between the media-raised expectations of public opinion and the prudent procrastination of the political and diplomatic segments of the international community.

The Missing Cavalry

Washington was embarrassed by the Darfur crisis, not least because it did not fit well within either of the two main camps in the administration and on Capitol Hill: the "realists" and the "Garang lobby" (that is, supporters of the SPLA leader John Garang). The "realists" were found mostly in the State Department, the CIA, and the Defense Intelligence Agency. They argued that, given the useful role that Khartoum was playing in the war on terrorism by supplying information about its erstwhile friends, it should at least be helped even if perhaps not fully supported, especially if it showed any signs of cooperation at Naivasha.

The "Garang lobby" was found mostly in Congress and at the US Agency for International Development. On June 1, 2004, members of Congress who sympathized with the SPLA sent President George W. Bush a list of 23 names of janjaweed supporters, controllers, and commanders who were either members of the Sudanese government or closely linked to it. The message was clear: do something about these people.

President Bush seemed discomfited by the implicit demand. Supporters of anti-Khartoum legislation tended to be more "on the left." Yet there was a core group of anti-Khartoum activists at the opposite end of the political spectrum from where he drew most of his electoral support. Many fundamentalist Protestant organizations had rallied to the anti-Khartoum lobby. By mid-2004, vocal Jewish groups such as the Committee for the Holocaust Memorial in Washington had also joined in the indignant chorus of protests about Darfur.

The president thus found himself under pressure from an array of public opinion elements too wide to be ignored during an election year. Yet, since the "realists" in the intelligence community kept insisting that Khartoum was too important to be harshly treated, these contradictory pressures led the White House to compromise on all fronts— supporting the Naivasha negotiations; not putting too much practical pressure on Khartoum, but nevertheless approving legislation that could be used as a sword of Damocles in case of noncompliance; becoming vocal on Darfur; putting a fair amount of money on its humanitarian aspect—but doing nothing at the military level.

This author was assured that Secretary of State Colin Powell had practically been ordered to use the term "genocide" during his high-profile September 9, 2004, testimony to the Senate Committee on Foreign Relations, but that he also had been advised to add in the same breath that this did not oblige the United States to undertake any sort of drastic action, such as a military intervention.

President Bush in short tried to be all things to all people on the Sudan/Darfur question. Never mind that the result was predictably confused. What mattered was that attractive promises could be handed around without any sort of firm commitment being made. Unsurprisingly, the interest level of US diplomacy on the Sudan question dropped sharply as soon as Bush was reelected.

Likewise, in its usual way of treating diplomatic matters, the European Union presented a spectacle of complete lack of resolve and coordination when it came to Darfur. The French only cared about protecting Idris Deby's regime in Chad from possible destabilization. The British blindly followed Washington's lead, finding this somewhat difficult since Washington was not very clear about which direction it wished to take. The Scandinavian countries and the Netherlands gave large sums of money and remained silent. Germany made anti-Sudanese government noises that it never backed up with any sort of action and gave only limited cash. And the Italians remained bewildered.

The result was a purely humanitarian approach to the crisis, with the EU and its member states giving $142 million (out of a total of $301 million; that is, more than the United States) without coming up with anything meaningful in terms of policy.

Everyone knew that a military operation was the only form of intervention that could have any drastic effect. But Brussels was quite incapable of mustering the energy to do in distant Darfur what it had failed to do without American or NATO prompting in neighboring Bosnia or Kosovo a few years earlier.

Even on the question of deciding on the nature of what was happening in Darfur, the union could not manage to speak with any clearly recognizable voice, its parliament only declaring that what was going on was "tantamount to genocide." During several Darfur "cease-fire" or "peace" talks in Abéché and Abuja, the Europeans pushed for a "no fly zone" above Darfur. But even when it was accepted, they did strictly nothing to try to enforce it.

The UN's Dilemma

The UN was in a terrible position regarding the Darfur crisis for a number of reasons. First, it was deeply involved in the Naivasha process, boosting the capacity and resolve of regional governments in what ended up being a saga of endless procrastination and obfuscation. Khartoum kept playing Darfur against Naivasha in order to win at both levels or, if a choice had to be made, at least to keep Darfur out of the military reach of the international community. Second, the UN was at the forefront of the humanitarian effort both in southern Sudan and in Darfur.

Third, UN Secretary General Kofi Annan knew that the US administration hated him (and the UN in general) and would do anything in its power to make the world body and its secretary general make a potentially fatal false move. Fourth, the Arab/black African split that was implicit in the Darfur crisis had many echoes inside the UN. And finally, the EU member states and America kept pushing the world body to act as if they were not themselves responsible for it.

Annan knew that the December 1948 genocide convention only obliged the member states to "refer" such a matter to the UN, but that once the world body had accepted the challenge, it became mandatory for it to act. Therefore, his permanent nightmare over Darfur was that member states would corner him into saying "genocide," thereby forcing him to act, and then fail to give him the necessary financial, military, and political means to do so. For the United Nations, which had been shaken by the United States' bypassing it on the Iraq question, such a debacle would have been a catastrophe.

Caught on the horns of so many dilemmas, Annan tried to act without upsetting things, to scold without being threatening, and to help without intruding too much. The result was that he appeared weak and irresolute at a time when the United Sates and some of his own staff were insisting on more "action," even if it was no more than symbolic. In June 2004, after he had been booed by demonstrators in Harvard Square, Annan declared: "Based on reports I have received, I cannot at this stage call it genocide or ethnic cleansing yet."

> **The Darfur tragedy will continue to unfold. And the cry of "never again" heard after the Rwandese genocide will ring hollowly as "once again."**

This was the worst of both worlds: he had uttered the big taboo words, but prevaricated over their relevance. The pressure kept building on the UN to come up with some radical solution. And the more the pressure built up, the more the secretary general resisted it, because he knew only too well that those who were applying it had no real intention of doing anything.

The more the crisis developed, the less the UN seemed capable of doing anything political about it, even though at the humanitarian level it carried over 60 percent of the financial burden. In many ways, this situation came to demonstrate the UN's practical limitations in crises where the heavyweight member states do not want to act. Blaming the UN was easy for those who were responsible for its inaction. Passing the buck to the African Union was another favorite resort to sophistry.

The Report of the UN Commission of Inquiry on the Darfur Violence provided an example of the world body and the United Sates each acting their parts in a coordinated show of egregious disingenuousness. The report documented violations of international human rights by "people who might have acted with genocidal intentions"; yet the situation was not a genocide, although it was definitely "war crimes." But the United States did not like the International Criminal Court (ICC), fearing that some of its own human rights violations, particularly in Iraq, might make it liable to prosecution. It therefore did not favor the UN suggestion that Darfur war crimes should be brought to the ICC, suggesting instead that a special tribunal might be set up in Arusha on the model of the Rwanda tribunal.

Off the record, everyone worried about naming names in an eventual prosecution because the perpetrators of the Darfur war crimes were the same people who, according to the January 9, 2005, "peace agreement," were now supposed to implement the Nairobi settlement and turn Sudan into a brave new world of peace and prosperity.

The African Union's Moment

Once the OAU had decided to shed its skin and be reborn as the African Union (AU), it had known that it would be judged, both by its member states and by the broader international community, on the basis of its competence in conflict management. Darfur was the first major crisis to face the organization since its transformation, and its commission chairman, Alpha Konare, and the AU chairman in 2004–2005, President Olusegun Obasanjo of Nigeria, knew that the moment of truth had arrived.

But the financial provisions under which the AU operated were highly unrealistic. Its 2003 budget had been a meager $43 million and out of this the member states had neglected to pay $26 million. This did not prevent Konare from requesting $1.7 billion for a "strategic plan" for the AU, which was to have its own peace fund, a pan-African parliament (based in South Africa), a court of justice, and even a standing army. When the dreaming stopped, the Addis Ababa-based organization finally settled for a budget of $158 million, with $63 million financed by obligatory payments and another $95 million by "voluntary contributions."

In the short term, the estimated cost of a peacekeeping operation in Darfur—nearly $250 million—had to be financed entirely by foreign donors. In many ways they were only too glad to contribute. Brussels promised $110 million and others, including Washington and the UN, pledged the rest. The AU decided to send 132 observers to Western Sudan, with 300 troops whose mandate would be restricted to protecting the observers.

It also declared that in its opinion, this was not ethnic cleansing in Darfur. This was to be a recurrent problem for the AU: in many ways it has not stopped being the "heads of state trade union," which President Julius Nyerere of Tanzania had denounced in 1978. Afraid of Darfur's

potential for splintering the organization between Arabs and black Africans, Konare tried his best to minimize the racial angle of the crisis. Worse, he systematically refused to condemn Khartoum or even to put the responsibility for the massacres squarely on the janjaweed. For the AU, Darfur remained a case of mass murder without any known perpetrators, and Khartoum was even discreetly advised on how to "handle the whites."

Obasanjo had offered 2,000 Nigerian troops, but only a fraction of them were going to be sent as part of the AU contingent. Khartoum's minister of the interior, Abd-er-Rahim Mohamed Hussein, one of the two or three most powerful figures in the government, retorted, "We will not tolerate the presence of any foreign troops, whatever their nationality." In Khartoum's usual style this meant, "We will accept foreign troops: all that matters is their nationality and their mandate."

Khartoum would be satisfied on both accounts, leading it to accept what it had at first so vociferously rejected. The troops would all be African. And their mandate—peacekeeping alone being acceptable—was satisfactory both for the Western countries, which were let off the hook easily, and for Khartoum, which was getting an impotent and probably mute witness to its "good faith."

As for the AU, it was also satisfied: it had been allowed to play in the big boy's league and would not have to pay for the privilege. "Africa" would be at the forefront of the Darfur crisis and any accusation of impotence or limitation of means would be beamed back at the donors.

In a way not completely unlike that of the UN, the AU has been scheduled for a "Mission Impossible." It is supposed to substitute itself for the coalition of the unwilling, to stop what it is only mandated to observe, to operate on a shoestring, and to keep the pretense of serious international involvement for its tight-fisted sponsors. Predictably, all it has achieved is a token presence.

The Usual Explanations

Once the principle of some kind of foreign intervention was decided, even one as limited as that given to the AU, the problem of "genocide" came back to the fore, not so much as a media term but as a legal label with potential consequences for international proceedings and criminal sanctions.

The number of victims is not a key factor in deciding whether large-scale killings constitute a genocide or not. But numbers are relevant, first in themselves (the magnitude of what the targeted group has suffered) and secondly because of their real or potential impact on world opinion. In the case of Darfur, however, numbers of victims have been both extremely difficult to compute and the object of fierce differences of opinion.

A more fundamental aspect of the problem is semantics, which not only goes to the heart of the matter but illuminates the way Darfur has been dealt with by the international community. Four types of explanations have been offered for the Darfur violence. The first is that it is an explosion of tribal conflicts exacerbated by drought. This has been usually (but not always) the Sudanese government's explanation.

Second, it is explained as a counterinsurgency campaign gone badly wrong because the government has used inappropriate means to fight back the insurrection. This is roughly the position of the Darfur specialist Alex de Waal and a number of Western governments. De Waal does not use the argument to exonerate Khartoum. But the Western governments adopting this position usually minimize Khartoum's responsibility, preferring to talk of "errors."

A third explanation posits a deliberate campaign of "ethnic cleansing," with the Sudanese government trying to displace or eliminate "African" tribes in order to replace them by "Arab" ones that it feels would be more supportive of "Arab" rule in Khartoum. Finally, there is the genocide hypothesis, supported by evidence of systematic racial killings.

The "ethnic conflict" explanation has to be looked at technically, not ideologically. Ethnic tensions and problems have existed in Darfur for a long time, though not along the lines of the present conflict. This is an essential point that makes Darfur not unlike Rwanda. Tensions between Tutsi and Hutu were already present when the first Europeans arrived in the 1890s. However, they had never been globalized in the way that occurred during the 1994 genocide. Ethnic tensions can slip into violence, but they involve local weaponry, do not present a relentless and systematic character, and do not entail large-scale cooperation from the administration.

When Darfur villages were bombed and strafed by government aircraft, this was not the work of spontaneously violent local nomads. When the janjaweed were organized into coordinated military units and assigned to camps they shared with the regular army, it was not possible to characterize what was happening as spontaneous violence. Ethnic tensions in Darfur were and still are real, and recurring droughts have made them worse. But they of themselves were not sufficient to unleash the violence we have seen. They were the raw material, not the cause.

Nevertheless, Khartoum has systematically resorted to this and other similar "explanations" in order to deny its involvement in the massacres. The problems of Darfur are caused by "bandits, not rebels"; in any case these bandits are "just a little gang, incapable of standing up to the regular army"; as for the janjaweed, they are "a bunch of thieves," just like the rebels. Actually, the rebels and the janjaweed are the same thing. There is "no rebellion in Darfur, just

a conflict among specific tribes. The government has not armed any militia. The propaganda in the West is trying to exaggerate what is happening." A list of such quotations would be almost endless.

If one discounts these unlikely "explanations," then what of the "counterinsurgency gone wrong?" In many ways, this is true, but is it the whole picture and, specifically, is it an excuse of some kind? Technically, Darfur is a bad case of poorly conceived counterinsurgency carried out with completely inadequate means. A "clean" counterinsurgency may even be impossible if a guerrilla movement has arisen from deep-seated economic, social, and cultural grievances.

But beyond this question of "counterinsurgency gone wrong," there is another point that causes the problem to slip into another dimension. In many ways the 1980s were a period of permanent counterinsurgency, when Arabs in Khartoum looked on the "African" tribes in Darfur as the enemy. The fact that the pace of the violence slowed down somewhat during the 1990s did not change that basic outlook. The state of ethnic relations resulting from frantic ideological manipulations of that period remained a permanent threat to non-Arabs in the province. Thus, any armed movement initiated by the non-Arab tribes of Darfur was like a red rag waved before the eyes of an excited bull.

Here again the parallel with Rwanda is striking. When Tutsi rebels entered Rwanda in October 1990 they probably did not realize the degree of danger they were creating for the other Tutsi living inside the country. In an atmosphere charged with racism an armed rebellion by the "inferior" group is fraught with enormous danger for the civilians of that group.

Indeed, counterinsurgency in Darfur could perhaps only have gone wrong. This was not "counterinsurgency" organized by a government trying to restore law and order. It was an answer with arms by a racially and culturally dominant group to the insurrection of a racially and culturally subject group. The hope that repression could be limited to combatants was completely unrealistic.

The Big-G Word

The two other explanations, "ethnic cleansing" and "genocide," are closely related. As a rough differentiation we could take "ethnic cleansing" to mean massive killings of a certain section of the population in order to frighten the survivors away and occupy their land but without the intent of killing them all. "Genocide" is more difficult to define. The December 1948 International Convention on the Prevention and Punishment of Crimes of Genocide says that what constitutes genocide is "deliberately inflicting on the group conditions of life calculated to bring about its physical destruction *in whole or in part.*"

Blaming the UN was easy for those who were responsible for its inaction.

I personally used another definition in my book, *The Rwanda Crisis*—namely, a coordinated attempt to destroy a racially, religiously, or politically predefined group in its entirety. I am attached to the notion of an attempt at *total* obliteration because it has a number of consequences that seem to be specific to a "true" genocide. First, the numbers tend to be enormous because the purge is thorough. Second, there is no escape. In the case of a racially defined group, the reason is obvious, but if the group is religiously defined no conversions will be allowed. And if it is politically defined, no form of submission will save its members.

Finally, the targeted group will retain for many years after the traumatic events a form of collective paranoia that will make even its children live with an easily aroused fear. This is evident among the Armenians, the Jews, and the Tutsi. But it is present also in less obviously acute forms in groups such as the North American Indians, French Protestants, and Northern Irish Catholics. It is this "fractured consciousness" that makes future reconciliation extremely difficult.

If we use the December 1948 definition it is obvious that Darfur is a genocide, but if we use the definition I proposed in my book on Rwanda, it is not. At the immediate existential level this makes no difference; the horror experienced by the targeted group remains the same, no matter which word we use. But this does not absolve us from trying to understand the nature of what is happening.

And whether the "big-G word" is used or not appears to make a considerable difference in terms of international reaction. It is a measure of the jaded cynicism of our times that we seem to think that the killing of 250,000 people in a genocide is more serious, a greater tragedy, and more deserving of our attention than that of 250,000 people in nongenocidal massacres.

The reason seems to be the overriding role of the media coupled with the mass-consumption need for brands and labels. Things are not seen in their reality but in their capacity to create brand images, to warrant a "big story," to mobilize television time high in rhetoric. "Genocide" is big because it carries the Nazi label, which sells well. "Ethnic cleansing" is next best (though far behind) because it goes with Bosnia, which was the last big-story European massacre. But simply killing is boring, especially in Africa.

The notion of "ethnic cleansing," implying that the Sudanese government has been trying to displace African tribes in order to give their land to "Arabs," was at first not backed by any evidence other than the shouts hurled at victims by the perpetrators themselves. The perpetrators might hope for such an outcome from their massacres, but such a policy probably was not clearly thought out in Khartoum.

It is possible, however, that in a diffuse and decentralized way there has been a deliberate attempt to "Arabize" Darfur. The few instances of "Arabs" settling on the land abandoned by the African peasants do not seem very convincing. The "Arabs" are mostly nomads who do not appear to be much interested in becoming agriculturalists. But they are desperate for pastureland, made more and more scarce by the southward movement of the desert. Blacks in Darfur might be dying in part so that camels and sheep can graze where men used to cultivate.

A Strange Ballet

As for the most prominent use of the word "genocide" in connection with Darfur, Secretary of State Powell seems to have based his thinking on the December 1948 definition when he said on September 9, 2004, that in his opinion Darfur was a genocide. Other spokesmen for world opinion danced a strange ballet around the big-G word. President Bush declared: "Our conclusion is that a genocide is under way in Darfur." British Foreign Minister Chris Mullin was more prudent, merely saying that a genocide "might have taken place." The spokesman for the French Foreign Ministry limited himself to saying that there had been "massive violations of human rights," while Walter Lindner, for the German Foreign Affairs Ministry, said that this was "a humanitarian tragedy . . . with a potential for genocide." In the end none of them went beyond talk. The UN, the AU, and the humanitarians were left holding the bloody babies.

This leaves open the question of "intent," which was at the center of the UN Commission of Inquiry's decision not to call Darfur a genocide. The commission wrote that there was "not sufficient evidence to indicate that Khartoum had a state policy intended to exterminate a particular racial or ethnic group," a definition that moved away from that of December 1948, but which in itself is acceptable.

However, the semantic play ended up supporting an evasion of reality. The notion that this was probably not strictly speaking a "genocide" seemed to satisfy the commission that things were not really too bad. Conclusions about "war crimes" could have serious consequences, but that would require translating them into ICC indictments.

From Bad to Worse?

What is the present situation in Darfur? It is bad and fast deteriorating. The massive humanitarian effort undertaken during 2004 enabled over 2 million people to survive in internal-displaced-person camps, precariously perched on the edge of death. But this effort is now seriously undermined because the means that the international community is ready to put into African catastrophes are limited. The drought now playing havoc with the economies of Tanzania, Kenya, Somalia, and parts of Ethiopia will require money, and that money is largely being culled out of the Darfur budget.

This financial shrinkage is occurring at a time when violence in Darfur is again on the rise. The fact that the AU is completely impotent has given a feeling to both the janjaweed and the rebels that they need not bother about the military tourists in their midst. As a result, the guerrillas have stepped up military operations and the janjaweed have gone back to attacking the civilian population, albeit on a smaller scale than in 2004.

In addition, Darfur is suffering spillover from what might be called "the Chadian war of succession." Curiously enough this was triggered, if not caused, by Darfur. The Zaghawa tribe, which lives on both sides of the Chad border, was one of those targeted by the janjaweed. President Deby of Chad is a Zaghawa but he chose to ally himself with Khartoum in helping the repression because some of his personal enemies had joined the rebellion on the Sudanese side.

This somewhat paradoxical alliance caused many Chadian Zaghawa to side against Deby, and he now faces a full-fledged insurgency. And most of the rebels belong not only to Deby's clan but even to his own family. In mid-March they attempted a second coup against him (the first had taken place in May 2005), and then took refuge in Darfur when they failed. Deby now accuses Khartoum of helping his rebellious relatives in order to punish him for abandoning the repression camp.

Whatever the reality of the accusations and counter-accusations currently flying between Khartoum and Ndjamena, the result is a translation of Chad's civil strife into Darfur, as if the martyred province had not suffered enough. In response, the UN has proposed replacing the inefficient AU monitors with European or NATO forces. But, since such forces could be efficient in stopping the violence, the Sudanese government has blocked the proposal by all available means—including the setting up of bogus "terrorist" organizations that "threatened" to kill UN representative Jan Pronk and the US chargé d'affaires in Khartoum.

In the face of this blackmail, the international community has backed down and prolonged the AU's impotent mandate until the end of this year. Short of a military intervention such as that of a UN force firmly equipped with sufficient guns and a clear mandate to use them, the Darfur tragedy will continue to unfold. And the cry of "never again" heard after the Rwandese genocide will ring hollowly as "once again."

GÉRARD PRUNIER is director of the French Center for Ethiopian Studies in Addis Ababa. His latest book is *Darfur: The Ambiguous Genocide* (Cornell University Press, 2005), from which this essay draws.

Reprinted from *Current History*, Vol. 15, No. 691, May 2006, pp. 195–202. Copyright © 2006 by Current History, Inc. Reprinted with permission.

Asia's Forgotten Crisis
A New Approach to Burma

Over the past decade, Burma has gone from being an antidemocratic embarrassment and humanitarian disaster to being a serious threat to its neighbors' security. The international community must change its approach to the country's junta.

MICHAEL GREEN AND DEREK MITCHELL

U.S. policy toward Burma is stuck. Since September 1988, the country has been run by a corrupt and repressive military junta (which renamed the country Myanmar). Soon after taking power, the State Law and Order Restoration Council (SLORC), as the junta was then called, placed Aung San Suu Kyi, the leader of the opposition party the National League for Democracy, under house arrest. In 1990, it allowed national elections but then ignored the National League for Democracy's landslide victory and clung to power. Then, in the mid-1990s, amid a cresting wave of post-Cold War democratization and in response to international pressure, the SLORC released Suu Kyi. At the time, there was a sense within the country and abroad that change in Burma might be possible.

But this proved to be a false promise, and the international community could not agree on what to do next. Many Western governments, legislatures, and human rights organizations advocated applying pressure through diplomatic isolation and punitive economic sanctions. Burma's neighbors, on the other hand, adopted a form of constructive engagement in the hope of enticing the SLORC to reform. The result was an uncoordinated array of often contradictory approaches. The United States limited its diplomatic contact with the SLORC and eventually imposed mandatory trade and investment restrictions on the regime. Europe became a vocal advocate for political reform. But most Asian states moved to expand trade, aid, and diplomatic engagement with the junta, most notably by granting Burma full membership in the Association of Southeast Asian Nations (ASEAN) in 1997.

A decade later, the verdict is in: neither sanctions nor constructive engagement has worked. If anything, Burma has evolved from being an antidemocratic embarrassment and humanitarian disaster to being a serious threat to the security of its neighbors. But despite the mounting danger, many in the United States and the international community are still mired in the old sanctions-versus-engagement battle. At the United Nations, Secretary-General Ban Ki-moon has appointed the former Nigerian diplomat and UN official Ibrahim Gambari to continue the organization's heretofore fruitless dialogue with the junta about reform. The U.S. State Department and the U.S. Congress have fought over control of U.S. Burma policy, leading to bitterness and polarization on both sides. Although the UN Security Council now does talk openly about Burma as a threat to international peace and security, China and Russia have vetoed attempts to impose international sanctions. And while key members of the international community continue to undermine one another, the junta, which renamed itself the State Peace and Development Council (SPDC) in 1997, continues its brutal and dangerous rule.

Regimes like the SPDC do not improve with age; therefore, the Burma problem must be addressed urgently. All parties with a stake in its resolution need to adjust their positions and start coordinating their approach to the problem. Although this may seem like an unlikely proposition, it has more potential today than ever before. Burma's neighbors are beginning to recognize that unconditional engagement has failed. All that is needed now is for the United States to acknowledge that merely reinforcing its strategy of isolation and the existing sanctions regime will not achieve the desired results either. Such a reappraisal would then allow all concerned parties to build an international consensus with the dual aim of creating new incentives for the SPDC to reform and increasing the price it will pay if it fails to change its ways.

Burmese Ways

After General Than Shwe became chair of the junta in 1992, repression grew more brazen. Thousands of democracy activists and ordinary citizens have been sent to prison, and Suu Kyi has been repeatedly confined to house arrest, where she remains today. Since 1996, when the Burmese army launched its "four cuts" strategy against armed rebels—an effort to cut off their access to food, funds, intelligence, and recruits among the population—2,500 villages have been destroyed and over one million people, mostly Karen and Shan minorities, have been displaced. Hundreds of thousands live in hiding or in open exile in Bangladesh, India, China, Thailand, and Malaysia. In 2004, the reformist prime minister Khin Nyunt was arrested. Two years ago, Than Shwe even moved the seat of government from Rangoon (which the junta calls Yangon), the traditional capital, to Pyinmana, a small logging town some 250 miles north—reportedly on the advice of a soothsayer and for fear of possible U.S. air raids. And this past summer, the government cracked down brutally on scores of Burmese citizens who had taken to the streets to protest state-ordered hikes in fuel prices.

Burma's neighbors are struggling to respond to the spillover effects of worsening living conditions in the country. The narcotics trade, human trafficking, and HIV/AIDS are all spreading through Southeast Asia thanks in part to Burmese drug traffickers who regularly distribute heroin with HIV-tainted needles in China, India, and Thailand. According to the U.S. Drug Enforcement Administration, Burma accounts for 80 percent of all heroin produced in Southeast Asia, and the UN Office on Drugs and Crime has drawn a direct connection between the drug routes running from Burma and the marked increase in HIV/AIDS in the border regions of neighboring countries. Perversely, the SPDC has been playing on its neighbors' concerns over the drugs, disease, and instability that Burma generates to blackmail them into providing it with political, economic, and even military assistance.

Worse, the SPDC appears to have been taking an even more threatening turn recently. Western intelligence officials have suspected for several years that the regime has had an interest in following the model of North Korea and achieving military autarky by developing ballistic missiles and nuclear weapons. Last spring, the junta normalized relations and initiated conventional weapons trade with North Korea in violation of UN sanctions against Pyongyang. And despite Burma's ample reserves of oil and gas, it signed an agreement with Russia to develop what it says will be peaceful nuclear capabilities. For these reasons, despite urgent problems elsewhere in the world, all responsible members of the international community should be concerned about the course Burma is taking.

Frustrated Neighbors

ASEAN may be the most important component of any international Burma policy. The organization invited Burma to join it in 1997 partly on the theory that integration would enhance ASEAN's influence over the junta more than would isolation (and partly out of concern over China's growing influence in the country). More recently, however, the ten-member organization has come to recognize that Burma is not only a stain on its international reputation but also a drain on its diplomatic resources and a threat to peace and stability in Asia. In 2005, ASEAN members began to pressure the SPDC to give up its turn to take over the group's rotating leadership, which was scheduled for 2007; they breathed a collective sigh of relief when Than Shwe allowed the Philippines to take Burma's spot. But particularly after Than Shwe's bizarre decision to move the capital and his rebuff of all international efforts, including by the Malaysian foreign minister, to persuade him to improve the junta's behavior, ASEAN states have only grown more concerned about Burma's direction.

Political liberalization in Indonesia and growing activism in Malaysia and the Philippines have also led ASEAN to redefine its mandate and apply greater pressure for change in Burma. When ASEAN was created four decades ago, its five founding states undertook not to interfere in each other's internal affairs as a way both to distance themselves from their colonial pasts and to avoid conflict in the future. But last January, ASEAN members prepared a new charter for the twenty-first century that champions democracy promotion and human rights as universal values, and they have established a human rights commission despite the SPDC's strong objections. With ASEAN's underlying principles under revision, leadership by Southeast Asian nations will become an even more essential component of any new international approach to the junta.

Japan will be another important force for reform. Tokyo and Washington perennially disagreed over their policies toward Burma in the 1980s and 1990s, but there has been a promising shift in Japan's attitude recently. Now that Tokyo has to contend with the slowdown in Japan's economic power and the rise in China's, it is articulating its foreign policy objectives and diplomacy in different terms. In November 2006, Japanese Foreign Minister Taro Aso made a speech promoting an "arc of freedom and prosperity" from the Baltics to the Pacific and touting Tokyo's commitment to human rights, democracy, and the rule of law. His speech conspicuously omitted any mention of Burma, but there is no question that Japan's Burma policy has been shifting significantly. In September 2006, Tokyo finally agreed to support a discussion on Burma in the UN Security Council. Members of the Diet have created the Association for the Promotion of Values-Based Diplomacy, which seeks to infuse Japanese foreign policy in Asia with a renewed emphasis on promoting democracy. And last May, former Prime Minister Junichiro Koizumi joined 43 other former heads of state in an open letter calling on the SPDC to unconditionally release Suu Kyi.

Securing Japan's cooperation will be especially important. The Burmese people generally have a positive memory of Japan's assistance in helping the country throw off British colonial rule in the 1940s. Both the junta and the democratic opposition see opportunities for Japanese aid to help rebuild the country (although they disagree on the conditions under which that aid would be welcome). Furthermore, Burma presents a unique opportunity for Japan to demonstrate its bona fides on promoting democracy, protecting human rights, and advancing regional security—especially at a time when the rhetoric and policies of China, the other Asian giant, continue to focus on outdated mercantilist principles.

Unhealthy Competition

If ASEAN and Japan are critical components of any international approach to Burma, China and India could be the greatest obstacles to efforts to induce reform in the country. China has many interests in Burma. Over the past 15 years, it has developed deep political and economic relations with Burma, largely through billions of dollars in trade and investment and more than a billion dollars' worth of weapons sales. It enjoys important military benefits, including access to ports and listening posts, which allow its armed forces to monitor naval and other military activities around the Indian Ocean and the Andaman Sea. To feed its insatiable appetite for energy, it also seeks preferential deals for access to Burma's oil and gas reserves.

Beijing's engagement with the SPDC has been essential to the regime's survival. China has provided it with moral and financial support—including funds and materiel to pay off Burmese military elites—thus increasing its leverage at home and abroad. By throwing China's weight behind the SPDC, Beijing has complicated the strategic calculations of those of Burma's neighbors that are concerned about the direction the country is moving in, thus enabling the junta to pursue a classic divide-and-conquer approach.

In its own defense, China continues to assert its fealty to the principle of noninterference. In early 2007, China and Russia cast their first joint veto in the UN Security Council in 35 years to block a measure that would have sanctioned the SPDC. The move was consistent with both states' historical objections to any attempts by the Security Council to sanction a country for human rights violations. It also aligned with Beijing's overall strategic goals of the past few years: to secure the resources, markets, and investment destinations to fuel China's remarkable economic development; to shun risky international moves that might destabilize its neighborhood and distract the Chinese leadership from urgent domestic challenges; and to promote noninterference as an alternative model for international diplomacy—all interests that will make it difficult to induce China to change its Burma policy.

But China's position could shift, particularly as Beijing considers its longer-term interests. China, like many other states on Burma's border, must be concerned about the effects of its neighbor's tortured development on its own security. In fact, Chinese officials in Beijing and the governor of Yunnan Province, which borders Burma, are reported to have been putting pressure on the SPDC to reform and urgently address drug trafficking and health issues. This quiet shift could track the recent change in Beijing's approach to another wayward neighbor: North Korea. As soon as Beijing realized that being hands-off did not prevent Pyongyang from testing nuclear weapons and ballistic missiles over its objections—thus damaging China's reputation and threatening its security—it agreed to UN Security Council sanctions to try to bring Pyongyang under control. The same could happen with Burma, and all the more readily because it occupies a less strategic position for China than does North Korea (China's northeastern border has historically been an area of strategic vulnerability and competition).

Another possible source of change is growing pressure from ASEAN nations, which have been suspicious of China's dealings with Burma over the last 15 years. Once Beijing comes to recognize that its current approach to Burma undermines its professed desire to be a responsible international actor, it will have good reason to redefine its real interests in Burma. The key will be for the United States and others to prioritize Burma in their diplomatic efforts with China in order to get Beijing to reach this conclusion.

It will also be a challenge getting India on board. Despite Prime Minister Manmohan Singh's trumpeting of democratic values, India has actually become more reticent when it comes to Burma in recent years. This is particularly regrettable considering that Congress was one of the Burmese democratic opposition's strongest supporters during much of the 1990s and that Suu Kyi continues to cite Mohandas Gandhi as a model for nonviolent resistance. The change occurred during the past decade, after New Delhi detected that China's political and military influence in Burma was filling the void left by the international community's deliberate isolation of the junta. Like China, India is hungry for natural gas and other resources and is eager to build a road network through Burma that would expand its trade with ASEAN. As a result, it has attempted to match China step for step as an economic and military partner of the SPDC, providing tanks, light artillery, reconnaissance and patrol aircraft, and small arms; India is now Burma's fourth-largest trading partner. Singh's government has also fallen for the junta's blackmail over cross-border drug and arms trafficking and has preferred to give it military and economic assistance rather than let Burma become a safe haven for insurgents active in India's troubled northeastern region.

Yet this shortsighted policy is clearly not in India's interests. Persistent repression and turmoil in Burma will continue to threaten India's security along its border. Internal political reform leading to a more open and reconciled Burma would be far more beneficial for India than anything that would result from India's current tactical accommodations. Of course, India is eager to counter Chinese influence and strengthen its linkages to ASEAN through Burma. But its efforts to become more integrated into East Asia would be better served by following the example of like-minded democracies such as Indonesia, which has spearheaded efforts to change ASEAN's positions on democratization and human rights, than by parroting outdated rhetoric advocating noninterference or pursuing pure mercantilism.

Coordinated Engagement

Given the differing perspectives and interests of these nations, a new multilateral initiative on Burma cannot be based on a single, uniform approach. Sanctions policies will need to coexist with various forms of engagement, and it will be necessary to coordinate all of these measures toward the common end of encouraging reform, reconciliation, and ultimately the return of democracy. To succeed, the region's major players will need to work together.

Bringing them together will require the United States' leadership. One way to proceed would be for Washington to lead the five key parties—ASEAN, China, India, Japan, and the United States—in developing a coordinated international initiative and putting forth a public statement of the principles that underlie their vision for a stable and secure Burma. The five partners should develop a road map with concrete goalposts that lays out both the benefits that the SPDC would enjoy if it pursued true political reform and national reconciliation and the costs it would suffer if it continued to be intransigent. The road map should present the SPDC with an international consensus on how Burma's situation affects international stability and the common principles on which the international community will judge progress in the country. One purpose of such a road map would be to reassure the SPDC of regional support for Burma's territorial integrity and security and demonstrate the five parties' commitment to provide, under the appropriate conditions, the assistance necessary to ensure a better future for the country. This would be an important guarantee given the Burmese military's traditional paranoia.

Clearly, any process of reform and national reconciliation in Burma will have to begin with the immediate release of Suu Kyi and other political prisoners, including other members of the National League for Democracy and ethnic leaders, and involve their full participation in the institution of democracy. The guidelines for a new constitution that were announced in September, ostensibly as a "road map to democracy," do not come close in this regard. Than Shwe and the SPDC despise Suu Kyi, of course, which is why some U.S. supporters of engagement with Burma argue that it would be imprudent to peg the international community's treatment of the SPDC on the junta's treatment of Suu Kyi. However, her party's success in the 1990 elections and the fact that Burmese society continues to venerate her mean that any legitimate and credible approach to reform in Burma will have to take her perspectives into account.

Potential chinks are also appearing in the SPDC's armor. Than Shwe's erratic behavior, his decision to imprison former Prime Minister Khin Nyunt and thousands of Khin Nyunt's military associates, and his efforts to create a Kim Il Sung-like cult of personality are signs of brittleness and division within the junta. If the SPDC were faced with an offer of new economic and political opportunities from other states in the region—or greater international pressure and isolation should it fail to reform—some of its members might eventually feel compelled to seek a different course for themselves and their country.

The five parties should not be expected to agree on everything or even on a single, uniform approach to the SPDC. Rather, the objective of such discussions would be to encourage a degree of compromise among the participants and coordination among their respective policies so that they may be channeled toward a common end. The current approach—with each party pursuing its individual policy with an eye as much toward competing with the others for its own advantage as toward promoting change in Burma—has clearly played into the junta's hands. It has allowed the Burmese government to avoid united international action while still gaining the resources necessary to hold on to power.

The participation of China and India, currently the SPDC's greatest enablers, will be critical. The United States could begin to influence both nations' thinking by making Burma a higher priority in bilateral dialogues. In discussions with Beijing, Washington could make China's Burma policy another test of its readiness to be a "responsible stakeholder," much as it has already done in regard to Darfur. With New Delhi, Washington could make India's Burma policy an important component of the two governments' evolving strategic dialogue and nascent partnership on international issues, including democracy promotion and regional stability. Even more important, the U.S. government should initiate a new approach with ASEAN, Japan, and actors outside of Asia, such as the European Union, which has had a long-standing interest in political reform in Burma. ASEAN alone does not have the cohesion or the clout to shape China's or India's policy toward Burma. But with help from the United States and others, it could take a leading role in spearheading a new coordinated, multilateral approach that neither Beijing nor New Delhi would be able to ignore. China was reluctant to host the six-party talks on North Korea at first, but it eventually preferred to take on that role rather than leave the job of dealing with Pyongyang's nuclear activities to the United States, Japan, and South Korea. Once a new multilateral approach to Burma begins to take shape, China will not want to be viewed as obstructing progress on an issue of importance to its neighbors.

In order to participate fully and effectively, the U.S. government, for its part, will need to relax its strict prohibition on official high-level contact with the SPDC. This will require close consultation between the White House, the State Department, and Congress; Congress should grant the administration diplomatic flexibility in exchange for appropriate oversight. The president should appoint a special adviser to serve as the coordinator of U.S. policy on Burma and as the United States' lead contact in its international outreach (and eventually as the U.S. envoy to the Burmese regime itself). In the meantime, U.S. sanctions regarding trade and investment should remain in place, both to avoid too sudden a shift in posture and to keep in reserve potential carrots that could later be offered to the SPDC to encourage reform. The United States should also continue to push for UN Security Council action on Burma in order to keep the issue at the top of its agenda with China.

The international community needs to act now to begin a process of concentrated and coordinated engagement for the benefit of the Burmese people and of broader peace and stability in Asia. As with the six-party talks on North Korea, a multilateral approach will require some compromise by all participants. The United States will need to reconsider its restrictions on engaging the SPDC; ASEAN, China, and India will need to reevaluate their historical commitment to noninterference; Japan will need to consider whether its economics-based approach to Burma undermines its new commitment to values-based diplomacy. But all parties have good reasons to make concessions. None of them can afford to watch Burma descend further into isolation and desperation and wait to act until another generation of its people is lost. In addition to humanitarian principles, there are strategic grounds for stepping up diplomatic efforts on Burma: it is now the most serious remaining challenge to the security and unity of Southeast Asia. Of course, change will eventually come to Burma. But without the coordinated engagement of the major interested powers today, that change will come at a great cost: to the stability of Southeast Asia, to the conscience of the international community, and, most important, to the long-suffering Burmese people, who languish in the shadows as the rest of the world concentrates its energies elsewhere.

MICHAEL GREEN is Associate Professor of International Relations at the Edmund A. Walsh School of Foreign Service at Georgetown University and a Senior Adviser and Japan Chair at the Center for Strategic and International Studies. **DEREK MITCHELL** is a Senior Fellow and Director for Asia Strategy at CSIS.

Men of Principle

Iran's Neoconservatives and Their "White Coup"

Last time *The Economist* visited Iran for a special report, in 2003, the so-called "Tehran spring"—a period of cautious political liberalisation under the presidency of the soft-spoken Mr Khatami—was drawing to a close. He had won a landslide election in 1997 and a renewed though smaller mandate in 2001. These victories had signalled that the people of Iran wanted change: freedom of thought and speech, political diversity, a more open economy, tolerance, the rule of law and a friendlier stance towards the outside world. But as president, Mr Khatami had limited powers to deliver what they wanted.

That was because the constitution drawn up under Ayatollah Khomeini adopted a doctrine known as *velayat-e faqih,* in which an Islamic jurist sits as "supreme leader" at the apex of politics. And over the course of the Khatami presidency the unelected part of the structure, directed by the present supreme leader, former president Ayatollah Ali Khamenei, systematically throttled most of the changes Mr Khatami and his fellow reformers proposed.

Dozens of newspapers opened during the Khatami period, only for many to be shut down on one pretext or another by the judiciary. Clerics who took advantage of the new atmosphere to question the doctrine of *velayat-e faqih* were imprisoned or otherwise cowed. Even as political debate blossomed, Iran's security services cracked down on religious and ethnic minorities. A number of the regime's critics fell victim to murders traced later to the interior ministry. In 1999 police reacted to a peaceful demonstration for freer speech by invading Tehran University, beating and arresting hundreds of students and killing at least one. In the *majlis* (parliament) much of the president's reforming legislation was vetoed by the Council of Guardians, a committee of clerics appointed by the supreme leader to ensure that laws conform with Islamic precepts.

By 2004 Mr Khatami's failure either to stand up to these assaults on his programme or to deliver economic progress had led to widespread disillusion. That year, hardliners won a big victory in parliamentary elections. And in 2005 presidential elections produced an unexpected victory for Mr Ahmadinejad, then a little-known former mayor of Tehran.

The Tehran spring of ten years ago has now given way to a bleak political winter. The new government continues to close down newspapers, silence dissenting voices and ban or censor books and websites. The peaceful demonstrations and protests of the Khatami era are no longer tolerated: in January security forces attacked striking bus drivers in Tehran and arrested hundreds of them. In March police beat hundreds of men and women who had assembled to commemorate International Women's Day.

The Consequences of Dissent

According to Human Rights Watch, an international lobbying group, detainees are routinely tortured in clandestine prisons operated by the judiciary, the information ministry and the Revolutionary Guards. The rate of executions appears to have speeded up, too. Iran now executes more people than any other country except China—often without giving defendants a fair trial. Homosexuality is one of the crimes punishable by death.

In recent months the slide back into authoritarianism has accelerated. Tehran's annual campaign against "bad *hijab*", when police harass or arrest women who show too much hair under their obligatory headscarves or make themselves up to look sexy, has been unusually severe. A series of high-profile arrests seems calculated to intimidate dissenters. Some of those arrested have been visiting American citizens with dual citizenship. (One, Haleh Esfandiari, from the Woodrow Wilson Centre in Washington, is the wife of Shaul Bakhash, a noted scholar and former writer for *The Economist.* She was detained and imprisoned while visiting her mother in Tehran.) More shocking inside the country was the arrest in April of Hossein Mousavian, a former Iranian ambassador to Germany and former nuclear negotiator, on suspicion of espionage. The arrest of a regime insider on such an outlandish charge sent a shudder through Iran's political establishment. Mr Mousavian is close to Akbar Hashemi Rafsanjani, a former president and Mr Ahmadinejad's defeated rival in the 2005 election.

If you are determined to give Iran the benefit of the doubt, one way to interpret these developments is to see them as the swing of a political pendulum—the sort of wobble you might expect in any country making a fitful transition to democracy. By 2005 Mr Khatami's reforming presidency had after all run out of steam. Mr Ahmadinejad won a popular election. The people seemed once again to want change, but change of a different kind: economic "justice" and redistribution rather than a political and cultural opening.

Mr Ahmadinejad, the austere son of a blacksmith, ran as an economic populist, adroitly harnessing the conviction of the *mostazafin*—Iran's "downtrodden"—that their basic needs had been neglected by the political reformers. A big part of his appeal was his promise to tackle the corruption many voters associated with the older brand of conservative, such as Mr Rafsanjani, whom many Iranians believe to be a billionaire as well as a cleric.

Nonetheless, says the pendulum theory, Iranian politics is still an affair of checks and balances. The new president is not invincible. His erratic economic policies—especially when combined with the impact of sanctions—will prevent him from satisfying the expectations he has aroused. By the time of the next *majlis* elections in 2008, or the presidential ones in 2009, the reformists will have regrouped and the pendulum may swing back.

In Iran, it is said, you can always dredge up plenty of evidence to support any theory you care to believe in. So it is with the theory of the pendulum. Mr Ahmadinejad has been in office for less than two years, but that has been time enough to produce plenty of evidence that his power is limited and his tenancy may be short. Despite the endorsement of the supreme leader (Ayatollah Khamenei has called him Iran's best president since the revolution), Mr Ahmadinejad has faced vehement opposition, not least from the *majlis* itself.

From the start, the *majlis* resisted many of his choices for cabinet jobs. It also rejected many of his spending plans. More than 30 *majlis* members have signed a petition that would summon the president to appear in parliament to explain his alleged policy failings. A year ago 50 prominent economists sent him an open letter attacking his economic policies. Last month they sent another, with additional signatories.

Mr Ahmadinejad's mounting bellicosity on the international stage—his threats against Israel, questioning of the Holocaust and nuclear defiance—has also run into robust internal criticism. This seemed to reach a crescendo last December when voters handed him a serious indirect rebuff. In municipal elections and elections for the Assembly of Experts (the body that elects and supervises the supreme leader), most of the candidates Mr Ahmadinejad supported were defeated.

Does this mean that the hardliners as a whole are in trouble? Not necessarily. In Iran's faction-based politics, the divisions between political blocks are not clear-cut. Factions tend to coalesce before elections and then break apart once they have got their man in. At the same time the defeated factions seek to form coalitions in the hope of reversing their defeat next time round. Right now the hardliners who rallied around Mr Ahmadinejad in 2005 are less concerned to maintain unity, whereas the main opposition groupings are feeling their way towards an alliance.

In the *majlis* these consist of a rump of Khatami-style reformists and a larger block of people who travel under the "conservative" banner but who are pragmatic in their approach and oppose Mr Ahmadinejad's brand of what many outsiders have come to call "neoconservatism".

Could the older-style conservatives such as Mr Rafsanjani and the reformists band together and win next time? That is what the pendulum theorists hope. This being Iran, however, plenty of evidence can also be found to prove that the pendulum theory is wrong.

A Parallel Universe

One of the theory's defects is its underlying assumption that power swings back and forth with election results. In Iran it doesn't quite. In 1997 Mr Khatami won a very handsome democratic mandate for reform, but by winning the presidency he did not win a free hand to govern.

Iran, remember, is at best a quasi-democracy: in parallel with the elected system exists another system that is unelected. Its elements include the armed forces (especially the Revolutionary Guards), the Council of Guardians, the judiciary, the senior conservative clerics and a vast administrative machine that reports directly to the supreme leader. By and large this unelected system is made up of strong believers in the original ideology of the revolution, or at least people who have a strong vested interest in it. A common self-description of these people is that they are *osoulgara*, or "principle-oriented".

The principle-oriented custodians of the revolution did not wait until the election of Mr Ahmadinejad before taking action against Mr Khatami's reforms, which they interpreted as a potentially lethal threat to its core values. With the connivance of the supreme leader, they simply used their executive power and a compliant judiciary to override the wishes of the legislature and the voters.

By these means President Khatami was deprived of his power long before he was deprived of his office. Nor did the men of principle think it safe to leave the choice of his successor to Iran's voters. The election took place only after legions of candidates had been disqualified by the Council of Guardians. By way of insurance there was also judicious fiddling on election day: reformists complain that the Revolutionary Guards and their associated Basij militia of perhaps a million young volunteers were drafted in to intimidate voters and stuff ballot boxes.

Take all this into account, and what is happening in Iranian politics begins to look more sinister than the swing of a pendulum. Some opposition politicians prefer to describe what Iran is experiencing as a "white" (i.e., bloodless) military coup. This did not start with President Ahmadinejad, though as a war veteran and former Revolutionary Guard commander he is typical of the class and generation behind it. It has been developing quietly ever since the men of principle began to fear that their revolution would not survive the encroachment of Western ideas, consumer habits, satellite television and the rise of a generation that had no direct memory of either revolution or war.

This is not the sort of coup in which the armed forces have to make an overt grab for power, because the supreme leader is part of the conspiracy. The fear, rather, is that with all the state institutions now in conservative hands the unelected centres of power are coalescing behind a single hard line and taking over all the top jobs. And in the name of principle this group (one *majlis* member calls it the "power in the shadow") has no qualms about bullying parliament or suborning the judiciary.

Mr Ahmadinejad is part of this group, but its survival does not depend on his. Indeed, many of the conservatives who supported his presidency are beginning to cast around for a more moderate, cooler-headed replacement (one possibility is Mohamed Baqer Qalibaf, the mayor of Tehran). "If necessary they will sacrifice him to protect themselves," says Isa Saharkhiz, the outspoken managing editor of *Aftab,* a reformist monthly. So strong is the military-clerical nexus under the supreme leader that Mr Saharkhiz dismisses the possibility of the reformists winning re-election. He says the Council of Guardians will simply disqualify their candidates.

A principal exhibit in the theory of the white coup is the relentless increase in the influence of the armed forces, especially the elite Revolutionary Guards. The Guards bared their teeth early in the reform period. Within a year of Mr Khatami's election as president their commander, General Rahim Safavi, was calling the reformers "hypocrites". In one notorious intervention he suggested that those reformers who (in his view) threatened the revolution should be beheaded.

Now that one of their own is president, the influence of the Guards has broadened. A large cohort of former Guards sits in the *majlis*. The Guards maintain their own intelligence agency and secret prisons. Men with close links to the Guards control principal media outlets such as the state broadcaster as well as the powerful Ministry for Islamic Guidance and Culture. Three years ago the Guards showed their strength by deciding on their own authority to close down the capital's new Imam Khomeini International Airport. They claimed that a decision to allow a Turkish consortium to operate the terminal had posed a threat to national security; but many Iranians think the real reason was that a company close to the Guards had lost its bid for the tender.

It may therefore be no coincidence that in the past two years the Guards' commercial interests have prospered. Their engineering arm, known as Ghorb, has been granted juicy slices of big state projects, including the building of gas pipelines and a new section of the Tehran metro.

Sayeed Laylaz, a former government official and now a private economist in Tehran, says simply that the Guards are "Iran's *nomenklatura*—a new social class formed by domination of the economy". Within ten months of Mr Ahmadinejad's election, he reckons, the value of civil contracts awarded to the Guards, many of them without going to competitive tender, had trebled from $4 billion to $12 billion. On top of this, the Guards are also thought to be in charge of Iran's nuclear-weapons programme, a political and technological responsibility conferring huge influence and prestige within the ruling system.

A Plot a Day Keeps Opposition Away

What makes Iran's future especially hard to predict right now is its testy relationship with the outside world, and particularly with the United States. That is because the direction Iran takes will depend not only on its own choices but also on what the world does to it. Many Americans, and many Iranians living in America, believe that the regime is so unpopular that it can indeed be reformed or even removed from within—if only the opposition receives a bit more help. To that end the American government has earmarked scores of millions of dollars to help Iranian "civil society" and pro-democracy groups.

But reformers inside the country dare not touch this money. Ebrahim Yazdi, leader of the Freedom Movement, which supported the revolution but is now a courageous voice for democracy, says that such programmes merely give the authorities an excuse to "intensify the repression". The government cites these American funds as proof that the United States is plotting its overthrow. Fearing (or claiming to fear) that America is fomenting a "velvet" revolution, it has used them to justify its arrest of foreign visitors.

In recent months almost all contacts between "civil society" and the West have fallen under real or manufactured suspicion. In May American would-be participants in an economic conference organised by the Ravand Institute, Tehran's first independent economic think-tank, set up by Iran's former ambassador to London, were denied visas. In June Iranians who had the temerity to attend a reception at the British embassy to mark the queen's birthday were harassed on their way in and out by police and rent-a-mob demonstrators. The regime is cutting down the number of foreign journalists based in Tehran and restricting the movements of those who remain. The country is being put on a "war footing", says one.

It is a familiar pattern. Writing from exile, Akbar Ganji, one of Iran's best-known dissidents, says the hardliners have consistently cited American policies towards Iran as an excuse to crack down on internal foes. "Politicians with close ties to the military establishment have taken control of the Iranian government and are trying to manage the cultural and political arena in the style of a police state," he says in the *Boston Review.* "These policies are, in turn, aggravating hostilities and allowing the Bush administration to justify its belligerence. Thus the vicious cycle continues."

A similar mechanism operates in the nuclear debate. Shahram Chubin, director of studies at the Geneva Centre for Security Policy, argues in a recent book that although Iran resumed the shah's nuclear programme for security reasons during the war with Iraq, its motivation now has at least as much to do with internal politics. As the revolution started to falter in the 1990s, he says, the nuclear option offered a way to rally nationalist opinion and "legitimate the regime".

So it has proved. Mr Ahmadinejad and his coterie have succeeded brilliantly in portraying the regime's quest for nuclear "technology" (it is careful never to speak of nuclear weapons) as a matter of national pride. Most Iranians do not see why a great nation such as theirs should be denied a technology others are allowed to have. This has wrong-footed the pragmatists, such as Ayatollah Rafsanjani, who supports the nuclear programme but would work harder to prevent it from antagonising the world and isolating Iran.

For Iran's men of principle it may be that antagonising the world and isolating Iran are very much part of the point.

Hermidas Bavand, a Tehran-based academic, says that just as revolutionaries in Russia and China took fright when their ideas stopped resonating with the people, those in Iran think that their survival depends on making Iranians feel surrounded, isolated and beset by foes. A particular group, he says, wants to make the revolution permanent "in order to retain their control of the power structure"—and for this it is helpful if they can point to enemies everywhere.

The more that outsiders meddle, the deeper the regime digs in. Better to let the country find its own way towards democracy, the reformers say. But can the world afford to leave Iran to its own devices? If they are nuclear devices, perhaps not.

Banning the Bomb
A New Approach

WARD WILSON

In July of 1945, U.S. president Harry Truman wrote in his diary, "It is certainly a good thing for the world that Hitler's crowd or Stalin's did not discover this atomic bomb. It seems to be the most terrible thing ever discovered, but it can be made the most useful." Terrible and useful. For sixty years, people have focused on the terrible aspects of nuclear weapons. They have made films about nuclear war, detailed the horrors of Hiroshima and Nagasaki, and imagined the end of life on earth. In those sixty years, on the other hand, people have rarely talked seriously about the usefulness of nuclear weapons. Do they really win wars? Are they effective threats? Fear—engendered by real and imagined cold war dangers—constrained real inquiry. Absorbed by images of destruction, most people didn't ask practical questions. But it turns out that the area that we've explored the most—the terribleness of nuclear weapons—is not the key to understanding them. The key is investigating whether or not they are really useful.

I am not urging the familiar argument that nuclear weapons are too dangerous to be useful; I am suggesting that even if one could use them with impunity, nuclear weapons would still have little practical value. Sixty years of experience, recent reevaluations of the track record of nuclear weapons, and reinterpretations of Hiroshima and Nagasaki based on new research make it possible to argue that there are very few situations in which nuclear weapons are useful. It might, in fact, be possible to demonstrate that nuclear weapons are functionally the equivalent of biological and chemical weapons: powerful and dangerous weapons, but with very few real applications. And therefore it might also be possible to make the case that—as with chemical and biological weapons—there are practical, prudential reasons for banning nuclear weapons.

Current Strategies

To date, two related strategies have been used to oppose the use of nuclear weapons: the horror strategy and the risk strategy. The former relies on moral feelings and tries to persuade people that using nuclear weapons is too immoral to contemplate. The latter relies on calculations of the possibility that a small war could become an all-out nuclear war and tries to persuade people that the danger is too great.

Those who use the horror strategy often make Hiroshima and Nagasaki the centerpiece of their case. They try to drive home the immorality of using nuclear weapons by forcing their listeners to experience vicariously the horror of these cities. Doctors increased the emotional impact of this approach in the 1980s by talking unflinchingly and in detail about the medical consequences of nuclear attacks.

The risk strategy has been more widely embraced than the horror strategy. Vividly given a story line by Nevil Shute in *On the Beach* (a novel later made into a movie in which a nuclear war extinguishes all human life), it has remained a staple of antinuclear argument, used by radicals and sober policymakers alike.

Jonathan Schell updated and expanded the risk strategy in *The Fate of the Earth*. Schell eschewed the normal tack of emphasizing the risks of escalation, arguing instead that an all-out nuclear war might lead to the destruction of all life on earth. So it didn't matter how big or small the risk of escalation was, the consequences were so terrible that no amount of risk was worth running. In 1983, Carl Sagan and four others further buttressed Schell's case with evidence suggesting that severe climatic disruption, dubbed "nuclear winter," could be triggered by a nuclear war.

Sound as their reasoning might be, both these strategies have weaknesses. The horror argument's weakness is that in a crisis necessity almost always trumps morality. People will say, "Yes, it's wrong. But we have to do it. We have no other choice." If the Bomb seems likely to be militarily effective most people will decide to use it, even if they know it is wrong to do so.

The risk strategy has been eroded by the end of the cold war, which led to lowered tensions and significantly reduced the likelihood of nuclear escalation. Another key—but often overlooked—change is the end of "extended deterrence"—the threat by the United States and the Soviet Union to respond to attacks on their client states with nuclear counterattacks. At one time, all of Europe, all of Latin America, some of Asia, and even parts of Africa were covered by extended deterrence. With the collapse of the cold war client-state system, many nations are now out from under the nuclear umbrella. It is now possible for the United States to attack, say, Syria, with nuclear weapons without the threat of a nuclear response from Russia. As the risk of escalation has decreased, the strength of the risk argument has also decreased.

Bigger Is Not Better

It is often said that every weapon that man has invented has been used in war. This statement misses the point. The important issue is not whether this or that weapon has ever been used, it is whether such a weapon—once tried—has become a fixture in the arsenals of warlike nations. Horrible weapons have been imagined and tried. But are they still used?

Consider the Paris Gun. Built by the Germans in World War I, it was more than 90 feet long, weighed 256 tons, and moved on rails. It fired a 210-pound projectile more than 80 miles. Often confused with its smaller cousin, the large mortar called "Big Bertha," in its day it was the largest cannon ever built. It was a terrifying weapon. From March until August of 1918, the Germans used it to rain shells down on Paris without warning. The Parisians were bewildered and terrified. In all, the Paris Gun fired about 360 shells, killing 250 people and wounding 620.

Only a handful of other superguns have since been built (Schwerer Gustav and V3 among them). Their impact on the wars in which they participated was minimal. Today, nations do not race to build their own superguns. African nations, torn by strife, do not try to trade their oil or diamond resources for superguns bought from arms dealers. There are no angry diatribes in liberal papers about the horror of these weapons and the necessity of banning them.

"But of course this is so," someone might say, "because these weapons were not very effective." And that is the point. Decisions about acquiring or banning weapons are not based on their horribleness but on their ability or inability to help win wars.

There are four general ways that nuclear weapons might be used: in a war intended to exterminate an opponent, in a war of coercion, as a threat, and to create terror. For two of these categories—coercion and threats—it is relatively easy to show that nuclear weapons are not ideal weapons and, in some circumstances, are so seriously mismatched to the task at hand as to be useless.

On the other hand, nuclear weapons are admirably suited for wars of extermination. If you have decided on a war in which your goal is to annihilate your opponent, nuclear weapons are your best choice. In this case it is necessary to argue not that the weapons wouldn't be useful, but that such wars are morally wrong. This is not a demanding task. No case can be made that the capability to wage a war of annihilation is valuable or necessary. And this moral judgment is borne out by the practical experience of history: the actual number of wars of extermination is small. (Wars of extermination are distinct from genocide or other murderous actions within a country's own boundaries.) A careful review of human history unearthed only one clear case, the Third Punic War.

The vast majority of wars are wars of coercion. The conventional wisdom has been that nuclear weapons are decisive in this kind of war. After all, they won the war in the Pacific. But when examined closely, the presumption of decisiveness evaporates. Recent reinterpretations of the Japanese surrender call into question the notion that the bombings of Hiroshima and Nagasaki were in any way connected with that decision. The Soviet intervention radically altered the strategic situation and was the decisive event.

The power to destroy cities is not the power to win wars. Freeman Dyson makes this point vividly in an example drawn from the Falklands War. Someone had said loosely about the war that if the British had wanted to they could have "blown Buenos Aires off the map." This was true, but Dyson points out that the British would still have had to send soldiers to re-conquer the Falklands. And destroying Buenos Aires would probably have made the Argentine soldiers defending the islands fight more fiercely. Or the British could have nuked the Falklands themselves, but that would have destroyed the islands. The British abstained from using nuclear weapons not because they have admirable restraint, but because there was no practical application for the weapons.

Sixty years of experience with nuclear weapons does not support the notion that they are singularly useful to their possessors. Despite its nuclear arsenal, the United States was fought to a draw in Korea, lost a war in Vietnam, did not stop genocides in Cambodia or Rwanda, and is currently mired in conflict in Iraq. Despite its sizable nuclear arsenal, the Soviet Union suffered humiliation in its own guerrilla war in Afghanistan. Nuclear nations have fought many wars, but these supposedly powerful weapons have not played a decisive role in any of them.

Nuclear weapons do not appear to be suited to the battlefield. This inutility has already been ratified by two of the most authoritative bodies in a position to make a judgment: the military establishments of the United States and the Soviet Union. If tactical nuclear weapons were really militarily useful, would these two military establishments have allowed almost all tactical weapons to be retired in the 1980s?

Nuclear weapons are also of questionable effectiveness in attacks on economic targets. Most economic targets are roughly building-sized, and with today's precision-guided munitions, conventional weapons are more than adequate. Nuclear weapons, on the other hand, require destruction of an area many times larger than the target. What is the point of destroying a quarter of a city in order to knock out an oil refinery? It is true that a large-scale nuclear attack could effectively shatter a nation's economic infrastructure, but at what point does this become a war of extermination?

Diplomatic Influence

When the United States first got nuclear weapons, there were high hopes that they would provide not just military might, but international influence as well. Truman, when he talked about nuclear weapons being "useful" in the diary entry quoted above, was probably thinking of the upcoming negotiations he faced with the Soviet Union over the shape of the post–World War II world. His secretary of state, James F. Byrnes, told him with a touch of euphoria that nuclear weapons would probably allow the United States to "dictate our own terms after the war." Byrnes returned from the bargaining table a chastened man. The Soviets, he reported ruefully afterward, "are stubborn, obstinate, and they don't scare." Perhaps this is not surprising. Joseph Stalin said in a 1946 interview in *Pravda,* "Atomic bombs are meant to frighten those with weak nerves."

The U.S. nuclear monopoly did not prevent communist domination of Eastern Europe in the years after the Second World War. It did not prevent the Berlin Crisis of 1948. It did not prevent the communist takeover of China in 1949. Of course, any threat will work some percentage of the time—some people scare easily. The question is, are nuclear weapons reliable tools of coercion? Clearly not.

Some people argue that nuclear weapons have kept the United States and other nations safe by deterring nuclear war. This is difficult to prove. Imagine a man who says that the lucky penny he keeps on his dresser has prevented nuclear war. When you ask for proof, he says, "Well, I've kept that penny on the dresser for sixty-two years and there's been no war, so it must be working!" Nuclear weapons may provide crucial safety and security, although it is hard to imagine how dangerous weapons that cannot be defended against are the best means of providing safety. Another—perhaps more certain—way to prevent nuclear war is to ban nuclear weapons.

Of What Use Today?

Another way to assess the usefulness of nuclear weapons is to think about the role they might play in a crisis today. Imagine, for example, that the North Koreans used a nuclear weapon to attack Seoul or Tokyo. The United States, Russia, Great Britain, France, or China would all be in a position to retaliate against Pyongyang. Some might argue that this would be the right way to deter future nuclear attacks against cities. But wouldn't a far more practical deterrent be for the United States, Russia, and China to form an alliance, invade North Korea, and set up a new government? Nuking Pyongyang only punishes the innocent. North Korea's leaders would surely have left the city shortly before the North Korean nuclear strike was launched. Nuking Pyongyang kills North Korean civilians, who, because they live under a dictatorship, have no responsibility for the decision to attack. Rogue states that use nuclear weapons are unlikely to be democratic states, and because what nuclear weapons do best is kill people, nuclear weapons will never be well suited to punishing such a regime.

Many people believe that the most likely use of nuclear weapons in the next few years (barring a war in the Middle East or the Asian subcontinent) is a terrorist attack against a city. Terrorists, whose aim is to coerce political change by irregular attacks on innocents, are the people most likely to imagine that nuclear weapons are useful. On the other hand, it is difficult to imagine nuclear deterrence against terrorists. Imagine that a nuclear bomb hidden in a cargo container is detonated in Baltimore Harbor. What effective nuclear retaliation options are there? It would be very difficult to identify the attackers. But even assuming that a terrorist group takes responsibility—say, al-Qaeda—how can nuclear weapons be used to redress this evil? Would you use a nuclear weapon against a city in Pakistan in which you think Osama bin Laden is hiding? Again, the vast majority of those who die will be innocent, and if faulty intelligence leads you to attack the wrong city you risk punishing *only* the innocent.

A good deal of energy has been devoted to imagining circumstances in which nuclear weapons would be exactly the right weapons to use. But why is it necessary to imagine unlikely or outlandish scenarios in order to justify these weapons?

The current U.S. administration supports research into developing "bunker buster" nuclear weapons that could destroy targets deeply buried or secreted in caves. There are two telling objections to such a weapon. First, as with most applications of nuclear weapons, conventional weapons already provide a fairly extensive bunker buster capability. Nuclear bunker busters would only extend existing capabilities a few hundred meters (to three hundred meters below the surface at most). It is within the capabilities of almost any enemy simply to dig deeper. The second is that the intelligence necessary for such a strike is unimaginable. Even with the sophisticated technology currently available to the U.S. government, for example, we were unable to identify chemical and biological facilities in Iraq, a country with barren, cloud-free, best-case topography. This is an indication of how hard it is to locate secret facilities. And we were looking for facilities on the surface.

The current administration also imagines that mini-nukes would be useful. These are weapons with roughly a third the destructive power of the bomb that destroyed Hiroshima—about the same destructive power that was deployed in the conventional raids against Japanese cities in the summer of 1945. Why build a nuclear weapon with an end result you can already achieve using conventional weapons?

In this connection, the size of nuclear weapons raises a question. Early on in the nuclear age, physicists warned that there was no theoretical limit to the size of hydrogen bombs. The Soviets tested a bomb with a yield of roughly fifty-two megatons in 1962. Larger bombs could have been built. Yet they have not been. In fact, the size of nuclear warheads in the U.S. and Russian arsenals has been shrinking. At one time one megaton (or larger) warheads were common, but today the yield of an average warhead in the U.S. strategic arsenal is only about a third of a megaton. How can nuclear bombs be shrinking if the greater the destructive power the greater the military usefulness? If nuclear weapons are useful, why is it that the trend is toward making them more like conventional weapons?

Benefits of Banning the Bomb

The benefits of a total ban are clear. The chief benefit is that it protects us against the danger that people are currently most concerned with in connection with these weapons: use by a terrorist group against a city. By banning nuclear weapons you substantially decrease the chances that they will fall into the hands of rogue states or terrorist organizations. The only reason that the director of the Pakistani nuclear project was able to sell nuclear technology to the North Koreans is that proliferation had gained such widespread acceptance. The more nations that have nuclear weapons, the more likely someone is to put them into the hands of irresponsible people. (As I write this in

October 2006, North Korea has just tested a nuclear weapon. The international reaction serves as a strong reminder that it is important to keep nuclear weapons out of the hands of unstable leaders.)

Any international ban would have to include careful monitoring of all formerly nuclear nations and inspection of nuclear power reactors. (If nuclear nations are unwilling to give up their weapons entirely, perhaps each could warehouse a small stockpile under UN administration in their own countries. The weapons could be retrieved by their owner, but only by publicly breaking the treaty.) With no military weapons floating around, and access to nuclear power monitored and controlled by international organizations, building a rogue bomb or stealing one becomes almost impossible.

None of the arguments sketched here is the final word on the usefulness of nuclear weapons. There is considerable work still to be done. The Hiroshima argument needs to be more thoroughly researched. The case against city attacks needs to be strengthened with historical examples. And along with work on each of its parts, a systematic treatment of the entire subject is needed. But it should be clear from the limited treatment here that there is enough substance in the approach to merit further work.

In 1775, Edmund Burke rose in Parliament to oppose the use of force against the American colonies. Burke believed strongly that the application of force was not the best way to bind the colonies to the British Empire. Burke said that he opposed force not because it was an "odious" instrument of policy but because it was a "feeble" one. His assertion must have been especially surprising because the British army and navy at that time were the most powerful in the world. Using force, he argued, could intimidate and coerce, but raw power alone would not create obedience in the colonies. In some situations brute force is less effective (or more "feeble") than other means.

It may seem paradoxical to think of them as "feeble," but I want to make something of the same argument about nuclear weapons. The strongest arguments against the use of nuclear weapons are not those that demonstrate that they are horrible or dangerous (although they are certainly both), but those that show that they aren't very useful. Weapons, like tools, are situational: their "power" is measured not by their raw force but by the extent to which their capabilities match the circumstances. A jackhammer is a very powerful tool; it's not much help in repairing a watch. A howitzer is of no use underwater; a shotgun blast doesn't help where stealth is required; a knife has little effect at a thousand yards. It's not the size of the bang, it's the match between the situation at hand and the weapon's capabilities. In most military situations, conventional weapons are better suited to the task at hand than nuclear ones. Only in blowing up cities are nuclear weapons singularly well suited to a task. This is an objective, however, that only terrorists pursue enthusiastically.

If there are hardly any circumstances in which nuclear weapons are militarily useful, and if it seems likely that the more nations that have nuclear arsenals the more likely the weapons are to fall into the hands of terrorists or madmen, then it makes practical sense to ban them.

WARD WILSON is an independent scholar living in Trenton, N.J. He is currently at work on a book about the military usefulness of destroying cities throughout history. He writes regularly at www.rethinking nuclearweapons.org.

UNIT 6

Cooperation

Unit Selections

Key Points to Consider

- Itemize the products you own that were manufactured in another country.

- What recent contacts have you had with people from other countries? How was it possible for you to have these contacts?

- How do you use the World Wide Web to learn about other countries and cultures?

- Identify nongovernmental organizations in your community that are involved in international cooperation (e.g., Rotary International).

- What are the prospects for international governance? How do trends in this direction enhance or threaten American values and constitutional rights?

- What new strategies for cooperation can be developed to fight infectious disease, terrorism, international narcotics trafficking and other threats?

- How can conflict and rivalry be transformed into meaningful cooperation?

Student Web Site
www.mhcls.com/online

Internet References
Further information regarding these Websites may be found in this book's preface or online.

Carnegie Endowment for International Peace
http://www.ceip.org
OECD/FDI Statistics
http://www.oecd.org/statistics/
U.S. Institute of Peace
http://www.usip.org

Arabian Eye/PunchStock

An individual can write a letter and, assuming it is properly addressed, be relatively certain that it will be delivered to just about any location in the world. This is true even though the sender pays for postage only in the country of origin and not in the country where it is delivered. A similar pattern of international cooperation is true when a traveler boards an airplane and never gives a thought to the issue of potential language and technical barriers, even though the flight's destination is halfway around the world.

Many of the most basic activities of our lives are the direct result of governments cooperating across borders. International organizational structures, for example, have been created to eliminate barriers to trade, monitor and respond to public health threats, set standards for international telecommunications, arrest and judge war criminals, and monitor changing atmospheric conditions. Individual governments, in other words, have recognized that their self-interest directly benefits from cooperation (in most cases by giving up some of their sovereignty through the creation of international governmental organizations, or IGOs).

Transnational activities are not limited to the governmental level. There are now tens of thousands of international nongovernmental organizations (INGOs). The activities of INGOs range from staging the Olympic Games to organizing scientific meetings to actively discouraging the hunting of seals. The number of INGOs along with their influence has grown tremendously in the past 50 years.

During the same period in which the growth in importance of IGOs and INGOs has taken place, there also has been a parallel expansion of corporate activity across international borders. Most

U.S. consumers are as familiar with Japanese or German brand-name products as they are with items made in their own country. The multinational corporation (MNC) is an important non-state actor. The value of goods and services produced by the biggest MNCs is far greater than the gross domestic product (GDP) of many countries. The international structures that make it possible to buy a Swedish automobile in Sacramento or a Korean television in Buenos Aires have been developed over many years. They are the result of governments negotiating treaties that create IGOs to implement the agreements (e.g., the World Trade Organization). As a result, corporations engaged in international trade and manufacturing have created complex transnational networks of sales, distribution, and service that employ millions of people.

To some observers these trends indicate that the era of the nation-state as the dominant player in international politics is passing. Other experts have observed these same trends and have concluded that the state system has a monopoly of power and that the diverse variety of transnational organizations depends on the state system and, in significant ways, perpetuates it.

In many of the articles that appear elsewhere in this book, the authors have concluded their analysis by calling for greater international cooperation to solve the world's most pressing problems. The articles in this section provide examples of successful cooperation. In the midst of a lot of bad news, it is easy to overlook the fact that we are surrounded by international cooperation and that basic day-to-day activities in our lives often directly benefit from it.

A Filled Balance

Europe as a Global Player

A Parliamentary Perspective

HANS-GERT POETTERING

In the 28 years since the European Parliament was first elected, it has developed from a largely advisory forum into a full-fledged branch of Europe's legislature. Since the Single European Act of 1986 and the Maastricht Treaty of 1992, the role of the European Parliament in EU decision-making has increasingly changed from one of marginality to one of centrality. Today, members of the European Parliament share law-making powers with the Council of Ministers across many policy areas. The Parliament has truly come of age.

The advent of co-decision between the Parliament and the Council has made the Parliament a major actor in the EU legislative process. The Parliament has become an integral part of a new European political system, in which the vast majority of decisions require explicit approval of the Parliament. Whether it be the liberalization of transport, regulation of financial markets, limits on carbon emissions, or product standards and consumer protection, the decisions of the Parliament are now as important as those of member states in setting EU law.

In recent years, our work as members of the Parliament has shaped and advanced European integration in many fields. We pushed forward the process of EU enlargement when there was reticence in some other quarters. The single market and the single currency would never have occurred without the early and sustained advocacy of Euro-parliamentarians. The political majority in the European Parliament is now critical in determining who is chosen as president of the European Commission. Furthermore, as a result of parliamentary pressure, foreign and security policy has become an integral part of EU activity.

When I first became a member of the European Parliament in 1979, the individual sovereign states guarded their own foreign and security policies, making the policy area something of a taboo subject at the supranational level. This disunity, however, changed in the mid-1980s, when the Single European Act formalized modest arrangements for "European political cooperation." The Maastricht Treaty converted them into a formal Common Foreign and Security Policy, for the first time raising the possibility of a European defense. Today, more than a dozen

EU military and policing missions can be found throughout the world. While deployment of EU troops or police forces outside the European Union was unheard of in 1979, it is a daily reality in 2007.

As the European Union becomes more involved in world affairs and as domestic integration deepens, it becomes more important that the European institutions function as effectively and democratically as possible. These objectives can most effectively be obtained through the ratification of the European constitutional treaty. We need the reforms espoused by the constitution to successfully fulfill our role in EU and world affairs.

European integration has gone through cycles of crisis and self-doubt in the past, but it has usually emerged stronger as a result. When the European Defense Community failed in 1954, it subsequently took less than three years to reach an agreement on the Rome Treaties. When the first effort to establish a common currency failed during the 1970s, the experience of further monetary crises pointed to the continuing necessity for a full economic and monetary union, a logic that led to the adoption of the euro in 2002. While the difficulties in securing ratification of the European constitutional treaty by all member states have been a blow to the development of the European Union, I believe that they can be overcome, just as European integration has cleared previous obstacles that initially seemed insurmountable in its 50-year history.

One clear lesson from the recent ratification crisis is that there is a need to connect more closely European citizens with the project of European integration. Some of the citizens of France and the Netherlands who voted against the constitutional treaty in referenda in the summer of 2005 did so because they regarded the European Union as insufficiently coherent, democratic, or transparent. Yet ironically, the constitutional treaty actually includes many of the changes that are necessary to strengthen democracy, coherence, and transparency in the Union. For example, it extends the mandate of the president of the European Council, gives the European Parliament even greater legislative power, clarifies the competences of the

Union, and simplifies the types of legislative action—all in an effort to improve the overall consistency, clarity, and accountability of EU institutions.

The foreign policy component of the constitutional treaty is especially important. Only an effective and democratic European Union along the lines foreseen in the constitutional treaty can be a credible actor in the world, and furthermore, a reliable partner for the United States. Though commentators like to distinguish between "soft" and "hard" power, I would prefer to distinguish between coherence and incoherence in foreign policy-making. The truth is that even though decision-making at the EU level is now integral to determining the foreign policy of the member states—and the global presence of the European Union is already an important reality in world affairs—the Union as such is not in the position to act coherently in its own right. This limitation stems in varying degrees from the Union's legal status, the institutional division between the Council and the Commission, and the Union's lack of free-standing military resources. The provisions of the constitutional treaty, which establish the post of European foreign minister and create a European external action service, are important for the emergence of a more comprehensive and credible EU foreign policy.

Responsible political leadership in the European Union is rightly committed to putting these provisions into practice. So far, the constitutional treaty has been ratified by two-thirds of the European Union's 27 member states. It is also supported by the vast majority of members of the European Parliament. Our common objective is to implement at least the core propositions enshrined in the treaty—the key substance of the original text—before the next elections to the European Parliament in June 2009.

Europe and Globalization

A constitutional treaty will make it easier for Europe to address the pressing issues of our time, at home and abroad. Globalization poses new challenges to European policymakers in the economic sphere and in many other fields. Europe has been slower in taking full advantage of the opportunities of globalization than the United States, let alone China or India. But the European Union has been fully aware that just as globalization brings new opportunities, as it empowers individuals and expands the global market, creating billions of new consumers, it simultaneously requires changes in European citizens' attitudes toward job security, welfare, and most importantly, investment in human capital through education and life-long learning. The majority of citizens in the European Union would resist any form of globalization that undermined the principles of human dignity, but this outcome need not materialize. The market dynamic can and should continue to be underpinned by a safety net for the weaker members of European society. This is an essential principle of a social market economy.

In a way, European integration has been, and continues to be, an anticipated form of regional globalization. It has been driven, by and large, by political decisions designed to support the freedom and cohesion of European societies, to facilitate the creation of a single European market, and to provide a greater measure

of legal certainty to activities in the European sphere. It is based on supranational law and therefore offers a sort of framework in which a free market can flourish to the benefit of more citizens. Based on this experience, we believe that globalization will progress most smoothly if it goes hand in hand with some legal rules—not ones that undermine the forces of the market, but rules that safeguard the interests of citizens, both as consumers and producers.

Projecting Stability into the World

To date, globalization has too often left out important parts of the world community, notably in the Arab world and sub-Saharan Africa. As both these regions are physically proximate to Europe, we are particularly sensitive to this situation. In fact, it is both a strategic and a moral obligation that we pay more attention to what is taking place in these regions. Poverty, insecurity, and fear can easily produce a dangerous combination of illegal migration, fanaticism, and violence.

The European Union is now the largest donor of development aid in the world. Some critics claim that this assistance is some kind of compensation for the legacy of European colonialism in lesser-developed countries. I think it emphasizes instead Europe's firm desire to be a constructive partner in building a better world.

Europe's political leaders and institutions are determined to fight terrorism and any form of political violence. We are gravely concerned about an ideology of Islamic radicalism that includes the use of violence as a means to succeed in its political and religious goals. We absolutely condemn terror in the name of politics or religion, and we are concerned that the continuation of any form of radical Islamic terror will undermine the chances of a dialogue among cultures that is more vital today than ever.

Europe is an immediate neighbor of the Arab world. The bulk of immigrants into the European Union originate from northern Africa and sub-Saharan Africa, with Spain being the biggest recipient. Muslims have become the second largest religious group in the Union, representing around 3.5 percent of the total population. Mosques are a common sight all over Europe. In our position, a cross-cultural dialogue is crucial. By the nature of our situation and our history, the European Union is absolutely determined to guarantee a peaceful cohabitation of Christians, Muslims, Jews, and all other religious, secular, and atheist people. We can only do this on the basis of mutual respect.

An important component of the emerging foreign policy of the European Union is the effort to project stability into the immediate neighborhood of the Union and into the wider world. The recent enlargement of the European Union was a spectacular example of the success of that policy: the prospect of EU membership played an important part in ensuring the democracy and prosperity of the former Soviet republics and client states which are now safely members of a democratic European family. An enlarged European Union has recently developed a complex web of policies to stabilize its immediate surroundings and to promote peace and affluence beyond its borders. Our partnerships with Russia and other Eastern European countries that are non-EU member states are designed to build a more stable relationship with that part of Europe's neighborhood.

Likewise, the European Union is part of the "Quartet" along with the United States, the United Nations, and Russia that designed the Road Map for Peace in the Middle East. Many obituaries have been written for this Quartet process. But in the end, I believe, a comprehensive solution to the vexing Middle East conundrum will have to follow the main elements of the established Road Map and, in fact, will need the commitment of the Quartet countries. We want a comprehensive, equitable, and lasting peace that recognizes the right of existence of both Israel and a viable Palestinian state. The Euro-Mediterranean Partnership—in which the European Parliament plays a leading role—is an important vehicle for bringing all European countries together with the Arab coastal states of the Mediterranean and with Israel.

Transatlantic Partnership

Rising to the challenge of globalization also requires deeper transatlantic cooperation. Most major global issues we face cannot be resolved solely by the actions of either the European Union or the United States. In general, when we cannot reach agreement across the Atlantic on major global challenges, policy simply fails to be enacted at the international level and the credibility of the Western world decreases. In order to resolve key issues from climate control to global terrorism, the European Union and the United States must be active partners in a common endeavor.

The ties that bind the United States and the European Union are deeply rooted. We are each other's largest economic partners, whether in terms of trade, capital flows, inward investments, or jobs. Ownership of many of our companies is now in effect vested jointly in the hands of both US and EU citizens. Our great universities cooperate actively. There is a regular, intense exchange of ideas, emails, and visitors across the Atlantic. At a political level, however, there is still much to be done. We have the achievements of the NATO Treaty, we have our regular EU-US summits and parliamentary exchanges, but we have no systematic framework within which to organize our overall relations. As early as 1962, President John F. Kennedy proposed a transatlantic treaty broadening the bases for our relationship for this very reason.

In the absence of such a framework, we can still work positively together on a common agenda. The current German presidency of the Council has already declared that strengthening transatlantic relations, particularly in the economic sphere, is one of its major external policy priorities. Chancellor Angela Merkel has talked of promoting "ever-closer economic cooperation" across the Atlantic, signaling that she particularly wants to see progress toward an EU-US Transatlantic Economic Partnership, based on some variant of a "Transatlantic Market." The latter concept is not a free-trade area or a customs union; rather, it is in effect a single market, in which EU and US technical standards, regulatory régimes, and competition policies would progressively converge. The idea has long been advocated in resolutions of the European Parliament. Indeed, it is a good example of how the Parliament has shifted the policy agenda, in this case, by going out in front of the member-state governments.

The concept of a transatlantic single market has, for the first time, been picked up by the president of the European Commission, José Manuel Barroso, in Brussels, and by the US president and administration in Washington. It is an idea whose time has come. Legislators in the European Parliament, together with senators and congressmen on Capitol Hill, will need to be closely involved. If Parliament and Congress are to approve the result and make all the legislative changes necessary to implement it, it is sensible that we be partners from the start in its design, negotiation, and delivery.

Maintaining the "Atlantic Civilization"

The future of European integration and of a strong transatlantic partnership are important political objectives and key components in maintaining our "Atlantic civilization." The European Union is developing new scenarios to advance both greater unity and stronger Euro-American relations. The German presidency of the Council currently is attempting to identify methods and timelines for achieving each. As a result, there is now a very serious possibility that Europe will overcome the crisis over the ratification of the European constitutional treaty and emerge strengthened by this process. The European Union needs the substance of the reforms enshrined in the treaty, not only to better manage its affairs as a union of 27 or more member states, but also to confront the new and pressing policy challenges posed by globalization and to discharge its responsibilities in the world. Equally, there is an increasing likelihood that we will see significant progress toward a closer transatlantic partnership, at least in the economic sphere, with the concept of a barrier-free single market across the Atlantic firmly on the agenda. These twin achievements would represent major stepping stones toward building a less dangerous and more prosperous world.

HANS-GERT POETTERING, MEP, is President of the European Parliament.

The Grameen Bank

A small experiment begun in Bangladesh has turned into a major new concept in eradicating poverty.

MUHAMMAD YUNUS

Over many years, Amena Begum had become resigned to a life of grinding poverty and physical abuse. Her family was among the poorest in Bangladesh—one of thousands that own virtually nothing, surviving as squatters on desolate tracts of land and earning a living as day laborers."

In early 1993 Amena convinced her husband to move to the village of Kholshi, 112 kilometers (70 miles) west of Dhaka. She hoped the presence of a nearby relative would reduce the number and severity of the beatings that her husband inflicted on her. The abuse continued, however—until she joined the Grameen Bank. Oloka Ghosh, a neighbor, told Amena that Grameen was forming a new group in Kholshi and encouraged her to join. Amena doubted that anyone would want her in their group. But Oloka persisted with words of encouragement. "We're all poor—or at least we all were when we joined. I'll stick up for you because I know you'll succeed in business."

Amena's group joined a Grameen Bank Center in April 1993. When she received her first loan of $60, she used it to start her own business raising chickens and ducks. When she repaid her initial loan and began preparing a proposal for a second loan of $110, her friend Oloka gave her some sage advice: "Tell your husband that Grameen does not allow borrowers who are beaten by their spouses to remain members and take loans." From that day on, Amena suffered significantly less physical abuse at the hands of her husband. Today her business continues to grow and provide for the basic needs of her family.

Unlike Amena, the majority of people in Asia, Africa and Latin America have few opportunities to escape from poverty. According to the World Bank, more than 1.3 billion people live on less than a dollar a day. Poverty has not been eradicated in the 50 years since the Universal Declaration on Human Rights asserted that each individual has a right to:

> A standard of living adequate for the health and well-being of himself and of his family, including food, clothing, housing and medical care and necessary social services, and the right to security in the event of unemployment, sickness, disability, widowhood, old age or other lack of livelihood in circumstances beyond his control.

Will poverty still be with us 50 years from now? My own experience suggests that it need not.

After completing my Ph.D. at Vanderbilt University, I returned to Bangladesh in 1972 to teach economics at Chittagong University. I was excited about the possibilities for my newly independent country. But in 1974 we were hit with a terrible famine. Faced with death and starvation outside my classroom, I began to question the very economic theories I was teaching. I started feeling there was a great distance between the actual life of poor and hungry people and the abstract world of economic theory.

I wanted to learn the real economics of the poor. Because Chittagong University is located in a rural area, it was easy for me to visit impoverished households in the neighboring village of Jobra. Over the course of many visits, I learned all about the lives of my struggling neighbors and much about economics that is never taught in the classroom. I was dismayed to see how the indigent in Jobra suffered because they could not come up with small amounts of working capital. Frequently they needed less than a dollar a person but could get that money only on extremely unfair terms. In most cases, people were required to sell their goods to moneylenders at prices fixed by the latter.

This daily tragedy moved me to action. With the help of my graduate students, I made a list of those who needed small amounts of money. We came up with 42 people. The total amount they needed was $27.

I was shocked. It was nothing for us to talk about millions of dollars in the classroom, but we were ignoring the minuscule capital needs of 42 hardworking, skilled people next door. From my own pocket, I lent $27 to those on my list.

Still, there were many others who could benefit from access to credit. I decided to approach the university's bank and try to persuade it to lend to the local poor. The branch manager said, however, that the bank could not give loans to the needy: the villagers, he argued, were not creditworthy.

I could not convince him otherwise. I met with higher officials in the banking hierarchy with similar results. Finally, I offered myself as a guarantor to get the loans.

In 1976 I took a loan from the local bank and distributed the money to poverty-stricken individuals in Jobra. Without exception, the villagers paid back their loans. Confronted with this evidence, the bank still refused to grant them loans directly. And so I tried my experiment in another village, and again it was successful. I kept expanding my work, from two to five, to 20, to 50, to 100 villages, all to convince the bankers that they should be lending to the poor. Although each time we expanded to a new village the loans were repaid, the bankers still would not change their view of those who had no collateral.

Because I could not change the banks, I decided to create a separate bank for the impoverished. After a great deal of work and negotiation with the government, the Grameen Bank ("village bank" in Bengali) was established in 1983.

From the outset, Grameen was built on principles that ran counter to the conventional wisdom of banking. We sought out the very poorest borrowers, and we required no collateral. The bank rests on the strength of its borrowers. They are required to join the bank in self-formed groups of five. The group members provide one another with peer support in the form of mutual assistance and advice. In addition, they allow for peer discipline by evaluating business viability and ensuring repayment. If one member fails to repay a loan, all members risk having their line of credit suspended or reduced.

The Power of Peers

Typically a new group submits loan proposals from two members, each requiring between $25 and $100. After these two borrowers successfully repay their first five weekly installments, the next two group members become eligible to apply for their own loans. Once they make five repayments, the final member of the group may apply. After 50 installments have been repaid, a borrower pays her interest, which is slightly above the commercial rate. The borrower is now eligible to apply for a larger loan.

The bank does not wait for borrowers to come to the bank; it brings the bank to the people. Loan payments are made in weekly meetings consisting of six to eight groups, held in the villages where the members live. Grameen staff attend these meetings and often visit individual borrowers' homes to see how the business—whether it be raising goats or growing vegetables or hawking utensils—is faring.

Today Grameen is established in nearly 39,000 villages in Bangladesh. It lends to approximately 2.4 million borrowers, 94 percent of whom are women. Grameen reached its first $1 billion in cumulative loans in March 1995, 18 years after it began in Jobra. It took only two more years to reach the $2-billion mark. After 20 years of work, Grameen's average loan size now stands at $180. The repayment rate hovers between 96 and 100 percent.

A year after joining the bank, a borrower becomes eligible to buy shares in Grameen. At present, 94 percent of the bank is owned by its borrowers. Of the 13 members of the board of directors, nine are elected from among the borrowers; the rest are government representatives, academics, myself and others.

A study carried out by Sydney R. Schuler of John Snow, Inc., a private research group, and her colleagues concluded that a Grameen loan empowers a woman by increasing her economic security and status within the family. In 1998 a study by Shahidur R. Khandker, an economist with the World Bank, and others noted that participation in Grameen also has a significant positive effect on the schooling and nutrition of children—as long as women rather than men receive the loans. (Such a tendency was clear from the early days of the bank and is one reason Grameen lends primarily to women: all too often men spend the money on themselves.) In particular, a 10 percent increase in borrowing by women resulted in the arm circumference of girls—a common measure of nutritional status—expanding by 6 percent. And for every 10 percent increase in borrowing by a member the likelihood of her daughter being enrolled in school increased by almost 20 percent.

Not all the benefits derive directly from credit. When joining the bank, each member is required to memorize a list of 16 resolutions. These include commonsense items about hygiene and health—drinking clean water, growing and eating vegetables, digging and using a pit latrine, and so on—as well as social dictums such as refusing dowry and managing family size. The women usually recite the entire list at the weekly branch meetings, but the resolutions are not otherwise enforced.

Even so, Schuler's study revealed that women use contraception more consistently after joining the bank. Curiously, it appears that women who live in villages where Grameen operates, but who are not themselves members, are also more likely to adopt contraception. The population growth rate in Bangladesh has fallen dramatically in the past two decades, and it is possible that Grameen's influence has accelerated the trend.

In a typical year 5 percent of Grameen borrowers—representing 125,000 families—rise above the poverty level. Khandker concluded that among these borrowers extreme poverty (defined by consumption of less than 80 percent of the minimum requirement stipulated by the Food and Agriculture Organization of the United Nations) declined by more than 70 percent within five years of their joining the bank.

To be sure, making a microcredit program work well—so that it meets its social goals and also stays economically sound—is not easy. We try to ensure that the bank serves the poorest: only those living at less than half the poverty line are eligible for loans. Mixing poor participants with those who are better off would lead to the latter dominating the groups. In practice, however, it can be hard to include the most abjectly poor, who might be excluded by their peers when the borrowing groups are being formed. And despite our best efforts, it does sometimes happen that the money lent to a woman is appropriated by her husband.

Given its size and spread, the Grameen Bank has had to evolve ways to monitor the performance of its branch managers and to guarantee honesty and transparency. A manager is not allowed to remain in the same village for long, for fear that he may develop local connections that impede his performance. Moreover, a manager is never posted near his home. Because of such constraints—and because managers are required to have university degrees—very few of them are women. As a result, Grameen has been accused of adhering to a paternalistic pattern. We are sensitive to this argument and are trying to change the situation by finding new ways to recruit women.

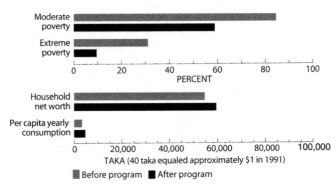

Figure 1 Household Well-Being before and after Participation in Grameen.

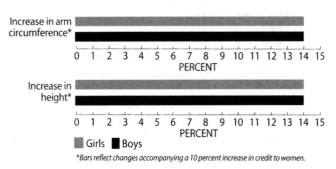

Figure 2 Impact of Grameen on Nutritional Measures of Children.

Grameen has also often been criticized for being not a charity but a profit-making institution. Yet that status, I am convinced, is essential to its viability. Last year a disastrous flood washed away the homes, cattle and most other belongings of hundreds of thousands of Grameen borrowers. We did not forgive the loans, although we did issue new ones, and give borrowers more time to repay. Writing off loans would banish accountability, a key factor in the bank's success.

Liberating Their Potential

The Grameen model has now been applied in 40 countries. The first replication, begun in Malaysia in 1986, currently serves 40,000 poor families; their repayment rate has consistently stayed near 100 percent. In Bolivia, microcredit has allowed women to make the transition from "food for work" programs to managing their own businesses. Within two years the majority of women in the program acquire enough credit history and financial skills to qualify for loans from mainstream banks. Similar success stories are coming in from programs in poor countries everywhere. These banks all target the most impoverished, lend to groups and usually lend primarily to women.

The Grameen Bank in Bangladesh has been economically self-sufficient since 1995. Similar institutions in other countries are slowly making their way toward self-reliance. A few small programs are also running in the U.S., such as in innercity Chicago. Unfortunately, because labor costs are much higher in the U.S. than in developing countries—which often have a large pool of educated unemployed who can serve as managers or accountants—the operations are more expensive there. As a result, the U.S. programs have had to be heavily subsidized.

In all, about 22 million poor people around the world now have access to small loans. Microcredit Summit, an institution based in Washington, D.C., serves as a resource center for the various regional microcredit institutions and organizes yearly conferences. Last year the attendees pledged to provide 100 million of the world's poorest families, especially their women, with credit by the year 2005. The campaign has grown to include more than 2,000 organizations, ranging from banks to religious institutions to nongovernmental organizations to United Nations agencies.

The standard scenario for economic development in a poor country calls for industrialization via investment. In this "top-down" view, creating opportunities for employment is the only way to end poverty. But for much of the developing world, increased employment exacerbates migration from the countryside to the cities and creates low-paying jobs in miserable conditions. I firmly believe that, instead, the eradication of poverty starts with people being able to control their own fates. It is not by creating jobs that we will save the poor but rather by providing them with the opportunity to realize their potential. Time and time again I have seen that the poor are poor not because they are lazy or untrained or illiterate but because they cannot keep the genuine returns on their labor.

Self-employment may be the only solution for such people, whom our economies refuse to hire and our taxpayers will not support. Microcredit views each person as a potential entrepreneur and turns on the tiny economic engines of a rejected portion of society. Once a large number of these engines start working, the stage can be set for enormous socioeconomic change.

Applying this philosophy, Grameen has established more than a dozen enterprises, often in partnership with other entrepreneurs. By assisting microborrowers and microsavers to take ownership of large enterprises and even infrastructure companies, we are trying to speed the process of overcoming poverty. Grameen Phone, for instance, is a cellular telephone company that aims to serve urban and rural Bangladesh. After a pilot study in 65 villages, Grameen Phone has taken a loan to extend its activities to all villages in which the bank is active. Some 50,000 women, many of whom have never seen a telephone or even an electric light, will become the providers of telephone service in their villages. Ultimately, they will become the owners of the company itself by buying its shares. Our latest innovation, Grameen Investments, allows U.S. individuals to support companies such as Grameen Phone while receiving interest on their investment. This is a significant step toward putting commercial funds to work to end poverty.

I believe it is the responsibility of any civilized society to ensure human dignity to all members and to offer each individual the best opportunity to reveal his or her creativity. Let us remember that poverty is not created by the poor but by the institutions and policies that we, the better off, have established. We can solve the problem not by means of the old concepts but by adopting radically new ones.

Further Readings

Grameen Bank: Performance and Sustainability. Shahidur R. Khandker, Baqui Khalily and Zahed Khan. World Bank Discussion Papers, No. 306. ISBN 0-8213-3463-8. World Bank, 1995.

Give Us Credit. Alex Counts. Times Books (Random House), 1996.

Fighting Poverty with Microcredit: Experience in Bangladesh. Shahidur R. Khandker. Oxford University Press, 1998.

Grameen Bank site is available at www.grameenfoundation.org on the World Wide Web.

MUHAMMAD YUNUS, the founder and managing director of the Grameen Bank, was born in Bangladesh. He obtained a Ph.D. in economics from Vanderbilt University in 1970 and soon after returned to his home country to teach at Chittagong University. In 1976 he started the Grameen project, to which he has devoted all his time for the past decade. He has served on many advisory committees: for the government of Bangladesh, the United Nations, and other bodies concerned with poverty, women, and health. He has received the World Food Prize, the Ramon Magsaysay Award, the Humanitarian Award, the Man for Peace Award, and numerous other distinctions as well as six honorary degrees.

Giving Globally

The Search for Solutions

A doctor, a banker, an engineer and a scientist are working separately—and together—to bring lifesaving vaccines to children around the world. How inspired individuals can take on and conquer some of the world's biggest problems.

MARY CARMICHAEL

In medicine there are three kinds of good ideas: the obvious ones, the not-so-obvious ones and the sort that Dr. Edward Jenner came up with in 1796. He had heard from his neighbors in rural Gloucestershire, England, that people who caught cowpox didn't get the more-lethal smallpox very often, and he suspected the first disease was triggering the body's defenses against the second. The notion must have sounded preposterous to his colleagues. At the time they didn't have words for the "immune system" and "germs" because they hadn't figured out either concept. Nonetheless, Jenner believed in his idea, and so did a mother who let him test it on her 8-year-old son, James Phipps, when cowpox broke out on her farm in the spring of that year. The doctor collected pus from an infected milkmaid, shot it into the boy, and waited. After six weeks he injected the boy with smallpox. He waited some more until he was sure James wouldn't get sick. Then he announced the dawn of an era. He had invented the vaccine. No doubt Jenner sounded crazy when he proposed his idea. Revolutionaries often do.

Vaccines have transformed the entire world by eradicating smallpox, and they have largely rid the developed world of polio and measles. If vaccination is one of the most important medical innovations of the past two centuries, it is also one of the most cost-effective. Vaccines do not cure disease; they prevent it, which is better. Immunize 100 people and you not only keep them healthy, you stop them from infecting thousands more. Each year, vaccines save uncountable numbers of lives, uncountable because in the West it is impossible to imagine life as we know it without them—which makes it all the more confounding that millions of people still can't get them. When it comes to immunization, much of the developing world is still stuck in the 18th century. In vast parts of rural Africa, Asia and Latin America, kids don't get any of the basic vaccines available in developed countries; they die because of that fact. And no one anywhere gets routinely and effectively immunized against

the big global killers—HIV, tuberculosis and malaria, which together take 6 million lives each year—because, even with all the technological prowess of modern medicine, good vaccines for those diseases do not exist.

Why this grim reality? There are challenges at every level. The science is hard: doctors struggle to run clinical trials in the shambles of the developing world, and biologists can't always outsmart bacteria and viruses. The logistics are hard: the path a vaccine takes from the lab to the patient is fraught with difficulty. The financing is hard: cost-effective though they are, vaccines are still too expensive for most poor countries to afford, and experience has shown that it doesn't work when rich countries just throw money at the problem. Considering the obstacles, it's kind of amazing that people get immunized at all.

And yet, 211 years after Jenner treated his first patient, those obstacles are starting to look a little more surmountable. The basic idea behind vaccines hasn't changed much; they work the same way, and the goal is still to use them to wipe out the world's worst diseases. But something else has changed: Jenner has a large new group of heirs, and they share his doggedly optimistic attitude. They include a doctor who's making it easier to do high-tech science in low-tech environments; a biologist who has spent 23 years failing to defeat HIV and trying, trying again; an engineer who thinks patients can ward off disease with a cheap inhalable powder, and a banker who has improved the health of poor people by getting rich people to invest in bonds. All four are given to unorthodox thinking. Put more bluntly, sometimes they sound a little crazy. But if they're crazy like Jenner, that's probably a good thing.

Dr. Fred Binka, 54, was standing at a hospital bed one day two weeks ago, looking down on a sleeping 4-month-old girl. Her name was Jennifer Mansua, and she had spent most of this day in the Kintampo Health Research Centre, in central Ghana, in the dark—the power kept going out. The nurses gave her blood transfusions by candlelight and tried as best they could to keep mosquitoes away from her. The mosquitoes, however, had already won. Jennifer had malaria. Her mother, Cecilia Nakabu, had tried to cure her with methods that didn't involve a costly hospital visit—over-the-counter meds, TLC, prayer. Now Jennifer was soothed and on her way back to health, but Nakabu still hovered near Binka, looking worried. Binka, meanwhile, was thinking about saving not just Jennifer but millions of other kids. "Imagine the stress on the whole system," he said. "If you could just develop a vaccine to prevent this disease, malaria, then, well, it would be fantastic."

That is precisely what Binka is trying to do. But he is not a guy who spends a lot of time hunched over a microscope. He's the executive director of INDEPTH, a network of 37 research centers across Africa, Asia and Central America. INDEPTH is creating a huge database on virtually every aspect of the lives of patients at these sites: their medical histories, their marriages, even their religions. At Kintampo alone it is tracking 140,000 people. The data, in many cases, are the only official record of their existence. Few Ghanaians register births or deaths with the government; fewer still have ID cards; some don't know how old they are. "Thousands of people are born here, grow up, live their life, retire and die, and no one outside their village even knows they existed," says Binka. "There simply is no information available."

Clinical trials are all about information. Without basic data, high-quality research will never come out of developing countries. Yet trials of vaccines for these countries must be conducted there, so doctors can see if their study subjects will catch whatever disease it is they're trying to prevent. Databases like Binka's can ensure that trials in the developing world live up to the standards set by the developed world. For any vaccine to be accepted worldwide, the trial behind it has to be perfect.

GlaxoSmithKline is currently testing a malaria vaccine in children across Africa. The early results look good. A lot of the credit goes to GSK scientists. But Binka's work—the databases, and also his efforts to improve infrastructure at the trial centers—has strengthened the operation. "This trial is getting the same scrutiny as it would if it were done in the U.S.," says Ripley Ballou, a GSK researcher who helped develop the trial vaccine. "Hiring staff, training them, improving blood cultures, and transportation and infrastructure—it's all being done."

The improvements to the Ghanaian health-care system will last long after the GSK team has gone home. They'll help all patients, not just the ones who take part in this trial or future ones. At least that's what Binka is hoping. He wants consistency—a health-care system that works even when there's no drug company in town. "You want to develop these people into laboratory scientists," he says. "Can you imagine that you'd do a trial in Ghana that brings about a good result, and then it's over and you say, 'OK, now the government can take over everything'?" Binka has allies at the PATH Malaria Vaccine Initiative, a nonprofit that supports promising vaccine candidates. "You can't just parachute into the middle of Africa and then leave," says John McNeil, the group's scientific director: it's not fair to the African people and it also means you lose the infrastructure you've just built. Next year, when GSK begins to announce

results from its trial, Binka will probably still be hard at work. That's how he wants it.

Emilio Emini, who oversees vaccine development at Wyeth Pharmaceuticals, is big in every way. He's 6 feet 4 and broad-shouldered, he thinks big and his scientific reputation is one of the biggest in Big Pharma. Still, even he can be humbled by the challenge of getting vaccines to the developing world. It has a way of making people feel small.

Emini, 53, met his lifelong nemesis for the first time in 1983, when he was a vaccine developer at Merck. He's a guy who doesn't so much speak as release a flood of arguments, facts and intimidating technical terms. Most people would not want to be his enemy. But then, his enemy isn't a person. It is a virus: HIV, which was discovered the same year Emini went to Merck.

At the time, Emini didn't expect to spend the next 24 years fighting the virus. No one else did, either. Yes, AIDS was bad, but Margaret Heckler, the secretary of Health and Human Services, predicted that an HIV vaccine would go into trials within two years. It did, then it flopped, and so has every other attempt since then. The problem, which scientists still don't fully understand, is that HIV thrives on immune-system activity—and nothing boosts immune activity as effectively as a vaccine. "The objective for those of us who make vaccines," says Emini, "is to kill the bastard before it has the chance" to exploit the body's response to it.

Until last Friday, Emini thought he might be able to kill the bastard, or at least cripple it. At Merck, in the mid-'90s, he worked on a vaccine, adding HIV genes to the "adenovirus" that causes the common cold. Tests on monkeys looked promising. Before human trials started, Emini left Merck, in 2003, to head the International AIDS Vaccine Initiative. In 2005, he moved to Wyeth Pharmaceuticals and launched more HIV vaccines there. But he kept track of his old vaccine. Many people did: it was probably the most promising candidate around. "Was," because last Friday, Merck pulled it. The vaccine was brilliantly designed and apparently safe, but like the string of failures that preceded it, it simply didn't work.

This is the biggest disappointment HIV researchers have had in years. A few scientists have even begun to suggest that the virus is vaccine-proof. Emini is not one of them. "This is not the time to give up," he says. His Wyeth team is now pursuing several approaches, and there are dozens more, based on every tactic scientists can think of. Most are percolating in petri dishes, but one, from SanofiPasteur, has gone slightly farther in clinical trials than Merck. Those who continue to do this kind of work have extraordinary faith that they'll succeed. If any of the new vaccines is even a little helpful, "we'll be happy, really happy," says Dr. Jose Esparza, an HIV expert at the Bill and Melinda Gates Foundation. "If we get one that's 40 percent effective we'll open a bottle of champagne."

In the meantime, Emini has plenty else to do. He's working on other vaccines at Wyeth, most notably "Prevnar 13," which he calls "the most complex biological product ever made." Its chemistry is remarkable: it is essentially 13 vaccines in one. A new variation on an existing shot, it targets 13 strains of the pneumonia-causing pneumococcus bacterium, some of which are found mainly in the developing world. It's currently in latestage trials.

There's a carrot on a stick for firms that work on pneumococcal vaccines: a unique type of funding called an "advance market commitment." Last year several wealthy countries, mostly in Europe, announced that they wanted a vaccine for pneumococcal disease. Make a good one that developing countries will want, the donors said, and we'll buy it from you and give it to them. You'll recoup your investment, they'll get their medicine, and we'll know our money made a difference. Future AMCs may target vaccines for malaria, TB and yes, AIDS. There's already plenty of incentive to develop an HIV vaccine: there's a Nobel Prize out there. But an extra push couldn't hurt. As Emini knows too well, defeating HIV may take every weapon the world has to offer.

As it happens, David Edwards, 46, is working on a new one, though it's not intended for HIV—yet. A biomedical engineer at Harvard University, he speaks softly and quickly, like a man who needs to finish talking because there are a thousand more important things he should be doing. His research, translated into action, could save millions of lives. But he is modest about it; praise him and he'll shrug, saying what he does is simply "a combination of art and science." His colleague, Barry Bloom, the dean of Harvard's School of Public Health, is more effusive: he calls Edwards's biggest innovation "way out."

Edwards's work is like his conversations: precise and economical. It's also, well, kind of technical. Basically, what he's done is taken a process that didn't work for making vaccines, stripped it to its essence and thus made it feasible. The process, "spray-drying," is the same one used to make pasteurized milk. It's usually done with chemicals that protect what's being dried from excessive heat. But when applied to live bacteria, those chemicals aren't protective—they're lethal. This was Edwards's insight. He and his graduate student Yun-Ling Wong took out the chemicals and spray-dried bacteria in a simpler solution of mostly water. The result, published in February, was a powdered version of *Mycobacterium tuberculosis*. It could replace the current TB vaccine. All a patient would have to do is breathe it in.

In theory, this could be huge. The spray-drying technology could make vaccines against any disease, not just TB. The powder is easy, fast and cheap to make, and it's stable at room temperature, unlike most traditional vaccines, which have to be kept cold—obviously a tricky task in the hot, shifting climates of tropical countries. It could also replace the unwieldy, if iconic, mechanism used to deliver most vaccines in the developing world today. "Getting rid of the needle would be great," says Edwards. "Getting a better vaccine would be even greater." He might get that, too. The powder contains 10 times as many live, replicating bacteria as the traditional vaccine. It's probably very potent.

That's the catch. Some people find the idea of voluntarily inhaling a giant cluster of TB germs a little discomfiting. The organisms in the powder are weakened, but they still might cause reactions in an organ as delicate as the lung, says Jerald Sadoff of the Aeras Global TB Vaccine Foundation. "There's a risk, and that risk has to be examined thoroughly," he says. So far, it's been examined only in guinea pigs. They did fine. But like Jenner, Edwards needs to test his idea on people.

That may happen soon. Last week, the Gates Foundation, which funds an enormous amount of vaccine research—it is impossible to write about the field without mentioning its name—expanded its reach even further. It announced a $200 million grant to Aeras for trials of six new TB vaccines, including the powder. Edwards also is moving ahead with plans to make the stuff on a large scale. Last year South African scientists visited his lab to learn how to build their own spray-drying facility. Someday, Edwards says, they could produce the world's annual supply of TB vaccine, an effort that would take about 50 days. Think he's just dreaming? Take a deep breath and think again.

Christopher Egerton-Warburton studied biochemistry at Oxford University. But he's not a scientist or a doctor or an engineer; academia is too precarious and ill-paid for him. He's a banker, and, at first glance, a pretty stereotypical one. Until recently, he worked in the London offices of Goldman Sachs, which he calls "the big bad bank." He goes by "Edge," wears cuff links with crests on them and is the picture of worldly success: there's a sharp-suited photo of him in the company's 2003 annual report. He knows you probably think Goldman Sachs types "eat babies for breakfast." It's unclear whether he cares. He's charming but ruthless; he says, for example, that doing charity work makes it "sometimes hard to meet your colleagues in the eye."

But Edge knows charity. When the British government needed advice on a decidedly unglamorous vaccine project, the task fell to him. His job was to transform the business of immunization into an investment opportunity glittery (and secure) enough to attract billions in risk-averse international capital. He did it, and how: among his investors were Bono, British Prime Minister Gordon Brown and the pope.

The project that Edge helped put together is called IFFIm, the International Finance Facility for Immunisation. It started with a phone call. In 2002, Brown was the Chancellor of the Exchequer, in charge of the treasury. His officials called up Goldman Sachs wanting a favor: could the bank help out with an innovative scheme for raising money on the bond markets? And could it do so in the next two months? Free of charge? Goldman Sachs said yes and handed over the responsibility to Edge. He was barely out of his 20s, but he had the right résumé for the job. He'd already done some similar bond work for post-apartheid South Africa.

Later, Edge would start wondering why someone hadn't done this sort of thing already for vaccines. The answer: it was hard. The project called for banking skills, but it also required some mediation. The money he raised was earmarked for the Global Alliance for Vaccines and Immunization (GAVI). The agency is market-oriented and famous for getting results fast. But it's still a nonprofit, and it wants to help people—not exactly the kind of value that always shows up on a balance sheet.

At one point, negotiations hit a bit of a snag. Several European governments had agreed to back IFFIm's first bond offering, but the tricky rules of budgeting stopped them from offering megabucks upfront. Edge offered what seemed to him like a reasonable solution: make the aid dollars conditional on financial good behavior. Legally, that would allow the governments to offer money in big lump sums. But to GAVI, Edge's clause was heresy. Failing states with messy finances were the ones who needed help the most; the agency didn't want to abandon poor people there. Edge scratched his head. Then he saw a loophole: GAVI could take care of the most chaotic countries with the part of its budget that didn't come from IFFIm. From that point things started to move.

IFFIM finally launched last November. Since then, it has sponsored efforts against measles, polio, tetanus and yellow fever. Edge is still a moneyman, now at RMB International. He looks back fondly on his vaccination project, and he says (maybe jokingly) that it helps him sleep at night. It was also a rare opportunity to do good while also doing well. No matter what his cuff links look like, that shouldn't tarnish them too much.

This week many of the world's smartest humanitarians will be in New York City for the Clinton Global Initiative, a gathering that is half policy briefing and half drum circle. On Wednesday, a panel will consider the problems that people like Binka, Emini, Edwards and Edge are facing. No one can say exactly when, or even if, these problems will be solved. What's clear, though, is that solutions are more likely now that people around the world are working together on them. The guest list includes several people mentioned in this article and many more who share their goals. It also includes Dr. Tachi Yamada, president of the Gates Foundation's Global Health Program. He'll be roaming the halls, listening for "ideas so novel that people might try to shoot them down." In other words, he'll be looking for Jenners.

Meetings like this happen all the time. Even as the Clinton conference gets underway, another, more scientific group of innovators will be assembling at the Massachusetts Institute of Technology for a different conference. But most of us won't be at either meeting and, for that matter, most of us don't work in global health.

What Yamada would like to get across is that it makes no difference. He will look for good ideas anywhere. If he hears one from, say, a banker, he'll take it, even if that banker hasn't thought much about vaccines before. He has a big idea of his own: to bring people together who don't usually talk about health and don't usually talk to each other. That, he says, is how you get a revolution. Hey, if a country doctor, a farm woman and an 8-year-old boy can start one, maybe we all can.

Teamwork Urged on Bird Flu
Conference Plots Global Strategy

Wealthy countries will have to provide hundreds of millions of dollars for virus surveillance and testing, vaccine production and antiviral stockpiling, many delegates said. Developing countries, particularly in Southeast Asia, where the H5N1 bird flu virus has circulated since 1997, must create compensation programs so that farmers won't conceal outbreaks in their flocks.

The latest outbreak of the H5N1 strain, which began in December 2003, has cost Southeast Asia more than $10 billion and depressed its GDP by 1.5 percent. Vietnam and Thailand have each lost about 15 to 20 percent of their poultry stocks from death and intentional culling of infected flocks.

Large numbers of dead or dying birds also mean that more people will be exposed to the H5N1 virus, which could theoretically "reassort" with a human flu virus in an infected person, forming a hybrid with new characteristics.

DAVID BROWN

Avian influenza is making the world a global village—or, more precisely, a global barnyard—in a way that demands international cooperation to a degree not seen previously on a health issue, experts said Monday as 600 people from 100 countries began a conference on how to prevent bird flu from becoming a human pandemic.

Wealthy countries will have to provide hundreds of millions of dollars for virus surveillance and testing, vaccine production and antiviral stockpiling, many delegates said. Developing countries, particularly in Southeast Asia, where the H5N1 bird flu virus has circulated since 1997, must create compensation programs so that farmers won't conceal outbreaks in their flocks.

In addition, several experts called for changes in the traditional ways poultry is raised and marketed in the developing world in order to put more distance between birds and their keepers. Scientists will also need to learn a lot more about the ecology of flu viruses in migrating wild birds, which apparently recently carried H5N1 from East Asia to Europe.

"We need to deal with this together. . . . If one country is inadequately prepared, it is a threat to every other country," said Bernard Vallat, head of the World Organization for Animal Health, an international agency known by the French acronym OIE.

OIE is sponsoring the meeting with the World Health Organization (WHO), the U.N. Food and Agriculture Organization (FAO) and the World Bank. It is being held at WHO's headquarters in Geneva.

The potential effects of an influenza pandemic are enormous. WHO estimates that a pandemic comparable to the mild Hong Kong flu of 1968 could kill as many as 7.4 million people. If it were as lethal as the 1918 Spanish flu virus, which killed 50 million, the toll would be much, much higher.

In 2003, a short-lived and well-controlled outbreak of SARS, or severe acute respiratory syndrome, caused a 2 percent drop in Southeast Asia's gross domestic product in a single quarter. A pandemic that lasted a year, as most do, would produce economic losses of $800 billion, said Milan Brahmbhatt, an economist with the World Bank.

The latest outbreak of the H5N1 strain, which began in December 2003, has cost Southeast Asia more than $10 billion and depressed its GDP by 1.5 percent. Vietnam and Thailand have each lost about 15 to 20 percent of their poultry stocks from death and intentional culling of infected flocks.

"The benefits of preventing or mitigating an outbreak are likely to be very high," Brahmbhatt told the delegates gathered in the round, wood-paneled assembly room at WHO's headquarters.

Virtually everyone agreed that, despite the 124 human cases and 63 deaths from the H5N1 strain since December 2003, the virus remains overwhelmingly an animal pathogen. However, the more animals that contract it, the more chances it has of developing mutations that might allow it to infect people more easily than it does now.

Large numbers of dead or dying birds also mean that more people will be exposed to the H5N1 virus, which could theoretically "reassort" with a human flu virus in an infected person, forming a hybrid with new characteristics.

"The control is at the level of the animal. The window of opportunity for doing that is still open. The virus has not yet reassorted or mutated," said Samuel Jutzi, an FAO official.

UNIT 7

Values and Visions

Unit Selections

Key Points to Consider

- Is it naive to speak of global issues in terms of ethics?

- What roles can governments, international organizations, and individuals play in making high ethical standards more common in political and economic transactions?

- How is the political role of women changing, and what impacts are these changes having on conflict resolution and community building?

- The consumption of resources is the foundation of the modern economic system. What are the values underlying this economic system, and how resistant to change are they?

- What are the characteristics of leadership?

- In addition to the ideas presented here, what other new ideas are being expressed, and how likely are they to be widely accepted?

Student Web Site

www.mhcls.com/online

Internet References

Further information regarding these Web sites may be found in this book's preface or online.

Human Rights Web
   http://www.hrweb.org
InterAction
   http://www.interaction.org

The final unit of this book considers how humanity's view of itself is changing. Values, like all other elements discussed in this anthology, are dynamic. Visionary people with new ideas can have a profound impact on how a society deals with problems and adapts to changing circumstances. Therefore, to understand the forces at work in the world today, values, visions, and new ideas in many ways are every bit as important as new technology or changing demographics.

Novelist Herman Wouk, in his book *War and Remembrance,* observed that many institutions have been so embedded in the social fabric of their time that people assumed that they were part of human nature. Slavery and human sacrifice are two examples. However, forward-thinking people opposed these institutions. Many knew that they would never see the abolition of these social systems within their own lifetimes, but they pressed on in the hope that someday these institutions would be eliminated.

Wouk believes the same is true for warfare. He states, "Either we are finished with war or war will finish us." Aspects of society such as warfare, slavery, racism, and the secondary status of women are creations of the human mind; history suggests that they can be changed by the human spirit.

The articles of this unit have been selected with the previous six units in mind. Each explores some aspect of world affairs from the perspective of values and alternative visions of the future.

New ideas are critical to meeting these challenges. The examination of well-known issues from new perspectives can yield new insights into old problems. It was feminist Susan B. Anthony who once remarked that "social change is never made by the masses, only by educated minorities." The redefinition of human values (which, by necessity, will accompany the successful confrontation of important global issues) is a task that few people take on willingly. Nevertheless, in order to deal with the dangers of nuclear war, overpopulation, and environmental degradation, educated people must take a broad view of history. This is going to require considerable effort and much personal sacrifice.

Getty Images

When people first begin to consider the magnitude of contemporary global problems, many often become disheartened and depressed. Some ask: What can I do? What does it matter? Who cares? There are no easy answers to these questions, but people need only look around to see good news as well as bad. How individuals react to the world is not solely a function of so-called objective reality but a reflection of themselves.

As stated at the beginning of the first unit, the study of global issues is the study of people. The study of people, furthermore, is the study of both values and the level of commitment supporting these values and beliefs.

It is one of the goals of this book to stimulate you, the reader, to react intellectually and emotionally to the discussion and description of various global challenges. In the process of studying these issues, hopefully you have had some new insights into your own values and commitments. In the presentation of the allegory of the balloon, the fourth color added represented the "meta" component, all of those qualities that make human beings unique. It is these qualities that have brought us to this "special moment in time," and it will be these same qualities that will determine the outcome of our historically unique challenges.

Humanity's Common Values

Seeking a Positive Future

Overcoming the discontents of globalization and the clashes of civilizations requires us to reexamine and reemphasize those positive values that all humans share.

Wendell Bell

Some commentators have insisted that the terrorist attacks of September 11, 2001, and their aftermath demonstrate Samuel P. Huntington's thesis of "the clash of civilizations," articulated in a famous article published in 1993. Huntington, a professor at Harvard University and director of security planning for the National Security Council during the Carter administration, argued that "conflict between groups from differing civilizations" has become "the central and most dangerous dimension of the emerging global politics."

Huntington foresaw a future in which nation-states no longer play a decisive role in world affairs. Instead, he envisioned large alliances of states, drawn together by common culture, cooperating with each other. He warned that such collectivities are likely to be in conflict with other alliances formed of countries united around a different culture.

Cultural differences do indeed separate people between various civilizations, but they also separate groups within a single culture or state. Many countries contain militant peoples of different races, religions, languages, and cultures, and such differences do sometimes provoke incidents that lead to violent conflict—as in Bosnia, Cyprus, Northern Ireland, Rwanda, and elsewhere. Moreover, within many societies today (both Western and non-Western) and within many religions (including Islam, Judaism, and Christianity) the culture war is primarily internal, between fundamentalist orthodox believers on the one hand and universalizing moderates on the other. However, for most people most of the time, peaceful accommodation and cooperation are the norms.

Conflicts between groups often arise and continue not because of the differences between them, but because of their similarities. People everywhere, for example, share the capacities to demonize others, to be loyal to their own group (sometimes even willing to die for it), to believe that they themselves and those they identify with are virtuous while all others are

wicked, and to remember past wrongs committed against their group and seek revenge. Sadly, human beings everywhere share the capacity to hate and kill each other, including their own family members and neighbors.

Discontents of Globalization

Huntington is skeptical about the implications of the McDonaldization of the world. He insists that the "essence of Western civilization is the Magna Carta not the Magna Mac." And he says further, "The fact that non-Westerners may bite into the latter has no implications for accepting the former."

His conclusion may be wrong, for if biting into a Big Mac and drinking Coca-Cola, French wine, or Jamaican coffee while watching a Hollywood film on a Japanese TV and stretched out on a Turkish rug means economic development, then demands for public liberties and some form of democratic rule may soon follow where Big Mac leads. We know from dozens of studies that economic development contributes to the conditions necessary for political democracy to flourish.

Globalization, of course, is not producing an all-Western universal culture. Although it contains many Western aspects, what is emerging is a *global* culture, with elements from many cultures of the world, Western and non-Western.

Local cultural groups sometimes do view the emerging global culture as a threat, because they fear their traditional ways will disappear or be corrupted. And they may be right. The social world, after all, is constantly in flux. But, like the clean toilets that McDonald's brought to Hong Kong restaurants, people may benefit from certain changes, even when their fears prevent them from seeing this at once.

And local traditions can still be—and are—preserved by groups participating in a global culture. Tolerance and even the celebration of many local variations, as long as they do not harm others, are hallmarks of a sustainable world community. Chinese food, Spanish art, Asian philosophies, African drumming, Egyptian history, or any major religion's version of the Golden Rule can enrich the lives of everyone. What originated locally can become universally adopted (like Arabic numbers). Most important, perhaps, the emerging global culture is a fabric woven from tens of thousands—possibly hundreds of thousands—of individual networks of communication, influence, and exchange that link people and organizations across civilizational boundaries. Aided by electronic communications systems, these networks are growing stronger and more numerous each day.

Positive shared value: Unity.

Searching for Common, *Positive* Values

Global religious resurgence is a reaction to the loss of personal identity and group stability produced by "the processes of social, economic, and cultural modernization that swept across the world in the second half of the twentieth century," according to Huntington. With traditional systems of authority disrupted, people become separated from their roots in a bewildering maze of new rules and expectations. In his view, such people need "new sources of identity, new forms of stable community, and new sets of moral precepts to provide them with a sense of meaning and purpose." Organized religious groups, both mainstream and fundamentalist, are growing today precisely to meet these needs, he believes.

Positive shared value: Love.

Although uprooted people may need new frameworks of identity and purpose, they will certainly not find them in fundamentalist religious groups, for such groups are *not* "new sources of identity." Instead, they recycle the past. Religious revival movements are reactionary, not progressive. Instead of facing the future, developing new approaches to deal with perceived threats of economic, technological, and social change, the movements attempt to retreat into the past.

Religions will likely remain among the major human belief systems for generations to come, despite—or even because of—the fact that they defy conventional logic and reason with their ultimate reliance upon otherworldly beliefs. However, it is possible that some ecumenical accommodations will be made that will allow humanity to build a generally accepted ethical system based on the many similar and overlapping moralities contained in the major religions. A person does not have to believe in supernatural beings to embrace and practice the principles of a global ethic, as exemplified in the interfaith

declaration, "Towards a Global Ethic," issued by the Parliament of the World's Religions in 1993.

Positive shared value: Compassion.

Interfaith global cooperation is one way that people of different civilizations can find common cause. Another is global environmental cooperation seeking to maintain and enhance the life-sustaining capacities of the earth. Also, people everywhere have a stake in working for the freedom and welfare of future generations, not least because the future of their own children and grandchildren is at stake.

Positive shared value: Welfare of future generations.

Many more examples of cooperation among civilizations in the pursuit of common goals can be found in every area from medicine and science to moral philosophy, music, and art. A truly global commitment to the exploration, colonization, and industrialization of space offers still another way to harness the existing skills and talents of many nations, with the aim of realizing and extending worthy human capacities to their fullest. So, too, does the search for extraterrestrial intelligence. One day, many believe, contact will be made. What, then, becomes of Huntington's "clash of civilizations"? Visitors to Earth will likely find the variations among human cultures and languages insignificant compared with the many common traits all humans share.

Universal human values do exist, and many researchers, using different methodologies and data sets, have independently identified similar values. Typical of many studies into universal values is the global code of ethics compiled by Rushworth M. Kidder in *Shared Values for a Troubled World* (Wiley, 1994). Kidder's list includes love, truthfulness, fairness, freedom, unity (including cooperation, group allegiance, and oneness with others), tolerance, respect for life, and responsibility (which includes taking care of yourself, of other individuals, and showing concern for community interests). Additional values mentioned are courage, knowing right from wrong, wisdom, hospitality, obedience, and stability.

The Origins of Universal Human Values

Human values are not arbitrary or capricious. Their origins and continued existence are based in the facts of biology and in how human minds and bodies interact with their physical and social environments. These realities shape and constrain human behavior. They also shape human beliefs about the world and their evaluations of various aspects of it.

Human beings cannot exist without air, water, food, sleep, and personal security. There are also other needs that, although not absolutely necessary for the bodily survival of individuals, contribute to comfort and happiness. These include clothing, shelter, companionship, affection, and sex. The last, of course, is also necessary for reproduction and, hence, for the continued survival of the human species.

Thus, there are many constraints placed on human behavior, if individuals and groups are to continue to survive and to thrive. These are *not* matters of choice. *How* these needs are met involves some—often considerable—leeway of choice, but, obviously, these needs set limits to the possible.

Much of morality, then, derives from human biological and psychological characteristics and from our higher order capacities of choice and reasoning. If humans were invulnerable and immortal, then injunctions against murder would be unnecessary. If humans did not rely on learning from others, lying would not be a moral issue.

Some needs of human individuals, such as love, approval, and emotional support, are inherently social, because they can only be satisfied adequately by other humans. As infants, individuals are totally dependent on other people. As adults, interaction with others satisfies both emotional and survival needs. The results achieved through cooperation and division of labor within a group are nearly always superior to what can be achieved by individuals each working alone. This holds true for hunting, providing protection from beasts and hostile groups, building shelters, or carrying out large-scale community projects.

Thus, social life itself helps shape human values. As societies have evolved, they have selectively retained only some of the logically possible variations in human values as norms, rights, and obligations. These selected values function to make social life possible, to permit and encourage people to live and work together.

Socially disruptive attitudes and actions, such as greed, dishonesty, cowardice, anger, envy, promiscuity, stubbornness, and disobedience, among others, constantly threaten the survival of society. Sadly, these human traits are as universal as are societal efforts to control them. Perhaps some or all of them once had survival value for individuals. But with the growth of society, they have become obstacles to the cooperation needed to sustain large-scale, complex communities. Other actions and attitudes that individuals and societies ought to avoid are equally well-recognized: abuses of power, intolerance, theft, arrogance, brutality, terrorism, torture, fanaticism, and degradation.

Positive shared value: Honesty

I believe the path toward a harmonious global society is well marked by widely shared human values, including patience, truthfulness, responsibility, respect for life, granting dignity to all people, empathy for others, kindliness and generosity, compassion, and forgiveness. To be comprehensive, this list must be extended to include equality between men and women, respect for human rights, nonviolence, fair treatment of all groups, encouragement of healthy and nature-friendly lifestyles, and acceptance of freedom as an ideal limited by the need to avoid harming others. These value judgments are not distinctively Islamic, Judeo-Christian, or Hindu, or Asian, Western, or African. They are *human* values that have emerged, often independently, in many different places based on the cumulative life experience of generations.

Human societies and civilizations today differ chiefly in how well they achieve these positive values and suppress negative values. No society, obviously, has fully achieved the positive values, nor fully eliminated the negative ones.

But today's shared human values do not necessarily represent the ultimate expression of human morality. Rather, they provide a current progress report, a basis for critical discourse on a global level. By building understanding and agreement across cultures, such discourse can, eventually, lead to a further evolution of global morality.

In every society, many people, groups, and institutions respect and attempt to live by these positive values, and groups such as the Institute for Global Ethics are exploring how a global ethic can be improved and implemented everywhere.

Principle for global peace: Inclusion.

The Search for Global Peace and Order

Individuals and societies are so complex that it may seem foolhardy even to attempt the ambitious task of increasing human freedom and wellbeing. Yet what alternatives do we have? In the face of violent aggressions, injustice, threats to the environment, corporate corruption, poverty, and other ills of our present world, we can find no satisfactory answers in despair, resignation, and inaction.

Rather, by viewing human society as an experiment, and monitoring the results of our efforts, we humans can gradually refine our plans and actions to bring closer an ethical future world in which every individual can realistically expect a long, peaceful, and satisfactory life.

Given the similarity in human values, I suggest three principles that might contribute to such a future: *inclusion, skepticism,* and *social control.*

1. The Principle of Inclusion

Although many moral values are common to all cultures, people too often limit their ethical treatment of others to members of their own groups. Some, for example, only show respect or concern for other people who are of their own race, religion, nationality, or social class.

Such exclusion can have disastrous effects. It can justify cheating or lying to people who are not members of one's own ingroup. At worst, it can lead to demonizing them and making them targets of aggression and violence, treating them as less than human. Those victimized by this shortsighted and counterproductive mistreatment tend to pay it back or pass it on to others, creating a nasty world in which we all must live.

Today, our individual lives and those of our descendants are so closely tied to the rest of humanity that our identities ought to include a sense of kinship with the whole human race and our circle of caring ought to embrace the welfare of people everywhere. In practical terms, this means that we should devote more effort and resources to raising the quality of life for the worst-off members of the human community; reducing disease, poverty, and illiteracy; and creating equal opportunity for all men and women. Furthermore, our circle of caring ought to include protecting natural resources, because all human life depends on preserving the planet as a livable environment.

2. The Principle of Skepticism

One of the reasons why deadly conflicts continue to occur is what has been called "the delusion of certainty." Too many people refuse to consider any view but their own. And, being sure that they are right, such people can justify doing horrendous things to others.

As I claimed in "Who Is Really Evil?" (*The Futurist,* March–April 2004), we all need a healthy dose of skepticism, especially about our own beliefs. Admitting that we might be wrong can lead to asking questions, searching for better answers, and considering alternative possibilities.

Critical realism is a theory of knowledge I recommend for everyone, because it teaches us to be skeptical. It rests on the assumption that knowledge is never fixed and final, but changes as we learn and grow. Using evidence and reason, we can evaluate our current beliefs and develop new ones in response to new information and changing conditions. Such an approach is essential to futures studies, and indeed to any planning. If your cognitive maps of reality are wrong, then using them to navigate through life will not take you where you want to go.

Critical realism also invites civility among those who disagree, encouraging peaceful resolution of controversies by investigating and discussing facts. It teaches temperance and tolerance, because it recognizes that the discovery of hitherto unsuspected facts may overturn any of our "certainties," even long-cherished and strongly held beliefs.

3. The Principle of Social Control

Obviously, there is a worldwide need for both informal and formal social controls if we hope to achieve global peace and order. For most people most of the time, informal social controls may be sufficient. By the end of childhood, for example, the norms of behavior taught and reinforced by family, peers, school, and religious and other institutions are generally internalized by individuals.

Principle for global peace: Skepticism.

Yet every society must also recognize that informal norms and even formal codes of law are not enough to guarantee ethical behavior and to protect public safety in every instance. Although the threats we most often think of are from criminals, fanatics, and the mentally ill, even "normal" individuals may occasionally lose control and behave irrationally, or choose to ignore or break the law with potentially tragic results. Thus, ideally, police and other public law enforcement, caretaking, and rehabilitation services protect us not only from "others," but also from ourselves.

Likewise, a global society needs global laws, institutions to administer them, and police/peacekeepers to enforce them. Existing international systems of social control should be strengthened and expanded to prevent killing and destruction, while peaceful negotiation and compromise to resolve disputes are encouraged. A global peacekeeping force with a monopoly on the legitimate use of force, sanctioned by democratic institutions and due process of law, and operated competently and fairly, could help prevent the illegal use of force, maintain global order, and promote a climate of civil discourse. The actions of these global peacekeepers should, of course, be bound not only by law, but also by a code of ethics. Peacekeepers should use force as a last resort and only to the degree needed, while making every effort to restrain aggressors without harming innocent people or damaging the infrastructures of society.

Expanding international law, increasing the number and variety of multinational institutions dedicated to controlling armed conflict, and strengthening efforts by the United Nations and other organizations to encourage the spread of democracy, global cooperation, and peace, will help create a win-win world.

Conclusion: Values for a Positive Global Future

The "clash of civilizations" thesis exaggerates both the degree of cultural diversity in the world and how seriously cultural differences contribute to producing violent conflicts.

In fact, many purposes, patterns, and practices are shared by all—or nearly all—peoples of the world. There is an emerging global ethic, a set of shared values that includes:

- Individual responsibility.
- Treating others as we wish them to treat us.
- Respect for life.
- Economic and social justice.
- Nature-friendly ways of life.
- Honesty.
- Moderation.
- Freedom (expressed in ways that do not harm others).
- Tolerance for diversity.

The fact that deadly human conflicts continue in many places throughout the world is due less to the differences that separate societies than to some of these common human traits and values. All humans, for example, tend to feel loyalty to their group, and may easily overreact in the group's defense, leaving excluded

Toward Planetary Citizenship

A global economy that values competition over cooperation is an economy that will inevitably hurt people and destroy the environment. If the world's peoples are to get along better in the future, they need a better economic system, write peace activists Hazel Henderson and Daisaku Ikeda in *Planetary Citizenship*.

Henderson, an independent futurist, is one of the leading voices for a sustainable economic system; she is the author of many books and articles on her economic theories, including most recently *Beyond Globalization*. Ikeda is president of Soka Gakkai International, a peace and humanitarian organization based on Buddhist principles.

"Peace and nonviolence are now widely identified as fundamental to human survival," Henderson writes. "Competition must be balanced by cooperation and sharing. Even economists agree that peace, nonviolence, and human security are global public goods along with clean air and water, health and education—bedrock conditions for human well-being and development."

Along with materialistic values and competitive economics, the growing power of technology threatens a peaceful future, she warns. Humanity needs to find ways to harness these growing, "godlike" powers to lead us to genuine human development and away from destruction.

Henderson eloquently praises Ikeda's work at the United Nations to foster global cooperation on arms control, health, environmental protection, and other crucial issues. At the heart of these initiatives is the work of globally minded grassroot movements, or "planetary citizens," which have the potential to become the next global superpower, Henderson suggests.

One example of how nonmaterial values are starting to change how societies perceive their progress is the new Gross National Happiness indicators developed in Bhutan, which "[reflect] the goals of this Buddhist nation, [and] exemplify the importance of clarifying the goals and values of a society and creating indicators to measure what we treasure: health, happiness, education, human rights, family, country, harmony, peace, and environmental quality and restoration," Henderson writes.

The authors are optimistic that the grassroots movement will grow as more people look beyond their differences and seek common values and responsibilities for the future.

Source: *Planetary Citizenship: Your Values, Beliefs and Actions Can Shape a Sustainable World* by Hazel Henderson and Daisaku Ikeda. Middleway Press, 606 Wilshire Boulevard, Santa Monica, California 90401. 2004. 200 pages. $23.95. Order from the Futurist Bookshelf, www.wfs.org/bkshelf.htm.

"outsiders" feeling marginalized and victimized. Sadly, too, all humans are capable of rage and violent acts against others.

In past eras, the killing and destruction of enemies may have helped individuals and groups to survive. But in today's interconnected world that is no longer clearly the case. Today, violence and aggression too often are blunt and imprecise instruments that fail to achieve their intended purposes, and frequently blow back on the doers of violence.

The long-term trends of history are toward an ever-widening definition of individual identity (with some people already adopting self-identities on the widest scale as "human beings"), and toward the enlargement of individual circles of caring to embrace once distant or despised "outsiders." These trends are likely to continue, because they embody values—learned from millennia of human experience—that have come to be nearly universal: from the love of life itself to the joys of belonging to a community, from the satisfaction of self-fulfillment to the excitement of pursuing knowledge, and from individual happiness to social harmony.

How long will it take for the world to become a community where every human everywhere has a good chance to live a long and satisfying life? I do not know. But people of [goodwill] can do much today to help the process along. For example, we can begin by accepting responsibility for our own life choices: the goals and actions that do much to shape our future. And we can be more generous and understanding of what we perceive as mistakes and failures in the choices and behavior of others. We can include all people in our circle of concern, behave ethically toward everyone we deal with, recognize that every human being deserves to be treated with respect, and work to raise minimum standards of living for the least well-off people in the world.

We can also dare to question our personal views and those of the groups to which we belong, to test them and consider alternatives. Remember that knowledge is not constant, but subject to change in the light of new information and conditions. Be prepared to admit that anyone—even we ourselves—can be misinformed or reach a wrong conclusion from the limited evidence available. Because we can never have all the facts before us, let us admit to ourselves, whenever we take action, that mistakes and failure are possible. And let us be aware that certainty can become the enemy of decency.

In addition, we can control ourselves by exercising self-restraint to minimize mean or violent acts against others. Let us respond to offered friendship with honest gratitude and cooperation; but, when treated badly by another person, let us try, while defending ourselves from harm, to respond not with anger or violence but with verbal disapproval and the withdrawal of our cooperation with that person. So as not to begin a cycle of retaliation, let us not overreact. And let us always be willing to listen and to talk, to negotiate and to compromise.

Finally, we can support international law enforcement, global institutions of civil and criminal justice, international courts and global peacekeeping agencies, to build and strengthen nonviolent means for resolving disputes. Above all, we can work to ensure that global institutions are honest and fair and that they hold all countries—rich and poor, strong and weak—to the same high standards.

If the human community can learn to apply to all people the universal values that I have identified, then future terrorist acts like the events of September 11 may be minimized, because all people are more likely to be treated fairly and with dignity and because all voices will have peaceful ways to be heard, so some of the roots of discontent will be eliminated. When future terrorist acts do occur—and surely some will—they can be treated as the unethical and criminal acts that they are.

There is no clash of civilizations. Most people of the world, whatever society, culture, civilization, or religion they revere or feel a part of, simply want to live—and let others live—in peace and harmony. To achieve this, all of us must realize that the human community is inescapably bound together. More and more, as Martin Luther King Jr. reminded us, whatever affects one, sooner or later affects all.

WENDELL BELL is professor emeritus of sociology and senior research scientist at Yale University's Center for Comparative Research. He is the author of more than 200 articles and nine books, including the two-volume *Foundations of Futures Studies* (Transaction Publishers, now available in paperback 2003, 2004). His address is Department of Sociology, Yale University, P.O. Box 208265, New Haven, Connecticut 06520. E-mail wendell.bell@yale.edu.

This article draws from an essay originally published in the *Journal of Futures Studies 6*.

The Politics of God

MARK LILLA

I. "The Will of God Will Prevail"

The twilight of the idols has been postponed. For more than two centuries, from the American and French Revolutions to the collapse of Soviet Communism, world politics revolved around eminently political problems. War and revolution, class and social justice, race and national identity—these were the questions that divided us. Today, we have progressed to the point where our problems again resemble those of the 16th century, as we find ourselves entangled in conflicts over competing revelations, dogmatic purity and divine duty. We in the West are disturbed and confused. Though we have our own fundamentalists, we find it incomprehensible that theological ideas still stir up messianic passions, leaving societies in ruin. We had assumed this was no longer possible, that human beings had learned to separate religious questions from political ones, that fanaticism was dead. We were wrong.

An example: In May of last year, President Mahmoud Ahmadinejad of Iran sent an open letter to President George W. Bush that was translated and published in newspapers around the world. Its theme was contemporary politics and its language that of divine revelation. After rehearsing a litany of grievances against American foreign policies, real and imagined, Ahmadinejad wrote, "If Prophet Abraham, Isaac, Jacob, Ishmael, Joseph or Jesus Christ (peace be upon him) were with us today, how would they have judged such behavior?" This was not a rhetorical question. "I have been told that Your Excellency follows the teachings of Jesus (peace be upon him) and believes in the divine promise of the rule of the righteous on Earth," Ahmadinejad continued, reminding his fellow believer that "according to divine verses, we have all been called upon to worship one God and follow the teachings of divine Prophets." There follows a kind of altar call, in which the American president is invited to bring his actions into line with these verses. And then comes a threatening prophecy: "Liberalism and Western-style democracy have not been able to help realize the ideals of humanity. Today, these two concepts have failed. Those with insight can already hear the sounds of the shattering and fall of the ideology and thoughts of the liberal democratic systems. . . . Whether we like it or not, the world is gravitating towards faith in the Almighty and justice and the will of God will prevail over all things."

This is the language of political theology, and for millennia it was the only tongue human beings had for expressing their thoughts about political life. It is primordial, but also contemporary: countless millions still pursue the age-old quest to bring the whole of human life under God's authority, and they have their reasons. To understand them we need only interpret the language of political theology—yet that is what we find hardest to do. Reading a letter like Ahmadinejad's, we fall mute, like explorers coming upon an ancient inscription written in hieroglyphics.

The problem is ours, not his. A little more than two centuries ago we began to believe that the West was on a one-way track toward modern secular democracy and that other societies, once placed on that track, would inevitably follow. Though this has not happened, we still maintain our implicit faith in a modernizing process and blame delays on extenuating circumstances like poverty or colonialism. This assumption shapes the way we see political theology, especially in its Islamic form—as an atavism requiring psychological or sociological analysis but not serious intellectual engagement. Islamists, even if they are learned professionals, appear to us primarily as frustrated, irrational representatives of frustrated, irrational societies, nothing more. We live, so to speak, on the other shore. When we observe those on the opposite bank, we are puzzled, since we have only a distant memory of what it was like to think as they do. We all face the same questions of political existence, yet their way of answering them has become alien to us. On one shore, political institutions are conceived in terms of divine authority and spiritual redemption; on the other they are not. And that, as Robert Frost might have put it, makes all the difference.

Understanding this difference is the most urgent intellectual and political task of the present time. But where to begin? The case of contemporary Islam is on everyone's mind, yet is so suffused with anger and ignorance as to be paralyzing. All we hear are alien sounds, motivating unspeakable acts. If we ever hope to crack the grammar and syntax of political theology, it seems we will have to begin with ourselves. The history of political theology in the West is an instructive story, and it did not end with the birth of modern science, or the Enlightenment, or the American and French Revolutions, or any other definitive historical moment. Political theology was a presence in Western intellectual life well into the 20th century, by which time it had shed the mind-set of the Middle Ages and found modern reasons for seeking political inspiration in the Bible. At first, this modern political theology expressed a seemingly enlightened outlook and was welcomed by those who wished liberal democracy well. But in the aftermath of the First World War it took an apocalyptic turn, and "new men" eager to embrace the future began generating theological justifications for the most repugnant—and godless—ideologies of the age, Nazism and Communism.

It is an unnerving tale, one that raises profound questions about the fragility of our modern outlook. Even the most stable and successful democracies, with the most high-minded and civilized believers, have proved vulnerable to political messianism and its theological justification. If we can understand how that was possible in the advanced West, if we can hear political theology speaking in a more recognizable tongue, represented by people in familiar dress with familiar names, perhaps then we can remind ourselves how the world looks from its perspective. This would be a small step toward measuring the challenge we face and deciding how to respond.

II. The Great Separation

Why is there political theology? The question echoes throughout the history of Western thought, beginning in Greek and Roman antiquity and continuing down to our day. Many theories have been proposed, especially by those suspicious of the religious impulse. Yet few recognize the rationality of political theology or enter into its logic. Theology is, after all, a set of reasons people give themselves for the way things are and the way they ought to be. So let us try to imagine how those reasons might involve God and have implications for politics.

Imagine human beings who first become aware of themselves in a world not of their own making. Their world has unknown origins and behaves in a regular fashion, so they wonder why that is. They know that the things they themselves fashion behave in a predictable manner because they conceive and construct them with some end in mind. They stretch the bow, the arrow flies; that is why they were made. So, by analogy, it is not difficult for them to assume that the cosmic order was constructed for a purpose, reflecting its maker's will. By following this analogy, they begin to have ideas about that maker, about his intentions and therefore about his personality.

In taking these few short steps, the human mind finds itself confronted with a picture, a theological image in which God, man and world form a divine nexus. Believers have reasons for thinking that they live in this nexus, just as they have reasons for assuming that it offers guidance for political life. But how that guidance is to be understood, and whether believers think it is authoritative, will depend on how they imagine God. If God is thought to be passive, a silent force like the sky, nothing in particular may follow. He is a hypothesis we can do without. But if we take seriously the thought that God is a person with intentions, and that the cosmic order is a result of those intentions, then a great deal can follow. The intentions of such a God reveal something man cannot fully know on his own. This revelation then becomes the source of his authority, over nature and over us, and we have no choice but to obey him and see that his plans are carried out on earth. That is where political theology comes in.

One powerful attraction of political theology, in any form, is its comprehensiveness. It offers a way of thinking about the conduct of human affairs and connects those thoughts to loftier ones about the existence of God, the structure of the cosmos, the nature of the soul, the origin of all things and the end of time. For more than a millennium, the West took inspiration from the Christian image of a triune God ruling over a created cosmos and guiding men by means of revelation, inner conviction and the natural order. It was a magnificent picture that allowed a magnificent and powerful civilization to flower. But the picture was always difficult to translate theologically into political form: God the Father had given commandments; a Redeemer arrived, reinterpreting them, then departed; and now the Holy Spirit remained as a ghostly divine presence. It was not at all clear what political lessons were to be drawn from all this. Were Christians supposed to withdraw from a corrupted world that was abandoned by the Redeemer? Were they called upon to rule the earthly city with both church and state, inspired by the Holy Spirit? Or were they expected to build a New Jerusalem that would hasten the Messiah's return?

Throughout the Middle Ages, Christians argued over these questions. The City of Man was set against the City of God, public citizenship against private piety, the divine right of kings against the right of resistance, church authority against radical antinomianism, canon law against mystical insight, inquisitor against martyr, secular sword against ecclesiastical miter, prince against emperor, emperor against pope, pope against church councils. In the late Middle Ages, the sense of crisis was palpable, and even the Roman Church recognized that reforms were in order. But by the 16th century, thanks to Martin Luther and John Calvin, there was no unified Christendom to reform, just a variety of churches and sects, most allied with absolute secular rulers eager to assert their independence. In the Wars of Religion that followed, doctrinal differences fueled political ambitions and vice versa, in a deadly, vicious cycle that lasted a century and a half. Christians addled by apocalyptic dreams hunted and killed Christians with a maniacal fury they had once reserved for Muslims, Jews and heretics. It was madness.

The English philosopher Thomas Hobbes tried to find a way out of this labyrinth. Traditionally, political theology had interpreted a set of revealed divine commands and applied them to social life. In his great treatise "Leviathan" (1651), Hobbes simply ignored the substance of those commands and talked instead about how and why human beings believed God revealed them. He did the most revolutionary thing a thinker can ever do—he changed the subject, from God and his commands to man and his beliefs. If we do that, Hobbes reasoned, we can begin to understand why religious convictions so often lead to political conflicts and then perhaps find a way to contain the potential for violence.

The contemporary crisis in Western Christendom created an audience for Hobbes and his ideas. In the midst of religious war, his view that the human mind was too weak and beset by passions to have any reliable knowledge of the divine seemed commonsensical. It also made sense to assume that when man speaks about God he is really referring to his own experience, which is all he knows. And what most characterizes his experience? According to Hobbes, fear. Man's natural state is to be overwhelmed with anxiety, "his heart all the day long gnawed on by fear of death, poverty, or other calamity." He "has no repose, nor pause of his anxiety, but in sleep." It is no wonder that human beings fashion idols to protect themselves from what they most fear, attributing divine powers even, as Hobbes wrote, to "men, women, a bird, a crocodile, a calf, a dog, a snake, an onion, a leek." Pitiful, but understandable.

And the debilitating dynamics of belief don't end there. For once we imagine an all-powerful God to protect us, chances are we'll begin to fear him too. What if he gets angry? How can we appease him? Hobbes reasoned that these new religious fears were what created a market for priests and prophets claiming to understand God's obscure demands. It was a raucous market in Hobbes's time, with stalls for Roman Catholics, Anglicans, Lutherans, Calvinists, Anabaptists, Quakers, Ranters, Muggletonians, Fifth Monarchy Men and countless others, each with his own path to salvation and blueprint for Christian society. They disagreed with one another, and because their very souls were at stake, they fought. Which led to wars; which led to more fear; which made people more religious; which. . . .

Fresh from the Wars of Religion, Hobbes's readers knew all about fear. Their lives had become, as he put it, "solitary, poor, nasty, brutish, and short." And when he announced that a new political philosophy could release them from fear, they listened. Hobbes planted a seed, a thought that it might be possible to build legitimate political institutions without grounding them on divine revelation. He knew it was impossible to refute belief in divine revelation; the most one can hope to do is cast suspicion on prophets claiming to speak about politics in God's name. The new political thinking would no longer concern itself with God's politics; it would concentrate on men as believers in God and try to keep them from harming one another. It would set its sights lower than Christian political theology had, but secure what mattered most, which was peace.

Hobbes was neither a liberal nor a democrat. He thought that consolidating power in the hands of one man was the only way to relieve citizens of their mutual fears. But over the next few centuries, Western thinkers like John Locke, who adopted his approach, began to imagine a new kind of political order in which power would be limited, divided and widely shared; in which those in power at one moment would relinquish it peacefully at another, without fear of retribution; in which public law would govern relations among citizens and institutions; in which many different religions would be allowed to flourish, free from state interference; and in which individuals would have inalienable rights to protect them from government and their fellows. This liberal-democratic order is the only one we in the West recognize as legitimate today, and we owe it primarily to Hobbes. In order to escape the destructive passions of messianic faith, political theology centered on God was replaced by political philosophy centered on man. This was the Great Separation.

III. The Inner Light

It is a familiar story, and seems to conclude with a happy ending. But in truth the Great Separation was never a fait accompli, even in Western Europe, where it was first conceived. Old-style Christian political theology had an afterlife in the West, and

only after the Second World War did it cease to be a political force. In the 19th and early 20th centuries a different challenge to the Great Separation arose from another quarter. It came from a wholly new kind of political theology heavily indebted to philosophy and styling itself both modern and liberal. I am speaking of the "liberal theology" movement that arose in Germany not long after the French Revolution, first among Protestant theologians, then among Jewish reformers. These thinkers, who abhorred theocracy, also rebelled against Hobbes's vision, favoring instead a political future in which religion—properly chastened and intellectually reformed—would play an absolutely central role.

And the questions they posed were good ones. While granting that ignorance and fear had bred pointless wars among Christian sects and nations, they asked: Were those the only reasons that, for a millennium and a half, an entire civilization had looked to Jesus Christ as its savior? Or that suffering Jews of the Diaspora remained loyal to the Torah? Could ignorance and fear explain the beauty of Christian liturgical music or the sublimity of the Gothic cathedrals? Could they explain why all other civilizations, past and present, founded their political institutions in accordance with the divine nexus of God, man and world? Surely there was more to religious man than was dreamed of in Hobbes's philosophy.

That certainly was the view of Jean-Jacques Rousseau, who did more than anyone to develop an alternative to Hobbes. Rousseau wrote no treatise on religion, which was probably a wise thing, since when he inserted a few pages on religious themes into his masterpiece, "Émile" (1762), it caused the book to be burned and Rousseau to spend the rest of his life on the run. This short section of "Émile," which he called "The Profession of Faith of the Savoyard Vicar," has so deeply shaped contemporary views of religion that it takes some effort to understand why Rousseau was persecuted for writing it. It is the most beautiful and convincing defense of man's religious instincts ever to flow from a modern pen—and that, apparently, was the problem. Rousseau spoke of religion in terms of human needs, not divine truths, and had his Savoyard vicar declare, "I believe all particular religions are good when one serves God usefully in them." For that, he was hounded by pious Christians.

Rousseau had a Hobbes problem, too: he shared the Englishman's criticisms of theocracy, fanaticism and the clergy, but he was a friend of religion. While Hobbes beat the drums of ignorance and fear, Rousseau sang the praises of conscience, of charity, of fellow feeling, of virtue, of pious wonder in the face of God's creation. Human beings, he thought, have a natural goodness they express in their religion. That is the theme of the "Profession of Faith," which tells the parable of a young vicar who loses his faith and then his moral compass once confronted with the hypocrisy of his co-religionists. He is able to restore his equilibrium only when he finds a new kind of faith in God by looking within, to his own "inner light" (lumière intérieure). The point of Rousseau's story is less to display the crimes of organized churches than to show that man yearns for religion because he is fundamentally a moral creature. There is much we cannot know about God, and for centuries the pretense of having understood him caused much damage to Christendom.

But, for Rousseau, we need to believe something about him if we are to orient ourselves in the world.

Among modern thinkers, Rousseau was the first to declare that there is no shame in saying that faith in God is humanly necessary. Religion has its roots in needs that are rational and moral, even noble; once we see that, we can start satisfying them rationally, morally and nobly. In the abstract, this thought did not contradict the principles of the Great Separation, which gave reasons for protecting the private exercise of religion. But it did raise doubts about whether the new political thinking could really do without reference to the nexus of God, man and world. If Rousseau was right about our moral needs, a rigid separation between political and theological principles might not be psychologically sustainable. When a question is important, we want an answer to it: as the Savoyard vicar remarks, "The mind decides in one way or another, despite itself, and prefers being mistaken to believing in nothing." Rousseau had grave doubts about whether human beings could be happy or good if they did not understand how their actions related to something higher. Religion is simply too entwined with our moral experience ever to be disentangled from it, and morality is inseparable from politics.

IV. Rousseau's Children

By the early 19th century, two schools of thought about religion and politics had grown up in the West. Let us call them the children of Hobbes and the children of Rousseau. For the children of Hobbes, a decent political life could not be realized by Christian political theology, which bred violence and stifled human development. The only way to control the passions flowing from religion to politics, and back again, was to detach political life from them completely. This had to happen within Western institutions, but first it had to happen within Western minds. A reorientation would have to take place, turning human attention away from the eternal and transcendent, toward the here and now. The old habit of looking to God for political guidance would have to be broken, and new habits developed. For Hobbes, the first step toward achieving that end was to get people thinking about—and suspicious about—the sources of faith.

Though there was great reluctance to adopt Hobbes's most radical views on religion, in the English-speaking world the intellectual principles of the Great Separation began to take hold in the 18th century. Debate would continue over where exactly to place the line between religious and political institutions, but arguments about the legitimacy of theocracy petered out in all but the most forsaken corners of the public square. There was no longer serious controversy about the relation between the political order and the divine nexus; it ceased to be a question. No one in modern Britain or the United States argued for a bicameral legislature on the basis of divine revelation.

The children of Rousseau followed a different line of argument. Medieval political theology was not salvageable, but neither could human beings ignore questions of eternity and transcendence when thinking about the good life. When we speculate about God, man and world in the correct way, we express our noblest moral sentiments; without such reflection we despair and eventually harm ourselves and others. That is the lesson of the Savoyard vicar.

In the aftermath of the French Revolution, the Terror and Napoleon's conquests, Rousseau's children found a receptive audience in continental Europe. The recent wars had had nothing to do with political theology or religious fanaticism of the old variety; if anything, people reasoned, it was the radical atheism of the French Enlightenment that turned men into beasts and bred a new species of political fanatic. Germans were especially drawn to this view, and a wave of romanticism brought with it great nostalgia for the religious "world we have lost." It even touched sober philosophers like Immanuel Kant and G. W. F. Hegel. Kant adored "Émile" and went somewhat further than Rousseau had, not only accepting the moral need for rational faith but arguing that Christianity, properly reformed, would represent the "true universal Church" and embody the very "idea" of religion. Hegel went further still, attributing to religion an almost vitalistic power to forge the social bond and encourage sacrifice for the public good. Religion, and religion alone, is the original source of a people's shared spirit, which Hegel called its Volksgeist.

These ideas had an enormous impact on German religious thought in the 19th century, and through it on Protestantism and Judaism throughout the West. This was the century of "liberal theology," a term that requires explanation. In modern Britain and the United States, it was assumed that the intellectual, and then institutional, separation of Christianity and modern politics had been mutually beneficial—that the modern state had benefited by being absolved from pronouncing on doctrinal matters, and that Christianity had benefited by being freed from state interference. No such consensus existed in Germany, where the assumption was that religion needed to be publicly encouraged, not reined in, if it was to contribute to society. It would have to be rationally reformed, of course: the Bible would have to be interpreted in light of recent historical findings, belief in miracles abandoned, the clergy educated along modern lines and doctrine adapted to a softer age. But once these reforms were in place, enlightened politics and enlightened religion would join hands.

Protestant liberal theologians soon began to dream of a third way between Christian orthodoxy and the Great Separation. They had unshaken faith in the moral core of Christianity, however distorted it may have been by the forces of history, and unshaken faith in the cultural and political progress that Christianity had brought to the world. Christianity had given birth to the values of individuality, moral universalism, reason and progress on which German life was now based. There could be no contradiction between religion and state, or even tension. The modern state had only to give Protestantism its due in public life, and Protestant theology would reciprocate by recognizing its political responsibilities. If both parties met their obligations, then, as the philosopher F. W. J. Schelling put it, "the destiny of Christianity will be decided in Germany."

Among Jewish liberal thinkers, there was a different sort of hope, that of acceptance as equal citizens. After the French Revolution, a fitful process of Jewish emancipation began in

Europe, and German Jews were more quickly integrated into modern cultural life than in any other European country—a fateful development. For it was precisely at this moment that German Protestants were becoming convinced that reformed Christianity represented their national Volksgeist. While the liberal Jewish thinkers were attracted to modern enlightened faith, they were also driven by the apologetic need to justify Judaism's contribution to German society. They could not appeal to the principles of the Great Separation and simply demand to be left alone. They had to argue that Judaism and Protestantism were two forms of the same rational moral faith, and that they could share a political theology. As the Jewish philosopher and liberal reformer Hermann Cohen once put it, "In all intellectual questions of religion we think and feel ourselves in a Protestant spirit."

V. Courting the Apocalypse

This was the house that liberal theology built, and throughout the 19th century it looked secure. It wasn't, and for reasons worth pondering. Liberal theology had begun in hope that the moral truths of biblical faith might be intellectually reconciled with, and not just accommodated to, the realities of modern political life. Yet the liberal deity turned out to be a stillborn God, unable to inspire genuine conviction among a younger generation seeking ultimate truth. For what did the new Protestantism offer the soul of one seeking union with his creator? It prescribed a catechism of moral commonplaces and historical optimism about bourgeois life, spiced with deep pessimism about the possibility of altering that life. It preached good citizenship and national pride, economic good sense and the proper length of a gentleman's beard. But it was too ashamed to proclaim the message found on every page of the Gospels: that you must change your life. And what did the new Judaism bring to a young Jew seeking a connection with the traditional faith of his people? It taught him to appreciate the ethical message at the core of all biblical faith and passed over in genteel silence the fearsome God of the prophets, his covenant with the Jewish people and the demanding laws he gave them. Above all, it taught a young Jew that his first obligation was to seek common ground with Christianity and find acceptance in the one nation, Germany, whose highest cultural ideals matched those of Judaism, properly understood. To the decisive questions—"Why be a Christian?" and "Why be a Jew?"—liberal theology offered no answer at all.

By the turn of the 20th century, the liberal house was tottering, and after the First World War it collapsed. It was not just the barbarity of trench warfare, the senseless slaughter, the sight of burned-out towns and maimed soldiers that made a theology extolling "modern civilization" contemptible. It was that so many liberal theologians had hastened the insane rush to war, confident that God's hand was guiding history. In August 1914, Adolf von Harnack, the most respected liberal Protestant scholar of the age, helped Kaiser Wilhelm II draft an address to the nation laying out German military aims. Others signed an infamous pro-war petition defending the sacredness of German militarism. Astonishingly, even Hermann Cohen joined the chorus, writing an open letter to American Jews asking for support,

on the grounds that "next to his fatherland, every Western Jew must recognize, revere and love Germany as the motherland of his modern religiosity." Young Protestant and Jewish thinkers were outraged when they saw what their revered teachers had done, and they began to look elsewhere.

But they did not turn to Hobbes, or to Rousseau. They craved a more robust faith, based on a new revelation that would shake the foundations of the whole modern order. It was a thirst for redemption. Ever since the liberal theologians had revived the idea of biblical politics, the stage had been set for just this sort of development. When faith in redemption through bourgeois propriety and cultural accommodation withered after the Great War, the most daring thinkers of the day transformed it into hope for a messianic apocalypse—one that would again place the Jewish people, or the individual Christian believer, or the German nation, or the world proletariat in direct relation with the divine.

Young Weimar Jews were particularly drawn to these messianic currents through the writings of Martin Buber, who later became a proponent of interfaith understanding but as a young Zionist promoted a crude chauvinistic nationalism. In an early essay he called for a "Masada of the spirit" and proclaimed: "If I had to choose for my people between a comfortable, unproductive happiness . . . and a beautiful death in a final effort at life, I would have to choose the latter. For this final effort would create something divine, if only for a moment, but the other something all too human." Language like this, with strong and discomforting contemporary echoes for us, drew deeply from the well of biblical messianism. Yet Buber was an amateur compared with the Marxist philosopher Ernst Bloch, who used the Bible to extol the utopia then under construction in the Soviet Union. Though an atheist Jew, Bloch saw a connection between messianic hope and revolutionary violence, which he admired from a distance. He celebrated Thomas Müntzer, the 16th-century Protestant pastor who led bloody peasant uprisings and was eventually beheaded; he also praised the brutal Soviet leaders, famously declaring "ubi Lenin, ibi Jerusalem"—wherever Lenin is, there is Jerusalem.

But it was among young Weimar Protestants that the new messianic spirit proved most consequential. They were led by the greatest theologian of the day, Karl Barth, who wanted to restore the drama of religious decision to Christianity and rejected any accommodation of the Gospel to modern sensibilities. When Hitler came to power, Barth acquitted himself well, leading resistance against the Nazi takeover of the Protestant churches before he was forced into exile in 1935. But others, who employed the same messianic rhetoric Barth did, chose the Nazis instead. A notorious example was Emanuel Hirsch, a respected Lutheran theologian and translator of Kierkegaard, who welcomed the Nazi seizure of power for bringing Germany into "the circle of the white ruling peoples, to which God has entrusted the responsibility for the history of humanity." Another was Friedrich Gogarten, one of Barth's closest collaborators, who sided with the Nazis in the summer of 1933 (a decision he later regretted). In the 1920s, Gogarten rejoiced at the collapse of bourgeois Europe, declaring that "we are glad for the decline, since no one enjoys living among corpses," and called for a new religion that "attacks culture as culture . . . that attacks the whole world." When the brownshirts began marching and torching books, he got his wish. After Hitler completed his takeover, Gogarten wrote that "precisely because we are today once again under the total claim of the state, it is again possible, humanly speaking, to proclaim the Christ of the Bible and his reign over us."

All of which served to confirm Hobbes's iron law: Messianic theology eventually breeds messianic politics. The idea of redemption is among the most powerful forces shaping human existence in all those societies touched by the biblical tradition. It has inspired people to endure suffering, overcome suffering and inflict suffering on others. It has offered hope and inspiration in times of darkness; it has also added to the darkness by arousing unrealistic expectations and justifying those who spill blood to satisfy them. All the biblical religions cultivate the idea of redemption, and all fear its power to inflame minds and deafen them to the voice of reason. In the writings of these Weimar figures, we encounter what those orthodox traditions always dreaded: the translation of religious notions of apocalypse and redemption into a justification of political messianism, now under frightening modern conditions. It was as if nothing had changed since the 17th century, when Thomas Hobbes first sat down to write his "Leviathan."

VI. Miracles

The revival of political theology in the modern West is a humbling story. It reminds us that this way of thinking is not the preserve of any one culture or religion, nor does it belong solely to the past. It is an age-old habit of mind that can be reacquired by anyone who begins looking to the divine nexus of God, man and world to reveal the legitimate political order. This story also reminds us how political theology can be adapted to circumstances and reassert itself, even in the face of seemingly irresistible forces like modernization, secularization and democratization. Rousseau was on to something: we seem to be theotropic creatures, yearning to connect our mundane lives, in some way, to the beyond. That urge can be suppressed, new habits learned, but the challenge of political theology will never fully disappear so long as the urge to connect survives.

So we are heirs to the Great Separation only if we wish to be, if we make a conscious effort to separate basic principles of political legitimacy from divine revelation. Yet more is required still. Since the challenge of political theology is enduring, we need to remain aware of its logic and the threat it poses. This means vigilance, but even more it means self-awareness. We must never forget that there was nothing historically inevitable about our Great Separation, that it was and remains an experiment. In Europe, the political ambiguities of one religion, Christianity, happened to set off a political crisis that might have been avoided but wasn't, triggering the Wars of Religion; the resulting carnage made European thinkers more receptive to Hobbes's heretical ideas about religious psychology and the political implications he drew from them; and over time those political ideas were liberalized. Even then, it was only after the Second World War that the principles of modern liberal democracy became fully rooted in continental Europe.

As for the American experience, it is utterly exceptional: there is no other fully developed industrial society with a population so committed to its faiths (and such exotic ones), while being equally committed to the Great Separation. Our political rhetoric, which owes much to the Protestant sectarians of the 17th century, vibrates with messianic energy, and it is only thanks to a strong constitutional structure and various lucky breaks that political theology has never seriously challenged the basic legitimacy of our institutions. Americans have potentially explosive religious differences over abortion, prayer in schools, censorship, euthanasia, biological research and countless other issues, yet they generally settle them within the bounds of the Constitution. It's a miracle.

And miracles can't be willed. For all the good Hobbes did in shifting our political focus from God to man, he left the impression that the challenge of political theology would vanish once the cycle of fear was broken and human beings established authority over their own affairs. We still make this assumption when speaking of the "social causes" of fundamentalism and political messianism, as if the amelioration of material conditions or the shifting of borders would automatically trigger a Great Separation. Nothing in our history or contemporary experience confirms this belief, yet somehow we can't let it go. We have learned Hobbes's lesson too well, and failed to heed Rousseau's. And so we find ourselves in an intellectual bind when we encounter genuine political theology today: either we assume that modernization and secularization will eventually extinguish it, or we treat it as an incomprehensible existential threat, using familiar terms like fascism to describe it as best we can. Neither response takes us a step closer to understanding the world we now live in.

It is a world in which millions of people, particularly in the Muslim orbit, believe that God has revealed a law governing the whole of human affairs. This belief shapes the politics of important Muslim nations, and it also shapes the attitudes of vast numbers of believers who find themselves living in Western countries—and non-Western democracies like Turkey and Indonesia—founded on the alien principles of the Great Separation. These are the most significant points of friction, internationally and domestically. And we cannot really address them if we do not first recognize the intellectual chasm between us: although it is possible to translate Ahmadinejad's letter to Bush from Farsi into English, its intellectual assumptions cannot be translated into those of the Great Separation. We can try to learn his language in order to create sensible policies, but agreement on basic principles won't be possible. And we must learn to live with that.

Similarly, we must somehow find a way to accept the fact that, given the immigration policies Western nations have pursued over the last half-century, they now are hosts to millions of Muslims who have great difficulty fitting into societies that do not recognize any political claims based on their divine revelation. Like Orthodox Jewish law, the Muslim Shariah is meant to cover the whole of life, not some arbitrarily demarcated private sphere, and its legal system has few theological resources for establishing the independence of politics from detailed divine commands. It is an unfortunate situation, but we have made our bed, Muslims and non-Muslims alike. Accommodation and mutual respect can help, as can clear rules governing areas of tension, like the status of women, parents' rights over their children, speech offensive to religious sensibilities, speech inciting violence, standards of dress in public institutions and the like. Western countries have adopted different strategies for coping, some forbidding religious symbols like the head scarf in schools, others permitting them. But we need to recognize that coping is the order of the day, not defending high principle, and that our expectations should remain low. So long as a sizable population believes in the truth of a comprehensive political theology, its full reconciliation with modern liberal democracy cannot be expected.

VII. The Opposite Shore

This is not welcome news. For more than two centuries, promoters of modernization have taken it for granted that science, technology, urbanization and education would eventually "disenchant" the charmed world of believers, and that with time people would either abandon their traditional faiths or transform them in politically anodyne ways. They point to continental Europe, where belief in God has been in steady decline over the last 50 years, and suggest that, with time, Muslims everywhere will undergo a similar transformation. Those predictions may eventually prove right. But Europe's rapid secularization is historically unique and, as we have just seen, relatively recent. Political theology is highly adaptive and can present to even educated minds a more compelling vision of the future than the prospect of secular modernity. It takes as little for a highly trained medical doctor to fashion a car bomb today as it took for advanced thinkers to fashion biblically inspired justifications of fascist and communist totalitarianism in Weimar Germany. When the urge to connect is strong, passions are high and fantasies are vivid, the trinkets of our modern lives are impotent amulets against political intoxication.

Realizing this, a number of Muslim thinkers around the world have taken to promoting a "liberal" Islam. What they mean is an Islam more adapted to the demands of modern life, kinder in its treatment of women and children, more tolerant of other faiths, more open to dissent. These are brave people who have often suffered for their efforts, in prison or exile, as did their predecessors in the 19th century, of which there were many. But now as then, their efforts have been swept away by deeper theological currents they cannot master and perhaps do not even understand. The history of Protestant and Jewish liberal theology reveals the problem: the more a biblical faith is trimmed to fit the demands of the moment, the fewer reasons it gives believers for holding on to that faith in troubled times, when self-appointed guardians of theological purity offer more radical hope. Worse still, when such a faith is used to bestow theological sanctification on a single form of political life—even an attractive one like liberal democracy—the more it will be seen as collaborating with injustice when that political system fails. The dynamics of political theology seem to dictate that when liberalizing reformers try to conform to the present, they inspire a countervailing and far more passionate longing for redemption in the messianic

future. That is what happened in Weimar Germany and is happening again in contemporary Islam.

The complacent liberalism and revolutionary messianism we've encountered are not the only theological options. There is another kind of transformation possible in biblical faiths, and that is the renewal of traditional political theology from within. If liberalizers are apologists for religion at the court of modern life, renovators stand firmly within their faith and reinterpret political theology so believers can adapt without feeling themselves to be apostates. Luther and Calvin were renovators in this sense, not liberalizers. They called Christians back to the fundamentals of their faith, but in a way that made it easier, not harder, to enjoy the fruits of temporal existence. They found theological reasons to reject the ideal of celibacy, and its frequent violation by priests, and thus returned the clergy to ordinary family life. They then found theological reasons to reject otherworldly monasticism and the all-too-worldly imperialism of Rome, offering biblical reasons that Christians should be loyal citizens of the state they live in. And they did this, not by speaking the apologetic language of toleration and progress, but by rewriting the language of Christian political theology and demanding that Christians be faithful to it.

Today, a few voices are calling for just this kind of renewal of Islamic political theology. Some, like Khaled Abou El Fadl, a law professor at the University of California, Los Angeles, challenge the authority of today's puritans, who make categorical judgments based on a literal reading of scattered Koranic verses. In Abou El Fadl's view, traditional Islamic law can still be applied to present-day situations because it brings a subtle interpretation of the whole text to bear on particular problems in varied circumstances. Others, like the Swiss-born cleric and professor Tariq Ramadan, are public figures whose writings show Western Muslims that their political theology, properly interpreted, offers guidance for living with confidence in their faith and gaining acceptance in what he calls an alien "abode." To read their works is to be reminded what a risky venture renewal is. It can invite believers to participate more fully and wisely in the political present, as the Protestant Reformation eventually did; it can also foster dreams of returning to a more primitive faith, through violence if necessary, as happened in the Wars of Religion.

Perhaps for this reason, Abou El Fadl and especially Ramadan have become objects of intense and sometimes harsh scrutiny by Western intellectuals. We prefer speaking with the Islamic liberalizers because they share our language: they accept the intellectual presuppositions of the Great Separation and simply want maximum room given for religious and cultural expression. They do not practice political theology. But the prospects of enduring political change through renewal are probably much greater than through liberalization. By speaking from within the community of the faithful, renovators give believers compelling theological reasons for accepting new ways as authentic reinterpretations of the faith. Figures like Abou El Fadl and Ramadan speak a strange tongue, even when promoting changes we find worthy; their reasons are not our reasons. But if we cannot expect mass conversion to the principles of the Great Separation—and we cannot—we had better learn to welcome transformations in Muslim political theology that ease coexistence. The best should not be the enemy of the good.

In the end, though, what happens on the opposite shore will not be up to us. We have little reason to expect societies in the grip of a powerful political theology to follow our unusual path, which was opened up by a unique crisis within Christian civilization. This does not mean that those societies necessarily lack the wherewithal to create a decent and workable political order; it does mean that they will have to find the theological resources within their own traditions to make it happen.

Our challenge is different. We have made a choice that is at once simpler and harder: we have chosen to limit our politics to protecting individuals from the worst harms they can inflict on one another, to securing fundamental liberties and providing for their basic welfare, while leaving their spiritual destinies in their own hands. We have wagered that it is wiser to beware the forces unleashed by the Bible's messianic promise than to try exploiting them for the public good. We have chosen to keep our politics unilluminated by divine revelation. All we have is our own lucidity, which we must train on a world where faith still inflames the minds of men.

MARK LILLA is professor of the humanities at Columbia University. This essay is adapted from his book *"The Stillborn God: Religion, Politics and the Modern West."*

First published by *The New York Times Magazine,* August 19, 2007. Copyright © 2007 by Mark Lilla. Reprinted by permission of The Wylie Agency.

What Lurks in Its Soul?

Google's colorful childlike logo, its whimsical appeal and its lightning-fast search results have made it the darling of information-hungry Internet users. Google has accomplished something rare in the hard-charging, mouse-eat-mouse environment that defines the high-tech world—it has made itself charming. We like Google. We giggle at the "Google doodles," the playful decorations on its logo that appear on holidays or other special occasions. We eagerly sample the new online toys that Google rolls out every few months.

Meanwhile, the Googlers spend countless hours tweaking Google's hardware and software to reliably deliver search results in a fraction of a second. Few Google users realize, however, that every search ends up as a part of Google's huge database, where the company collects data on you, based on the searches you conduct and the Web sites you visit through Google. The company maintains that it does this to serve you better, and deliver ads and search results more closely targeted to your interests. But the fact remains: Google knows a lot more about you than you know about Google.

Microsoft also worries that Google is raiding the ranks of its best employees. That was threatening enough when Google operated exclusively in Silicon Valley. But it grew worse when Google opened an outpost in the suburbs of Seattle, just down the road from Microsoft headquarters, and aggressively started poaching. Microsoft finally sued Google for its hiring of Kai-Fu Lee, a senior technologist who once headed Microsoft's Chinese operations. Lee is now recruiting in Asia for Google, despite a court order upholding aspects of a non-compete clause that Lee signed while at Microsoft.

DAVID A. VISE

The soul of the Google machine is a passion for disruptive innovation.

Powered by brilliant engineers, mathematicians and technological visionaries, Google ferociously pushes the limits of everything it undertakes. The company's DNA emanates from its youthful founders, Sergey Brin and Larry Page, who operate with "a healthy disregard for the impossible," as Page likes to say. Their goal: to organize all of the world's information and make it universally accessible, whatever the consequences.

Google's colorful childlike logo, its whimsical appeal and its lightning-fast search results have made it the darling of information-hungry Internet users. Google has accomplished something rare in the hard-charging, mouse-eat-mouse environment that defines the high-tech world—it has made itself charming. We like Google. We giggle at the "Google doodles," the playful decorations on its logo that appear on holidays or other special occasions. We eagerly sample the new online toys that Google rolls out every few months.

But these friendly features belie Google's disdain for the status quo and its voracious appetite for aggressively pursuing initiatives to bring about radical change. Google is testing the boundaries in so many ways, and so purposefully, it's likely to wind up at the center of a variety of legal battles with landmark significance.

Consider the wide-ranging implications of the activities now underway at the Googleplex, the company's campuslike headquarters in California's Silicon Valley. Google is compiling a genetic and biological database using the vast power of its search engines; scanning millions of books without traditional regard for copyright laws; tracing online searches to individual Internet users and storing them indefinitely; demanding cell phone numbers in exchange for free e-mail accounts (known as Gmail) as it begins to build the first global cell phone directory; saving Gmails forever on its own servers, making them a tempting target for law enforcement abuse; inserting ads for the first time in e-mails; making hundreds of thousands of cheap personal computers to serve as cogs in powerful global networks.

Google has also created a new kind of work environment. It serves three free meals a day to its employees (known as Googlers) so that they can remain on-site and spend more time working. It provides them with free on-site medical and dental care and haircuts, as well as washers and dryers. It charters buses with wireless Web access between San Francisco and Silicon Valley so that employees can toil en route to the office. To encourage innovation, it gives employees one day a week—known as 20 percent time—to work on anything that interests them.

To eliminate the distinction between work and play—and keep the Googlers happily at the Googleplex—they have volleyball, football, puzzles, games, rollerblading, colorful kitchens stocked with free drinks and snacks, bowls of M&Ms, lava lamps, vibrating massage chairs and a culture encouraging

Googlers to bring their dogs to work. (No cats allowed.) The perks also include an on-site masseuse, and extravagant touch-pad-controlled toilets with six levels of heat for the seat and automated washing, drying and flushing without the need for toilet paper.

Meanwhile, the Googlers spend countless hours tweaking Google's hardware and software to reliably deliver search results in a fraction of a second. Few Google users realize, however, that every search ends up as a part of Google's huge database, where the company collects data on you, based on the searches you conduct and the Web sites you visit through Google. The company maintains that it does this to serve you better, and deliver ads and search results more closely targeted to your interests. But the fact remains: Google knows a lot more about you than you know about Google.

If these were the actions of some obscure company, maybe none of this would matter much. But these are the practices of an enterprise whose search engine is so ubiquitous it has become synonymous with the Internet itself for millions of computer users. And if the Google Guys have their way, their presence will only grow. Brin and Page see Google (its motto: "Don't Be Evil") as a populist force for good that empowers individuals to find information fast about anything and everything.

Part of Google's success has to do with the network of more than 100,000 cheap personal computers it has built and deployed in its own data centers around the world. Google constantly adds new computers to its network, making it a prolific PC assembler and manufacturer in its own right. "We are like Dell," quipped Peter Norvig, Google's chief of search quality.

The highly specialized world of technology breaks down these days into companies that do either hardware or software. Google's tech wizards have figured out how to do both well. "They run the largest computer system in the world," said John Hennessy, a member of Google's board of directors, a computer scientist and president of Stanford University. "I don't think there is even anything close."

Google doesn't need all that computer power to help us search for the best Italian restaurant in Northern Virginia. It has grander plans. The company is quietly working with maverick biologist Craig Venter and others on groundbreaking genetic and biological research. Google's immense capacity and turbo-charged search technology, it turns out, appears to be an ideal match for the large amount of data contained in the human genome. Venter and others say that the search engine has the ability to deal with so many variables at once that its use could lead to the discovery of new medicines or cures for diseases. Sergey Brin says searching all of the world's information includes examining the genetic makeup of our own bodies, and he foresees a day when each of us will be able to learn more about our own predisposition for various illnesses, allergies and other important biological predictors by comparing our personal genetic code with the human genome, a process known as "Googling Your Genes."

"This is the ultimate intersection of technology and health that will empower millions of individuals," Venter said. "Helping people understand their own genetic code and statistical code is something that should be broadly available through a service like Google within a decade."

Brin's partner has nurtured a different ambition. For years, Larry Page dreamed of tearing down the walls of libraries, and eliminating the barriers of geography, by making millions of books searchable by anybody in the world with an Internet connection. After Google began scanning thousands of library books to make them searchable online, book publishers and authors cried foul, filing lawsuits claiming copyright infringement.

Many companies would have reached an amicable settlement. Not Google. Undaunted, Google fired back, saying copyright laws were meant to serve the public interest and didn't apply in the digital realm of search. Google's altruistic tone masked its savvy, hard-nosed business strategy—more books online means more searches, more ads and more profits. Google recently began displaying some of these books online (print.google. com), and resumed scanning the contents of books from the collections of Harvard, Stanford, the University of Michigan, the New York Public Library and Oxford. But legal experts predict that the company's disruptive innovation will undoubtedly show up on the Supreme Court's docket one day.

From Madison Avenue to Microsoft, Google's rapid-fire innovation and growing power pose a threat of one kind or another. Its ad-driven financial success has propelled its stock market value to $110 billion, more than the combined value of Disney, Ford, General Motors, Amazon.com and the media companies that own the *New York Times,* the *Wall Street Journal* and *The Washington Post.* Its simplified method of having advertisers sign up online, through a self-service option, threatens ad agencies and media buyers who traditionally have played that role. Its penchant for continuously releasing new products and services in beta, or test form, before they are perfected, has sent Microsoft reeling. Chairman Bill Gates recently warned employees in an internal memo of the challenges posed by such "disruptive" change.

Microsoft also worries that Google is raiding the ranks of its best employees. That was threatening enough when Google operated exclusively in Silicon Valley. But it grew worse when Google opened an outpost in the suburbs of Seattle, just down the road from Microsoft headquarters, and aggressively started poaching. Microsoft finally sued Google for its hiring of Kai-Fu Lee, a senior technologist who once headed Microsoft's Chinese operations. Lee is now recruiting in Asia for Google, despite a court order upholding aspects of a non-compete clause that Lee signed while at Microsoft.

Google's success is neither accidental nor ephemeral. Brin and Page—the sons of college professors who introduced them to computing when they were toddlers—met in 1995 at Stanford, where they were both Ph.D candidates in computer science and technology. They became inseparable and set out to do things their own way. Professors laughed at Page when he said one day that he was going to download the Internet so he could improve upon the primitive early search engines.

Seven years ago, Google didn't exist in any form beyond a glimmer in the eyes of Brin and Page. Then in the fall of 1998, they took leaves of absence from Stanford, and moved their hardware into the garage and several rooms of a house in nearby Menlo Park. Armed primarily with the belief that they could build a better search engine, they have created a company unlike any other.

With Brin and Page setting the tone, Google's distinctive DNA makes it an employer of choice for the world's smartest technologists because they feel empowered to change the world. And despite its growing head count of more than 4,000 employees worldwide, Google maintains the pace of innovation in ways contrary to other corporations by continuing to work in small teams of three to five, no matter how big the undertaking. Once Google went public and could no longer lure new engineers with the promise of lucrative stock options, Brin invented large multi-million-dollar stock awards for the small teams that come up with the most innovative ideas.

A good example is Google's latest deal—a far-reaching, complex partnership with NASA, unlike any agreement between a private firm and the space agency, to share data and resources and employees and identify ways to create new products and conduct searches together in space. Although NASA is a public entity, many of the details of the partnership remain hidden from public view.

Despite all that has been achieved, Google remains in its infancy. Brin likes to compare the firm to a child who has completed first grade. He and Page gaze into a glittering globe in the Googleplex that shows billions of Google searches streaming in from around the world, and notice the areas that are dark. These are the places that have no Internet access.

Quietly, they have been buying up the dark fiber necessary to build GoogleNet, and provide wireless Web access for free to millions or billions of computer users—potentially disruptive to phone and cable companies that now dominate the high-speed Internet field. Their reasoning is straightforward: If more people globally have Internet access, then more people will use Google. The more books and other information that they can translate into any language through an automated, math-based process they are developing now, the more compelling the Google experience will be for everyone, and the more wealth the company will have to invest in their vision.

Supremely confident, the biggest risk that Brin, Page and Google face is that they will be unable to avoid the arrogance that typically accompanies extraordinary success. Amazon.com founder Jeff Bezos jokes that Brin and Page are so sure of themselves, they wouldn't hesitate to argue with a divine presence.

But the fact remains that they are human beings, and inevitably, both they and Google will make mistakes. Unless any of these prove lethal, however, Google—through its relentless focus on disruptive innovation—appears likely to wreak havoc on established enterprises and principles for many years to come.

DAVID VISE is a *Post* business reporter and the co-author with Mark Malseed of *"The Google Story,"* published this week by Random House.

A Deeper Shade of Green

At times he can seem like a biblical prophet, lamenting how our human failings are destroying the planet. Yet listen more carefully to Bill McKibben—environmental essayist, activist, and author of the best seller *The End of Nature*—and you'll hear a redeeming message that transforms the idea of what "green" can mean.

BILL MCKIBBEN

This is the year when we finally started to understand what we are in for. Exactly 12 months ago, an MIT professor named Kerry Emanuel published a paper in *Nature* showing that hurricanes had slowly but steadily been gaining in strength and duration for a generation. It didn't attract widespread attention for a few weeks—not until Katrina roared across the Gulf of Mexico and rendered half a million people refugees. The scenario kept repeating: Rita choking highways with fleeing Texans; Wilma setting an Atlantic Ocean record for barometric lows; Zeta spinning on New Year's Day. Meanwhile, other data kept pouring in from around the planet: Arctic sea ice melting past an irrevocable tipping point; thawing permafrost in northeastern Siberia creating so much methane that lakes didn't freeze even in the depths of boreal winter; the NASA calculation that 2005 had been the warmest year on record.

In January, a trinity of announcements sealed the mood. First, British scientist James Lovelock, who invented the instrument that allowed us to detect our eroding ozone layer, published an essay predicting that we'd already added too much CO_2 to the atmosphere and that runaway global warming was inevitable. He predicted that billions will die this century. A few days later came a less dramatic but equally alarming announcement. The steady and long-serving NASA climatologist James Hansen defied federal attempts to gag him and told reporters that new calculations about, among other things, the instability of Greenland's ice shelf showed "we can't let it go on another ten years like this." If we did? Over time, the buildup of CO_2 emissions would "imply changes that constitute practically a different planet." Less than ten years to reverse course. Not our kids' lifetimes, or our grandkids'. Ours.

Finally, at month's end, even President Bush, as faithful a friend as the fossil fuel industry has ever had, announced America was "addicted to oil." Historians, I think, will look back on this as the time when denial finally began to crumble. When we finally began to understand that the planet as we've known it was at stake—and not from a possible scenario, like nuclear war, but from the consumption of the coal and oil and gas that power most of the actions of our lives. This is new. Humans have never faced a civilization-scale challenge before. Whether we deal with it gracefully or not depends, I believe, on what happens to that creed we call environmentalism.

Environmentalism is mostly an American invention, one of the most powerful ideas we've offered to the rest of the planet. It arose here for a simple reason. We came to full consciousness while we were still in the process of subduing the nation's forests and prairies. In much of Asia and Europe, the woods were cut and the rivers tamed before the age of writers. Here, though, Henry David Thoreau could see the line between man and nature on his daily walks. George Perkins Marsh could watch what happened to the flow of streams when New England forests were cut down. Aldo Leopold could look on as the fierce green fire turned dull in the eyes of a gunned-down wolf.

None of these environmentalists, or the hundreds of thousands of other women and men who believed passionately in such ideas, were able to slow the economic juggernaut that rushed across this continent, however. Most didn't think of that as their role; it didn't even cross their minds. They set up small islands of park and wilderness for the tide to rush around. And they worked, especially after Rachel Carson, to cure modernity's most toxic side effects, making sure certain chemicals were banned and the Clean Air Act passed. This movement has been remarkably effective. Even as our economy has grown larger, smog has also abated. We can swim in most of our rivers again. And our model has spread to the rest of the world. Other countries have adopted their own clean air acts, built their own national parks. And environmentalists can still win great victories: The Sierra Club and the Wilderness Society and all the rest have managed so far, for instance, to preserve the Arctic National Wildlife Refuge from drilling.

But when it came time to deal with global warming, this kind of environmentalism flunked. Despite 20 years of increasingly dire warnings, American carbon emissions continue to grow; we won't even engage in the Kyoto Protocol, the one international effort to bring carbon emissions under some kind of control. A few western European nations are doing better, but even they are having trouble meeting their reduction targets. And the developing world is starting to flood the atmosphere with CO_2 on an almost American scale. From 1990 to 2004, China's carbon emissions increased by 67 percent, nearly all of it the result of coal.

We're now starting to realize this failure was almost inevitable. Environmentalism's method of handling global warming is flawed.

The old paradigm works like this: We judge just about every issue by asking the question, Will this make the economy larger? If the answer is yes, then we embrace whatever is in question—globalization, factory farming, suburban sprawl. In this paradigm, the job of environmentalism is to cure the worst effects, and endless economic growth makes that job easier. If you're rich, you can more easily afford the catalytic converter for the end of the tailpipe that magically scrubs the sky above your city.

But it turns out that, above all else, endless economic growth is built on the use of cheap fossil fuel. The industrial revolution began the day in 1712 that Thomas Newcomen figured out how to use a steam engine to pump water out of a coal mine, so that it could be mined more cheaply and easily, thus allowing more steam engines. Coal, oil, and natural gas were, and are, miraculous—compact, easily transportable, crammed with Btu, and cheap. Dig a hole in the ground, stick a pipe in the right place, and you get all the energy you could ever need.

Precisely the same fuels that gave us our growth now threaten our civilization. Burn a gallon of gas and you release five pounds of carbon into the atmosphere. And as China demonstrates every day, the cheapest way to spur growth is by burning more fossil fuel. Even Benjamin Friedman, the Harvard economist who wrote a brilliant book last year defending the morality of economic growth, conceded that carbon dioxide is the one major environmental contaminant for which no study has ever found any indication of improvement as living standards rise.

Which means we might need a new idea. We need to stop asking, Will this make the economy larger? Instead, we need to start asking, Will this pour more carbon into the atmosphere? Some of the shift would be technological. If carbon carried a real price, then we'd be building windmills far faster than we are now. All cars would be hybrid cars, and all lightbulbs would be compact fluorescent. Every new coal plant would be paying the steep price to separate carbon from its exhaust stream and store it underground. All that would help—but not enough to meet Hansen's ten-year prognostication, not enough to reduce worldwide carbon emissions by the 70 percent required to stabilize the climate at its current degree of disruption.

For that to happen, we'd need to change as dramatically as our lightbulbs. We'd need to see ourselves differently—identity and desire would have to shift. Not out of a sense of idealism or asceticism or nostalgia for the '60s. Out of a sense of pure pragmatism.

For instance, we've gotten used to eating across great distances. Because it's always summer somewhere, we've accustomed ourselves to a food system that delivers us fresh produce 365 days a year. The energy cost is incredible—growing and transporting a single calorie of iceberg lettuce from California to the eastern U.S. takes 36 calories of energy. What would it take to get us back to eating more locally, to accepting what the seasons and smaller scale local farmers provide?

Or think about the houses we now build. They're enormous—more than double the size they were in 1950, despite the fact that the number of people in the average home continues to fall. Even a technologically efficient furnace or air conditioner struggles to heat or cool such a giant space—and the houses can only be built on big suburban lots, guaranteeing that their occupants will be entirely car-dependent. What would it take to make us consider smaller homes, closer to the center of town, where we could use the bus or a bike for daily transportation?

It would require, I think, a movement that takes people's aspirations for good and secure and durable lives seriously. That takes those desires more seriously even than the consumer economy has taken them. We would need a kind of cultural environmentalism that asks deeper questions than we're used to asking.

How deep? Here's a data set just as interesting as the ongoing spike in planetary temperatures—and almost as depressing. Since researchers started trying to measure such things in the years after World War II, the percentage of Americans who consider themselves "very happy" with their lives has remained steady, even though the material standard of living has nearly tripled in the same period. More stuff is not making us happier—but we can't break out of the cycle that offers more stuff as our only real goal.

What we really seem to want, according to the economists and psychologists conducting such research, is more community. Standard economic theory has long assured us that we're insatiable bundles of desires. That may be true, but more and more it feels like our greatest wish is for more contact with other people. We've built the most hyper-individualized society the world has ever seen: According to some surveys, most Americans don't know their next-door neighbors, which is a truly novel idea for primates. That's contributed to the great success of our economy—each of us rises and falls based on our own efforts, which is a great motivator. But it's also contributed to that gathering sense of dissatisfaction, and to that cloud of carbon dioxide. If everyone has to drive their own car everywhere (and the biggest car possible, to maximize their own safety), then it's hard to reduce emissions. If our idea of paradise remains a 4,000-square-foot house on its own isolated lot, it's hard to imagine really rapid change.

But there are at least glimmers of another possible future. Consider food again. Last winter I conducted an experiment: Could I get through the cold months in my northern valley eating just the food grown in my county? As it turned out, I didn't simply survive; I thrived. There were plenty of potatoes and onions and beets and beef and cider and beer and wheat and eggs, and just enough tomatoes canned in the heat of summer, to see me through. I'm sure I saved lots of energy, though I can't calculate just how much. What I can list, though, are the new friends I made, and they numbered in the dozens. My food cost more in terms of time; it wasn't as convenient to go to the farmers market as to the Shop 'n Save. But that cost, thought of differently, was actually the biggest benefit of the whole experiment.

And I'm not alone. The number of farmers markets in the country has doubled in the past decade. Sales are growing at least 10 percent annually, making it among the fastest expanding parts of the food sector. A Saturday in Madison, Wisconsin, finds nearly 18,000 people shopping in the streets around the state capitol. In Burlington, Vermont's largest city, about 7 percent of the fresh food the populace eats is grown on just a hundred acres of community-supported farmland near the town's old dump. Some farmers markets cater to yuppies, and some are in housing projects; all bring people closer together.

And you can do the same kind of rethinking about many other parts of daily life, from transportation to housing to energy itself: Imagine a windmill at the end of your cul-de-sac, powering the ten homes along the street. You wouldn't be generating much carbon, and you would be generating lots of companionship.

Environmentalism has often been a somewhat grim business. (There is, after all, plenty to be grim about.) But a convivial environmentalism, one that asks us to figure out what we really want out of life, offers profound possibilities. Perhaps the most important of those possibilities is a new link with communities of faith in this country. Though they don't always live up to their ideals, churches and synagogues and mosques are among the few institutions that can posit some idea for human existence other than accumulation. They understand that it's not just, as Bill Clinton's campaign asserted, "the economy, stupid." Their political help is crucial for making necessary legislative change—maybe the best news of the year was that some 90 prominent evangelical leaders broke ranks with Pat Robertson and his ilk to announce that they wanted to fight global warming, and fight it with their particular set of tools. "This is God's world," they said, which is a shocking idea for a culture that's come to think of everything as ours. It's precisely this ability of religious leaders of all stripes to see individuals as part of something larger than themselves that's so important. And also their commitment to taking care of the needy, because of course there are lots of people in the world who aren't rich. If we can't help them figure out some path to dignity other than our hyper-individualism, the math of global warming will never work.

We don't need to erase individualism; it is one of the glories of the American character. But environmentalists desperately need to learn how to celebrate community, too.

Environmentalism isn't dying. In fact, the need for it has never been greater. But it has to transform itself into something so different that the old name really won't apply. It has to be about a new kind of culture, not a new kind of filter; it has to pay as much attention to preachers and sociologists as it does to scientists; it has to care as much about the carrot in the farmers market as it does about the caribou on the Arctic tundra. That's what the printouts on atmospheric concentrations of carbon dioxide tell us, and it's a message echoed by the researchers studying happiness and satisfaction. We don't need a slightly rejiggered version of the world we now inhabit; we need to start working on changes on the scale of the problems we face.

Fear of what will happen unless we shift, desire for what might happen if we do—together they're creating new openings for a more thorough shake-up than any American thinker since Thoreau has envisioned. But ten years is not a lot of time; we'd best get started.

Test-Your-Knowledge Form

We encourage you to photocopy and use this page as a tool to assess how the articles in *Annual Editions* expand on the information in your textbook. By reflecting on the articles you will gain enhanced text information. You can also access this useful form on a product's book support Web site at *http://www.mhcls.com/online/*.

NAME:

DATE:

TITLE AND NUMBER OF ARTICLE:

BRIEFLY STATE THE MAIN IDEA OF THIS ARTICLE:

LIST THREE IMPORTANT FACTS THAT THE AUTHOR USES TO SUPPORT THE MAIN IDEA:

WHAT INFORMATION OR IDEAS DISCUSSED IN THIS ARTICLE ARE ALSO DISCUSSED IN YOUR TEXTBOOK OR OTHER READINGS THAT YOU HAVE DONE? LIST THE TEXTBOOK CHAPTERS AND PAGE NUMBERS:

LIST ANY EXAMPLES OF BIAS OR FAULTY REASONING THAT YOU FOUND IN THE ARTICLE:

LIST ANY NEW TERMS/CONCEPTS THAT WERE DISCUSSED IN THE ARTICLE, AND WRITE A SHORT DEFINITION:

We Want Your Advice

ANNUAL EDITIONS revisions depend on two major opinion sources: one is our Advisory Board, listed in the front of this volume, which works with us in scanning the thousands of articles published in the public press each year; the other is you—the person actually using the book. Please help us and the users of the next edition by completing the prepaid article rating form on this page and returning it to us. Thank you for your help!

ANNUAL EDITIONS: Global Issues 08/09

ARTICLE RATING FORM

Here is an opportunity for you to have direct input into the next revision of this volume.
We would like you to rate each of the articles listed below, using the following scale:

1. **Excellent: should definitely be retained**
2. **Above average: should probably be retained**
3. **Below average: should probably be deleted**
4. **Poor: should definitely be deleted**

Your ratings will play a vital part in the next revision.
Please mail this prepaid form to us as soon as possible.
Thanks for your help!

RATING	ARTICLE	RATING	ARTICLE
	1. A Special Moment in History		23. Nuclear Now!
	2. It's a Flat World, After All		24. Looking into the Sun
	3. Can Extreme Poverty Be Eliminated?		25. Terrorist Rivals
	4. The Ideology of Development		26. State of Denial
	5. Feminists and Fundamentalists		27. The Long March to Be a Superpower
	6. Unipolar Stability		28. North Korea Takes on the World
	7. The Century Ahead		29. Lifting the Veil
	8. Africa's Restless Youth		30. Changing Course on Nuclear Talks
	9. Continuing the Green Revolution		31. The Politics of Death in Darfur
	10. Bittersweet Harvest		32. Asia's Forgotten Crisis
	11. Deflating the World's Bubble Economy		33. Men of Principle
	12. The Great Leap Backward?		34. Banning the Bomb
	13. Water Is Running Out		35. Europe as a Global Player
	14. Plastic Bags Are Killing Us		36. The Grameen Bank
	15. Cry of the Wild		37. The Search for Solutions
	16. Globalization and Its Contents		38. Teamwork Urged on Bird Flu
	17. Why the World Isn't Flat		39. Humanity's Common Values
	19. Political Graft: The Russian Way		40. The Politics of God
	20. Promises and Poverty		41. What Lurks in its Soul?
	21. Where the Money Went		42. A Deeper Shade of Green
	22. Ensuring Energy Security		

ABOUT YOU

Name

Date

Are you a teacher? ❏ A student? ❏
Your school's name

Department

Address

City

State

Zip

School telephone #

YOUR COMMENTS ARE IMPORTANT TO US!

Please fill in the following information:
For which course did you use this book?

Did you use a text with this ANNUAL EDITION? ❏ yes ❏ no
What was the title of the text?

What are your general reactions to the Annual Editions concept?

Have you read any pertinent articles recently that you think should be included in the next edition? Explain.

Are there any articles that you feel should be replaced in the next edition? Why?

Are there any World Wide Web sites that you feel should be included in the next edition? Please annotate.

May we contact you for editorial input? ❏ yes ❏ no
May we quote your comments? ❏ yes ❏ no